Informatik aktuell

Herausgeber: W. Brauer
im Auftrag der Gesellschaft für Informatik (GI)

H. P. Frei   P. Schäuble (Hrsg.)

Hypermedia

Proceedings
der Internationalen Hypermedia '93 Konferenz
Zürich, 2./3. März 1993

Springer-Verlag
Berlin Heidelberg New York
London Paris Tokyo
Hong Kong Barcelona
Budapest

Herausgeber

H. P. Frei
P. Schäuble
Institut für Informationssysteme, ETH Zürich
CH-8092 Zürich

Programmkomitee:

A. Aders, Technikum Winterthur
R. Albrecht, Universität Innsbruck
G. Coray, EPF Lausanne
R. Cordes, Telenorma Frankfurt
H. P. Frei, ETH Zürich (Vorsitz)
N. Fuhr, Universität Dortmund
W. Irler, Università di Trento
W. Janko, WU Wien
G. Knorz, Fachhochschule Darmstadt
R. Kuhlen, Universität Konstanz
H. Maurer, TU Graz und IMMIS Graz
J. Nievergelt, ETH Zürich
B. Plattner, ETH Zürich
W. Rauch, Universität Graz
P. Schäuble, ETH Zürich
W. Schaufelberger, ETH Zürich
H.-J. Schek, ETH Zürich
N. Streitz, GMD-IPSI Darmstadt
P. Stucki, Universität Zürich
B. Teufel, ART, Ueberlingen
A. Ventura, UBILAB, SBG Zürich
C. Womser-Hacker, Universität Regensburg

CR Subject Classification (1992): H.3, H.5.1, H.5.2, I.7.2, J.1, J.2, J.3, J.5

ISBN-13: 978-3-540-56477-5   e-ISBN-13: 978-3-642-78086-8
DOI: 10.1007/978-3-642-78086-8

Satz: Reproduktionsfertige Vorlage vom Autor/Herausgeber

33/3140-543210 – Gedruckt auf säurefreiem Papier

Preface

The Hypermedia '93 is the fourth in a series of Hypertext/Hypermedia conferences that have taken place in Basel, Darmstadt, and Graz. All these conferences--including the Hypermedia '93--were jointly organized by the respective Special Interest Groups of the Information Technology Associations of Austria (OCG), Germany (GI), and Switzerland (SI).

The term *hypermedia*--as it is used at the present time--stands for information that is organized with links that connect portions of information. At the same time, hypermedia signifies that these information portions may be of an arbitrary medium type like text, graphics, image, sound, video, or executable code. We also refer to 'pure' hypertext and to 'pure' multimedia as hypermedia. The former is of a uniform medium type, namely text, and the latter may be arranged in a strictly linear way, i.e. without links. Because we consider hypertext and multimedia as special cases of hypermedia, we have called this conference simply *'Hypermedia'*.

The international involvement has grown significantly since the last conference. The preceding three conferences were predominantly for researchers from the German speaking areas of Austria, Germany, and Switzerland. This is still the case; however, many researchers from non-German speaking countries submitted papers successfully. We are convinced that this will be an excellent opportunity for our researchers to broaden their views, allowing them to compare their results against the work done by researchers from other countries. As a consequence, this volume contains contributions from seven countries. Another consequence is that many papers are written in English.

The principal purpose of the Hypermedia '93 and of these proceedings is to disclose new and exciting research results. Even though we had this objective in mind, the ubiquitous question is whether there are enough novel results to be presented at the increasing number of hypermedia workshops and conferences. We never intended to compete with the large international conferences such as the ACM Hypertext Conference that takes place every year, alternatively in Europe and the USA. We have rather aimed for a small, yet exciting, conference to give the participants the opportunity to communicate and discuss new ideas in a stimulating environment. At the same time, we have tried our best to attract contributions for the Hypermedia '93 that live up to international standards.

These proceedings are proof that this goal was achieved. A great number of papers were submitted by many a project team. The reviewers performed a careful evaluation, and the program committee had to make the final decision of accepting or rejecting a paper, a task which was not always easy. We would like to thank them all for the excellent job they did.

Also, we would like to thank everyone who contributed to the success of the Hypermedia '93. This includes the program committee, the organizers, and in particular Rita Jenny, Madeleine Bernard, and Silvia Wertli. Without their assistance the Hypermedia '93 would not have been possible. Last but not least, we thank Springer-Verlag for publishing these proceedings.

H.P. Frei   P. Schäuble
Zurich, March 1993

Inhaltsverzeichnis

Short Contributions

Designing Hypermedia Representations from Work Domain Properties

Annelise Mark Pejtersen

Risø National Laboratory

Dk 4000 Roskilde Denmark

This paper argues that associative, semantic networks in hypermedia systems cannot be based only on the individual users' associative relationships as they occur during interaction with the system. Instead they should be chosen to represent different semantic relationships and structures derived from an analysis of the properties of the work domain , the task situation, and the user characteristics, which constitute the predominant features of a work system. Such semantic relationships should be identified for the different perspectives of the work system in order to support the user's activities at the different levels of representation at which the user chooses to perform. In addition, the interface formats should allow different perception of the information presented as required by semantic analysis, associative problem solving, navigation in the problem domain , and procedural interactions. This approach is illustrated with the Book House hypermedia system for libraries.

1. Introduction

Hypermedia system design reflects an increased attention to the development of applications for more complex work domains. From a start as a novel way of supporting information retrieval and text processing and as the basis for experiments in conceptual issues related to research in a promising new technology, hypermedia designs have progressed into areas of software development, education and training, community information, museums etc. Currently hypermedia systems are being developed for a variety of domains such as patent law, auditing, post office work, business management, case handling. However, as will be shown below, all these hypermedia designs are being introduced into domains which share common characteristics to a great extent.

Meyrowitz, (1989, 1992) Nielsen (1990), Romiszowski (1990) and many others put forward claims for systems with "interesting content" rather than hypermedia systems for the purpose of experimenting with hypermedia concepts. Since the latest developments have shown - and hopefully will even more so in the future - a growing number of systems with "interesting content", this paper discusses some of the analytical perequisites for rendering modern, complex, real world work domains *representable* in hypermedia systems. Shneidermann (1989) suggests that hypermedia systems are particularly well suited for domains where a large body of information can be organized into numerous, related fragments.

Many modern work domains are defined by a relatively high degree of information complexity. The size of the problem space and the number of different, potentially relevant factors to take into account are large and often require simultaneous attention. At the same time, domain information can be dynamically changing because of environmental influences. In complex and unstable domains, rigourous rule-based task procedures have to be replaced by problem solving, decision making and coordinating activities.This will give users more *degrees of freedom* and fewer *constraints* regarding their possibilities for taking action. Users' discretionary, explicit *explorations* of goals and constraints will be required in order to ensure that the system is maintained within the boundaries of acceptable performance.

These tendencies and the accompanying needs for users to be able to explore actively the domain constraints and goals require systems with hypermedia features. Support is required for the identification of the degrees of freedom left for users' improvisations, associations and inventiveness as limited by the domain constraints. From this follows the idea of a transparent system which directly makes visible to the users the network of domain relations and constraints and encourages the utilization of the alternatives available for action depending on personal characteristics and subjective preferences. However the prevailing need for support is heavily dependent on the domain.

Secondly, studies of user performance in actual task situations have uncovered several different forms for "natural decision making." Users in familiar situations are not likely to categorize or process multiple attributes of information in a normative way as system designers often expect them to. Nor do they sequentially carry out a formal situation analysis, goal formulation, priority judgment and planning (Klein 1989, Pejtersen 1984, Rasmussen 1986). Depending on their expertise, they will resort to browsing and search within the context of their task environment in the hope that they will recognize information matching their mental model of the case in question. Without the need for a deep analysis of the information presented, users with some training have the skill to directly perceive the meaning of the information and act upon it immediately (Rasmussen and Vicente 1990). From a different perspective, Bush's assumptions about associative information processing being the most natural way for humans to solve problems fit into these findings. (Bush 1945, Nyce and Kahn 1992).

An extension of this is that problem solving can take place at *several levels of abstraction* ranging briefly from goal to functional to physical considerations. There is thus a need to expand the initial hypermedia attention to associative recognition based information processing as a unique natural approach to also include *multiple levels* of processing. Information about the semantic relationships in the domain networks needs to be displayed in ways that support this multi-modal type of analytical and associative information processing behaviour.

These features of user behaviour in modern work systems with their associated needs for the exploration of domain constraints and action possibilities in network structures which are easily perceptible at multiple levels will make the hypermedia concept an appropriate vehicle for many system designs - also in domains which have not previously been considered.

2. Outline

The purpose of this paper is to put forward some arguments for the implementation of the hypermedia concept in advanced system design for complex work domains. The basic assumption is that hypermedia is a cognitive concept (and only secondarily a particular category of software) which was developed and implemented in a period when retrieval and control of information was no longer feasible with traditional procedures due to the rapidly increasing complexity and amount of the information to be processed.

In addition the paper will demonstrate the growth in the development of hypermedia systems during the last four years and indicate that this increase is limited to a relatively narrow variety of domains and indeed has its peak domains possessing common characteristics. Some reasons are given for this trend both in relation to the nature of the hypermedia concept and in relation to the different characteristics of various work domains.

Thirdly, the paper suggests a framework for the design of hypermedia representations based on an analysis of work system properties which can be useful for all kinds of domains. Without such a framework, it is difficult to see how hypermedia designs can emerge from their present limitations to applications in a restricted number of domains and thus achieve their deserved impact on new system developments. This framework also offers a solution to some of the most frequently discussed problems in the hypermedia literature about how to overcome users'"disorientation" and "cognitive overhead" (Conklin 1987). It is claimed that non-sequential, unconstrained associative behaviour is an efficient way of problem solving for skilled users, but for users in unfamiliar situations, analytical, even sequential, reasoning on symbolic structures is a more efficient problem solving behaviour.

Finally, the paper includes a running discussion of the Book House system designed for end users' information retrieval in libraries. It is used to exemplify how the framework for cognitive work analysis presented in this paper was employed for empirical domain analyses in libraries in the late 70's and the beginning of the 80's before hypermedia tools and concepts became familiar. Although they were carried out independently of this technique, the studies identified user behaviours which actually could only be adequately supported by hypermedia structures and representations. Thus years of empirical studies of cognitive user behaviour based on a different perspective pointed to a need for system features that actually turned out to be equivalent to a hypermedia system concept. The strength of this concept was confirmed by a successful user evaluation of the Book House in real life environments.

3. Hypermedia

The success of hypermedia systems is based on the concept of free and flexible navigation in semantic relationships which enable the tailoring and design of connections and relationships matching the semantics of the problem space with the semantics of users' cognitive worlds. It allows the design of a rich, multidimensional resource envelope for multiple associative activities as an alternative to the support of a particular normative interaction procedure. The strength of hypermedia systems for representing information is the ability of links to explicitly represent flexible semantic structures, and the ability of nodes to generate a natural correspondence between objects in the world and the nodes in the hypertext database (Conklin 1987, Begoraj, 1990). Others see important features in the "non-linear access to information, varied information access, integrated information access, ease of access and free access of information" (Duchastel, 1990).

There are numerous definitions of typical hypertext/hypermedia features which distinguish hypermedia applications from another computer systems and place varying and selective emphasis on their characteristics. From an <u>artefacts</u> point of view: "Windows on a screen associated with objects in a database, and links provided between these objects, both graphically (i.e. labelled as icons) and in the link database (i.e. as pointers)" (Conklin 1987). "Data stored in a network of nodes connected by links" (Smith and Weiss,1988); as a <u>design concept:</u> "a set of abstractions that provide a conceptual framework for creating, storing, retrieving information in a hypermedia" (Leggett et al, 1990); and finally from a <u>pragmatic "look and feel" user point of view</u> "when users' interactively take control of a set of dynamic links among units of information" (Nielsen 1990). For the purpose of the present paper, which discusses the Book House within a cognitive design framework and as an actual artefact, any of these and most other definitions are equally representative.

The hypermedia language uses application-dependent terminology, but basically it consists of *nodes* which are the single database entities containing the information content to be processed, stored, retrieved and of *links* connecting the attributes of node contents in *graph* structures which are collections of nodes in a network which can be further divided into subcategories such as *subgraphs* or *webs*. Interaction with the database is enabled by navigating in (part of) the total network of nodes by browsing through links, keyword searching or browsing through a selective collection of link and nodes in the network with a *browser* , and thus creating individual user *paths*. of associations.

Important for this discussion is that there are no constraints on nodes or semantic structures; any assembly of nodes and links is possible; multiple structures are possible for the same content information. It is possible to present and view content information from different perspectives and in different contexts; links and network structures can be easily modified. Thus a multidimensional "resource envelope" can be easily created mapping features from the work environment onto user characteristics and vice-versa. Another advantage is found in the flexibility of free navigation in the semantic network subject to the users' own discretionary choice. In many modern work domains it is becoming increasingly evident that users need a rich semantic network which corresponds to their preferences within the work domain constraints. Secondly, it is important to provide users an individual access to unlimited navigation in an associative network representing the work domain while keeping minute track of their activities.

4. Related work

The concept of appropriate *semantic network structures* is generally agreed upon as essential to support domain information without loosing control of goal related activities, and has gained much attention in design studies (Shneidermann 1989 Waterworth 1989 et al., Streitz 1990, Stieger 1990.).The importance of structure in the representation of information has motivated a cross disciplinary convergence of typical structures in information science, psychology, AI, and education (Churcher, 1989). Comprehension and learning suffer from the lack of integrating information into a coherent cognitive structure with cohesion among elements (Duchastel, 1990). A theoretical general framework for collaborative hypertext functionality using a cognitive model taken from a theory of the structure of the intellect based on psychological testing has been suggested. The correspondence of hypertext to the structure of an intellect model is suggested as a classification methodology useful to make designs that "help users understand large and complex databases, and to help to remove the ambiguity in the meaning of links and nodes, if they are too broadly defined to differentiate types of relationships" (Roa and Turof 1991). *Navigation* and *interaction* structures have received a similar amount of attention due to the phenomenon of "getting lost in hyperspace" and losing one's sense of location (Conklin 1987). A model of hypermedia interactions including the user, the task (goals, intentions, motives or purposes) and the domain in question in terms of teaching materials used is suggested for the domain of learning by Fischer and Mandl (1990). From the characteristics in their model, they identify three types of possible interactions: user-goal-domain interactions, user-domain-intellectual activities, intellectual activities-task-domain characteristics. The basic assumption is that when learning by use of hypermedia systems, structure and meaning given to the hypermedia is dependent on the interplay between user, domain and goal characteristics. Romiszowski (1990) follows up on this and provides design suggestions for a deeper goal and task analysis by taking into consideration both general "real world" educational values and specific task goals. A cognitive approach is found in Streitz (1990) to the authoring process. He considers writing during research tasks as a complex "design" problem solving activity with multiple constraints. His work addresses the need for cognitively compatible interfaces illustrated in SEPIA, which is structured by a number of activity spaces supporting different cognitive processes during the writing task, such as planning space, content space, argumentation space, rhetorical space, travelling space etc. Based on a number of experiments, Shneiderman (1989) experienced that there was a need for designing hypertext structures that were specific for each domain involved in an application.

In conclusion, recent research trends emphasize the need for a design framework based on a cognitive approach with inclusion of domain and task structures.

5. Hypermedia Domains and Applications

Three classes of hypermedia systems have been developed so far *active* and *passive* systems and a combination of both. *Active/dynamic* systems aim at letting the user create his/her own semantic networks by adding nodes (content) and adding/changing new links thus developing new relationships in the network entirely according to his/her own goals and subjective preferences. At the opposite end, *passive/static* systems are designed with pre-established links in the network and without user access to node contents. In between are systems where a combination of active/passive is found.The Book House belongs to this category.

Active systems serve professional users who need to adapt the system to their particular needs. This was the case in the early hypertext systems used by experts in document writing who could organize their good ideas with little or no constraints. In most other domains and tasks, there will be many more constraints on acceptable ideas and solutions and, in these cases, a combination of passive/active system features will be appropriate. What kind of system is most appropriate in a given design will depend on the total work system including the *domain constraints* to be adhered to, the *task situations* and the *role* of the users.

To make a proper choice, a framework is required to help designers identify the character of the domain. They need to be able to identify users' action possibilities and their degrees of freedom in the light of the behaviour-shaping constraints of the work system in order to ensure a balance in the design between users' action and exploration possibilities in pre-established database networks and the users' possibilities for changing both content and relational information.

For this purpose, it is useful to identify the structural relationships arising from the concepts of *constraints, coupling and user control,* which characterize and distinguish different types of networks appropriate for different domains. These three aspects are tightly coupled themselves but for operational purposes, their attributes can be separately described. (figure 1).

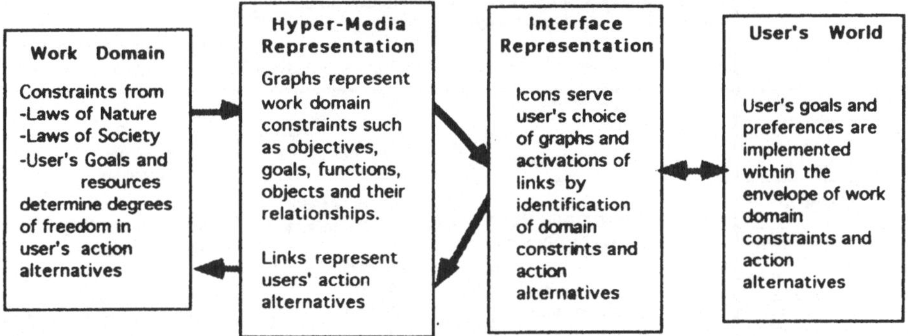

Figure 1 shows the different types of work domain constraints which may be used to impose structure on database networks in hyperspace representations; and to define the degrees of freedom left for users' own choice among action possibilities within the domain constraints according to the user's own goals and preferences.

The domain *constraints* on users' action possibilities and the corresponding *degrees of freedom* left for users' choice of actions are related to 1) the source of the constraints - i.e. from laws of nature in technical systems, legislation and other laws in society or the intentions of the user him/herself, 2) the degree of invariance, viability for change and susceptibility in the information for negotiation and interpretation by users. The *degrees of freedom* left for users' personal preferences; actions and goal formulation can be considered as that part of the workspace or network remaining after these constraints have been satisfied.

The *tightness of coupling* among domain concepts refers to 1) the degree of interaction among information, task functions, objects of work and cooperating users involved in task activities and 2) the degree of coordination of task functions, tightly coupled in a continuous work process, moderately coupled in interrupted work functions, or loosely coupled in single, separate activities. Simple descriptors are time, stress and degree of pacing.

The *user's role* involves the degree of *control* and *autonomy* which the user has on task, goal formulation and functional activities. This is highly dependent on and closely connected to the domain constraints.

Work systems differ and vary within this three dimensional description, a many-to-many mapping exists; within the same domain, multiple types of features may be found. Conversely, given features are common to more than one domain.

These general properties of work systems are important in order to determine the degrees of freedom a designer may give the user for making nodes, links and graphs in addition to those already provided to couple functions controlled by users, without violating the purpose of the system. An identification of these properties is an important source for organising hypermedia network structures and for comparing existing systems with potential domains for new hypermedia systems.

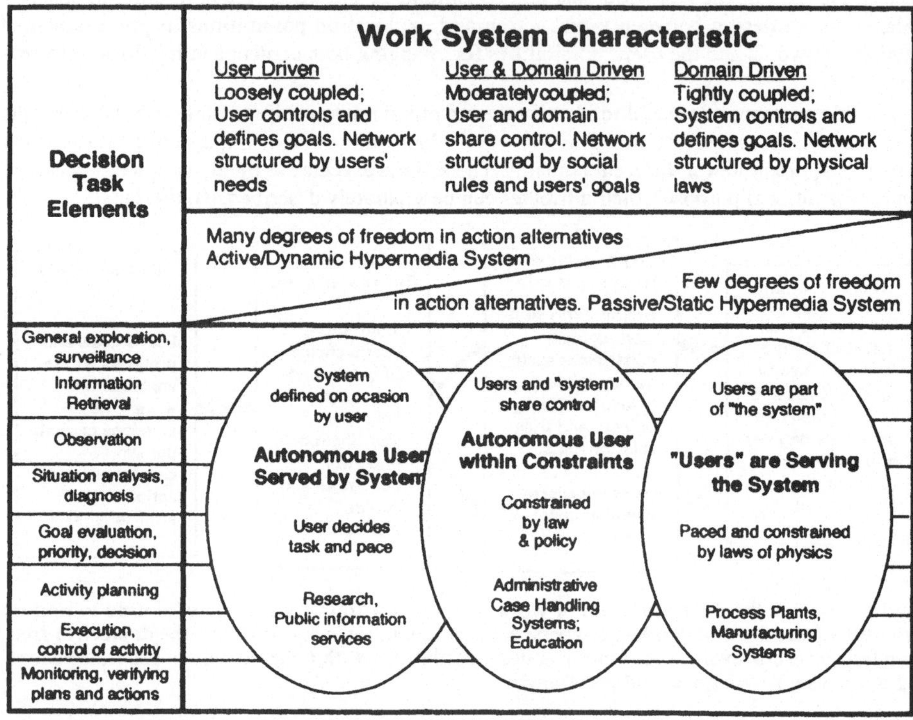

Figure 2. Some basic properties of different work domains. The properties of work domains and tasks vary along many dimensions which underlie the work. However some of the properties can be gathered together to generate typical cases. Thus the figure illustrates a continuum within which a particular domain can be placed.

The use of the three dimensional domain aspects of constraints, coupling and user control on actual hypermedia applications is discussed below in broad terms to give an impression of how hypermedia systems have become useful in complex domains, both in the most loosely coupled/unstructured domains as well as in domains with more tightly coupled network structures. A continuum stretching from user driven domains constituted by loosely coupled assemblies of objects on one hand to highly structured and tightly coupled system driven domains at the other extreme is illustrated in figure 2. The system design considerations at these two extremes will, of course, have to be very different.

5.1 Work Systems Structured by Users

The first hypermedia systems were envisioned and developed in a category of work domains without any inherent or explicit constraints on users' action possibilities. In most cases, relatively few external constraints (organizational, domain-related, etc) on action possibilities can be formulated. Users are autonomous and determine themselves the goals, the task and their approach to work. Users are often the general public, who bring to the system their own personal formulation of goals and constraints related to professional or to leisure activities. In such loosely coupled work systems, there exists much free room for action possibilities. Often, the organisational principles consist of conventional, arbitrary, simple information structures and labels (time, place, numerical, alphabetical, chronological, geographical order or crude topical classification schemes). Typical examples are services for the general population concerning cultural information in museums (Shneidermann 1989), community information in public information centres and tourist bureaus (Baird 1989), communication of news (Frenkel 1989), scientific and cultural information in libraries (Pejtersen 1989) or transportation (DSB Ticket Reservations 1991) etc..

Bush's *Memex* (Bush 1945), Engelbart and Nelson's (Nyce and Kahn 1992) hypertext work belong to the domain of scientific work and focussed originally on the large corpus of information in the Library of Congress. The goal was to avoid research workers being bogged down by the sheer mass of new knowledge and to support the selection of information, i.e. research findings, in a different way than that afforded by formal, hierarchical library classification and indexing schemes . Users were supposed to be domain specialists, scientists, knowledge workers. The underlying task was to write, read, comment, review, annotate, compare, edit, publish, advertise, distribute etc. through a network of publicly accessible hyperdocuments. Memex was envisioned as an *individual's device* for creating new associative structures through his/her personal, individual associations among items. Personal, individual associations were to be the basic principle to be applied in accessing and using records instead of those generally applied for the entire library collection and to be used by the general population of users.

In some user driven work systems, users are hardly constrained by other factors than the boundaries of the domain and the availability of information resources needed for choice of action. In that case, domain constraints are invisible, internal, and implicitly embedded in users' individual creativity and intellectual capacity as shaped within a long time span by shifting external constraints such as intellectual cultures, group norms, paradigms and fashions. Typical tasks are those concerned with creating art and cultural works.

Typical examples of hypermedia systems where the functionality depends entirely on the goals and intentions in the activities of single individuals are some research applications (Schnase 1989), idea analysis and organisation (Fischer 1990), authoring (Streitz 1990, Rada 1991). Many of these systems were built experimentally in the particular work domains of their developers.

For systems in which users are autonomous and determine the goals, task and approach to work, the source of constraints to represent in the information system design is the problem space as defined by user needs. This does not imply that these systems cannot be highly organised by a structured concept; however the design should be based on an analysis of the relational structure of the users' needs. If sufficiently comprehensive user structures cannot be identified, familiar metaphors can provide an "artificial structure" which provides an semantically analogical "glue" to connect relationships. The Book House combines these two approaches.

5.2 Work Systems Structured by Social Laws

Typical work system examples in this category are numerous and include some very early, hypermedia systems for educational tasks in the teaching of students. Constraints exist in this category of domains in the form of governmental laws, ministerial policies, institutional policies, and curicula plans. However given broad educational goals, teachers of a subject domain are left with many degrees of freedom in their choice of materials and exercises and, in particular, in choice of pedagogical methods, didactic approaches, etc. Equally important is the inherent advantage of giving students freedom to formulate their own goals and learning paths according to their own cognitive style and subjective preferences. (Landow 1989).

Other examples are office systems for training workers in business management (Andersen et al.1992), case handling of work accidents (Carstensen 1990), legal work in patent cases, auditing,which is a complex domain with tightly coupled networks of information (DeYoung 1989), writing legal documents (Thomas and Mital 1992), many examples of training of technicians in mechanical repair, and mail sorting machinery in post offices (Passang 1992), design work in human factors (Boff 1991) and in software development (Bocker 1990). Publishing has been a particularly fruitful domain for the development of hypermedia systems e.g., in the development of optic disc technologies.

5.3 Work Systems Structured by Physical Laws

A third category are domains involving the control of tightly coupled physical processes in technical systems - e.g., power plants and chemical process plants. The basic constraints underlying the behavior of this category of work domains is the physical functionality governed by laws of nature. The functional degrees of freedom in these tightly coupled systems are constrained by the physical anatomy and the resulting well defined functional structure. This leaves the user with practically no influence on the constraints or on task/problem formulation. Personal user semantics are irrelevant for system interactions; there are few degrees of freedom for choice among action alternatives during task performance. This is probably the reason why no hypermedia systems have been found in this domain by the author. However hypermedia is a relevant design concept for this domain - in particular because users need information systems with flexible facilities for exploring system state and eventual action possibilities in the case of unforeseen events. These are very critical for these domains due to the potentially extreme consequences of system malfunctions (Vicente and Rasmussen 1992).

It is a fundamental issue in hypermedia designs to give the user the control of the domain structure as well as control of the interaction with the system. This implies a shift from the traditional control of the user by interactive limitations to giving the user control of domain information by imposing personal semantic structures onto the domain structures. Therefore most hypermedia systems are found in domains characterized by a high degree of user control.

In conclusion, an attempt to place some actual hypermedia applications into these categories are found in figure 3. Complex domains structured by laws, legislation, social policies etc. together with complex domains structured on occasion by users' goal related needs have received most attention in hypermedia design.

HYPERMEDIA DOMAIN STRUCTURES

Physical Structures	Policy Structures	User Structures
	Accounting	Authoring
	Administration	Community infor-
	Authoring	mation
	- Collaborative	Conferences
	- Courseware	Design
	Computers	Entertainment
	- Documentation	- Interactive fiction
	- Interfaces	Intellectual Work
	- Manuals	Journalism
	- User Assistance	- Magazines
	Costumer Service	Research
	Design	- Biology
	Education	Tourism
	- Archeology	Transportation
	- Biology	- Railways
	- Dictionary	
	- Encyclopedia	
	- History	
	- Hypertext	
	- Language	
	- Literature	
	- Reference Book	
	Law	
	- Patent	
	- Social security	
	Mechanics	
	- Cars	
	- Ships	
	- Trains	
	Museums	
	- Exhibits	
	Office	
	Publishing	
	Software Use	
	Work Accidents	

Figure 3 shows some typical examples of domains for hypermedia systems placed within three typical types of structures. See appendix A for a list of applications summarized within the labels of Domain-Task-User categories.

6. Cognitive Framework for Analysis and Design

The framework described in this paper to support hypermedia designs is an analytical tool for cognitive work analysis which relates the conceptual model behind hypermedia software tools to the semantic network of concepts and relations in a work domain as well as to the cognitive characteristics of the users. The benefits of integrating the cognitive work analysis with the hypermedia conceptual model works both ways actually since the hypermedia concept provides a powerful language for describing the transfer of an analysis of work domain networks into functional system properties. This mutual benefit has a natural explanation. The origin of the hypermedia concept or paradigm sprang obviously from a desire to satisfy users' personal information needs by imposing a subjective, individual structure on general information systems in order to improve their abilities to satisfy the individual users' goals and intentions. This original purpose also explains the choice of domains and tasks for existing hypermedia systems - i.e., domains where no explicit constraints or structures can be/have been identified which require conformance by users in order to obtain an acceptable result.

The cognitive work analysis concept or paradigm was initiated by a need to understand the interaction between the complex relational structures and constraints of work domains and end users' cognitive activities and subjective preferences during computer-mediated task performance. These complex relational domain concepts play a major role - not only in stipulating goals and resources (i.e., ends and means) within which action possibilities and constraints can be identified; to a great extent they also structure users' cognitive activities and shape their mental models during task interactions (Rasmussen 1986).

---

1. WORK DOMAIN CHARACTERISTICS

Means/ends network
Goals, functions and objects of work domain

Constraints,tightness of coupling

Autonomous users' world of goals, intentions, constraints

2. TASK CHARACTERISTICS

Means/ends network in a task situation

Cognitive decision tasks

Task Strategies

3. USER CHARACTERISTICS

Mental Models

Cognitive and Perceptual Capabilities

Figure 4. The three basic properties of particular importance for hypermedia representations vary along many dimensions which underlie the analysis of work domains, task situations and user characteristics .

However the intent of designing hypermedia systems to match users' cognitive structures is for many applications a too limited approach. Task actions and users' cognitive structures are interrelated, and several different cognitive structures will be activated during interactions with a domain through a hypermedia system. Hence, to support users in coping with external task constraints, hypermedia representations also need to represent work domain structures and properties. That is, in complex work domains, associative, semantic networks cannot be generated purely from the individual users' associative relationships as they occur during interaction with the system. Instead they have to be based on semantic relationships and structures derived from an analysis of the properties of the totality comprising *work domain-task situation-user characteristics*. These are three dimensions from a theoretical framework for cognitive work analysis which has been developed recently to encompass from a cognitive perspective 1) the properties of different work domains, including organisational and management principles and 2) the resource and preference profiles of individual users who are placed in a given work domain. The framework offers principles within eight dimensions that can systematize designers' knowledge and use of theories, methods, models, concepts and relationships about human work activity that are relevant for the analysis, design and evaluation of advanced information systems. (Rasmussen, Pejtersen and Goodstein 1992). A short introduction of dimensions and features of the framework for design decisions can be found in Rasmussen and Pejtersen (1992).

Before the presentation of each of these three principles, a short overview of the Book House design decisions is given below.

7 The Book House System

The Book House is a library system designed to support both indexing and retrieval of fiction in libraries for the general public and in school libraries as well. The basic structure of the information flow during these two tasks is shown in figure 6. The first version of the system was a prototype developed in C running on a PC under DOS, containing 3.500 books. Fifty percent of a typical bookstock of a branch library close to Copenhagen. The second version is a commercial product developed in cooperation with Apple Computers A/S in Denmark in Supercard and C++ to be distributed to the Scandinavian countries. As mentioned above, the Book House was originally conceived before the arrival of hypermedia tools and as such was not driven by the new and fascinating possibilities of this technology.

Due to the cross disciplinary education in schools, and to the influence of TV and other Mass Media, requests in public libraries for specific subjects in fiction are becoming increasingly frequent, such as "books about jealousy in marriage, about feelings, not about divorce laws, with a happy ending, no divorces, and preferably with a philosophical attitude" or "critical books about physical demands in modern sports". Today no retrieval tool exists to solve these topical information needs. The Book House was designed to solve this retrieval problem.

Similar problems have been found in current online public access systems (adopted from Hildreth, 1989):

-Users fail to match their own need formulation with the subject vocabulary.of the system. The vocabulary in bibliographic records is incompatible with the needs and language brought to the systems by their users.

-Lacking understanding and use of system facilities. Partial use of the options provided by systems and missing opportunities to complete initiated searches.

-Navigational confusion and frustration for the user during the search process caused by bad interfaces and unsupportive user-system dialogues.

The Book House system concept was initiated as a means to circumvent such problems and to improve the general public's access to information in libraries.

As described elsewhere, (Pejtersen 179, 1980) from studies of five hundred user-librarian interactions in information retrieval followed by structured interviews recorded in a real life environment emerged a system with hypermedia features. In order to cope with user behaviour and user interactions with intermediaries as they occurred in the large amount of empirical data, the Book House system had to be designed so as to *achieve four types of match :*

1) The semantic network of the information sources in fictional literature was designed to match users' goals and intentions. Based on an analysis of user queries in cognitive decision tasks in information retrieval situations, a multifacetted classification scheme representing book content at several levels of abstraction corresponding to users' ways of asking for information was developed for indexing books in the database. This user-oriented indexing gave a fine granularity of information in book nodes with a high number of specific keywords as embedded links. A number of precision and recall experiments tested the indexing policy. As a result, a very tight relationship existed among the representational structure of book content/links and users' queries and categorisation of information.

2) The navigational interactions were designed to match the search strategies which proved to be natural to users for a given problem situation. The users' information processing, the

mental models they applied when searching within a given strategy, the requirements of these strategies for database content and for users' mental resources were also important for the design of the supporting retrieval functionality.

3) The content and structure of the interface were designed to match users' cognitive and perceptual capabilities during shifts among several retrieval strategies. Based on this, an iconic, direct manipulative interface with separate display formats was chosen for each of the implemented search strategies. A "Book House" metaphor was used as an overall structure underlying the content of the various displays in order to support users' navigation through the varied functionality of the system and to control the search.

4) The form of the icons in the interface displays was designed to match the user population's cultural background and knowledge in an attempt to design an interface which could easily be understood and operated by the occasional, possibly computer illiterate user.

An introduction of some of the design decisions and their underlying investigations within the domain -task - user perspective will be found in the following sections.

Design Decisions for the Book House	
1. Design of the database network with book content structures corresponding to the structure of library users' reading needs	*Database Content and structure* The representation of the book stock. i.e., the space in which search is to be performed
2. Design of computer functions to be activated by users' queries within one of several search strategies into proper selection of database network and retrieval algorithms	*Navigation and Retrieval Functionality:* Transformation of user strategies and procedures into access to database network and retrieval operations.
3. Design of a metaphor to determine structure and content of interface displays needed to control navigation and retrieval functionality	*Interface structure & content:* Structure on interface content to control elements and sequence of all interface displays
4. Design of the visual coding/icons used for the presentation of the elements of displays according to the user population's cultural background and capabilities	*Visual form of Interface Displays:* Form of visual presentation in displays of action possibilities: database network, strategies and retrieval operations

Figure 5. The basic design choices in the approach to the Book House design.

8 Use of the Framework for the Book House Design

Deriving semantic relationships from structures in one or more of the perspectives *work domain - task situation - user characteristics* formed the analytical basis for the design of the Book House. Only those of the dimensions displayed in figure 4 which were important for the design of the Book House system will be introduced. These perspectives include (a) analysis of the work system to uncover the *means/ends network* of work items and information sources that give structure to and describe the "resident knowledge-base" of the entire work system - including domain goals, constraints and action possibilities, (b) the information needs for cognitive decision tasks in particular work situations and appropriate task strategies, (c) users' cognitive and perceptual resource profiles, levels of expertise and subjective preferences.

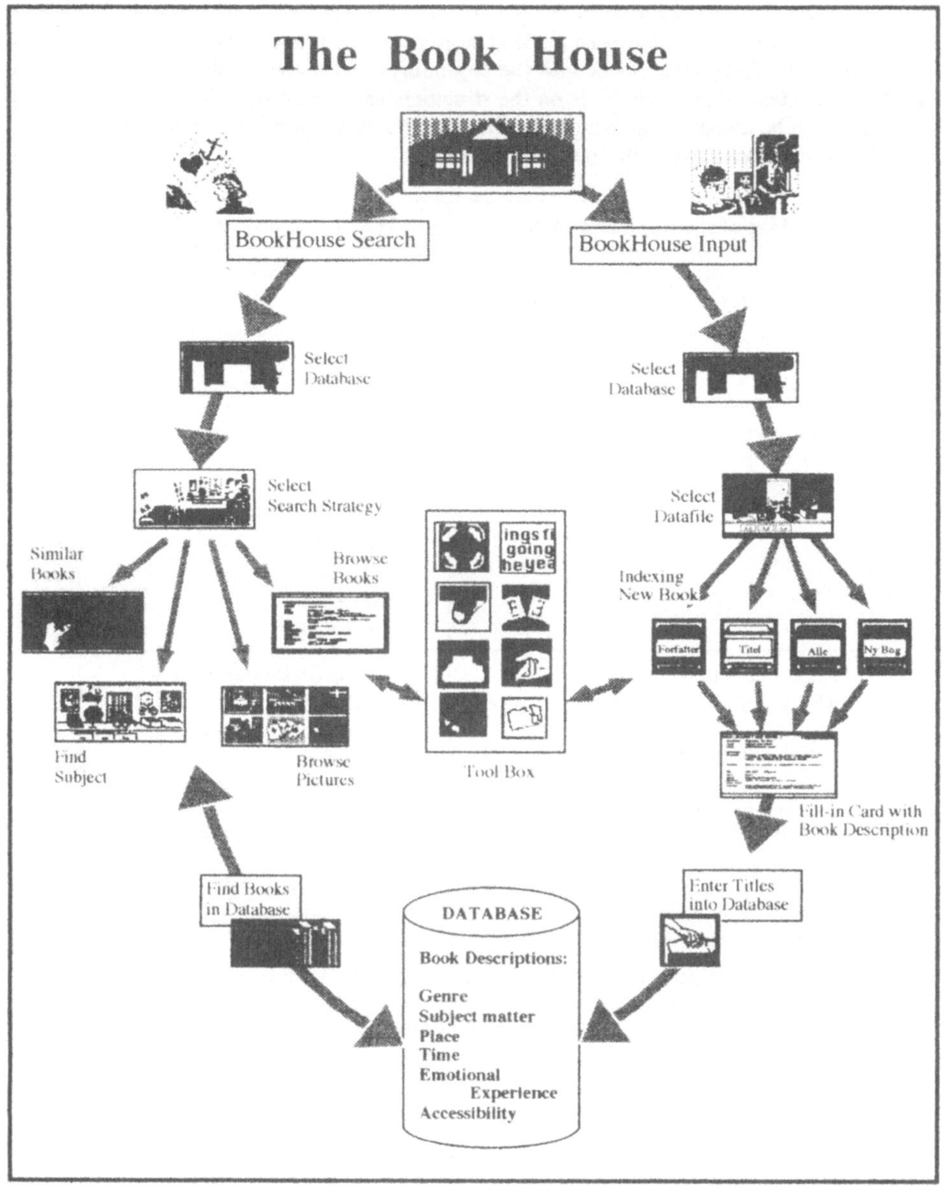

Figure 6 shows the two types of user interactions with the database. The left side shows retrieval of books from the database, the right side shows the option for writing a new book description or editing descriptions in the database.

Each of these three principles will first be outlined shortly in general terms, then followed by a second paragraph with a specific example from the Book House design. Then follows a short reference to the possible usefulness of these three main perspectives to hypermedia concepts.

For the purpose of the presentation of this paper at a hypermedia conference and for the benefit of its readers, a first attempt has been made at transferring the Book House design decisions as well as the underlying framework into the beginnings of a hypermedia system terminology/design context. The emphasis is on the structures as gleaned from a cognitive analysis which then can be mapped onto a hypermedium for structuring and representing information. Figure 5 gives an indication of this potential mapping.

Hypermedia Concepts	Work System Analysis

Database Network Content
    (Ex. Nodes, Links)
	Work Domain Concepts/Information sources:
	    Means/ends relations among
	    Goals,functions,objects
	    Constraints, Coupling, Control

Categories of Network Content
    (Ex.Graphs,Subgraphs, Link clusters,
    Composite nodes, Node types)
	Task Situation/ Decisions:
	    Information for
	    -Exploration
	    -Information Retrieval
	    -Goal setting
	    -Analysis
	    -Evaluation
	    -Monitoring

Navigational Interactions
    (Ex.Paths)
 	
Retrieval functionality
	Users' Task Strategies:Mental Models for:
	    Formal, Attribute Analysis
	    Associative, Prototypes
	    Intuitive, Pattern Recognition

Interface Representation Content/form
    (Ex.Nodes, Links, Graphs,Webs)
	Users Resources/Capabilities
	    Knowledge
	    Mental Models and Resources
	    Cognitive/Perceptual capabilities

Figure 7 A simplified illustration of the coupling between the work system analysis in terms of domain, task and user characteristics and the hypermedia software elements. The figure shows the many different types of representations from the cognitive work analysis.

8.1 Library Domain: The Book House Database Structure

Analysis of a work system is focused on the goal relevant constraints governing the work domain, which will then in turn be the constraints governing the development of a database network structure.If the domain in question has tightly coupled constraints, the analysis of the domain properties can be represented by the means/ends relations found in the actual domain. Analysis of the informational basis relevant for different task activities includes analysis of *why* a work activity exists, i.e. goals and constraints, *what* functions should take place, and *how* it should be done, i.e. tools to be used. This analysis provides the information resource territory in which a user has to navigate for exploration of the objectives and the options available to comply with work requirements. In user driven domains a similar analysis can be performed with focus on users' goals, intentions and possible constraints.

The Book House represents a user driven domain. Information retrieval is controlled by the end users' goals, intentions and pragmatic experiences as they are dynamically activated during retrieval interactions. The user should be autonomous in his/her control of the system. Most constraints on the retrieval process originates in the user's world. The only constraints originating in libraries are the, often rigid, classification schemes that do not reflect end users' perspectives. Hence, the domain analysis preceding the Book House design focussed on the means/ends aspect of the user's world. The focus was on the users' *intentionality* as culled mainly from the analysis of user queries arising during their cognitive decision making in actual information retrieval negotiations in libraries. (Figure 8)

Document Content	User Needs
Author Intention; Information; Education; Enjoyable Experience.	Reader's Ultimate Goal
Literary or Professional Quality; Paradigm; Style or School.	Value Criteria Related to Reading Process and/or Product
General Frame of Content; Cultural Environment, Historical Period, Professional Context.	General Topical Interest of Historical or Social Setting.
Specific, Factual Content. Episodic Course of Events; Factual Descriptions.	Topical Interest in Specific Content
Physical Characteristics of Document; Form, Size, Color, Typography, Source, Year of Print.	Reading Ability

Figure 8. Means/ends representation for the decision task in information retrieval. The figure illustrates that information retrieval essentially is an activity which attempts to achieve a "match" between two multi-level entities, one representing the user/reader with his / her needs / goals / values and the other a document collection describable at various corresponding levels.

Five main levels were identified in users' requests. The highest "why" level in the user's own means-ends representation expresses his/her *goals for reading documents* in terms of various kinds of emotional experiences and/or education and cognition/information. Next, the user's affiliation with scientific or *cultural paradigms* and subscription to professional schools or writing styles. These of course depend on the user's current task and/or product-oriented intentions with reading books. These goal related "why" motivations are also correlated with various *types of content-related factors* such as events, plot, subject-matter, social, geographical and time frames (comprising the so-called "what level"), and depend likewise on the user's current task and situation. A further decisive factor for a successful reading experience is the *accessibility of books* with regard to the level of communication employed by the author in relation to the user's reading abilities, the "how" level. This includes typically difficulties in language and/or substance matter content or in literary form relating to the social use of texts. It includes further *the physical appearance* of the documents, such as colour and cover or front page illustrations as well as the name, age and other characteristics of the main characters in the story. Similar levels have been defined in users' writing documents for hypertext systems (Dillon 1990).

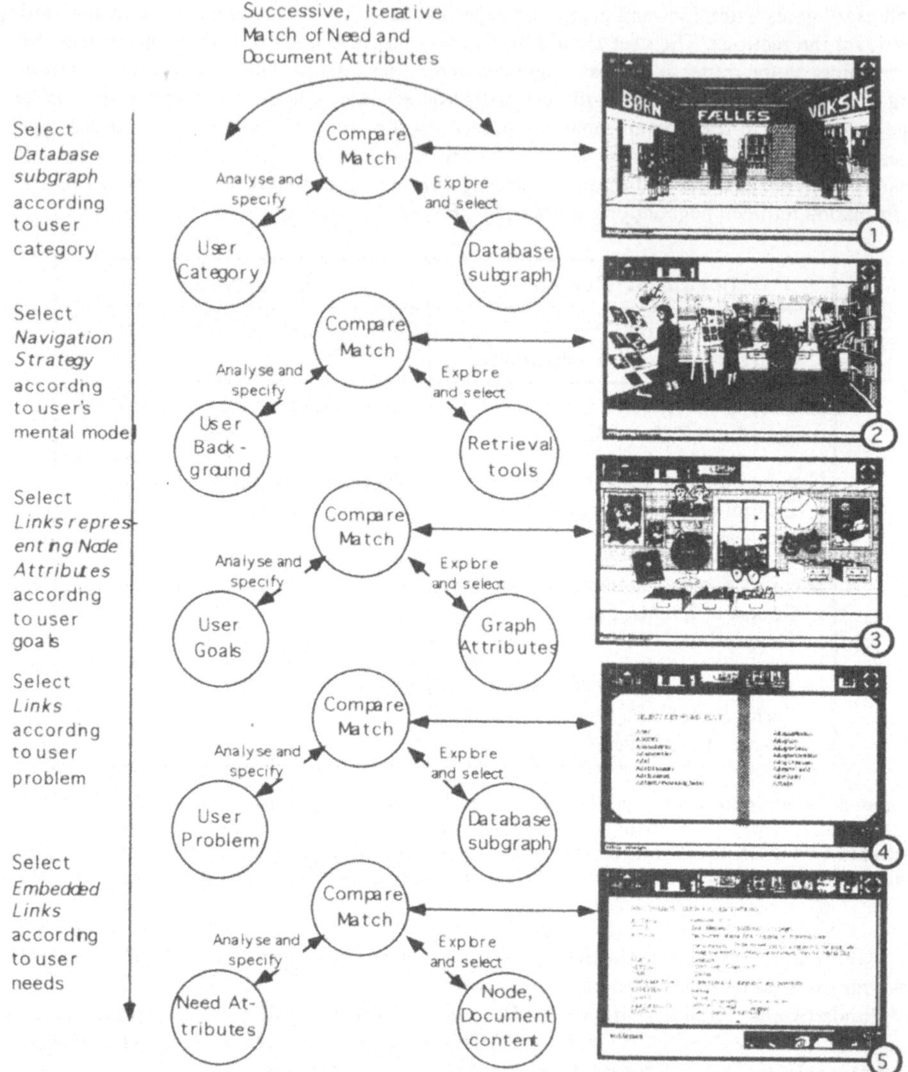

Figure 9 shows the levels of increasingly detailed information attributes involved in the decision task of match in information with user's need during navigation within the analytical strategy. If no match is found when multiple attributes of book content are compared with a need, action possibilities are shown as embedded links or as icons. The user can select among link types with different attributes represented in the display as icons: Red keywords can be selected or omitted from the book description and selected keywords can be deleted in a continuation of the analytical strategy. A search for books similar to the book on the screen can be initiated, browsing through the current set of books, or a shift to a different room for choice of another database or strategy.

Reference to hypermedia concepts: Since all five levels are of importance to the user, each book node in the Book House comprises information about all these dimensions. The content of each book node is structured according to these five levels of the means/ends representation. Each book node is an instantiation of the dimensions related to the various levels in the basic means-ends representation. The granularity of each book node is similarly given by this representation of users' level of information needs.

8.2 Framework: Task Situation Representation

Information gained from a task situation analysis will identify the knowledge items from the means/ends network which are relevant in a particular activity. The task situation analysis breaks down work activities into subunits which can be related to cognitive activities, such as information retrieval, situation analysis and diagnosis, priority judgments and goal evaluation, planning, execution and monitoring. These so called decision functions define categories within which the behaviour of the individual users takes place. They represent linked processes that presuppose one other, i.e. one decision process results in a "state of knowledge" that is the prerequisite for the next process.

In practise, these individual decision functions will not so be clearly separated and sequential. Instead the actual task will reflect user inclinations, experience and tendencies to introduce shifts of thought. Nevertheless, it is important to identify a set of generic decision functions and the resulting "states of knowledge" in order to be able to link the different decision functions.

These two insights are useful in identifying the queries which are likely to be made by users for retrieving information. They are particularly relevant for linking nodes into meaningful semantic units of subgraph structures matching each decision function. They can also be used for selecting links to database information in the shape of keywords, strings, icons, etc. This approach was used in the Book House design - and to some extent in Conklins (1987) system "Design Journal" based on a model ISAAC developed to meet the internal structure of design decisions during analysis and evaluation in order to support designers in a constrained task situation.

8.3 Framework: Task Situation in Decision Making Terms

This level of analysis transfers the task description to an information processing language. As shown in figure 9, the task of information retrieval is essentially an activity which attempts to achieve a "match" between two multi-level entities, one representing the user/reader with his/her needs/goals/values and the other a document collection describable at corresponding levels. A typical information retrieval activity can be decomposed into a number of generic information processing functions connected by various 'states of knowledge' about the problem domain. This will involve some or all of the following decision elements in various sequences and iterations will typically take place.

Situation analysis /diagnosis - generating a user need based on current goals, background activities.

Exploration - database information and constraints of match of users' needs with book features

Planning - goals to pursue, priorities of search paths and outcomes, preparation and translation of query formulation search strategies, search tactics and procedures.

Execution of search, control of retrieval activities, search tactics and strategies

Examining - evaluating/judging the relevance and compatibility of retrieved documents with needs.

Verification of result, possible revision, new activity planning, execution.

Reference to hypermedia concept: For the task of examination, verification of match of user's need with node contents and a subsequent revision of planning, choice of strategy and tactics, users were allowed untailored, free iterations and access to all subgraphs and links types: Means/ends subgraphs, database subgraphs, links, node structures.See figure 9 for an example of a decision task .

8.4 Framework: Task Strategies

Several cognitive strategies are available for most information processing tasks. Each strategy is based on a particular kind of mental model, a set of tactical rules and a related mode of interpretation of observations. A mental model is defined as a particular representation of the means/ends levels of the domain activated by choice of strategy. As for decision tasks, a sequential, formalized description of users' processing of information and observations is an idealized structure of a class of mental processes. The actual implementations of a particular strategy during a task situation will be different on each occurrence with frequent shifts among segments of strategies. But they will share important characteristics - i. e., a particular kind of mental model, a certain kind of interpretation of the observed information and a set of tactical planning rules for navigation in the information space of means and ends.

Different strategies demand very different resource profiles of a user with respect to knowledge, capacity, time, etc. The characteristics of the various strategies can therefore be further described with reference to subjective performance criteria such as time needed, cognitive strain, amount of information required, cost of failure, etc.. Resource conflicts can be resolved and mental work load relieved by shifts to another strategy possessing different resource requirements.

Momentary mental confusions and difficulties due to cognitive overload can normally be circumvented by a shift of strategy. Thus not only do the strategies themselves have to be known. In addition, designers have to be aware of the users' criteria for choosing among them as well as the cues initiating a choice of strategy or a shift between strategies in an actual situation, such as for instance memory requirements, spatial capabilities, and background knowledge.

Another, and equally important, reason for shifting strategy is the non linear, associative problem solving activities of users so often advocated by hypermedia researchers. A user can shift perspectives and strategies several times in response to new ideas and the changing priorities of different task objectives during task performance. Thus associative navigation can be undertaken following the links in the different networks underlying each individual strategy.

It will relieve users' disorientation if all of the strategies which are likely to be chosen by a user are implemented in the user-system interaction as usable navigational paths to database content. If the information content and structure necessary to follow a trail is tailored to match users' mental models underlying their current choice of strategy, their information processing will be recognition-based. In searching by recognition, the context is only implicitly known in terms of the pool of episodic experiences of the user, who will look for information to confirm or update the current model of his/her domain as a basis for choice among action possibilities. If this is not possible, the user is forced to resort to backtracking, to analytical reasoning about prior events and to remembering/understanding the attributes of the semantic, multilevel structures of the domain.

REVIEW OF STRATEGIES	
1. Bibliographical Strategy User: selects and decides author/title, explores retrieved items,compares bibliographical data with need and compares content with bibliographical data.	Computer: assists with identification, verification and location of retrieved items. Communicates information contents for verification of identified items.
2.Analytical Strategy User: communicates information on need. Accepts and rejects proposed documents.	Computer: explores user's need. Compares need with representation of information contents of documents in the database and selects documents. Displays document contents for user's consideration.
3.Empirical Strategy User: communicates characteristic demographic, personal characteristics. Accepts and rejects proposed documents.	Computer: explores user characteristics by questions and proposals. Classifies user according to user characteristics and associates to stereotypical sets of items.
4. Search by Analogy User: communicates information on need through a model document. Accepts and rejects proposed documents.	Computer: explores attributes of contents of model document, compares to document representations in database and selects, suggests documents for user's consideration. OR:classifies document and associates to stereotypical set of items in the database.
5.Browsing Strategy User: selects and skims subsets of database information. Communicates field of interest and explores potentials of the database.	Computer: scans through information content of subsets of database and compare match with profile of user interest.

Figure 10. The different search strategies identified during information retrieval in libraries, and the allocation of roles between user and computer, when navigation is supported by the display of information at various levels matching the different search strategies. Of the identified strategies shown in the figure only the empirical strategy was not implemented in the current version of the Book House system.

Book House Example: Strategies for Navigation. In much hypermedia literature, it is claimed that *browsing* is what hypermedia essentially provides most efficiently to users who thereby can navigate easily by selecting links (McAleese 1989). A main criterion in the Book House has been the support of interaction in terms of browsing links and book nodes within the contextual structure of different mental search strategies.

The system offers the opportunity to choose freely among an *analytical strategy, a search by analogy* and a *browsing strategy* (figure 10). Providing several search strategies together with a navigational metaphor has proven to be a very efficient solution to the disorientation problem.

The *analytical search* is a knowledge-based search in a network of relations between document attributes and attributes of user needs in order to achieve a match between the two.The mental model activated during this process must be based on knowledge about the users' world and a corresponding list of categorial attributes of book contents derived from user intentions.

Information during retrieval is perceived and interpreted at a symbolic level to develop, support and revise the current model of the actual domain of books and user needs.

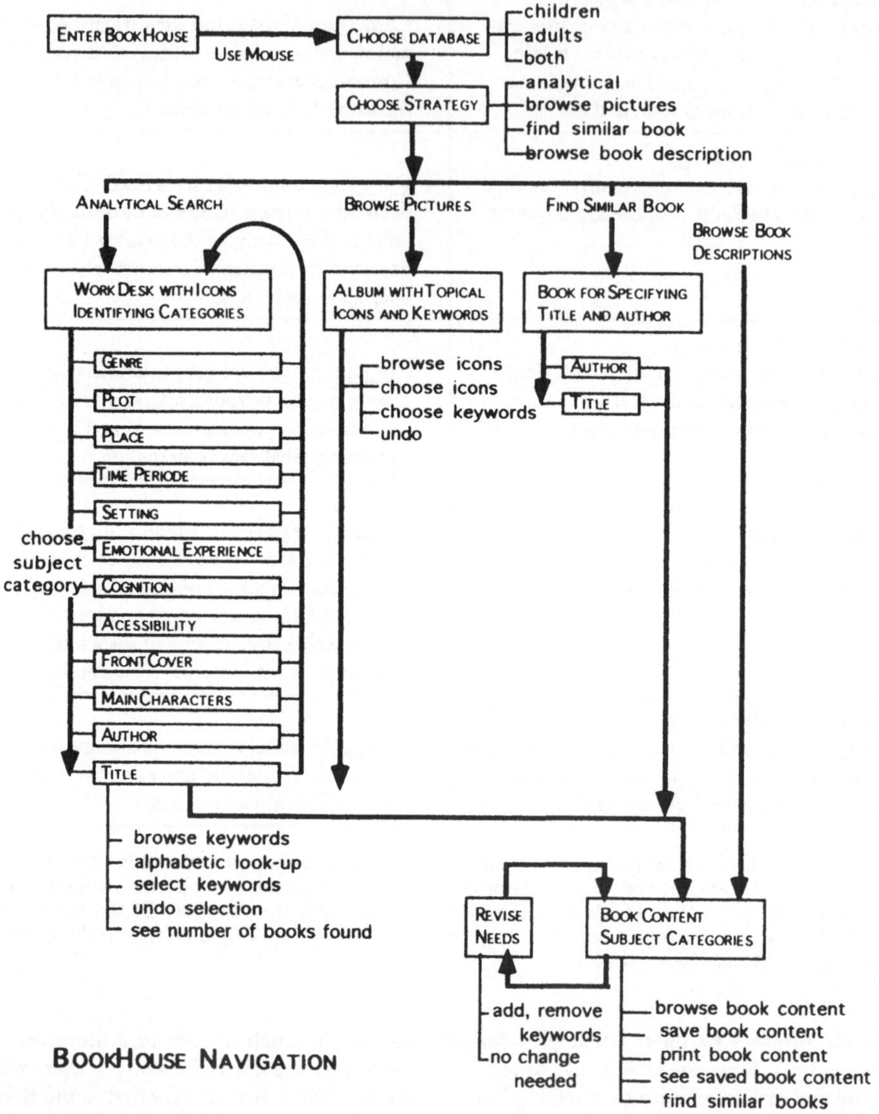

Figure 11 shows four different navigational paths The "see books" phase of the dialogue for comparison and evaluation of match with need, is entered from each of the four strategies: After either the analytical specification or the browse in pictures selection has been made, after a model book title has been specified in a find similar books dialogue, or after the user has desired to browse in book descriptions.A description of the first book of the current set is then displayed on the screen. A host of options now become available independent of the search strategy selected.The user can now repetitively select icons for search actions from the repertoire displayed on the top or bottom of displays in figure 9.

The search *by analogy* is more of a rule-based search using a prototypical, previously successful example from the user's reading repertoire which triggers associations to *patterns of book attributes*. The mental model consists of patterns of book attributes derived from intuitive judgements of similarity from past instances of similarity searches. Empirical experience rather than formal information is used to identify common attributes of individual examplars in a category.

Browsing and *exploration* is an intuitive process of scanning the database network hoping for a spontaneous recognition of relevant concepts and familiar cues and signs for action. Little is formally planned; the user's need is usually vaguely defined There is no explicit mental model of the user's domain and any intentions activated during browsing; browsing works primarily on the user's tacit knowledge of the domain of books and his/her own domain of intentions and goals. All kinds of pragmatic values, associations and experiences are involved when looking for a match with users' previous experiences. When browsing, there is a need for some kind of an organisation of information matching users' knowledge domain into operational subsets for browsing. A browsing strategy is appropriate in unfamiliar situations when no explicit characterization of the specific information to be retrieved is available. Browsing usually demands few mental resources and meets few constraints; a switch to browsing will often take place in any kind of search as a means for associative exploration, formulation and even revision of anticipated needs. Figure 11 shows different search strategies for navigation.

As discussed in a later paragraph, when information is displayed so as to support a recognition-based perception of cues for action, a browsing will be an efficient problem solving strategy. The Book House interface displays information to allow users to process information in a browsing mode while, at the same time, they navigate within an analytical strategy. This approach utilizes the benefits of a browsing mode requiring few mental resources without users losing any support of their search using a domain model which makes the attributes of the database network of book content explicit. The effect is a reduction of disorientation and cognitive overload.

Reference to hypermedia concepts: When searching within a strategy, computed links determined during system development will be changing as the user navigates. In each window, users' only have access to those procedural links of relevance for a given strategy. Book nodes have varied contents matching the individual strategy.

8.5   Framework: Representation of User Characteristics and Users' Cognitive Resources

Analysis of user characteristics are important for interface design, and will normally involve demographic features, profession, training, education, sex, age, etc.. In this paragraph the focus is on cognitive capabilities and perceptual characteristics in relation to users' level of *expertise*, which are naturally correlated with the other characteristics.

Depending on the users' varying expertise and domain knowledge, they will have different and more or less complete mental models of the means/ends network structure of their domain. Knowledge about novice and expert users' mental domain models is important for the user interface design because it supplies information about the content and format needed in the interface. Each model has its own set of requirements for a representation of the domain.

Users' preferences for task strategies will depend upon their competence and familiarity with their task. Novices and trained experts will therefore usually prefer different strategies.

When users navigate through choosing different strategies, they activate different mental domain models which should be represented accordingly in the interface to obtain compatibility between desired navigational strategy and interface displays.

Information displayed in the interface will be perceived, processed and interpreted in different ways depending on the user's expertise and familiarity with the problem at hand.The kind of information processing behaviour to be expected from users depending on their knowledge background and expertise is important for designing the content and form of interface representations. Three general levels of information processing are relevant in this context, the so called skills - rules and knowledge based behaviours (Rasmussen, 1986).

1.Analytical, knowledge based problem solving behaviour

Information is interpreted as symbols and thus depends upon a symbolic representation of domain properties. Analytical problem solving is slow and proceeds in a sequential fashion, and it is based on a fundamental understanding of the domain. It is therefore typical for experts in an unfamiliar situation or novice users when learning about a domain. Users in unfamiliar situations have no repertoire of heuristic short-cuts by-passing the analytical, symbolic way of perception of information. Normative structures of information are helpful in providing users with proper mental models of the domain. As they become more proficient, users will progress with task updates and modify their domain model.

To support the novice users and experts in unfamiliar situations, it is important to represent the properties of the work domain in the form of the means/ends network structure activated in the task in question. This network containing concepts of constraints, goals and means for task functions will serve as an "externalized" mental model. It will support novice users' attempts to create a proper mental model of the domain while learning the domain structures.

2. Perceptual, rule-based problem solving behaviour

Information will be interpreted as signs for action when the user is functioning in an associative mode. In this case, problem solving is not isolated from action and users will search for information to select among the perceived alternatives for action the one matching the case in question. Perception - action processing is recognition-based, fast and effortless and is typical for expert users in a familiar situation. If the environment is well structured and transparent, users in familiar situations will perceive only a small amount of information, enough to resolve the choice among action alternatives. This behaviour is primarily based on learning from frequently encountered events. To support expert users' associative perception - action behaviour, it is important to implement a unique one-to-one mapping between the network properties of the work domain in terms of constraints, goals and means for relevant functions and the signs for action selection provided by the interface.

3. Skill Based Behaviour

The level of skilled routines rely on direct perception and manipulation of information as time space signals. A direct manipulation interface with a pointer like a mouse supports users in quickly developing efficient sensory motor skills.

From this follows that interfaces displayed in the form of a one-to-one mapping between symbols and signs for action, may for all kinds of users support direct perception and become easy and fast to perceive and learn. (Rasmussen and Vicente 1990). The evaluation of the Book House system clearly demonstrated this.

In the current context this understanding of different behaviours is particularly important because one of the most frequently claimed objectives of interface designs for hypermedia systems is to solve problems with (1) users' disorientation and their loosing track of location and direction in a hyperspace, (2) cognitive overload due to the extra effort necessary to maintain several trails simultaneously (Conklin 1987) and (3) cohesion deficit (Duchastel, 1990). One reason for these problems are that several levels of information processing are necessary: Users have to reason about their problem in a task and domain dependent context while, at the same time, they attempt to operate within the confines of the existing, but often invisible and unstable, semantic structures of the system.

A frequently used way of solving the problems of disorientation and cognitive overload is the use of metaphors, such as travelling metaphors and walking around a town metaphors etc.. (Mcknight 1990, Hammond et al. 1990, Akscyn et al. 1987). Acksyn experienced that disorientation is not reduced significantly by more hierarchical structures, but that providing navigational commands give good help. However it was even better to provide navigational metaphors with immediate feedback, when an item has been accessed. A navigational metaphor is a very efficient support in providing users with an understanding of the structure of the hypermedia information system itself, if it is based on easily comprehensible analogies to a familiar concept. This makes it straightforward for users to build a mental model of the system in which they are navigating. The most important purpose is to give users a sensible, daily life congruent structural concept that keeps windows and screen displays with variable content together in a context that invites actions on the information by "walking around" screen displays to select information that affords action.

However, although this is a necessary representation if a system user needs a mental model of the hypermedia system, it has its limits in effectiveness as long as it does not also represent the pertinent semantic structural relationships of the various levels of domain content.

8.6 Interface Representation in the Book House

Novice and casual users of the Book House are likely to interpret information as symbols when trying to build a mental model of their problem space and its representation in the system. Embedded in the metaphor of a house, the semantics of the fiction retrieval domain are displayed in a work room as iconic tools and objects to be perceived as symbols used to classify and retrieve books in the database in a way which reflect users' needs and intentions (figure 12).

Pictures in the semantic network of icons called the "Picture Association Thesaurus" for supporting the browsing strategy are designed as symbols, which refer to users' prototypical concepts and needs culled from the general population's own world and knowledge (figure 13). The effectiveness of these icons in supporting prediction and symbolic reasoning depends on the user's familiarity with their content and form. Therefore the design was based on controlled, multiple choice *association tests* conducted with users in libraries. Only those icons whose meaning could be immediately perceived by naive users in two seconds or less were accepted for system design. (Pejtersen, 1991).

In addition to being interpretable in several ways as symbols for reasoning in unfamiliar situations, with properly chosen icons these two interface displays can also serve as sign cues for action. Novices can identify their meaning through an inference related to the underlying conceptual relations based on their associations and recognition from previous experiences.

Furthermore, to support signs for action, a great number of icons are chosen in the form of metaphors having functional analogies to a familiar context.

Reference to hypermedia concepts: The complex database network structures activated during retrieval sessions in terms of links among book nodes is therefore not displayed to users in the interface. It basically operates by presenting displays of iconic representations of link source and target as well as book node contents within the house metaphor with reference to users' needs and personal world. For users, the current computer network structure is irrelevant.

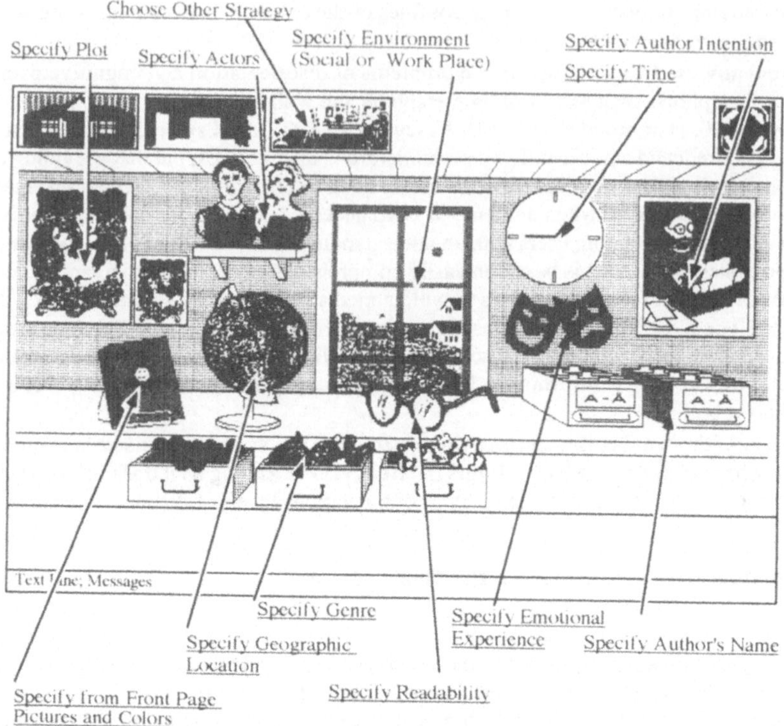

Figure 12. A further support of the user's explicit formulation of reading needs is given through the display of a work desk with icons which identify the various dimensions of need found from field studies. By making these dimensions explicit, the display probes the user's memory for aspects to consider. At the same time, the icons function as command icons which allow the specific dimensions to be used for search to be specified by direct manipulation. The intended level of cognitive control is skill-and rule based support.

9. Principles for Hypermedia Representations

From the experiences gained with the design of the Book House system employing a cognitive work system analysis using the perspective of work domain-task situation-user analysis, some preliminary principles for hypermedia systems are put forward for further investigation and discussion. They are put forward with reference to hypermedia concepts, and some are most appropriate for domains driven by user structures.

1. Hypermedia *networks* should be developed from a *work domain-task situation analysis* and represented as means/ends networks. Organising nodes into a multilevel means/ends link structure comprising goals, constraints, functions and objects will provide users with a global mental model based on an actual, basic domain structure. A means/ends graph structure provides *context* and may help users locate and deal with a task in the landscape in which work takes place.

Figure 13 shows semantic networks of icons based on users' associations of perception of meaning. While browsing six pages of pictorial representations of book content users' recognize attributes of needs. A textual representation with clusters of keywords linked to each icon is displayed in a textline at the bottom of the screen as the user touches the icon. When an icon is selected the category of books represented by keywords related to the icon is retrieved.

2. Depending on the character of the domain, a means/ends network covering the work domain and the task situation may have different information sources based on the degree and character of *goal relevant constraints and intentions:* e.g., physical laws, legislation, institutional and company policies and rules, social culture, and users' goals and intentions.

3. Hypermedia with types of nodes organized in subgraphs should be represented as parts of means/ends networks based on information needs and queries derived from *users' cognitive decision tasks* in a task situation. Typed nodes and subgraphs fitting decision tasks will provide a regularity that may help to reduce the cognitive information overload.

4. Hypermedia interfaces should be based on an analysis of *users' cognitive and perceptual characteristics*. Semantic domain networks should be represented in interface displays as symbolic information referring to the semantic content of nodes but, at the same time, they should be represented as signs for for action/link selection. This has the advantage of presenting to users one unit of information that can serve information processing based on perception for action or symbolic reasoning. Which way will then depend entirely on the individual user's cognitive capacity and the current task activity. In addition, when selected, they should be followed by immediate feedback.

5. There will usually be several strategy-related *domain models*, one for each strategy. Each of these models consists of graphs with collections of nodes relevant for cognitive decision tasks. Similarly, these should be displayed with a *symbolic representation* that, at the same time, can be perceived as a sign for action/link selection. Strategy-related procedural interactions should be displayed as signs representing to users a cue-action relationship.

6. *Task strategies* and their tactical rules should be used to form a set of *pre-established interactive paths* with associated procedures, which activate a selected content of the database network involved in the mental model related to a strategy. Cognitive strategies used as the basis for structuring *navigation* in the hyperspace will lead to different types of navigation. To improve learning and memory, metaphors providing domain and task analogies to structure the interface displays and enhance navigation through a walking or travelling around in the domain should be offered to users. This offers users the possibility for choosing strategies

according to subjective preferences and expertise. At the same time, it removes disorientation and solves problems caused by limitations in users' cognitive resources.

It is important to note that providing symbolic representations which render inherent domain constraints, functional structures and objects of work visible and transparent for knowledge-based reasoning is the most important requirement for content design of hypermedia representations. Secondly, it is important that the design of interfaces takes advantage of the fact that, under suitable circumstances, humans can immediately perceive the meaning and value of objects involved in task activities without any deep analysis of the data presented. The choice of the interface form should support a rapid progression from knowledge-based reasoning to rule-based reasoning for familiar events. The evaluation of the Book House system during a six months period in libraries favoured the system features derived from these principles, and end users had no problem with disorientation or cognitive overload (Goodstein and Pejtersen, 1989).

10. Conclusion

The argument behind the fascination with the hypermedia concept is its effectiveness in supporting users' natural, associative ways of solving a problem. Phrased in another way, Bush and his disciples argued against information systems requiring purely knowledge-based behaviour. He argued for information systems that would also support perception and action-based or recognition-based information processing. The related criticism of information systems requiring purely analytical, formal knowledge based behaviour has proven to be correct. Hypermedia systems are widely accepted by their users for allowing associative, recognition based behaviour.

For further development of the hypermedia concept it is suggested that more attention is payed to representation of the means/ends relations of the work domain and task situation, in addition to users' knowledge structures. Stimulating users' direct perception of the semantic structures in a domain at the level most appropriate to current needs helps users associate and generate several cue-action networks directly from, and across, interface displays, and this, in turn, supports the development of cognitive maps of the domain. Cue action signs during system interactions should be immediately followed by a system feature that enables users to actually act on these signs by marking them as connected with a current item without deep analysis of a relationship, once recognized as being connected.

The philosophy behind the hypermedia experiments led to a new kind of hypermedia system and software functionality, but it might as well be followed by a similar principle for representation of information in the user interface.

11. Acknowledgements

The contribution of many colleages, who have been involved both in library investigations, tdesign of the Book house system, and in the development of the theoretical framework for cognitive system design, to which this paper relate, is gratefully acknowledged. Especially the cooperation has been very helpful with the Royal Academy of Fine Arts on the design of interfaces and with Len Goodstein and Jens Rasmusen on our book dealing with the framework for work analysis: "Cognitive Engineering Concepts and Applications."

12. References

Andersen, N.B et al.. (1992): Qulis: Quality of Life Information System. In Proceedings from NORDDATA, Copenhagen 1992.

Baird, P. and Percival, Mark (1989): Glasgow Online: Database Development using Apple's Hypercard.in McAleese (1989) Hypertext. Theory into Practice. Blackwell Scientific Publications, England.

Begoray, J.A. (1990): Hypermedia Issues, Systems, Application Areas. In: Journal of Man Machine studies. vol. 33, p. 121-147.

Bodtker et al (1990): Hypadapter: An adaptive Hypertext System for Presentation of Teaching Content. In: Gloor, P.A. and Streitz, N. A (eds): Hypertext und Hypermedia. Von Theoretischen Konzepten zur Praktischen Anwendung. Springer-Verlag. Informatik Fachberichte 249. Germany.

Boff, Kenn (1991): CASHE. Computer Aided Systems Human Engineering: A Hypermedia Tool. Paper presented at RIAO , Barcelona, 1991.

Bush, V (1945): As We May Think. Atlantic Monthly, 176, p.101-108.

Carsten, P.(1990): ASK Work Accident System.(Internal Report) FCI, Denmark

Churcher, P.R.(1989): In. A Common Notation for Knowledge Representation, cognitive models, learning and hypertext.Hypermedia, vol.1, no.3. Taylor Graham

Conklin, J.(1987): Hypertext: An Introduction and Survey. IEEE Computer 20, (9), 17-41.

De Young, l.(1989): Hypertext Challanges in the Hypertext Domain. IN. Proceedings of ACM Hypertext 89 Conf. p.-169-189.

Dillon, A and McKnight, C.(1990): Towards a classification of text types: a repertory grid approach. In: Int.J. Man-Machine Studies, Vol.33, 623-636

Duchastel, P. (1990): Examining Cognitive Processing in Hypermedia Usage. In: Hypermedia; vol. 2 no. 3, 1990.

Edwards, D. and Hardman, L. (1989): Lost in Hyperspace: Cognitive Mapping and Navigation in a Hypertext Environment. in McAleese (Hypertext. Theory into Practice. Blackwell Scientific Publications, England.

Fischer et al. (1989): Design Environments for Constructive and Argumentative Design.In: Proceedings of ACM CHI 1989. p.269-275

Fischer, P.M. and Mandl, H.: Towards a Psychophysics of Hypermedia. In: Designing Hypermedia for Learning. Ed.: Jonassen, D.H. and Mandl, H. Heidelberg, Springer-Verlag, XVIIII-XXV

Frenkel, K.A. (1989): The Next Generation of Interactive Technologies. In: Communications of the ACM, 32, 7 p.872-881.

Goodstein L.P.and Pejtersen A.M.(1989): The BOOK HOUSE. System Functionality and Evaluation. RISØ National Laboratory. RISØ-M-2793, 198 p.

Hammond, N. and Allinson, L. (1987): The Travel Metaphor as Design Principle and Training Aid for Navigating around Complex Systems. In: People and Computers. Eds.: Diaper, D et al., 75-90

Hildreth, Charles R.(ed.) (1989): The Online Catalogue: Development and Directions. London: Library Associations.

Klein, G. A. (1989): Recognition-Primed Decisions. In Rouse W.B. (Ed.): Advances in Man-Machine System Research, 5, 47-92. Greenwich, CT: JAI Press.

Landow, G.P. (1989): Hypertext in Literary Education, Criticism and Scholarship. In: Computers and the Humanities, Vol. 23, 173-198

Legett et al. (1990): Hypertext for Learning. In: Designing Hypermedia for Learning. Ed.: Jonassen, D.H. and Mandl, H. Heidelberg, Springer-Verlag, XVIIII-XXV

McAleese, Ray (1989): Hypertext: Navigation and Browsing. In McAleese: Hypertext. Theory into Practice. Blackwell Scientific Publications, England

McKnight, C.; Dillon, A. and Richardson, J. (1989): Problems in Hyperland? A Human Factors Perspective. In: Hypermedia, Vol.1(2), 167-178

Meyrowitz, (1992) Hypertext: does it Reduce Cholesterol, too? in: Nyce, J.M. and Kahn, P. (1992): From Memex to Hypertext: Vannevar Bush and the Mind's Machine

Nielsen (1990), Hypertext and Hypermedia. Academic Press. London.

Nyce, J.M. and Kahn, P. (1992): From Memex to Hypertext: Vannevar Bush and the Mind's Machine.

Pasang, Linda: Hypermail. The Danish Institute of Technology. Private communication.
Pejtersen, A. M (1984).: Design of a computer-aided user-system dialogue based on an analysis of users' search Behavior. In: Social Science Information Studies, no. 4, p. 167-183
Pejtersen, A. M. (1980): Design of a classification scheme for fiction based on an analysis of actual user-librarian communication, and use of the scheme for control of librarians' search Strategies. In: Theory and Application of Information Research. Ed. Harbo, O. and Kajberg, L.. London, Mansell, p. 167-183.
Pejtersen, A. M. (1986): Implications of users' value perception for the design of a bibliographic retrieval System. In: Empirical Foundation of Information and Software Science. Ed.: J. C. Agrawal and P. Zunde. New York and London, Plenum Press, 1986, pp. 23-39.
Pejtersen, A. M. (1989): A Library System for Information Retrieval based on a Cognitive Task Analysis and Supported by an Icon Based Interface. In: ACM, SIGIR Conference Proceedings, Boston.
Pejtersen, A. M. (1990):Interfaces based on Associative Semantics for browsing in Information Retrieval Risø M-2794.
Pejtersen, A. M. (1991): Icons for Organization and Representation of Domain Knowledge in Interfaces. Published in: Tools for Knowledge Organization and the Human Interface. Proceedings 1st International ISKO Conference. Advances in Knowledge Organization, vol. 2. Ed: Fugmann, R. Indeks Verlag, Frankfurt.
Pejtersen, A. M. and Rasmussen, J.R. (1990): Intelligent Systems for Information Retrieval and Decision Support in Complex Work Domains. In: Expert Systems in Agricultural Research. Eds.: Fl.Skov et al.. Statens Planteavlsforsøg og Statens Husdyrbrugsforsøg.
Pejtersen, A. M., and Austin, J (1984): Fiction Retrieval: Experimental design and evaluation of a search system based on users' value Criteria. Part 1 and part 2. In: Journal of Documentation, Vol. 39, no. 4, p. 230-246 and vol. 40 no. 1, p. 25-35. London.
Pejtersen, A. M., Olsen, Sv. E. and Zunde, P. (1987): A Term Association Thesaurus: Development of a system for automatic search in bibliographic databases based on users' word associations. In: Empirical Foundations of Information and Soft Ware Science. Ed.: Rasmussen, J and Zunde, P.. New York and London, Plenum Press.
Pejtersen, A. M.:(1979) Investigation of search strategies in fiction based on an analysis of 134 user-librarian Conversations. In: IRFIS 3. Ed.: Henriksen, T. Oslo, p. 107-132.
Pejtersen, A.M. (1989): The BOOK HOUSE. Modeling users' needs and search strategies as a basis for system design. RISØ National Laboratory. RISØ-M-2794, 98 p.
Pejtersen, A.M. (1992): A New Model for Multimedia Interfaces to Online Public Access Catalogues. In The Electronic Library, International Journey.December. Learned Information, England.
Pejtersen, A.M. (1992): The Book House. An Icon Based Database System for Fiction Retrieval in Public Libraries. In: The Marketing of Library and Information Services 2. Ed: Cronin, B., ASLIB, London. 572-591.
Pejtersen, A.M. and Goodstein, L.P.(1990): Beyond the Desk Top Metaphor: Information Retrieval with an Icon Based Interface. In: M.J.Tauber and P.Gorny (eds): Proceedings of the 7th Interdisciplinary Workshop on Informatics and Psychology on Visualization in Human-Computer Interaction, Sharding, Austria , May 1988. Springer Verlag 1990.
Pejtersen, A.M.(1988): Search Strategies and data base design. In: L.P.Goodstein, H.B.Andersen and S.E.Olsen (eds.): Tasks, Errors and Models, Taylor and Francis Ltd..
Rada, R. (1991): Hypertext: from Text to Expertext.: McGraw-Hill Book Company, Maidenhead, Berkshire, England
Rao,U.and Turoff, M.(1991): Hypertext Functionality: A Theoretical framework. In: Human Computer Interaction, vol. 2, 1991.
Rasmussen, J.(1986): Information Processing and Human-Machine Interaction: An Approach to Cognitive Engineering. North Holland, 1986.
Rasmussen, J., and Vicente, K. J. (1990). Ecological interfaces: A technological imperative in high tech systems? International Journal of Human-Computer Interaction, 2, 93-111.
Rasmussen, J., Pejtersen, A.M. and Goodstein, L.P. (1992): Cognitive Engineering: Design Concepts and Applications. Wiley. In press.

Romiszowski, A. (1990): The Hypertext, Hypermedia Solution - But What is Exactly the
    Problem. In: Designing Hypermedia for Learning. Ed.: Jonassen, D.H. and Mandl, H.
    Heidelberg, Springer-Verlag, XVIIII-XXV
Schnase, J.L. and Leggett, J. (1989): Computational Hypertext in Biological Modelling. In:
    proceedings of ACM Hypertext
Shneidermann (1989): Reflections on Authoring, Editing, and Managing Hypertext. In: Barrett,
    E.(ed.):The Socity of Text, MIT press, Cambridge, MA, 989, pp. 115-131
Shneidermann et al. (1989): The hyperties Elecxtronic Encyclopedia: An Evaluation based on
    Three Museum Installations. In: Jurnal of American Society of Information Science 40, 3,
    p.172-182.
Smith and Weiss (1988): Hypertext. In: Communications of the ACM, 31 (7), 816-819.
Streitz, N.A. and Hannemann, J. (1990): Elaborating Arguments: Writing, Learning and
    Reasoning in a Hypertext Based Environment for Authoring. In: Designing Hypermedia for
    Learning. Eds.: D. Jonassen & H.Mandl, Heidelberg, Springer Verlag. 407-437
Streitz, N.A. Hypertext (1990): Hypertext und Hypermedia. Ein innovatives Medium zur
    Kommunikation von Wissen. In: Gloor, P.A. and Streitz, N. A (eds): Hypertext und
    Hypermedia. Von Theoretischen Konzepten zur Praktischen Anwendung. Springer-Verlag.
    Informatik Fachberichte 249. Germany.
Thomas, P. and Mital, V. (1992): Hypertext Document Retrieval and Assembly in Legal
    Domains. In: People and Computers VII. Eds.: Monk, A.; Diaper, D. and Harrison, M.D.
    243-269
Vicente, Kim and Rasmussen, J.(1992): Ecological Interface Design: Theoretical Foundations.
    IEEE Transactions on Systems, Man, and Cybernetics, vol. 22, no.4.
Waterworth, John and Chignell, M. (1989): A Manifesto for Hypermedia Usability Research.
    In. Hypermedia, vol.1, no.3. P 205-234.
Wilson, K. S. Palanque (1988): An Interactive Multimedia System Digital Video Interactive
    Prototype for Children. In: Proceedings of teh ACM CHI 1988. p.275-279.

Appendix A:Examples of Hypermedia Applications

Hypermedia Systems Domains	Tasks		Users
A la Recontre de Philippe	Foreeign languages	Learning	Students
ABS News Interactive	Television news	Browsing	Public
ACCESS	Tourist guide	Infomation retrieval	Public
ACM hypertext	Computers	Research	Scientists
Afternoon	Fiction	Reading	Public
ASK	Work accidents	Casehandling	Case workers
Aspen Movie Map	City map	Travelling	Public
BIT Journal	Human factors	Reading	Scientists
Book House	Library	Information retrieval	Public
Cassins Sparrow	Natural Science	Research	Scientists
CDWORD	Bible	Research	Scientists
Crompton's Enclycopedia	Universal	Learning, retrieval	Public
CSEM	Eletronic Magazine	Reading	Students, scientists
Design Museu	Modern design	Information retrieval	Public
DSB Manual	Mechanics	Repair	Technicians
Eastgate Press	Publication	Writing, reading	Students
Encuentros	Education	Learning	Students
EUCLID	Document writing	Idea organisation	Scientists
Expertext / MUCH	Education	Reading, writing	Teachers
Mcmahon	Education	Reading, writing	Pupils
Fress	Education	Learning	Students
g IBIS	Computer software	Idea organisation	Software engineers
Glasgow Online	Community	Information Retrieval	Public
Guide	Documents	Reading, writing	Scientists
Guide BSD	Computers	Design	Software engineers
Guide/ICL	Computer company	Service	Public
HIS	Computers	Learning	Students
Hypercat	Library	Infomation retrieval	Public
HyperlTDF	Research Institute	Management	Director, staff

Hypernews	Computer conference	Research	Scientists
Hypernotary	Legal documents	Writing	Lawyers
Hypertext 87	Computers	Reading, writing	Scientists
Hyperties	Museum	Information retrieval	Public
IDEX	Document database	Infomation retrieval	Public
IGD	Navy	Repair	Technicians
Inigogo gets out	Fiction	Reading, playing	Public
Interactive Nova	Education	Learning	Students
Intermedia Context 32	Education	Learning	Students
Intermedia tool	Education	Writing, reading	Students
Patents	Law office post office	Casehandling	Lawyers
Hypermail		Learning	Auditors
Audit	Business	Auditing	
Linktext	Publishing	Writing, editing	Universal
LSE Learning support	Education	Learning	Students
LYRE	Education	Learning	Students
Manual	Education	Learning	Students
Manual of medical Therapeuts	Medicine database	Information Retrieval	Students, scientists
Memex	Research libraries	Information Retrieval	Scientists
Movie manual	Mechanic manuals	Repair	Technicians
Navietext/DRUID	Computers	Design	Scientists
Neptune Hypertext	Computer software	Design	Software engineers
Newspeak	Television news	News watching	Public
NLS/Augment	Computers	Reading, writing	Software engineers
Notebook	Mathematics	Research	Scientists
Notecards	Universal	Writing	Researchers
OED	Universal	Reading	Public
Palenque	Education	Learning	Pupils
Peruses	Education	Learning	Students
SEPIA	Documentwriting	Writing	Scientists
Shakespeare	Education	Learning	Students
Soft Ad	Business	Marketing	Public
Symbolic DOC	Computer software	Learning	Engineers
SYNVIEW	Universal	Idea organization	Scientists
Team Work Station	Computer conference	Research	Scientists
Textnet	Library/documents	Writing referencing	Researchers

The election of 1912	Education	Learning	Students
The manhole	Fiction	Reading, playing	Public
The `88 vote	Education	Learning	Students
TWB Termbanle	Technical language	Translation	Translators
WE	Universal	Writing, reading	Scientists
Webster Dictionary	Universal	Learning, retrieval	Public
Whole earth Catalogue	Education	Learning	Students
Zanadu	Publishing	Writing, reading	Scientists
ZOG/KMS	Aircraft	Information management	Military staff

Appendix A shows a sample of hypermedia systems represented within the categories of Domain-Task-User. A few applications don't have names in which case the domain/task name has been used. The literature was not always specific about these three aspects of an application, in which case it was more or less cleraly implied. It includes some general tools, but primarily specific applications, and many examples had to be omitted for lack of space.

Computational Aids for Query Improvement

Jan Pedersen
Xerox Palo Alto Research Center
3333 Coyote Hill Rd.
Palo Alto, CA 94304
USA

Abstract

Information access tools are no better than the queries that drive them. Yet, the user is typically not provided any automated assistance to help formulate better queries. Two access methods that attempt to address this issue are discussed. The first, Snippet Search, permits search over the set of possible queries while the second, Scatter/Gather, enables query-free browsing over large document collections.

1   Introduction

Information access seeks to make available from a large collection of online documents items (i.e. documents or parts of documents) likely to be of use to the user at the time.

There are two basic approaches to this problem. The first, pursued in the hypertext and hypermedia literature, considers explicit links authored between associated items. This has the advantage that connections are only limited by the insight of the author, but has the disadvantage of requiring expert labor time proportional to the size of the collection. The second approach, pursued by the information retrieval community and in the literature on computed links, attempts to analyze the contents of items in order to apply heuristic notions of similarity between items and between queries and items. The goal is to avoid explicit authoring of links by instead computing them implicitly from the automatically analyzed substance of a query or an item. The cost is the construction of inappropriate links due to errorful heuristic matching and the omission of relevant links due to inadequate content analysis.

This paper will describe methods for both improving the accuracy of these implicit links and extending the range of their application by focussing computational resources on the query rather than the search mechanism. That is, many heuristic search methods will perform very well given an appropriate query; however, very little help is provided to the user to construct such a query. The discussion will consider recent work in information retrieval, and will restrict itself to collections of free text documents. However, the general observations apply to any content-based retrieval setting.

2 Information Retrieval Models

An information retrieval situation has two components, a user with an *information need* and a collection, or *corpus*, of natural language text documents. Note that the information need may not be expressed, or expressible, as a query in any particular query language. The task is to satisfy the need, typically by delivering one or more *relevant* documents, or alternatively, by indicating persuasively that no such documents exist in the corpus. This is typically accomplished by automatically extracting from each document a feature set, and providing the user with a tool which enables search over these features in some prescribed fashion. For example, in boolean search the feature set is one or more words extracted from the text of the document, and the query language is boolean expressions involving those words.

Conventional information retrieval techniques are studied within the *library-automation paradigm* motivated by the problems faced by librarians equipped with online card catalogues and other information professionals. It is assumed that there is an intelligent intermediary willing to formulate a complex query given a casually stated request and that the major cost to be minimized is online connect time. This implies that each search request must return as high quality, and as complete, a response as possible and is reflected in evaluation criteria that discount the cost of query formulation and place a premium on exhaustive recall [9]. It is also assumed that queries are of the sort processed by librarians, i.e. fairly focussed requests on a wide variety of different topics. Specific requests for particular documents or more general explorations are assumed to be handled through some other means, such as browsing through the stacks. Since retrieval is performed through an intelligent intermediary who is presumably trained in the use of thesauri and other query reformulation strategies, the query is taken to be a fair representation of the information need.

The recent distribution of information access tools to the desktop suggests that this assumption is unreasonable since most individuals cannot afford the luxury of a trained search assistant. Instead the intelligent intermediary must be replaced by more capable software. An alternative information access paradigm, *information theatre*[3], suggests that the now relatively cheap, dedicated computing resource should be invested in a way that minimizes user time rather than search time. The user may be a domain expert, but is assumed to be otherwise naive. Hence, the initial query is considered a radically incomplete representation of the information need requiring several levels of refinement. This is accomplished by extracting information from the corpus that will help sharpen the query, perhaps in multiple iterations, rather than directly addressing the information need. For example, a boolean search system can assist the user by providing intelligent access to the dictionary of indexed terms. Another example is relevance feedback which employs user relevance assessments over a sample result set to improve the next iteration of a near-neighbor search [10].

A Desktop information access system must also consider a wider range of specificity in queries since they are used in a wider variety of situations. For example, the user exposed to a new database may not have a specific question, but may instead simply wish to browse, in order to gain an understanding of what is available. This suggests that an effective desktop information access system will employ multiple search methods since no one method is likely to work well across the range.

This paper describes two new information access methods that exemplify the information theatre paradigm. The first method, *Snippet Search* [8], an interactive boolean search with proximity method, is directed toward improving queries that begin with a few descriptive words. The second method, *Scatter/Gather*, a cluster-based document browsing tool, addresses less specific information needs. Both employ a display/filtering loop to interactively arrive at a point satisfactory to the user and take advantage of both the high-interaction user interfaces and the considerable computing power available on modern workstations.

3 Snippet Search

Boolean keyword search presumes that a set of terms, typically individual words, or word stems, can be extracted from the unrestricted text of each document in a corpus. Search then proceeds by forming, as a query, a boolean expression in terms of these keywords, which is resolved by finding the set of documents that satisfy that expression. Proximity search adds to this by introducing a proximity operator that places nearness constraints on otherwise standard boolean conjunctions. For example, a two-word query may be narrowed by requesting that the words appear within one word of each other, either in any order or in the given order.

Proximity search enables the user to form phrase-like queries; that is, a local combination of terms is treated as a single unit. This can be quite valuable because individual words out of context are unreliable carriers of meaning. In contrast, compound nouns and short nound phrases are rarely ambiguous. Boolean conjunctions allow for the partial expression of these sorts of combinations, but they also allow many unwanted matches. Higher precision is achievable by making use of nearness constraints that filter out disconnected occurrences, yet also account for trivial language variations, such as inconsequential differences in word order.

Traditional applications of boolean or proximity search within the library-automation paradigm result in a candidate set of documents which satisfy the search criterion — the "hits". The user must then judge the effectiveness of the query by perusing these documents, a potentially time consuming operation. In fact, there is empirical evidence that boolean searches tend to fall into two classes, those whose results consist of very few hits (a narrow query), and those that result in a great many hits (a broad query) [1, 7]. In the case of only a few hits, the user is left with the uncomfortable feeling that something may have been missed, which leads to a desire to broaden the existing query. However, if the query is too broad, the user is presented with far too many hits, and the task of separating out the relevant documents from the mass becomes daunting.

The problem with boolean search is that the user is provided with little or no assistance in query reformulation. A dictionary of available search terms can aid the search for alternative terminology, as can an online domain-specific thesaurus

[5], however, the help of a highly trained intermediary, such as a research librarian, is required to reach a desirable reformulation.

One solution is to provide enough information about each hit that the user can rapidly determine the contextual usage, and hence arrive at a relevance judgement and, possibly, a reformulation, without necessarily scanning the entire text. Paper-based keyword-in-context indices (and other styles of permuted indices) offer a solution for the case of single term queries. The user enters the index with a single term, the "gutter word", and finds single lines of text for each occurrence, with the gutter word aligned in a column and lines ordered alphabetically by the text appearing after the gutter word, with wraparound [6]. Computerized versions of these sorts of indices exists in a variety of different forms [2, 12], yet few, if any, elaborate on the basic query and display strategy.

Snippet Search addresses these issues by allowing the user to directly inspect the space of phrases generated by a set of terms of interest. The intention is to aid query reformulation by exposing the user to the range of variation present in the corpus. For example, a snippet search keyed by the single term "information" might display phrases such as "information storage and retrieval", "advances in information retrieval", "sensory information", and "genetic information" among others, each of which occurs in the corpus.

From the user's perspective, Snippet Search resembles a phrase search where the query specifies constituents and results are returned which contain these and new constituents, organized in a fashion that emphasizes the new rather than the old. Query formulation consists of specifying one or more "constituents" in a way that requires little or no query syntax. These constituents are then matched against the corpus using a heuristic which interprets them as a boolean conjunction with a proximity constraint. Then, instead of returning matching documents and treating the search as if it were complete, as would a standard boolean search, Snippet Search returns returns a short textual context surrounding the matches. These *snippets* are intended to contain sufficient context to distinguish usage, but not so much as to distract the reader or clutter the display.

The current heuristic returns the text surrounding the search terms plus one other "significant" word, where significance is operationally defined by *not* being on some prespecified list of non-topic-influencing words (a *stop list*). The neighboring non-stop word provides distinguishing context and is highlighted in the display to draw the user's attention to what is new, rather than what was input (the query terms). If this context is insufficient to distinguish usage, the user is encouraged to ask for more (a snippet operation called "extend"). If the context shows a word combination which is *a priori* uninteresting, all snippets with similar word structure can be deleted (an operation called "forget"). Note that the "forget" operation is effectively boolean negation by example.

Since the time required for each of these operations can be made small, the overall effect is to encourage incremental query reformulation based on occurrences as they appear in the corpus of interest. In the case where a short context is sufficient to indicate that the snippet is indeed relevant, the user may proceed directly to the corresponding document (an operation called "view").

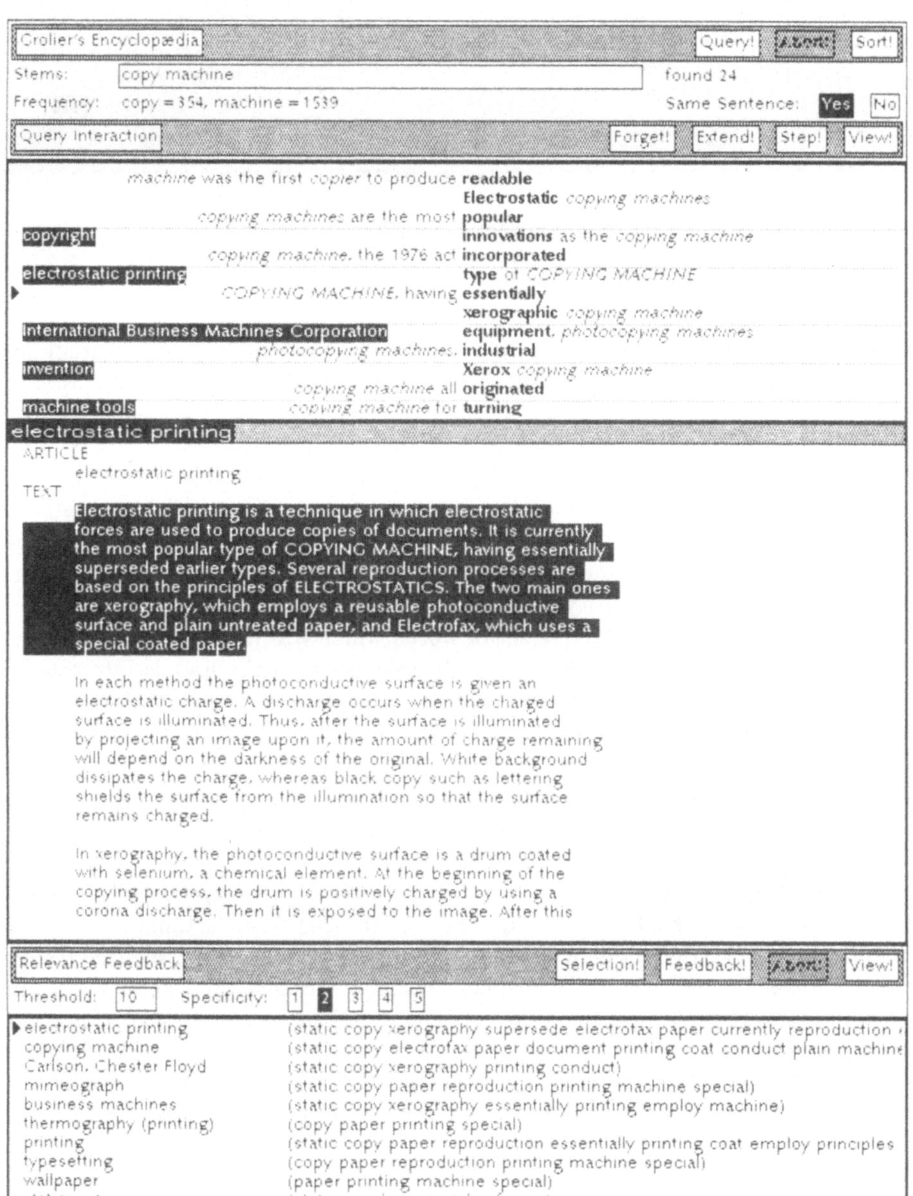

Figure 1: The Text Browser

Figure 2: Snippet Query Specification

3.1 An Example

We have implemented a version of Snippet Search which realizes the strategy just outlined [8] (see Figure 1). Currently, two search modes are supported over the same corpus, Similarity Search and Snippet Search. The first two panels concern themselves with snippet query specification and the presentation of results. The third panel is for the scrollable display of documents. The last two panels are concerned with Similarity Search [11]. The ordering is not particularly significant, although it is anticipated that Snippet Search will be most useful for bootstrapping starting with a few query words. The results can then seed a methods requiring a longer query, such as Similarity Search.

Search proceed by specifying a set of words which will form the components of a phrase match criterion (see Figure 2). In this example the user is interested in phrases that include the word "movie" (or its inflectional variations). Note that the interface reports the marginal frequency of the search term, and the number of hits currently found. The query is resolved by interpreting it as a boolean conjunction with a proximity constraint; a match occurs if the all query terms occur with no more than one content word gap between them. In the example, since there is only one query term, all instances of "movie" match.

The result of a query is a set of text snippets, each satisfying the phrase match criterion (see Figure 3). In the example each of the 263 total instances of "movie" generates up to two overlapping snippets. These are presented in a stylized fashion to aid perusal by the user. The display heuristic presents the query terms plus one additional non-stop word and all the intervening (unindexed) text, containing spaces, punctuation and stop words. The additional non-stop word is intended to provide distinguishing context. The inclusion of the intervening unindexed text provides useful syntactic information, especially through function words.

To focus the user's attention on new information, snippets are formatted so that the additional non-stop word, is placed adjacent to an easily recognizable location. This has the effect of columnating these contexts next to a vertical strip of white space, known as the "gutter". The gutter word is highlighted with a bold font, and the query terms are distinguished, but not as heavily emphasized, with an italic font. The final display is reminiscent of a keyword-in-context index, with the crucial difference that each gutter word is new information (not just part of the match criterion), and that each line may be the result of a multi-term query.

As with boolean search, no particular ordering of snippets is implied by the

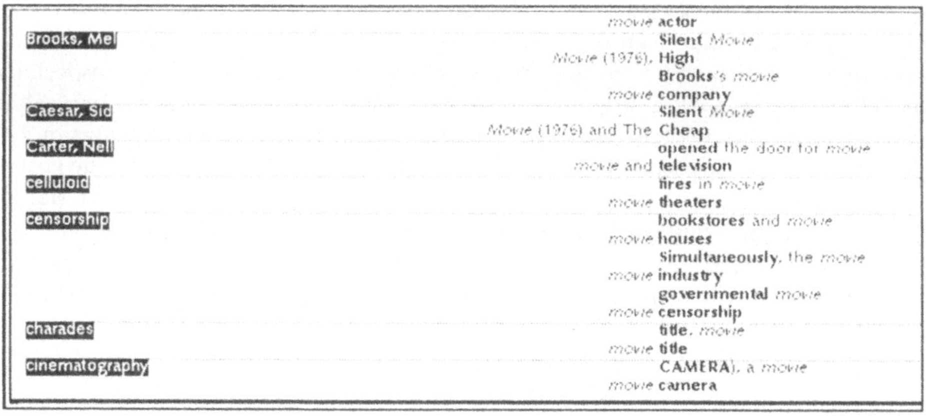

Brooks, Mel — movie actor / Silent *Movie* / *Movie* (1976), High / Brooks's movie / movie company
Caesar, Sid — Silent *Movie* / *Movie* (1976) and The Cheap
Carter, Nell — opened the door for movie / movie and television
celluloid — fires in movie / movie theaters
censorship — bookstores and movie / movie houses / Simultaneously, the movie / movie industry / governmental movie / movie censorship
charades — title, movie / movie title
cinematography — CAMERA), a movie / movie camera

Figure 3: Results of "movie" Query

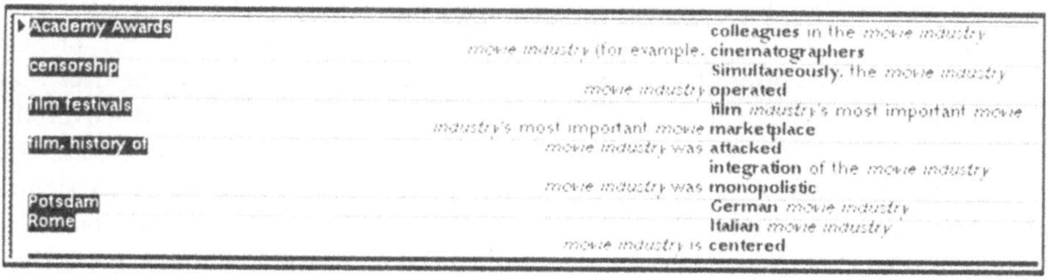

Academy Awards — colleagues in the movie industry / movie industry (for example, cinematographers
censorship — Simultaneously, the movie industry / movie industry operated
film festivals — film industry's most important movie / industry's most important movie marketplace
film, history of — movie industry was attacked / integration of the movie industry / movie industry was monopolistic
Potsdam — German movie industry
Rome — Italian movie industry / movie industry is centered

Figure 4: Results of "movie industry" Query

query resolution mechanism. It is often convenient to organize snippets to correspond to a particular scan order through an inverted index, since partial results may then be returned before the completion of the entire query. This is especially useful for queries with a large number of hits, since the user may begin perusal of the partial results without waiting for search termination. Other presentation orderings may also be useful. In particular, snippets may also be sorted by the gutter word, or by schemes that extract a sort key from the sequence of content words. This could be accomplished either incrementally or after search termination.

In this example, the user can easily see by inspection that "movie" occurs in phrases such as "silent movie", "movie theater", "movie industry", as well as many others. To view more snippets without scrolling, the user at this stage may choose to eliminate phrases similar (in the sense of having the same gutter word) to the one currently selected by buttoning "forget" in the query panel. Alternatively, the user may narrow the query by picking one of the completions for further study. If the user re-formulates the query adding "industry" as an additional term, twelve hits are returned (see Figure 4). Again, it is easy to see that the article titled "Rome" has a reference to the Italian movie industry. The snippet "*movie industry* **operated**" is not especially revealing; however, the user may button "extend" to enlarge the viewed context "*movie industry* operated under a self-imposed **code**". Any one of the snippets may be selected, and the associated document viewed (with the snippet highlighted) by buttoning "view" in the query panel.

4   Scatter/Gather

The concept of a query expressing an information need is central to information access. Yet, it is not difficult to imagine a situation in which it is hard, if not impossible, to formulate such a query precisely. For example, the user may not be familiar with the vocabulary appropriate for describing a topic of interest, or may not wish to commit himself to a particular choice of words. Indeed, the user may not be looking for anything specific at all, but rather may wish to discover the general information content of the corpus. Access to a document collection covers an entire spectrum: at one end is a narrowly specified *search* for a particular document, given something as specific as its title. At the other end is a *browsing* session driven by a desire simply to learn more about the document collection. Standard information access techniques tend to emphasize the search end of the spectrum; Scatter/Gather uses document clustering to attack the opposite end.

Drawing its inspiration from the initial pages of any conventional paper textbook, Scatter/Gather presents a dynamic table-of-contents metaphor for navigating a large collection of documents. Initially the system *scatters* the collection into a small number of document groups, by *document clustering*, and presents short summaries of them to the user. Based on these summaries, the user selects one or more of the groups for further study. The selected groups are *gathered* together to form a subcollection. The system then applies clustering again to scatter the new subcollection into a small number of document groups, which are again presented to the user. With each successive iteration the groups become smaller, and therefore more detailed. Ultimately, when the groups become small enough, this process bottoms by enumerating individual documents. Based on documents found in this process, or on the terms used to describe document groups, the user may, at any time, switch to a more focussed search method. We anticipate that the browsing tool will not be used to find particular documents, but will instead help the user formulate a search request, which will then be serviced by some other means.

Scatter/Gather depends on the existence of two facilities. First, since clustering and reclustering is an essential part of the basic iteration, an algorithm for clustering a large number of documents within a time tolerable for user interaction (*c.g.*, less than a minute) is required. Second, given a group of documents, some method for automatically summarizing that group must be specified. This cluster description must be sufficiently revealing for to give the user a sense of the topic defined by the group, yet short enough for many descriptions to be appreciated simultaneously.

We have developed algorithms to satisfy these requirements. *Fractionation* is a fast document clustering algorithm suitable for the online reclustering essential for Scatter/Gather [4]. We also employ a *cluster digest* consisting of a small set of topical words and typical titles as an easy to generate, concise cluster description.

4.1 An Illustration

The following section describes a Scatter/Gather session, where the text collection consists of about 5000 articles posted to the *New York Times News Service* during the month of August 1990, and summarized in Figure 5. To simplify the Figure, we manually assigned single-word labels based on the full cluster descriptions. A typescript of the first scatter of the session is provided as Appendix A.

Suppose the user wants to find out what happened that month. Several issues prevent the application of conventional search techniques:

- The information need is too vague to be described as a single topic.

- Even if a topic were available, the words used to describe it may not be known to the user.

- The words used to describe a topic may not be those used to discuss the topic and may thus fail to appear in articles of interest. For example, articles concerning international events need never use the words "international event".

- Even if some words used in discussion of the topic were available, documents may fail to use precisely those words, *e.g.*, synonyms may be used instead.

With Scatter/Gather, rather than being forced to provide terms, the user is presented with a set of clusters, an outline of the corpus. He need only select those clusters which seem potentially relevant to the topic of interest. In the example, the big stories of the month are immediately obvious from the initial scattering: Ir: vades Kuwait, and Germany considers reunification. This leads the user to

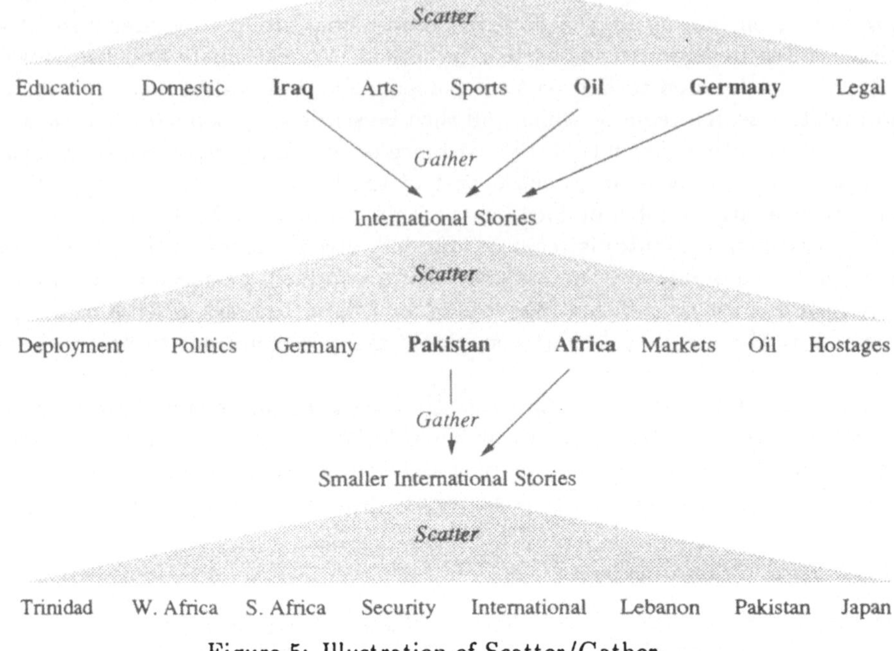

Figure 5: Illustration of Scatter/Gather

focus on international issues: he selects the "Kuwait" and "Germany" and "Oil" clusters. These three clusters are gathered together.

This reduced corpus is then reclustered on the fly to produce eight new clusters covering the reduced corpus. Since the reduced corpus contains a subset of the articles, these new clusters reveal a finer level of detail than the original eight. The articles on the Iraqi invasion and some of the 'Oil' articles have now been separated into clusters discussing the U.S. military deployment, the effects of the invasion upon the oil market, and one about hostages in Kuwait.

The user feels his understanding of these large stories is adequate, but wishes to find out what happened in other corners of the world. He selects the "Pakistan" cluster, which also contains other foreign political stories, and a cluster containing articles about Africa. This reveals a number of specific international situations as well as a small collection of miscellaneous international articles. The user thus learns of a coup in Pakistan, and about hostages being taken in Trinidad, stories otherwise lost among the major stories of that month.

5 Conclusion

Two retrieval methods have been presented that concentrate on providing the user with adequate information to formulate more effective queries, rather than expecting the user to derive good queries through introspection alone. In the first case,

```
> (time (setq first (outline (all-docs tdb))))
cluster 4970 items
global cluster 199 items...sizes: 18 24 53 5 25 47 13 14
move to nearest...sizes: 517 1293 835 86 677 1020 273 269
move to nearest...sizes: 287 1731 749 275 481 844 310 293
0 (287) CRITICS URGE NEW METHODS; PROGRAMS FOR PARENTS THE; TEACHING
  school, year, student, child, university, state, program, percent
1 (1731) FEDERAL WORK PROGRAMS HE; RESORT TAKES STEPS TO PR; AMERICANS
  year, state, york, city, million, day, service, company, week, official
2 (749) PENTAGON SAYS 60,000 IRA; BUSH ''DRAWS A LINE'' IN; BUSH SAYS
  iraq, iraqi, kuwait, american, state, unite, saudi, official, military
3 (275) Trillin's Many Hats; New Musical from the cre; After Nasty Teen
  film, year, music, play, company, movie, art, angeles, york, american
4 (481) TWISTS AND TURNS MAY MEA; SAX LOOKING FOR RELIEF I; PAINTING THE
  game, year, play, team, season, win, player, day, league, hit, right
5 (844) CRISIS PUSHES OIL PRICES; WHY MAJOR PANIC OVER A M; OIL PRICES
  price, oil, percent, market, company, year, million, stock, day, rate
6 (310) LEADERS OF TWO GERMANYS ; REPRESENTATIVES OF TWO G; SECURITY
  government, year, state, party, political, country, official, leader
7 (293) U.S. APPEALS ORDER FREEI; DID JUDGE MOVE TOO HASTI; MAYOR BARRY
  case, court, charge, year, judge, lawyer, attorney, trial, jury, federal
real time  131258 msec
```

Figure 6: Initial Scattering

Snippet Search's basic underlying assumption is that short queries, consisting of a few search terms, are by their very nature radically incomplete. Hence, query repair and elaboration through user interaction and iteration are essential to achieve the desired result, as is the presentation of information in a manner that can be quickly appreciated.

In the second case, Scatter/Gather enable the user to browse through very large document collections, without presuming that the collection has been manually categorized, in such a way that vocabulary appropriate for describing a particular topic is presented to the user, rather than *vice versa*. Here browsing is a process of discovery; the user modifies his information need based on the information made available about the corpus contents.

A   A Scatter/Gather Session

In Figure 6, we present the full output of the initial scatter of the Scatter/Gather session described in section 4.1. The corpus is the set of articles distributed by the *New York Times News Service* during the month of August 1990. This consists of roughly 30 megabytes of ASCII text in about 5000 articles. Some articles are repeated due to updates of news stories.

Each cluster is described with the two line display of its cluster digest. The first line contains the number of the cluster, the number of documents in the cluster, and titles of documents near the centroid. The second line contains words frequent in the cluster.

References

[1] D. C. Blair and M. E. Maron. An evaluation of retrieval effectiveness for a full-text document-retrieval system. *CACM*, 28(3):289–299, March 1985.

[2] ATT Corporation. Global regular expression program. Licensed software, 1979.

[3] D. R. Cutting, P.-K. Halvorsen, J. O. Pedersen, and M. Withgott. Information theater versus information refinery. In *AAAI Spring Symposium on Text-based Intelligent Systems*, Stanford University, Stanford, CA, March 1990. Also available as Xerox PARC technical report SSL-89-101.

[4] D.R. Cutting, J. Pedersen, D. Karger, and J.W. Tukey. Scatter/gather: A cluster-based approach to browsing large document collections. In *Proceedings of the Fifteenth Annual International ACM SIGIR Conference*, pages 318–329, June 1992. Also available as Xerox PARC technical report SSL-92-02.

[5] H.P.Frei, M.Bärtschi, and J.-F. Jauslin. Caliban: Its user-interface and retrieval algorithm. Technical Report 62, Institut für Informatik, ETH, Zürich, April 1985.

[6] H.P. Luhn. Keyword-in-context for technical literature. ASDD Report RC-127, IBM Corporation, Yorktown Heights, N.Y., August 1959.

[7] Gary Marchionini. Information-seeking strategies of novices using a full-text electronic encyclopedia. *Journal of the American Society for Inforamtion Science*, 40(1):54–66, 1989.

[8] J. O. Pedersen, D. R. Cutting, and J. W. Tukey. Snippet search: a single phrase approach to text access. In *Proceedings of the 1991 Joint Statistical Meetings*. American Statistical Association, 1991. Also available as Xerox PARC technical report SSL-91-08.

[9] G. Salton. *Automatic Text Processing*. Addison-Wesley, 1989.

[10] G. Salton and C. Buckley. Improving retrieval performance by relevance feedback. *Journal of the American Society for Information Science*, 41(4):288–297, June 1990.

[11] G. Salton, A. Wong, and C.S. Yang. A vector space model for automatic indexing. *Communications of the ACM*, 18(11):613–620, November 1975.

[12] Mark Zimmerman. Texas. Public Domain software, 1989.

Server Support for Cooperative Hypermedia Systems

Helge Schütt, Jörg M. Haake
GMD-IPSI
Postfach 104326
W–6100 Darmstadt
Federal Republic of Germany

e–mail: {schuett, haake}@darmstadt.gmd.de

Abstract: While current hypertext technology usually is restricted to single user systems, it is obvious that actual work environments require multi-user systems which support cooperating co-workers. However, previous research prototypes have concentrated either on the support for group work or on appropriate datamodels and storage policies for hypermedia objects. In this paper we discuss the CHS hypermedia engine which combines both approaches: It not only provides shared access to hypermedia objects but also supports cooperating clients in flexible ways.

Keywords: Cooperative Hypermedia Systems, Databases, Computer-Supported Cooperative Work

1   Introduction

In today's workplace there is virtually no task which is solved by an individual alone. Instead, it is teams of people who work together to solve a case, to prepare a document, or to complete a design. If hypermedia systems (cf. [Bus45, Nel65, Con87, Nie90, Kuh91]) want to enter the real world, it is therefore a prime requirement that they support multiple users who work concurrently on the same set of data (cf. [MPS91, LØS92]). Their work has to be synchronized, and they must be allowed to employ different cooperation models. From an architectural standpoint, it is clear that it is desirable to provide a (distributed) server for that purpose. Such a server would

- provide a shared database where hypermedia objects can be stored persistently,
- handle transactions, i.e. schedule concurrency control, perform recovery, and ensure data consistency during multi-user updates to the database,
- provide persistent and non-persistent activity markers on selected data,
- notify cooperating clients when data is updated so that they share the same view of the database.

In the German National Research Center for Computer Science — Integrated Publication and Information Systems Institute (GMD-IPSI), the CHS *Cooperative Hypermedia Server* has been designed and implemented to provide these services. While previous efforts on the *HyperBase* hypermedia engine have concentrated on the first two requirements and have been discussed elsewhere (cf. [SS90, Sch92]), CHS also provides the latter two services.

The paper is organized as follows: First we give an overview of the problem and related work. In the main section of this paper we explain CHS's datamodel and describe its system architecture. We then describe the hypermedia authoring environment SEPIA which is the largest application of CHS to date. Finally, we summarize our results and discuss some extensions to CHS.

2   Cooperative Hypermedia Servers

First, we give an overview of how working groups of people cooperate with the help of computers and draw some requirements from this discussion. We then review other research activities in the area of cooperative hypermedia systems and server support for hypermedia systems.

2.1   Cooperation Models

When a group of collaborating people works on a task (see [EGR91, Rod91] for an overview of CSCW systems), its members need to access a shared information base (e.g., a document base for co-authoring, or a pool of software modules and documentation for joint software development). Different situations of collaboration arise during the group work process: Sometimes co-workers work on separate parts of the information base (in parallel or at different times), or the way in which documents are processed ensures that at most one person at a time works on a document. We call such a situation an **individual work** situation. At other times several co-workers may concurrently access some part of the information base but still wish to work as independently as possible. In this **loosely-coupled work** situation awareness of co-workers' presence and activities is necessary to detect possible conflicts and coordination needs. If several co-workers wish to work in a synchronized way, they engage in **tightly-coupled work** where they cooperate and coordinate their work in synchronous conference-like "meetings". Here they should be provided with direct communication channels and a shared environment including a common view of the information base (the WYSIWIS principle: "What You See Is What I See").

Actual collaboration proceeds by shifting between these three collaboration modes. The transitions are often prompted by needs for coordination which arise from individual work or through observing activities of co-workers in loosely-coupled work. Therefore, **smooth transitions between the modes** must be supported.

A groupware application supporting the above collaboration modes requires access to a shared information base. Transactions are needed to synchronize concurrent access and to ensure a consistent state of the information base. To implement synchronization strategies among different sites of a groupware application, activity markers are needed to signal the current status of an object (e.g. is being edited, is checked out, etc.). Update notifications are needed to inform all concurrent sites of new states of the information base to ensure a common view of the information base. This applies not only to data objects but (in tightly coupled mode) also to display information (e.g., position on the screen and display style of information objects).

Furthermore, to support the tightly-coupled mode one needs shared views (WYSIWIS), which can be implemented by communication protocols among cooperating groupware sites. Additional communication facilities, like shared drawing tools, digital audio connections and video networks between distributed workstations, can be used to support informal communication.

To support smooth transitions between the three modes, the shared information base should include additional information which describes the status of the collaboration (e.g., who uses which information, which subgroups work in loosely or tightly-coupled mode). This kind of information can then be used to trigger state transitions among concurrent applications when changes occur. For example, a new co-worker may join a loosely or tightly-coupled session which is already in progress, or someone enters a part of the information base currently used by another co-worker working in individual work mode. In the latter case both applications should shift into loosely-coupled mode.

2.2   Related Work

Three prominent hypertext systems which were designed for group use are Neptune [DS86], the *Knowledge Management System* (KMS, [AMY88]) and *Intermedia* [HKR+92]. While the latter two are not based on a client/server architecture, Neptune is based on the *Hypertext Abstract Machine* (HAM, [CG88]). However, neither of these systems supports different users who want to be informed about updates done by other users. Only by inspecting an object, users can determine whether a change was made, and users cannot be made aware of other users who work "in the neighborhood" (as expressed by the link structure etc.) of the objects they currently work on.

Aquanet [MHRJ91] is a system which supports multiple authors in structuring a knowledge base. It uses a database server to store all relevant information, but apparently it does not exploit its database functionality. For example, although Aquanet maintains locks on objects, it does not provide persistent locks which would allow users to lock objects across database sessions. Similarly, Aquanet does not support transactions on the client side. Instead of synchronized group work, Aquanet only supports "semi-synchronous" group work: Clients may poll a "change log" to find out which data has been changed. Although Aquanet broadcasts display information among its clients, this broadcast seems to rely exclusively on the X window server. Aquanet does not have the notion of a display object where clients may decide whether they want to have their display objects synchronized or not.

In more recent work, several research groups are now engaged in the development of hypermedia engines. The HB1 hyperbase management system [SLH91] and the *Distributed Graph Server* (DGS, [SSS92]) aim at supporting cooperating hypermedia authors. Both systems are designed as servers which provide shared databases of hypermedia objects to collaborating users. However, neither system has a notion of a transaction (i.e. they do not allow to cluster several basic operations into one atomic operation which is made visible to the global database only when all basic operations have been executed successfully), and neither system supports the notification of collaborating users about changes to the database.

The most advanced system which concentrates on these group work aspects is the EHTS system [Wii91]. This system is based on a hypermedia engine HyperBase (which was named independently from the one we have developed at GMD-IPSI). This HyperBase is a server which not only maintains a database of shared hypermedia objects but also allows clients to subscribe to events and to lock objects. Clients can thus decide whether they want to be notified about changes to the global database. However, all this collaboration information is not stored persistently but only stored with the server process. Therefore, clients cannot recover when that process goes down. Furthermore, EHTS does not support transactions and does not provide persistent locks.

3   CHS, a Cooperative Hypermedia Server

To support collaborating authors of hypermedia documents, we have designed the CHS cooperative hypermedia server. Previous research concentrated on a datamodel for hypermedia objects, the sharing of objects, appropriate transaction schemata, balancing the load between clients and the server, and caching strategies for the clients, and has been reported elsewhere [SS90, Sch92]. This research has resulted in the implementation of the *HyperBase* hypermedia engine. In this section we first explain the data model of CHS and the enhancements to *HyperBase*'s architecture which are necessary to allow synchronized, collaborating client applications.

3.1   The Datamodel of CHS

The datamodel of CHS consists of hypermedia objects (nodes, links, and composite objects), and collaboration information (users and activity markers). Each of these concepts is described below. Hypermedia objects are discussed in detail in [SS90] so that we only briefly review them.

Hypermedia object is an abstract class which defines the basic properties of all hypermedia objects. These include the following four features:

♦ Each hypermedia object is uniquely identified through an object identifier (an OID).

♦ Each hypermedia object can be linked to any other hypermedia object.

♦ Each hypermedia object can be a subobject of any number of composite objects.

♦ Each hypermedia object can carry an arbitrary number of user-defined attributes which can be added and deleted at run time.

Nodes are hypermedia objects which carry a content. This content is of some basic type (string, byte array, etc.) and is not interpreted by the server. Thus nodes are the basic hypermedia objects and roughly correspond to *cards* in HyperCard [Sha91] or *frames* in KMS [AMY88].

Links are directed references between two hypermedia objects (including other links). Although links are directed, CHS offers functions to retrieve both the links which start and those which end in any given object, and it can also retrieve the objects which are the source or destination of these links.

Composite objects are partially ordered collections of other hypermedia objects. For each composite object, CHS offers functions which retrieve the immediate subobjects or recursively all subobjects of that object. In addition to this, for each hypermedia object CHS provides functions which retrieve the composite objects it is a subobject of, or recursively all composite objects it is an indirect subobject of.

CHS supports the creation, deletion, and update of these objects. In addition to this, CHS allows to navigate along chains of linked objects or through clusters represented by composite objects (hypertext functionality). CHS also provides closed nested transactions which allow a client to group operations into one atomic operation. For example in SEPIA (see below) each object that is visible at the user interface corresponds to two objects in the internal representation. One object is the hypermedia object the user is conceptually aware of, the other is a *visual container* object that carries all display information (location on the screen, color, etc.) for that object. Here every create- and delete-operation uses transactions to ensure that no incomplete objects are created in the database.

CHS maintains *collaboration information* to enable clients to exchange information. On the one hand this means that CHS must keep a database of current users. On the other hand, clients must be able to protect objects so that no other client modifies them during a given time span.

In CHS, a *user record* consists of the name of the user, the machine he works on, and a port through which his client is willing to accept external communication requests. Through that port it opens a socket communication channel to exchange data with other clients. Each such user record can be identified through a user-id (UID) which is unique for the given database. Using UIDs ensures that even if the same user runs two client applications on the same machine, these clients can still be distinguished.

The port number of a user record can either be a valid port or a distinguished null value HBNO-PORT. CHS does not require that clients be able to talk to each other, but if they choose to, they can do it. A user record is automatically created by CHS when a client logs into a database. The only information a client has to provide is its port number; everything else is determined by CHS. As additional functions (compared to *HyperBase*), CHS allows clients to read a specific user record or all user records.

Cooperating users must inform each other about the objects they (intend to) modify in the global database. To do this, CHS offers *activity markers* which can be placed on hypermedia objects. Each hypermedia object may carry an arbitrary number of activity markers, where each activity marker consists of an owner (given by his UID) and a severity value. Activity markers can be persistent or non-persistent. The distinction between the two is that markers of the first category survive across sessions while markers of the second category are released when a client logs out from the database.

Wiil's HyperBase offers locks both on whole objects and on single attributes [Wii91]. Wiil has observed that these locks should not be interpreted as strict locks in the sense of database locks because this would inhibit the desired cooperation behavior. Therefore, he allows clients to read locked objects so that a user can navigate through a hyperdocument even while it is being edited.

In CHS we carry this approach further and do not constrain the way in which clients react to activity markers. As an example, consider a node which carries a HBWRITEMARKER. As one policy, clients may decide that this object is invisible to other clients, similar to a write lock in conventional databases. As another policy, other clients might still be allowed to read the marked data, for example to copy the object and derive a new version of it. Still going further, an application may even allow other clients to read and write the marked object, for example when that object is subject to shared editing. Here the marker affects only those users who do not participate in the shared editing session.

Clients can create a marker both unconstrained and in an atomic test-and-set operation. They can read markers of everybody and delete the markers they own both individually and clustered by severity value. When clients log out from a database, CHS ensures that all non-persistent markers of that client are removed. If a user does not own any persistent markers, his user record is also removed from the database. Otherwise, the user record is only marked as HBNOTLOGGEDIN and is deleted when the user resumes his session. Resuming a session means that all markers which are owned by the old UID are now transferred to the new UID.

3.2   Architecture

To fulfill the requirements discussed in the previous sections, we propose the following system architecture (cf. figure 1). The user interface is handled by client workstations. Each workstation maintains a set of tools through which a user interacts with the hypertext objects. These clients use a shared hyperdocument database to persistently store their objects. This database also maintains the activity markers which prevent users from interfering with each other, and it handles concurrency control on critical regions. In addition to this, clients notify each other about changes which occur. These notifications are distributed by a central broadcast server process which ensures that updates are transmitted safely and sequentially. In the remainder of this section we discuss how these components interact.

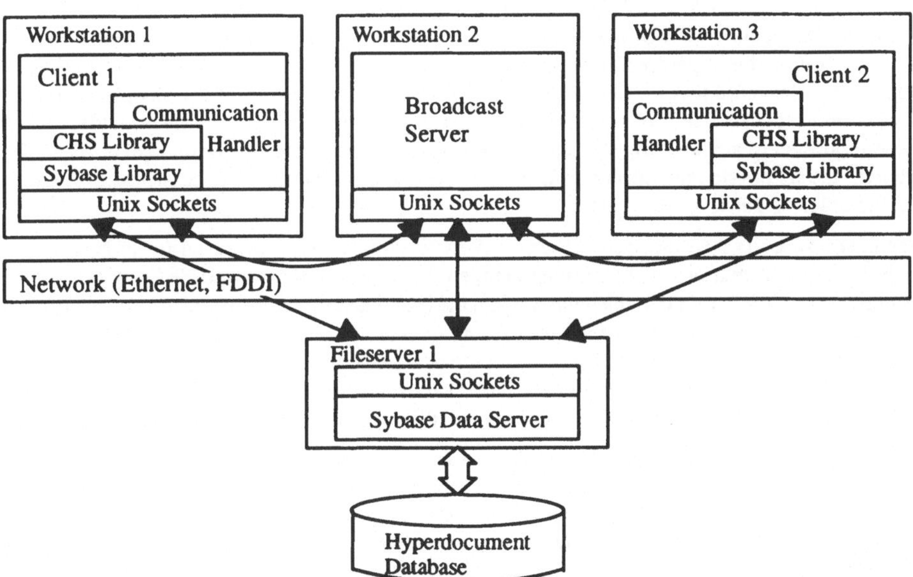

Figure 1: System Architecture

When a user wants to run an application, the following actions happen: First, he logs into the system and specifies a database he wants to work on. CHS then records him in the database together with his workstation and the port through which the client process can be reached. The client then searches the database for a broadcast server which is registered in the database and is willing to accept broadcast requests. If no such broadcast server is found, the client asks to start a new one. An atomic test-and-set operation offered by CHS ensures that only one such request is acknowledged so that at most one broadcast server exists for each database. Now the client connects itself to the broadcast server, which in turn informs the other registered clients about the new user. These can then retrieve the new user information from the database.

Note that with this approach the client process does not need to know any information about the broadcast server or other client processes in advance. It only specifies the database it wants to work on, and all other information about the broadcast server and the other clients (machines they run or, port numbers, etc.) is maintained by CHS.

As all information (including collaboration information) is stored persistently in the database, this architecture survives crashes of the broadcast server or of any client process. (This is one main advantage over systems like the HyperBase of Aalborg University [Wii91] where collaboration information is stored with the communication process and is lost when that process dies.) With our approach, any number of clients can restart a broadcast server at any time. CHS offers an atomic test-and-set operation to find out whether a second broadcast server process exists, and a broadcast server will shut itself down if this is the case. A restarted broadcast server then can access the database to retrieve the information it needs to communicate with the client processes.

Similarly, the broadcast server notices when a client can no longer be reached, and it can then close its corresponding socket and remove the client's user record from the database. As a side effect, this also releases all activity markers of that client. The data server also recognizes a client which crashes. It then rolls back all transactions which were not committed by the client and ensures that the global database stays consistent. The only situation which cannot be recovered is a failure of the database server process. But in this case a client can no longer access the data it needs, and it should go down gracefully anyway.

The user now wants to change a piece of data on his client. Data here can be the contents of a node, the structure of the hyperdocument, or the way in which objects and browsers appear on the screen. In order to do this, he first selects the objects that are affected by the change. This leads to selection requests that are issued to the database. If no other user currently edits the objects, these requests are acknowledged and activity markers are attached to these objects. The client receives the acknowledgement and informs the user that the selection is successful, e.g. by changing the color of the selected objects.

The user now edits the objects. This can be done through an appropriate editor or by changing their display information e.g. by moving them around. On completion of the editing process, the changed data is transmitted to the database and the broadcast server is informed that a change has happened. The broadcast server then informs all clients that a change has occurred. The clients then decide whether they need to know about the changed data and, if necessary, access the database to retrieve the changed pieces of data. Note that usually this does not involve any disk access: The data has just been written by a client and is still in main memory of the database server.

Note that the completion of the edit operation does not imply that the activity marker on the objects is also released. From CHS's perspective, markers do not prevent other clients from reading or writing the data. It is the clients' decision which cooperation policy they choose. For SEPIA (see below), we decided that other clients still can read data from a marked object but cannot edit it. Furthermore note that markers can be removed independently from other operations. There is no automatic release of markers after a move / edit operation has been completed. Clients may chose an appropriate policy here as well.

Note also that clients can employ different caching strategies. For some applications it may be desirable to load a snapshot of the hyperdocument database to the client process and not care about changes that occur later. Or, as is done in SEPIA, a client application can have the policy that all cached data is updated at the client side as soon as possible so that a client always displays the latest available state of the database. As frequent updates are costly, such an application would load as little data to the client side as needed to keep the number of forced updates at a minimum.

In our current implementation, all workstations are SUN SPARC-2 workstations running SUN OS 4.1.2 UNIX. The CHS library is written in C and uses the Sybase DB-library [Syb90] as a database. The broadcast server is also written in C and uses the standard UNIX socket communication. The networks we use are both a LAN based on an Ethernet and a MAN based on FDDI.

4   The SEPIA Cooperative Hypermedia Authoring Environment

A major application of CHS is the SEPIA cooperative hypermedia authoring environment. In this section first we briefly introduce the concepts of SEPIA. After that, we explain SEPIA's cooperation model and describe its implementation using the concepts presented in the previous section.

4.1   SEPIA at a Glance

SEPIA is a cooperative hypermedia authoring environment. Its purpose is to support groups of authors who collaboratively create hyperdocuments [HW92]. For the purpose of this paper, we will only explain SEPIA's data model and its cooperation model, but not its cognitive foundation [SHT89] or the construction kit which is available to authors [THH91]. Neither will we discuss the external communication lines (audio- and video links) which allow users to talk to each other while collaboratively working on a hyperdocument. A full description of SEPIA has been published in [SHH+92].

In SEPIA, the largest unit of data is a *project*. Such a project roughly corresponds to a book together with all background material in traditional publishing. Each project consists of four *activity spaces*. These are dedicated workspaces which serve different purposes.

Associated with each activity space is a dedicated *browser* which offers a certain set of functions on the objects it presents. These objects are hypertext objects, i.e., nodes, links, and composite objects. In SEPIA, nodes are typed, and each activity space provides specific types for nodes. Similarly, links are first-class objects, and each activity space offers a set of link types which are relevant in its context. Composite objects are used in all activity spaces to cluster information. One can also open a browser on a composite object to display its subobjects. For all browsers, a construction kit offers several basic options on how information can be arranged.

SEPIA clients have been implemented in Smalltalk-80, Release 4. SEPIA's data model and transaction schema has been implemented with the help of the SFK frame system [FR92]. The CHS library has been integrated into SEPIA as user-defined primitives of the Smalltalk system.

4.2   Cooperation in SEPIA

As browsers are the interaction facility of SEPIA, we decided that the most natural way of introducing cooperation into the system is to bind it to the use of browsers. In the following section we explain how this is done at the user interface level, and how it is implemented with the help of CHS's facilities described above. For a more detailed discussion of SEPIA's collaboration model see [HW92].

As illustrated in figure 2, users view SEPIA as a distributed system in which activity space browsers are linked together through a communication channel. Through browsers, we have introduced the concept of a neighborhood in the hypertext network: A user Y works in the neighborhood of user X iff Y works on objects in the same browser as X. (Strictly speaking, these are not the same browsers but different browsers which display the same composite object.) X is informed when Y enters his neighborhood. The sound of a doorbell is used to make X aware of Y entering his browser, and the names of X and Y are displayed in a status line of the browser. In most cooperative systems, a user is only informed when someone else tries to access the same node he is currently working on. In SEPIA, he is already made aware of other people working in the neighborhood of that node.

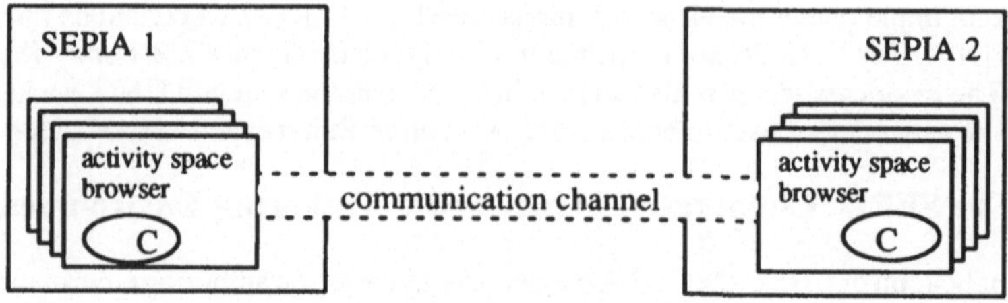

Figure 2: The user's view of cooperating clients

Within each browser, SEPIA uses different colors to represent the activity markers of an object. A white node is not marked by anybody, nodes that have been marked by that client are displayed in yellow, and nodes marked by other clients are displayed in red. Each operation that edits an object (moves it on the screen or actually edits its content) first leads to marking the object before the edit operation can be executed.

Apart from just being aware of others working in his neighborhood, a user may enter a tightly coupled session with a number of collaborating users. In tightly coupled mode, the individual browsers of the users are connected. All resizing of the browser window or scrolling within such a window is immediately transmitted to the other tightly coupled browsers. Here the WYSIWIS (What You See Is What I See) principle is in effect.

From the user's point of view, the architecture presented in the previous section is completely transparent. He only sees his work environment, which is a SEPIA project. Such a project consists of the four activity spaces explained above, each of which is represented on the screen by an activity space browser. Without worrying about the consistency of the shared database or safe communication among the clients, a user can be certain that the changes he makes are not overwritten by others and that the state he sees on his screen is the actual state of the database.

All this is taken care of by CHS. When a client starts, it first opens a socket through which it is willing to exchange information with other clients. The client then logs into a database maintained by CHS. Here it is registered as a user, and the broadcast server informs the other clients about the newcomer. Whenever data is changed, CHS first uses its transactions to ensure that the global database is in a consistent new state before the broadcast server process informs other clients that a change has occurred.

4.3   Transactions in SEPIA

CHS provides nested transactions to its clients, and this is one of the features which distinguish CHS from other approaches. In this section, we discuss how this feature is used and what the client has to observe here.

As an example, consider two nodes N_1 and N_2 which exist in the global database. A user running client C_1 now wants to create a link between these nodes. In SEPIA, this translates into the creation of four objects: A link object, a visual container which contains the display information of the link, and two link anchors, one for the source and one for the destination of the link. The global database is in a consistent state only if either none of these four objects exist, or all four of them exist. Therefore, the SEPIA client C_1 must ask CHS to ensure that no other client process can read the intermediate states of the database.

Similarly, C_1 must have a notion of a *local transaction* which ensures that on the client side either all four objects or none of these objects exist. To achieve this, a client must keep a log of the objects that have been created or modified during an interaction with a user, and it must be able to rollback the interaction at any point and undo the changes which have been done until this point.

Note that this log is not subject to multi-user access, i.e. the local transactions need not provide a notion of concurrency control. Note also that the log can be kept in main memory because the global transactions in CHS allow for full recovery. If a client process goes down, its log is lost, but its intermediate state is also lost and has not been committed to the global database. The database realizes that the client went down and rolls back the incomplete transactions.

SEPIA uses a nested commit schema to handle both local and global transactions. C_1 first starts a local transaction and a transaction in CHS. It then creates the four objects one after the other. Each of these operations starts subtransactions both on the client side and in CHS. During each operation, C_1 checks that the integrity constraints defined among the nodes and links are observed (e.g. that the types of the nodes are legal for the type of link which the user has selected). If such a constraint is not observed, both the local and the global transactions are rolled back. Similarly, if a transaction in CHS fails and is rolled back, the client rolls back its local transactions. When all subtransactions have been committed on the client side, C_1 asks CHS to commit the global transaction. After successful completion of this global transaction, C_1 commits its local transaction as well.

Local transactions on the client side are a feature of the SFK frame system [FR92] which has been developed at GMD-IPSI. Note that the transactions on the client side must also allow nesting. However, they have two choices on how they integrate the transaction schema of CHS, and with SEPIA we have done experiments with both of these choices. They may either have each transaction on the client side correspond to one transaction in CHS, or they may collect all changed data on the client side first, and use CHS's transactions only when a user operation has been completed successfully. E.g. a user may choose the "create link ..." option from a menu, select a start node for the link, and then decide to cancel this operation. Here the link, the visual container for the link, and one of the link anchors have already been created and must be removed from the client, and CHS need not be involved at all. The current version of SFK supports this kind of local logging which should decrease communication overhead with the global database maintained by CHS.

As both local and global transactions can be nested to arbitrary depth, clients can cluster any number of operations into new transactions. In our example, SEPIA may introduce a macro operation which creates a node and a link, given an existing node. (There are several examples where this is actually done). Here, SEPIA does not need to redefine the transaction which creates a link (e.g. convert this "main transaction" into a "subtransaction" by shifting the "commit transaction" statement from the "create link"operation to the macro operation), but it merely uses this transaction as a subtransaction of the macro operation without any change to the "begin transaction" / "commit transaction" which has been defined for the "create link" operation.

4.4   Policies in SEPIA

As explained in the previous section, a client which uses CHS has to decide on its storage, caching, and update policy with respect to its data objects, and it has to define semantics of the activity markers it uses. In this section we explain SEPIA's choices on these issues.

Our overall goal in the development of SEPIA has been that a user always sees the most recent consistent state of the database. For the *storage policy* of SEPIA this means that changes are propagated to the database as early as possible. For most updates, this is done as part of the update operation as it appears on the user interface. For continuous updates, however, (e.g. when an object is dragged across the screen) we do not store and broadcast each intermediate step but only propagate the final state of the object. In our example, objects then "jump" across the screens of those users who are only loosely coupled to the user who drags the object. This solution is not completely satisfactory but is reasonable with respect to the speed of current local area networks.

The *caching policy* of SEPIA says that as few objects as possible are to be loaded from the database. This ensures that very little update communication among the clients is necessary, and data is only transferred across the network as it is actually needed. The way this is done in SEPIA is through *dummy objects* which on the client side take the place of objects which are referenced by other objects but are not yet needed themselves. Such a dummy object replaces itself by an actual object which is retrieved from the database when it is needed by the client.

The *update policy* of SEPIA is such that every client accepts update requests at any time. It checks whether it has loaded the changed object and loads it from the database if necessary. A client ignores update requests for objects which are not used by it. Each client broadcasts login and logoff requests immediately. Changes to its data objects are broadcast as soon as the corresponding transaction has been completed successfully (i.e. the changed data has been stored with the database). We do not queue or cluster events on the client side; they are sequentialized by the database and the broadcast server.

If a client C goes down before it can broadcast update notifications, the other clients are in an inconsistent state with respect to the global database. But this is not crucial as transactions ensure that the global database always is in a consistent state and a client which reads an object from the database retrieves this consistent state. In their current status, objects which have been created by C are not visible to other clients, i.e. they will not wind up in an error. If a client tries to access an object which C has deleted, CHS will inform that client that this object no longer exists, and the client will remove it from its local cache. If another client modifies an object which already has been modified by C, it overwrites the changes done by C, just as it would if C were still there.

To support the loosely coupled mode, SEPIA notifies other clients when a new browser is opened or an existing one is closed. As browsers are not hypermedia objects, this cannot not done directly. Instead, each hypermedia object which is displayed by a browser carries an attribute with the list of users who concurrently have opened the object. Thus, instead of broadcasting the changes that are done to a browser, SEPIA broadcasts the changes to this attribute.

SEPIA employs a rather soft *locking policy*. Each object needs to be marked in order to be changed. An atomic test-and-set operation ensures that only one client has write access to that object. Other clients then recognize the activity marker and start their editors (on nodes) and browsers (on composite objects) in read-only mode. These clients can still read the marked data but not change them.

5 Discussion and Future Work

In this paper we have described the cooperative hypermedia server CHS (*HyperBase*, Release 4), which has been designed and implemented at GMD-IPSI. The main features of CHS which support cooperating clients are:

- ◆ CHS maintains a shared database of hypermedia objects. The generic datamodel of CHS has proven to be sufficient for hypermedia client applications like SEPIA.

- ◆ CHS provides transaction management and both temporary and persistent activity markers. Through these flexible means, client applications can define macro-operations and locking schemata which are appropriate for their corresponding tasks.

- ◆ CHS automatically maintains a database of users. Client applications can refer to that database to decide with whom they have to exchange update information, and users can resume sessions in which they had defined persistent activity markers.

The main extension to CHS will be the CoVer context-based version server [Web91] which is being developed at GMD-IPSI. CoVer not only maintains versions of individual objects but also maintains *tasks* which are the contexts in which these objects are used. It will be integrated into CHS later this year. An application interface then can define a versioning policy which is supported by CHS.

At first glance, it is a good idea to assign access control lists to shared objects, as has been done with the HAM [CG88] and DGS [SSS92]. These lists are additional attributes which restrict access to an object to certain people (i.e. either a single person or a group of collaborating authors). However, Akscyn et al. [AMY88] have reported that such a feature is rarely used in practise, and we therefore do not give it a high priority in our work.

Instead we propose an integration of an organizational database into the server. This database would assign roles to each user of the server and associate access rights with that role. For example, if X is a manager of Y then X has read and write access on all documents written by Y. Furthermore, this database would maintain process structures which describe the way in which documents are created and processed or distributed. For example, if authors X and Y want to submit a paper to a conference, the managers of both X and Y must be informed about this intended publication, and the paper must not be changed once these managers have released it. In this scenario the datamodel for hypertext objects must be extended such that each object is assigned one or more authors and a role (memo, internal paper, publication, etc.) within the organization.

CHS is currently being reimplemented with the help of the VODAK database management system [KNF+92]. This is a distributed object-oriented database management system which has been developed at GMD-IPSI. With the extended modeling capabilities of VODAK a large part of the application interface (e.g. the mapping of SEPIA objects to CHS objects and the storage policy) can directly be implemented inside the database system. In addition to this, VODAK offers an extended functionality with respect to multimedia data [KNS90] and an improved transaction schema [MRKN92] for better performance.

Acknowledgements

This paper did greatly benefit from the comments of Norbert Streitz and Erich Neuhold. We wish to thank Boris Bokowski and Christian Schuckmann for their help with the implementation of the clients' interface for SEPIA and their implementation of the broadcast server. And last but not least we wish to thank Lothar Rostek and Dietrich Fischer for their support when we used the SFK and CCK toolkits which proved to be extremely valuable for the development of our system.

References

[AMY88]   R. M. Akscyn, D. L. McCracken, and E. A. Yoder. KMS: A Distributed Hypermedia System for Managing Knowledge in Organizations. *CACM*, 31(7):820 – 835, July 1988.

[Bus45]   V. Bush. As We May Think. *Atlantic Monthly*, 176(1):101 – 108, June 1945.

[CG88]   B. Campbell and J. M. Goodman. HAM: A General Purpose Hypertext Abstract Machine. *Communications of the ACM*, 31(7):856 – 861, July 1988.

[Con87]   J. Conklin. Hypertext: An Introduction and Survey. *IEEE Computer*, 20(9):17–41, September 1987.

[DS86]   N. M. Delisle and M. D. Schwartz. Neptune: a Hypertext System for CAD Applications. In Carlo Zaniolo, editor, *Proceedings of the 1986 ACM-SIGMOD International Conference on Management of Data*, pages 132 – 143, Washington, D.C., May 28 – 30, 1986.

[EGR91]   C. A. Ellis, S. J. Gibbs, and G. L. Rein. Groupware: Some Issues and Experiences. *Communications of the ACM*, 34(1):38 – 58, January 1991.

[FR92]   D. H. Fischer and L. Rostek. *SFK: A Smalltalk Frame Kit – Concepts and Use*. Internal working paper, GMD-IPSI, February 17, 1992.

[HKR+92]   B. J. Haan, P. Kahn, V. A. Riley, J. H. Coombs, and N. K. Meyrowitz. IRIS Hypermedia Services. *Communications of the ACM*, 35(1):36 – 51, January 1992.

[HW92]   J. M. Haake and B. Wilson. Supporting Collaborative Writing of Hyperdocuments in SEPIA. In *Proceedings of the ACM 1992 Conference on Computer Supported Cooperative Work*, Toronto, Ontario, November 1 – 4, 1992.

[KNF+92]   W. Klas, E. J. Neuhold, P. Fankhauser, M. Kaul, P. Muth, T. Rakow, and V. Turau. VML — The VODAK Model Language, Version 2.0. Working Paper, 1992.

[KNS90]   W. Klas, E. J. Neuhold, and M. Schrefl. Using an Object-Oriented Approach to Model Multimedia Data. *Computer Communications* 13(4), 204–216, May 1990.

[Kuh91]   R. Kuhlen. *Hypertext — Ein nicht-lineares Medium zwischen Buch und Wissensbank*. Edition SEL-Stiftung. Springer-Verlag, 1991.

[LØS92]   D. B. Lange, K. Østerbye, and H. Schütt. Hypermedia Storage. Technical report R 92-2009, Aalborg University, Department of Mathematics and Computer Science, Fredrik Bajers vej 7E, 9220 Aalborg, Denmark, June 1992.

[MHRJ91] C. C. Marshall, F. G. Halasz, R. A. Rogers, and W. C. Janssen Jr. Aquanet: A Hypertext Tool to Hold Your Knowledge in Place. In *Proceedings of the 3rd ACM Conference on Hypertext*, pages 261 – 275, San Antonio, TX, December 15 – 18, 1991.

[MPS91]   K. C. Malcolm, S. E. Poltrock, and D. Schuler. Industrial Strength Hypermedia: Requirements for a Large Engineering Enterprise. In *Proceedings of the 3rd ACM Conference on Hypertext*, pages 13 – 24, San Antonio, TX, December 15 – 18, 1991.

[MRKN92] P. Muth, T. C. Rakow, W. Klas, and E. J. Neuhold. A Transaction Model for an Open Publication Environment. In A. K. Elmagarmid, editor, *Database Transaction Models for Advanced Applications*, chapter 6, pages 159 – 218. Morgan Kaufmann, 1992.

[Nel65]   T. H. Nelson. A File Structure of the Complex, the Changing, and the Indeterminate. In *Proceedings of the 20-th National ACM Conference*, pages 84 – 100, Cleveland, OH, August 24 – 26, 1965.

[Nie90]   J. Nielsen. *Hypertext and Hypermedia*. Academic Press, 1990.

[Rod91]   T. Rodden. A survey of CSCW systems. *Interacting with Computers*, 3(3):319 – 353, December 1991.

[Sch92]   H. Schütt. *HyperBase*: Eine Hypertextmaschine im praktischen Einsatz. In R. Cordes, editor, *Proceedings of Hypertext und Hypermedia '92*, Munich, September 14 – 16, 1992.

[Sha91]   D. Shafer. *The Complete Book of HyperCard 2*. Addison-Wesley, 1991.

[SHH+92] N. A. Streitz, J. Haake, J. Hannemann, A. Lemke, W. Schuler, H. Schütt, and M. Thüring. SEPIA: A Cooperative Hypermedia Authoring Environment. In *Proceedings of the Fourth ACM Conference on Hypertext (ECHT-92)*, Milan, November 30 – December 4, 1992.

[SHT89]   N. A. Streitz, J. Hannemann, and M. Thüring. From Ideas and Arguments to Hyperdocuments: Travelling through Activity Spaces. In *Proceedings of the 2nd ACM Conference on Hypertext*, pages 343 – 364, Pittsburgh, PA, November 5 – 8, 1989.

[SLH91]   J. L. Schnase, J. Leggett, and D. L. Hicks. HB1: Initial Design and Implementation of a Hyperbase Management System. Technical Report TAMU-HRL 91-002, Texas A&M University, Computer Science Department, Hypertext Research Lab, October 1991.

[SS90]   H. Schütt and N. Streitz. *HyperBase*: A Hypermedia Engine Based on a Relational Database Management System. In A. Rizk, N. Streitz, and J. André, editors, *Hypertext: Concepts, Systems, and Applications: Proceedings of the First European Conference on Hypertext*, pages 95 – 108, Versailles, France, November 28 – 30, 1990. Cambridge University Press, The Cambridge Series on Electronic Publishing.

[SSS92]   D. E. Shackelford, J. B. Smith, and F. D. Smith. A Distributed Graph Storage System for Artifacts in Group Collaborations. Technical Report TR 92-010, The University of North Carolina at Chapel Hill, March 1992.

[Syb90]   Sybase, Inc., 6475 Christie Avenue, Emeryville, CA 94608, USA. *DB-Library Reference Manual, Release 4.2*, May 1990.

[THH91]   M. Thüring, J. Haake, and J. Hannemann. What's ELIZA doing in the Chinese Room — Incoherent Hyperdocuments and how to Avoid them. In *Proceedings of the 3rd ACM Conference on Hypertext*, pages 161 – 177, San Antonio, TX, December 15 – 18, 1991.

[Web91]   A. Weber. Publishing Tools Need Both: State-Oriented and Task-Oriented Version Support. In *Proceedings of the 15th Annual International Computer Software and Applications Conference (COMPSAC-91)*, pages 633 – 639, Tokyo, Japan, September 11 – 13, 1991.

[Wii91]   U. K. Wiil. Using Events as Support for Data Sharing in Collaborative Work. In K. Gorling and C. Sattler, editors, *Proceedings of the International Workshop on CSCW*, pages 162 – 177, Berlin, April 9 – 11, 1991.

The Hypermedia Presentation Composer: A Tool for Automatic Hyperdocument Delivery

Christoph Hüser, Anja Haake
Integrated Publication and Information Systems Institute (IPSI)
Gesellschaft für Mathematik und Datenverarbeitung (GMD)
Dolivostraße 15, D - 6100 Darmstadt
e-mail: {hueser, ahaake} @darmstadt.gmd.de

This paper introduces the design and architecture of the Hypermedia Presentation Composer, a knowledge-based tool for automatic hyperdocument delivery. The Hypermedia Presentation Composer follows the general design principle of an integrated publishing environment: the logical document structure is separated from all kinds of semantics. In doing so, the Hypermedia Presentation Composer serves as a vehicle to experiment with the presentation and delivery of electronic documents to different hypermedia systems.

1 Introduction

The department Publication and Visualization Environment (PaVE) at the Integrated Publication and Information Systems Institute (IPSI) is building an integrated publishing environment. The aim of this environment is not only to support the electronic publishing process of paper documents. In particular we aim at the improvement and development of tools needed for publishing hypermedia publications.

Two innovative hypermedia publications, the Individualized Electronic Newspaper [13] and the hypermedia lexicon ipsiLex, serve as driving forces delivering requirements for such an integrated publishing environment. The Individualized Electronic Newspaper is part of the European RACE (Research and Development in Advanced Communications Technologies in Europe) project 1075 TELEPUBLISHING [19], [24]. IpsiLex [8] is an experimental publication developed by PaVE and serves as the starting point for our contribution to an electronic version of the Dictionary of Art, which is part of the European RACE project 2042 EUROPUBLISHING.

Both innovative hypermedia publications show the potential hypermedia offers to publishers. Electronic publications profit from the various media and in particular can be individualized and active. But the design of these publications also reveals two severe problems.

On the one hand, a central problem of hypermedia is disorientation. Good design rules for hyperdocuments are still missing. The presentation of information communicates its function to the reader. Such presentation forms for communicating knowledge have been developed within hundreds of years for conventional publications (for example see [23] for newspaper layout rules), but are still missing for hyperdocuments. Our approach to alleviate the problems of disorientation and getting lost in hyperdocuments is to apply document metaphors for the presentation of hyperdocuments in a consistent manner.

On the other hand, the production and delivery of large volumes on demand requires the automatic composing of hypermedia documents. Thereby, it must be possible to present hyperdocuments on various hypertext systems, depending on the reading software available at the customer's site. In addition, the problem of automatic layout generation is aggravated by the presentation requirements of electronic publications following document metaphors.

Taking the Individualized Electronic Newspaper and ipsiLex as examples of innovative hypermedia publications, we discuss requirements for hyperdocument delivery (Section 2). Then, we introduce the design and architecture of the Hypermedia Presentation Composer, a knowledge-based tool for automatic hyperdocument delivery (Section 3). Section 4 discusses differences to related work. Finally, Section 5 concludes on first experiences gained from our approach and discusses future work.

2   Two innovative Hypermedia Publications: The Individualized Electronic Newspaper and ipsiLex

The Individualized Electronic Newspaper [13] is an experimental publication which is individualized and composed on demand for a reader, and then delivered electronically. The content of the IEN is automatically selected according to a profile of the reader's particular interests from a continually developing pool of "up to the minute" articles and features. To fully exploit the possibilities for electronic delivery, the reader can receive the IEN both as a printable and as a hypermedia product. In this paper, we will focus on our contribution to the RACE project TELEPUBLISHING, the hypermedia IEN.

We designed the customized IEN as a fully integrated hypermedia product for access on a multi-media computer terminal or notebook. In addition to enhancing articles with high quality images, animations, and video, the IEN increases the current newspaper functionality. It offers access to background material, to databases of classified advertisements, or enables the publisher to provide extended news related services.

Figure 1 Example of a Front Page of the Hypermedia IEN

Figure 1 shows an IEN front page composed for a reader with interest in current affairs and a special interest in science. The current prototype is implemented in HyperNeWS [22]. While the front page is made to look much like a traditional newspaper, its functionality is enhanced to provide access to the content of a hypermedia newspaper: e.g. its different multimedia contents (in the right lower corner left to the contents bar the reader can activate a news video clip), the background information, and the extended services. According to his/her mood and information needs the reader can choose to flip pages by clicking on the arrows. He may reach sections of his interest directly or make use of the lexicon look-up by pressing the bullet buttons in the Contents bar.

The article on "Fusion Fraud" (containing new developments on the issue of cold fusion) provides the reader with different background material: clicking the buttons here will reveal a chronicle of events, i.e. a series of published articles dealing with this topic (Background); a transcript of an interview, which may eventually be shown as a video (Interview), a collection of bibliographic references (Literature), and a number of controversial contributions acquired directly by electronic mail (Netnews).

Figure 2 Rapid-lookup of an ipsiLex lexicon entry (on term "bookmark") popping up

"A Cheap and Easy Second Shot" is an example of a scrollable text with embedded buttons. Clicking on a sensitized phrase will bring up a lexicon entry containing its translation (e.g. into German) and explaining its meaning. Actually, ipsiLex has been integrated into the IEN as a lexicon service. Figure 2 shows the rapid-lookup of an ipsiLex lexicon entry.

The above figures show the application of document metaphors to the presentation of hyperdocuments in order to avoid disorientation and getting lost in hyperspace. Rather than defining the appearance of hyperdocuments on the basis of the system's technical capabilities, we exploit the technical features of the hypertext target system to realize the best presentation form for each kind of hypermedia publication. For example employing the newspaper metaphor means that newspaper articles are not mapped straightforward onto single HyperNeWS cards. Rather, a set of articles is arranged on a card representing a newspaper page. In contrast, background information pops up (e.g. the lexicon) and is presented according to the needs of the kind of publication.

The rapid-lookup shown in Figure 2 is only one presentation of ipsiLex [8]. Publishing information on demand for different purposes and users also implies the use of different parts of the information and different presentation forms according to the actual purpose. Figure 3 shows the comprehensive-lookup of ipsiLex which comprises – in addition to the term, its translation and its popular definition – additional information related

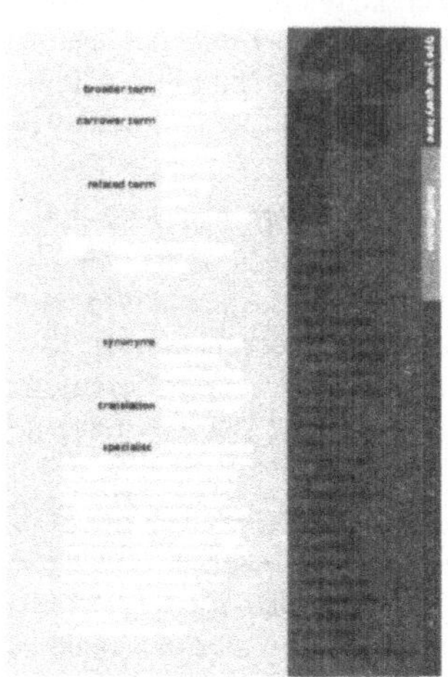

Figure 3
Comprehensive-lookup
of an ipsiLex lexicon entry

to a term (dark gray area in the middle). Clicking on the information items will bring up the information on the light gray area in the left. Beside the term and its translation, Figure 3 shows a definition addressing specialists instead of casual users, shows related synonyms of the term and additional thesaurus relations (broader, narrower and related term) maintained in the lexicon. These strings are active and can be used for navigating the lexicon.

Moreover, visual information illustrating the term can be invoked (waves left to the term "document type definition") and will pop up, or an audio pronunciation aid can be requested (left parentheses left to the term). In addition, an alphabetic list of lexicon entries and classifications of the lexicon entries can be requested, or the lexicon can be queried directly. These services are offered in the right bar and will pop up windows offering the requested support. The comprehensive-lookup of ipsiLex is an publication on its own which is in particular useful for authors, or may also be offered to IEN-readers that are interested in terminology.

3 The Design of the Hypermedia Layout Composer

3.1 Design Issues

Looking at the innovative electronic publications introduced in the previous section, we can identify four major issues of hypermedia publications that affect hyperdocument delivery.

First of all, both publications rely on the *reuse of material*. The various information contained in and related to a daily newspaper is used to compose an indeterminate amount of individualized newspaper issues. The total amount of lexicon entries including the relationships between those entries is used to produce different publications (rapid-lookup for casual users and comprehensive-lookup for experts).

Second, one key problem particularly imposed by the IEN is the *automatic presentation of documents*. Previewing of hundreds of individual newspaper issues is not possible. The issues have to be produced without manual corrections. As for ipsiLex, the indeterminate amount of entries have to be mapped to the different presentations with respect to the layout of the respective publications. Following the navigation operations of the readers, an incremental update of the well-designed document surface must be possible.

Third, it is generally required to *deliver hyperdocuments to different hypermedia systems*, depending on the reading software available at the reader's site. Potential readers can not be forced to buy various hypertext systems just to be able to subscribe to different electronic publications provided by different publishers. However, these hypermedia systems have to be suitable hypertext reading systems and have to support a minimum of the presentation facilities required by the specific publication design.

Fourth, the *hyperdocument presentation has to be adaptable according to different presentation preferences or whole document designs*. The experimental designs introduced in Section 2 are only a starting point to address the issue of hyperdocument design and good design rules for electronic publications are still missing. Therefore, it must also be possible to experiment with different presentations of a newspaper issue in a single hypertext system. Moreover, it may be required to slightly change the presentation according to enhancements or restrictions of various hypermedia target reading systems (cf. also Section 3.2.3).

To support the reuse of information (first issue) in different publishing contexts and phases of the publishing process, the design of the integrated publishing environment being developed by PaVE is based on a publishing model centered around a typed hypertext data model. The idea of the publishing model is to separate the logical content structure from all kinds of semantics, as they appear for printed and electronically delivered documents [13]. Our implementation of this model covers the logical document structure by SGML (Standard Generalized Markup Language) [3] *document type definitions*. Concrete typed hyperdocuments are represented by SGML *document instances* conforming to a certain document type definition (cf. [1] or [13] how to deal with hypertext links in SGML). The semantics beyond the logical structure are covered by declarative rules, so-called style definitions, that present knowledge about presentation or other task management in general and can be associated to the logical document structure.

This publishing model implies a layered architecture for the overall publishing environment as introduced in [12]. Publishing task specific tools share data maintained in shared databases. The analysis of the production tools – required for example for the production of the IEN – has shown that the application tools should be programmed on the basis of the knowledge contained in the document type definitions and should not be forced to deal with complex database schemas [13]. Therefore, we built the Structured Document Base (SDB) [11], a database application available on relational database management systems offering SGML-conformant storage, manipulation, navigation and querying of hyperdocuments (cf. Figure 4).

The Hypermedia Presentation Composer (HPC) is an example for such a publishing task-specific tool being build on top of the SDB, dedicated to the task of automatic document presentation and delivery (second issue). Presenting individualized hypermedia publications automatically according to document metaphors aggravates the layout problem for hypermedia publications. A column-based layout (e.g. newspaper) is in general not as easy as the layout of a continuous text (e.g. conference proceedings). Unconditional style sheets as offered by many document preparation systems do not suffice. Our approach is to apply knowledge-based techniques. Conditional rules cover a typical layout style and react on the individuality of each issue. This approach is also a prerequisite to make the HPC adaptable to various presentation styles (fourth issue).

However, to make the HPC work for different hypertext target systems (third issue) and to support various presentation styles (fourth issue), the architecture of the HPC has to be modular and well-designed. The HPC is based on an object-oriented formatter model separating the overall composing process into different subprocesses. Taking the composition and delivery of an IEN newspaper issue as an example, the next two sections will explain the HPC in detail.

3.2   The Overall Architecture

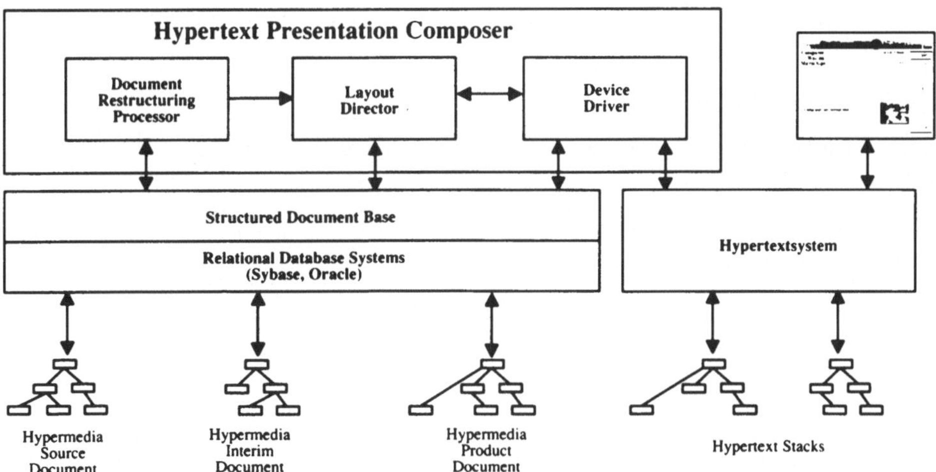

Figure 4 Overall Architecture of the Hypertext Presentation Composer

Figure 4 shows the overall architecture of the Hypermedia Presentation Composer. The overall composing process consists of three tasks: restructuring, publication assembling and interaction generation. These tasks are performed by three components that interact and communicate by sharing typed hyperdocuments stored in the SDB as SGML-conformant documents. An overall coordinator process of the Hypermedia Presentation Composer controls and guides these three components.

According to a set of restructuring rules, first the Document Restructuring Processor transforms the set of documents to be delivered, the so-called *Hypermedia Source Documents* (HSD), into the so-called *Hypermedia Interim Document* (HID) (cf. also Figure 6). Then, following a selected presentation style, the Layout Director together with the Device Driver perform the publication assembling and interaction generation by mapping the HID into the *Hypermedia Product Document* (HPD) which describes the final publication (cf. also Figure 7). In doing so, the Device Driver concurrently controls the generation of the concrete document to be delivered in the target hypertext system, for example as hypertext stacks in HyperNeWS or HyperCard. In the sequel we explain the different components and hypermedia documents in detail.

3.2.1 Document Restructuring Processor

According to a set of restructuring rules, the Document Restructuring Processor transforms the set of documents to be delivered, the HSD, into the HID which is used for publication assembling and interaction generation. Not all of the content has to be used for a certain publication and the presentation of the content does not have to follow the structure of the information units. These decisions, which are independent from the chosen presentation style, are taken by the Document Restructuring Processor.

Since restructuring documents for various purposes and document views is a general problem, the Document Restructuring Processor is embedded into SDB. It is a general tool for the transformation of (source) documents or parts of them conforming to a document document type definition (or schema) into a new (target) document conforming to another document type definition (or schema). This is achieved by traversing the document parse tree of the source document and then executing for every parsed element appropriate rules (cf. Section 3.3.1) that create or modify document elements in the target document. The transformation rules mapping an IEN source document into a HID are described in [14]. The transformation rules are specified in a language corresponding to a subset of the general language transformation process defined in the Document Style and Semantics Specification Language (DSSSL) [2], a companion standard of SGML. Due to the document manipulation, query and navigation functionality of SDB, the rules are able to directly access and modify any document element in the database.

3.2.2 Layout Director

The Layout Director guides the composition using a system independent presentation style. A presentation style consists of a set of general layout objects and an associated set of rules describing the arrangement, navigation and browsing behavior of the final publication. These rules cover the layout design of the publishing house as well as the personal preferences of the IEN reader stated in his profile.

general layout objects	
layout controller objects	abstract device objects
issue controller part controller page controller region controller content structure controller (CSC) content controller (CC)	stacks backgrounds cards textfields buttons ...
Hypermedia Interim Document	**Hypermedia Product Document**

Figure 5 General layout objects managed by the layout director

The set of *general layout objects* to be defined in a presentation style can be divided into two classes: *abstract device objects* describe basic layout entities such as laid out text strings, buttons, graphical elements or pictures while *layout controller objects* describe the arrangement of basic layout entities to a complex design (cf. Figure 5). The abstract device objects are stored persistently as the Hypermedia Product Document (HPD) and the layout controller objects are stored persistently as the Hypermedia Interim Document (HID) in the SDB.

Examples for complex designs are a caption laid out in conjunction with an image, or an article body laid out together with its headline and byline, a whole page and eventually the design of the overall publication. Therefore, to reflect the final layout of a whole publication, a presentation style may define additional properties and rules for at least the layout controller objects. These layout controller objects constitute a use hierarchy, each level dealing with a special class of composition aspects.

On top of the hierarchy an issue controller deals with general directives for the generation of a whole issue, for example the maximum amount of pages, part ordering, or connections to other publications. Parts of publications to be laid out differently are managed by part controllers belonging to the issue controller. To enable the flexible use of different layout rules for every page, a part controller owns a set of page controllers. A page controller has a page layout plan for one or a sequence of pages, defining layout aspects such as the grid and special typographic rules. A page controller describes the information to be presented as one unit, say screen or card, to the user. It consists of several region controllers dividing the page into functional areas.

A region controller has a set of content structure controllers (CSCs) (which could be shared among different region objects). A content structure controller aggregates several content controllers (CCs) into one logical layout unit. Thus, a content controller performs the rendering of atomic hyperdocument elements, for example a headline, a paragraph, or an image. The content structure controller glues and arranges these basic units into the first compound layout controller objects, for example an image with a caption.

All these controllers may define abstract device objects, i.e. the part controllers may define abstract stacks and backgrounds, page controllers may define backgrounds, cards or basic rendering objects covering the page numbering, and content controllers define the basic objects rendering content. These abstract device objects constitute a system-independent description of the final publication, the HPD.

3.2.3   Device Driver

The Device Driver performs the mapping of the abstract device objects onto concrete device objects such as stacks, backgrounds, cards, buttons, menus, text fields, canvases etc. provided by the target system, for example HyperNeWS or HyperCard. This mapping assigns to each abstract device object class one or a set of concrete device object classes implementing a fixed set of basic functions (e.g. positioning, sizing, value setting, typographic aspects) needed to compute the concrete layout. Thus, the Device Driver delivers concrete values needed for the composition process of the Layout Director by controlling the target system. The Device Driver asks the target system to generate corresponding concrete device objects and then requests concrete object extensions (position, size etc.) from the target system. These values will then be returned to the Layout Director to guide further composing decisions.

If the set of concrete device objects offered by the target system does not provide counterparts for all abstract device objects assumed by a presentation style two strategies are applicable. Either, the Device Driver may map one abstract object onto a group of concrete ones that will be treated as one entity by the Device Driver [17]. Or, the presentation style may be changed into a new presentation style adhering to the deficiencies of the target system. Thus, a presentation style is not totally system independent, but applicable to a class of hypertext systems, namely all those systems offering at least meaningful counterparts for the abstract device objects.

So on the one hand, to configure the HPC for a different target system (issue 3), only the Device Driver has to be reprogrammed. All presentation styles defined so far can be rerun for this new target system if the target system supports the relevant abstract device objects. On the other hand, to experiment with a different design for a publication (issue 4), only the presentation style has to be redefined.

3.3 The Composing Process

The coordinator process of the HPC controls the process flow of and communication between the three components described above. In the following, the three phases restructuring, publication assembling, and interaction generation are explained in detail.

3.3.1 Restructuring

In this first phase the publication described by its SGML document instance, for example an IEN newspaper issue including references to its articles, will be mapped by the Document Restructuring Processor to layout controller objects needed by the Layout Director (cf. Figure 6). Following a selected presentation style, an issue of the IEN will be restructured into a controller object hierarchy. The result of this phase is a controller structure described as an SGML document, i.e. the Hypermedia Interim Document (HID).

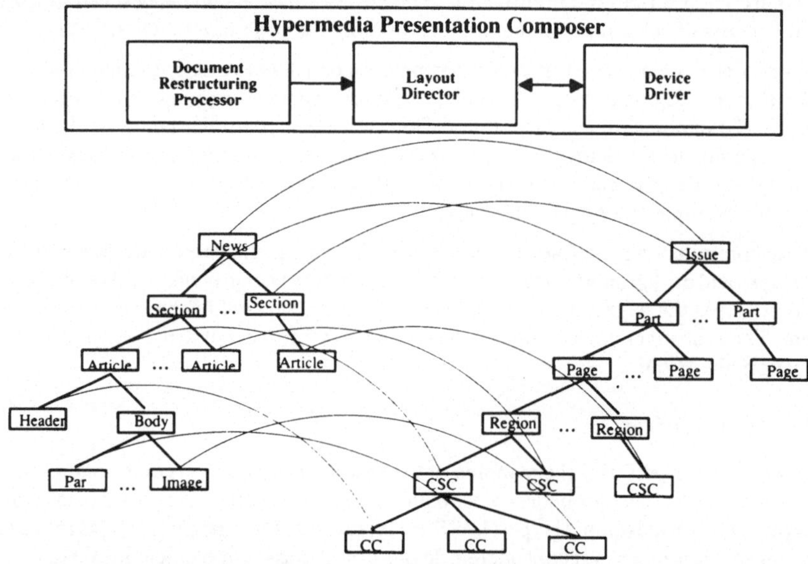

Figure 6 Generation of the Hypermedia Interim Document (HID)

As for an IEN issue, one issue controller will be created. Its properties will be defined according to the attributes of the IEN issue and the specifications of the presentation style. If the IEN issue provides a lexicon service, also an issue controller controlling the lexicon presentation will be generated.

Next, for every newspaper section (e.g. topic section, science, sport, culture, background information, interviews, literature) a part controller will be created. For the newspaper, some part controllers have two different page controllers, one for the front page of each section and the other controller for additional section pages. According to the part and type of page, each page controller will get assigned several region controllers. For example the overall IEN front page has a region controller for the contents bar at the right side, a lead article controller for the upper left part of the page, and an opinion controller defined left to the contents bar controller. The kinds of page and region controllers are defined by the restructuring rules for each type of newspaper section and will be generated as additional structure (cf. shaded area of the HPD in Figure 6).

In a next step, concrete newspaper articles will be mapped onto content structure controllers and their components will be mapped onto the respective content controllers. Here, structural information of the HSD that is not required for the layout process will be eliminated with respect to the HID (cf. shaded area of the HSD in Figure 6). Each content structure controller will be assigned to one region controller.

3.3.2 Publication Assembling

Publication assembling requires communication between the Layout Director and the Device Driver (cf. Figure 7). The problem of publication assembling may be characterized as packaging problem that is aggravated by the many constraints arising from a good layout and from profile restrictions and preferences. According to the layout directives stated in the presentation style the layout controllers driven by the Layout Director will generate the abstract device objects. In order to define the actual size of the objects to be rendered, they will request the Device Driver to compute the actual values. The Device Driver will associate concrete layout objects to every abstract device object and compute the needed information by controlling and consulting the hypertext target system (cf. Section 3.2.3). So in parallel to the abstract layout generation performed by the Layout Director, the device objects such as stacks, cards and card objects – and thus the final publication in the hypertext target system – are produced. For example, for an HyperNeWS issue of the IEN the part controller generate the stacks which are needed for the card generation of the page controllers.

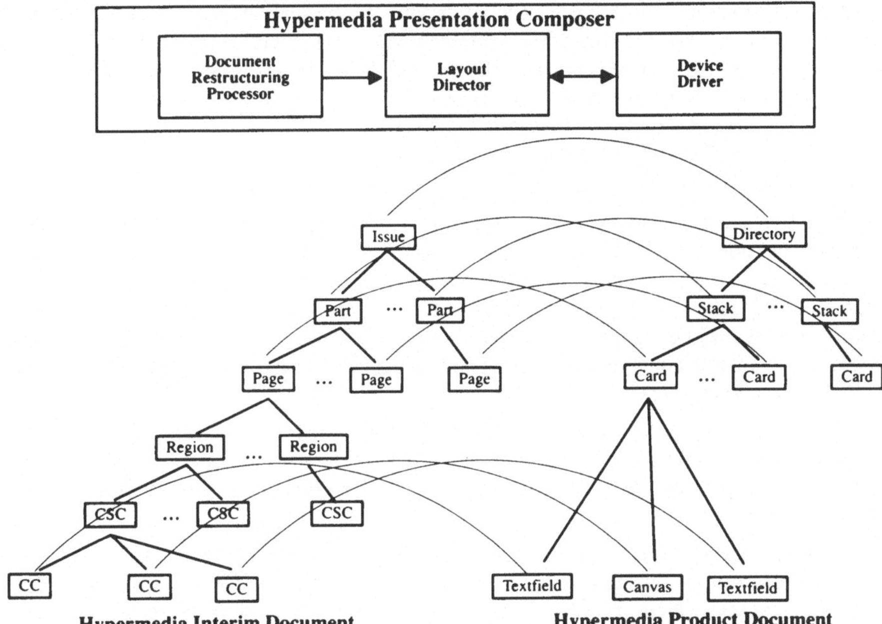

Figure 7 Generation of the Hypermedia Product Document (HPD)

Examining priority values of the IEN constituents the Layout Director controls the controller objects. In priority order the page controllers are requested to assemble their pages. The assembling of a page starts with the creation of an empty page according to the controller's page plan. The region controllers request their content structure controllers to compute the amount of size needed for the selected content to be rendered. The used parts of the newspaper constituents such as headline, byline, abstract, paragraphs or images are rendered by the content controllers onto text fields or canvases, or an anchor of a hypertext link may be mapped onto a sensitized string or a button.

The presentation rules will be applied to render the articles according to their priority until the region is filled. The best layout for each article has to be determined depending on the size and content of the article. Based on the size of their content computed by the content structure controllers and space required by neighboring region controller the regions may extend and shrink within their maximum and minimal extensions. Controlled by presentation rules for the whole page design, the region controllers are working in a competitive fashion to get the best positions and best amount of space defined by their properties. In case of conflicts, single articles can be laid out once again in an alternative and also sub-optimal fashion in order to fill the region without overlaps. Small gaps will be filled with so-called "filler articles" which are managed by a special region controller. Not all of the articles associated to a region controller have to be positioned. Too large or backlog articles may be assigned to new region and page controllers and thus drive the generation of additional pages. Thus, the cooperation between region and content structure controllers (cf. shaded area of the HID in Figure 7) defines the mapping of content to concrete hypertext objects (textfields etc.) and defines the amount of publication pages (cards).

3.3.3 Interaction Generation

This phase can be compared to generating a table of contents performed by document formatting systems. If the publication assembling is finished and all device objects are generated and known, the Layout Director can start the interaction generation. Knowing now all references between the generated device objects, the Layout Director will instruct the Device Driver to generate scripts for buttons realizing the switching of cards or calling of other publications. As for the IEN, the flipping of pages, the functionality of the contents bar, buttons referring to related articles, background information or extended services like the lexicon service will be generated by defining the corresponding HyperNews scripts for the respective concrete device objects.

4 Differences to related work

Others [5], [7] have proposed to learn from paper documents in order to alleviate disorientation problems in hypertext, too. The consistent application of document metaphors to hyperdocument presentation has not been pursued by many approaches. The Digital News System [10] maps each newspaper article manually onto a separate HyperCard card. The NewsPeek system [18] uses the metaphor of a newspaper front page for an news-oriented information retrieval system. The interface functionality may be compared to the comprehensive-lookup developed for ipsiLex. But the NewsPeek system only considers the incremental update and delivery of one kind of publication to a single, tailored target system.

DynaText [15] is an approach to deliver reference work described as SGML-conformant documents as electronic books to various window systems. It offers a simple default presentation for each document. More complex presentations have to be programmed explicitly using the Dyna-Text System Integrator Toolkit.

The HPC differs in many ways from formatters for print products or conventional editor systems. It does not perform type setting on character level. The focus of the HPC is rather the delivery of well-designed hyperdocuments to various systems. The type setting functionality, for example determining the extensions of a textfield given a selected font and content, is performed by the hypertext target system which is guided and controlled by the Device Driver. But the modular architecture allows to configure the HPC easily to new extensions and facilities of hypertext systems.

The controlling of the layout controller objects uses the model of boxes and glue as described in [16]. But the rules used to determine the size and place may differ according to the specific requirements of a publication, such as the IEN, which are stated in the presentation style.

[20] and [2] introduce the separation of the formatting process into separate tasks, which is also been pursued by [6]. In [20] a multi-level multi-stream formatting model is described. The for-

matter hierarchy can be compared to the controller hierarchy of the Layout Director. The algorithm of the hierarchical formatter corresponds to our page assembly task but it is paper- or print-oriented and does not contain a model for hypertext composing, i.e. it is not able to address hypertext systems or control the interaction generation. [20] further describes formatting techniques such as incremental formatting, which are implicitly given by our approach.

[4] discusses the problem of dynamic (during editing processes) and static type transformations in structured editing systems. A structure comparison tool is introduced that compares two structured document schemas and generates conversion rules for restructuring documents from one format to the other. These rules can be used by a conversion tool. This conversion tool can only restructure a single document instance into another. Since our Document Restructuring Processor exploits the full document access functionality of the SDB, also contents from various document instances can be restructured into a new publication. The automatic generation of conversion rules performed by the comparison tool would be an important extension to the restructuring support of the SDB.

5   Conclusion and Future Work

A first monolithic version of the HPC has been implemented for the two publications of ipsiLex. These experiences guided the design of the HPC introduced in this paper. The Document Restructuring Processor has been implemented and successfully been used to restructure, among other documents, IEN issues [14]. We have implemented a Device Driver for HyperNews. The Layout Director is currently under development. All implementations are done in C++.

Focusing at a good design of the IEN, we have extended HyperNeWS to support embedded links. The association of concrete device objects of a hypertext systems to abstract device objects being stored as SGML-conformant documents in the Hypermedia Product Document allows to build whole libraries of abstract device objects for each hypertext target system. These can be reused easily for the presentation of other documents or even be assembled into more complex layout objects e.g. graphical browsers.

The development of presentation styles has shown to be a complex task [14]. The rules of the presentation styles can be structured into different classes of rules (e.g. optimal layout of single entities; local, optimal arrangement of certain types of entities on one page; global estimation of the quality of the overall page layout; reconfiguration rules for suboptimal layout). The effort can be compared to the development of document type definitions. The design of the IEN layout rules will be published elsewhere.

Moreover, good design rules for hyperdocuments are still missing. New concepts supporting the reception of electronic documents – for example flipping of long newspaper articles that do not fit into an assigned textfield instead of using scrollbars or turning to another page – may challenge hyperdocument delivery further.

Recently, the HyTime [9], [21] standard has been published, extending SGML towards hypermedia applications. Besides standardized link types which are defined similar to the approaches in [1] and [13], HyTime proposes to implement a hypermedia document model by associating meta-interpretations to SGML document type definitions and also proposes the development of composing technology. The association of presentation styles via layout controller objects can be regarded as one step in the proposed direction. A next step is to extend our approach towards the functionality standardized in HyTime.

References

[1] *Guidelines for the Encoding and Interchange of Machine-Readable Texts.* Text Encoding Initiative, Document Number: TEI P1, July 1990.

[2] *Information Processing – Text and Office Systems – Document Style Semantics and Specification Language (DSSSL), ISO/IEC JTC 1/SC 18 (Draft Proposal).* Int. Org. for Standardization, 1989.

[3] *Information Processing – Text and Office Systems – Standardized Generalized Markup Language (SGML), ISO 8879–1986 (E).* Int. Org. for Standardization, 1986.

[4] Extase Akpotsui and Vincent Quint. *Type Transformation in Structured Editing Systems.* In Proc. of the Int. Conf. on Electronic Publishing (EP 92), Swiss Federal Institute of Technology, 1992.

[5] Mark Bernstein. *The Bookmark and the Compass: Orientation Tools for Hypertext Users.* SIGOIS Bulletin, Vol. 9, No. 4, pp. 34-45, Oct. 1988.

[6] Dick Bulterman. *CWI's Multimedia Research focuses on Synchronisation.* ERCIM News, No. 9, p. 9, April 1992.

[7] Fred Cole and Heather Brown. *Standards: What Can Hypertext Learn From Paper Documents?* Proc. of the HT Standardization Workshop, Jan. 16-18, National Inst. of Standards and Technology (NIST), Gaithersburg, MD, PB 90-215864, March 1990.

[8] Dietrich Fischer and Wiebke Möhr. *Lexikon-Redaktion: eine Herausforderung für Computer-Assistenz beim Publizieren.* GMD-Spiegel. Informationen aus der wissenschaftlichen Arbeit der Gesellschaft für Mathematik und Datenverarbeitung, März 1991.

[9] Charles F. Goldfarb (project editor). *Committee Draft Int. Standard 10744 Information Technology – Hypermedia/Time-based Structuring Language (HyTime).* Technical Report ISO/IEC CD 10744, ISO, April 1991.

[10] Eric M. Hoffert and Greg Gretsch. *The Digital News System at EDUCOM: A Convergence Of Interactive Computing, Newspapers, Television and High-Speed Networks.* Comm. of the ACM, Vol. 34, No. 4, pp. 113-116, April 1991.

[11] Christoph Hüser. *Report on a prototypical interface for structured documents and its application to the IEN scenario.* Technical Report 75/GMD/IPS/DS/L/047/b0, TELEPUBLISHING Project, RACE–Programme, Aug. 27, 1991.

[12] Christoph Hüser and Erich J. Neuhold. Knowledge-Based Cooperative Publication Systems. Proceedings of the Internationaler GI-Kongress: Wissensbasierte Systeme – Verteilte künstliche Intelligenz, Oct. 23-24, 1991.

[13] Christoph Hüser and Anja Weber. *The Individualized Electronic Newspaper: An application challenging hypertext technology.* Hypertext und Hypermedia 1992: Konzepte und Anwendungen auf dem Weg in die Praxis, München, 14.- 16. Sept. 1992, Informatik Aktuell, Springer Verlag.

[14] Gerhard Ihnofeld. *Spezifikation eines Hypertext Composing Prozesses und Entwicklung der Regelsprache für die Transformation von strukturierten Dokumenten anhand einer beispielhaften Anwendung.* Diploma Thesis, TH Darmstadt, Fachbereich Informatik, Dec. 3, 1991.

[15] Carl Kelley. *DynaText (TM) Product Overview.* Electronic Book Technologies, One Richmond Square, Providence, RI 02906, April 1992.

[16] Donald E. Knuth. *The T_EXbook.* Addison-Wesley Publishing Company, 1984

[17] John J. Legget and Ronnie L. Killough. *Issues in hypertext interchange.* Hypermedia, Vol. 3, No.3, pp. 159-186, 1991.

[18] Andrew Lipman and Walter Bender. *News and Movies in the 50 Megabit Living Room.* Paper presented at Globecom, IEEE, Tokyo, Japan, 1987.

[19] Roberto Minio. *Publishing as a broadband application.* IEE Conf. Integrated Broadband Services and Networks, pp. 153-159, London, Oct. 1990.

[20] Makoto Murata and Koichi Hayashi. *Formatter Hierarchy for Structured Documents.* Proc. of the Int. Conf. on Electronic Publishing (EP 92), Swiss Federal Institute of Technology, 1992.

[21] Steven R. Newcomb, Neill A. Kipp and Victoria T. Newcomb. *The "HyTime" Hypermedia/Time-based Document Structuring Language.* Comm. of the ACM, Vol. 34, No. 11, pp. 67–83, Nov. 1991.

[22] The Turing Institute. *HyperNeWS 1.4.* 36 North Hanover Street, Glasgow G1 2AD, UK.

[23] Verlag Frankfurter Algemeine Zeitung. *Alles über die Frankfurter Allgemeine Zeitung.* Verlag Frankfurter Allgemeine Zeitung, Hellerhofstraße 2-4, 6000 Frankfurt am Main, 1989.

[24] Anja Weber and Erich J. Neuhold. *Distributed Publishing of Electronic Newspapers and Mailorder Catalogues.* Technical Report "Arbeitspapiere der GMD" 574, Sept. 1991.

Verbesserung der Kantenbeschreibung in Hyperkollektionen durch Relevanzrückkoppelung

D. Stieger
Eidgenössische Technische Hochschule (ETH) Zürich
Institut für Informationssysteme
CH - 8092 Zürich

Kanten liefern nicht nur die Grundlage für das manuelle Navigieren in Hyperkollektionen, sie können - sofern sie geeignet deskribiert sind - auch für das automatische Retrieval gewinnbringend verwendet werden. Ein spezieller Ansatz zur Berücksichtigung von solchen Kanten wird aufgezeigt. Vor allem wird gezeigt, wie existierende Kantenbeschreibungen mit Hilfe von Relevanzrückkoppelungsmethoden verbessert werden. Diese Verbesserung wird nachgewiesen durch Experimente auf einem Hypertext und die Resultate werden diskutiert.

1. Einleitung

Die in Dokumenten enthaltene Information kann von einem Leser nur dann richtig interpretiert und damit genutzt werden, wenn dieser um die Zusammenhänge (den Kontext) des Inhalts weiss. Dieser Kontext setzt sich zusammen aus dem Vorwissen des Lesers über das Gebiet und aus dem neuen Wissen, welches während des Lesevorgangs vermittelt wird. Die Kanten in Hyperkollektionen haben - neben einer organisatorischen Referenzfunktion - die Aufgabe, die Knoten *semantisch* einzubetten. Somit hat der Leser die Möglichkeit, sich fehlendes Wissen um die Zusammenhänge durch Navigation selbst anzueignen.

Die Erstellung und Organisation von Hyperkollektionen ist ein komplizierter Vorgang; so muss sich der Autor z.B. überlegen, wie er die Information - möglichst arm an Redundanz - auf Knoten verteilt und wie er diese Knoten zueinander in Beziehung stellt. Oft werden in Hypertexten logische, hierarchische Gliederungen, wie sie in linearen Dokumenten anzutreffen sind, nur sparsam angewendet. Dadurch geht der Gesamtzusammenhang (das übergreifende Thema) verloren [HAA 91, MAR 89]. Bei einer rein intellektuellen Navigation in grossen und komplexen Hypernetzen führt dies zu Orientierungsproblemen [CON 87]; zudem ist die Kantenbezeichnung (oft sogar nur der Kantentyp) und die Bezeichnung des Zielknotens das einzige, worauf der Leser seinen Entscheid, ob er eine Kante verfolgen soll stützen kann.

Ein Information Retrieval System (IRS), welches in der Lage ist auf Hypernetzen zu arbeiten, sollte die durch die Kanten ausgedrückte semantische Einbettung der Knoten ausnutzen. Dies kann nur gewinnbringend vorgenommen werden, wenn das System die Bedeutung der Kanten mit Hilfe einer Beschreibung erfassen kann. Die

Zielsetzungen eines solchen IRS sind entweder eine bessere Bewertung der Knoten (bessere Effektivität, verglichen mit dem Retrieval ohne Verwendung von Kanten) oder eine Unterstützung beim Navigieren *(browsing)*. Zum letzteren gehört das Finden eines geeigneten Startknotens oder - falls sich der Leser bereits auf einem Knoten befindet - das Finden von geeigneten Nachfolgeknoten.

2. Eine geeignete Kanteninformation für das Retrieval

Es gibt mehrere Möglichkeiten, um in Hyper-Systemen Kanten zu charakterisieren. Diese Kanteninformation dient bis heute praktisch ausschliesslich dazu, dem Leser - während des Navigierens - bei der Bestimmung geeigneter Nachfolgeknoten behilflich zu sein. Wir unterscheiden folgende Arten von Kanteninformation:

- Typisierung mit vorgegebenen Kanten-Typen
- Benennung mit anwenderspezifischen Begriffen
- 'angeheftete' Information

Die *Typisierung* stellt eine einfache und - sofern sich die Anzahl Typen in Grenzen hält - eine für den Leser kompakte Art von Kanteninformation dar. Als grösster Vorteil ist die wirkungsvolle Darstellbarkeit zu nennen; der Kantentyp widerspiegelt sich meist in dem für die Repräsentation der Kante verwendeten Piktogramm. Die Motivation eine Kante zu verfolgen ergibt sich - sofern *nur* die Typisierung zur Anwendung kommt - nur aus dem aktuellen Kontext.

Die *Benennung* von Kanten bietet den Vorteil, dass der Leser bereits eine Idee bekommt, was das Verfolgen der Kante an neuer Information bringen könnte und stellt somit eine differenziertere Art von Information dar als die reine Typisierung. Die Qualität der Benennung hängt stark vom Autor ab. Oft wird dazu nur eine einzige Phrase verwendet; trotzdem wird die damit verbundene Arbeit oft als kognitive Mehrbelastung empfunden [CON 87, S. 40].

Die Beschreibung der Kante mit *angehefteter Information* erlaubt einem Leser festzustellen, ob sich ein Navigieren zum nächsten Knoten lohnt oder nicht. Ein Retrieval Algorithmus, welcher automatisch entlang von Kanten navigieren soll, benötigt zur Beantwortung dieser Frage eine *Kantenbeschreibung (Kantendeskribat)*. Diese wird analog zur Deskribierung der Knoten erstellt [FRE 92]. Folgende Ansätze für die Deskribierung drängen sich auf:

- automatische Generierung aus der Kanteninformation
- automatische Generierung aus den zur Kante gehörigen Knoten
- Resultat einer Relevanzrückkoppelung

Diese Ansätze schliessen sich gegenseitig nicht aus. Es ist denkbar, dass eine erste, automatisch generierte Kantenbeschreibung durch Relevanzrückkoppelung nachträglich modifiziert wird. Wir gehen davon aus, dass eine *direkte Modifikation* der Beschreibung durch den Anwender selbst (z.B. mit Hilfe eines speziellen Editors) eine grosse Belastung und (bei ungeübten Anwendern) eine kognitive Ueberforderung darstellt.

Die *automatische Generierung* des Kantendeskribats aus den umliegenden Knoten rechtfertigt sich durch die Tatsache, dass Kanten verantwortlich sind für die semantische Einbettung der Knoten. Es sollte daher möglich sein, eine Kantenbeschreibung durch Einbezug von zumindest Quell- und Zielknoten automatisch ableiten zu können. Es ist zu erwarten, dass wenn zusätzlich weitere Knoten (und damit Kanten) berücksichtigt werden, die damit gewonnene Kantenbeschreibung an Qualität gewinnt.

Die Motivation eines Anwenders, Relevanzinformation zu geben, ist gross, wenn er für weitere Anfragen, eine höhere Effektivität des Systems erwarten darf. Die Relevanzinformation ergibt ein vom aktuellen Kontext geprägtes, anwenderbezogenes Bild der Kanten und wird daher - ausser in speziellen und homogenen Benutzerkreisen - oft nur für eine kleinere Anwendergruppe oder gar nur einen spezifischen Anwender benutzt. Bei der Nutzung der Relevanzinformation zur *Unterstützung der Navigation* ist darauf zu achten, dass der aktuelle Kontext des Lesers (d.h. das neu akquirierte Wissen durch bereits gelesene Passagen) angemessen berücksichtigt wird.

3. Ein Ansatz zur Berücksichtigung der Kantenbeschreibung

Wir unterscheiden zwei Arten von Kanten und damit implizit zwei Arten von Retrieval Systemen, welche diese Kanten verwenden:

- referentielle Kanten
- semantische Kanten

Referentielle Kanten erlauben im wesentlichen das komfortable Lesen von Texten, enthalten jedoch keine zusätzliche Kantenbeschreibung [FRE 91a]. Beispiele sind z.B. Verweise vom Inhaltsverzeichnis zum entsprechenden Beginn der Kapitel oder vom Text zu bibliographischen Referenzen. Retrieval Methoden, welche auf referentiellen Kanten basieren, wurden bereits mehrfach untersucht und beschrieben [SAL 86, KWO 88, FRI 88, SAV 92]. Die Methoden basierten entweder auf der Uebertragung von Merkmalen oder Merkmalsgewichten von den Zielknoten- auf die Quellknotenbeschreibungen, oder auf der Korrektur eines initialen *Retrieval Status Value (RSV)* des Quellknotens aufgrund seiner Zielknoten [COH 87]. Es zeigte sich, dass *generelle* Aussagen in Bezug auf die zu erwartende Effektivität problematisch sind.

Semantische Kanten weisen auf ähnliche, detailliertere, weiterführende oder widersprechende Information und besitzen Kantenbeschreibungen, welche typischerweise aus gewichteten Merkmalen bestehen. Retrieval Methoden, welche diese Art von Kanten unterstützen, sind noch relativ neu. G.A. Boy stellte einen *regelbasierten* Ansatz zur Unterstützung des *browsing* vor [BOY 91]. B. Croft beschrieb einen vielversprechenden probabilistischen Ansatz, welcher nach Kenntnis des Autors nie evaluiert wurde [CRO 89]. In [FRE 92] stellten wir einen Ansatz vor, der auf automatisch generierten Kantenbeschreibungen basiert und auf einer modifizierten, herkömmlichen Testkollektion gute Resultate zeigte. Eine Erweiterung dieses Ansatzes soll im folgenden aufgezeigt werden. Dabei soll der Begriff 'Kante' stets im Sinne einer *semantischen Kante* aufgefasst werden.

Damit der Ansatz einfach qualifizierbar ist, beschränken wir uns bei der Effektivitätsbeurteilung auf die Situation, wie sie ein Anwender antrifft, welcher in einer Kollektion geeignete Knoten sucht, aber selbst wenig über die Kollektion weiss. Die Beurteilung von Retrieval Resultaten, welche aus einem *browsing* Vorgang hervorgegangen sind, wäre mit Schwierigkeiten verbunden, da der aktuelle Wissensstand des Anwenders mitberücksichtigt werden müsste. Zudem hängt dort die Relevanz-Beurteilung nicht nur von dem durch das Retrieval gelieferten Knoten ab, sondern auch von dessen Umgebung und der Bereitschaft des Lesers diese zu explorieren.

Das Modell:

Eine Kante ist gerichtet und besteht aus folgenden Komponenten:

$\lambda = <I, ls, ld>$, wobei   I die Kanteninformation,

ls der zur Kante gehörige Quellknoten und

ld der entsprechende Zielknoten darstellt.

Sowohl die Anfrage q, die Knoten n_i, als auch die Kanten λ (n_i, n_j) werden deskribiert. Dies führt zu den Deskribaten

$$\vec{q}, \vec{n}_i, \vec{\lambda} \in \mathbf{R}^m,$$

wobei die Vektor-Komponenten jeweils Merkmalsgewichte darstellen.

Während die Anfrage- und Knotenbeschreibungen wie im Information Retrieval üblich erhalten werden, ist das Kantendeskribat das Resultat einer Deskribierfunktion i, von der wir hier annehmen, dass sie nur auf die Beschreibungen des Quell- und Zielknotens zugreife. In [FRE 92] stellt diese Funktion die *Summe* der Beschreibungsvektoren des Quell- und des Zielknotens der Kante dar. Aus speicherökonomischen Gründen und zur Erhöhung der Effizienz werden nur die am höchsten gewichteten Merkmale verwendet, d.h. niedrige Merkmalsgewichte werden auf 0 gesetzt.

Eine durch i erhaltene initiale Kantenbeschreibung kann später modifiziert werden. Wir führen dazu eine Modifikationsfunktion i_u ein, welche die Kantenbeschreibung modifizieren darf:

$$i_u : \mathbf{R}^m \times \mathbf{R}^m \rightarrow \mathbf{R}^m \ , \ (\vec{\lambda}, \vec{u}) \mapsto i_u(\vec{\lambda}, \vec{u}) := (\vec{\lambda} + \vec{u}), \text{ wobei } \vec{u} \in \mathbf{R}^m$$

Ein Retrieval Algorithmus soll eine Kante verfolgen, wenn die Aehnlichkeit zwischen der Anfrage- und der Kantenbeschreibung einen Wert v überschreitet. Ein zusätzliches Prädikat P, welches direkt auf der Kanteninformation I (z.B. dem Kantentyp) operiert, kann eine Navigation verhindern. Dieses Prädikat P spielt jedoch in den folgenden Betrachtungen eine untergeordnete Rolle. Für die im folgenden bezeichnete Aehnlichkeitsfunktion σ kann z.B. das Skalarprodukt zur Anwendung gelangen. Das Entscheidungsprädikat e auf die Frage, ob eine Kante verfolgt wird, lautet:

$$e : ((\sigma (\vec{q}, \vec{\lambda}) > v) \ \text{AND} \ P(I))$$

Das Verfahren unter Verwendung von Kanten beruht auf der Korrektur eines initialen RSVs. Der initiale $RSV_0^{q,n}$ des Knotens n wird durch eine klassische Retrieval

Funktion $\rho(\vec{q}, \vec{n})$ bestimmt. Die Korrektur kann durch eine gewichtete Hinzunahme der RSV_0^{q,n_i} aller Zielknoten n_i - welche über das Entscheidungsprädikat e besucht werden dürfen - vorgenommen werden:

$$RSV_0^{q,n} := \rho\,(\vec{q}, \vec{n})$$

$$RSV_{korr}^{q,n} := RSV_0^{q,n} + w_d \cdot \frac{1}{|n_i|} \cdot \sum_i \left(\xi\!\left(n, n_i, \sigma\!\left(\vec{q}, \vec{\lambda}(n, n_i)\right)\right) \cdot RSV_0^{q,n_i} \right)$$

Die Funktion ξ erlaubt eine gewichtete Berücksichtigung der Zielknoten in Abhängigkeit von der Kantenbeschreibung. w_d stellt eine kollektionsabhängige Konstante dar (siehe [FRE 92]), welche den Einfluss der berücksichtigten Zielknoten skaliert.

4. Verbesserung des Kantendeskribats durch Relevanzrückkoppelung

In klassischen Ansätzen wird die Relevanzrückkoppelung entweder zur Modifikation der Anfrage oder - etwas unüblicher - auch zur Modifikation der Beschreibung der gefundenen Informationseinheit [SAL 90] verwendet. Hier wird die Relevanzinformation zur Modifikation der Kantenbeschreibung benützt.

Wie bereits ausgeführt, gibt das Prädikat e an, ob eine Kante λ zum Informationsbedürfnis q des Anwenders ergänzende Information verspricht. Eine Relevanzrückkoppelung, welche auf Kanten einwirkt, kann den durch das Prädikat e bestimmten Effekt positiv oder negativ beeinflussen; dazu werden in den Kanten die Merkmals-Gewichtungen entsprechend modifiziert. Werden mit gewissen Merkmalen 'schlechte Erfahrungen' gemacht, so sollen tiefe Gewichtungen dieser Merkmale dafür sorgen, dass die betreffende Kante in ähnlichen Zusammenhängen eher nicht verfolgt wird. Das Umgekehrte gilt, wenn mit Merkmalen 'gute Erfahrungen' gemacht werden.

In einem Initialzustand sind entweder alle Kantenbeschreibungen leer, oder sie enthalten das Resultat einer Kantendeskribierfunktion i. Liegt Relevanzinformation bezüglich eines Knotens vor, so kann eine Veränderung der Kantenbeschreibung Verschiedenes bewirken:

- eingehende Kanten

  Die Erreichbarkeit des Knotens wird verändert. Der Knoten wird unter ähnlichen Bedingungen - diese werden bestimmt durch die Anfrage - von anderen Knoten her besser oder schlechter erreichbar gemacht.

- ausgehende Kanten

  Das Navigieren von diesem Knoten aus wird in der aktuellen Form unterstützt bzw. erschwert. Dadurch wird die Chance, dass sich der RSV einer Anfrage an dieser Stelle durch Berücksichtigung der umliegenden Knoten erhöht, verändert.

Wird ein Knoten als relevant beurteilt, so werden in *allen* von diesem Knoten ausgehenden und *im letzten Retrieval-Vorgang berücksichtigten* Kanten die zu den Anfragemerkmalen gehörenden Einträge erhöht, dasselbe geschieht mit *allen* eingehenden

Kanten (unabhängig davon, ob sie im letzten Retrieval-Vorgang verwendet wurden).
Ist der Knoten nicht relevant, so werden die Einträge erniedrigt (sie können auch negativ werden). Die im Prädikat e enthaltene Aehnlichkeitsfunktion σ wird somit diejenigen Kanten bevorzugen, welche in ähnlichen Situationen 'gut abgeschnitten' haben.

Die Relevanzinformation wird aus praktischen Gründen auf die Angabe von Präferenzklassen beschränkt. Damit der Anwender bei der Bewertung nicht überfordert wird, aber dennoch eine genügend grosse Anzahl von Präferenzen für die Auswertung resultiert, schlagen wir vor, mit den vier folgenden Klassen zu operieren:

++	der Knoten stellt genau das gewünschte Resultat dar	$\beta \geq 1$
+	der Knoten ist in einer gewissen Hinsicht nützlich	$\beta = 1$
~	der Knoten ist weder besonders nützlich noch absolut ungeeignet	$\beta = 0$
-	der Knoten ist nicht relevant bezüglich der Anfrage	$\beta = -1$

Die Modifikation der Kantenbeschreibung würde nach den üblichen Relevanzrückkoppelungs-Methoden folgendermassen vorgenommen: $\vec{\lambda'} := \vec{\lambda} + \beta \cdot \vec{q}$. Die Wahl des Parameters β bei der Berücksichtigung der Präferenzklasse ++ hängt einerseits von der Anfrage, andererseits aber auch von der Hyper-Kollektion ab. Je besser Knoten als 'wirklich zutreffend' bestimmt werden können, desto höher darf das Gewicht bei der Bewertung dieser Klasse sein.

Es liegt auf der Hand, dass beim längeren Einsatz eines nach dieser Methode operierenden Systems, die jeweils oft gleich bewerteten Kantenmerkmale 'explodieren' und somit die selten bewerteten Merkmale 'überdecken'. Zwei Massnahmen sind möglich:

- Das Inkrement/Dekrement der Gewichte nimmt bei einer gewissen Sättigung ab.
- Die Gewichte werden von der Aehnlichkeitsfunktion interpretiert.

Da die Aehnlichkeitsfunktion öfter ausgeführt wird als die Relevanz-Rückkoppelung, entscheiden wir uns für den ersten Weg. Die Kantenbeschreibung wird mit Hilfe der folgenden (symmetrischen) Funktion modifiziert:

$$\lambda'_i := \text{sign}\left(\text{sign}(\lambda_i) \cdot \left(2^{|\lambda_i|} - 1\right) + \beta \cdot q_i\right) \cdot \log_2\left(1 + \left|\text{sign}(\lambda_i) \cdot \left(2^{|\lambda_i|} - 1\right) + \beta \cdot q_i\right|\right) \quad \forall i = 1...m$$

Analog zu den bekannten Rückkoppelungs-Verfahren können bei grösseren Anfragen - anstelle aller Anfrage-Merkmale - auch nur die am höchsten gewichteten Merkmale verwendet werden. Da die Kantenbeschreibung semantisch und formal der Knotenbeschreibung entspricht, kann für die Funktion σ eine der üblichen Aehnlichkeitsfunktionen zum Einsatz kommen.

5. Experimente

Die Effekte einer automatisch generierten Kantenbeschreibung wurden in [FRE 92] diskutiert. Wir beschränken uns hier auf die Ueberprüfung, inwiefern mit dem vorgestellten Relevanzrückkoppelungs-Verfahren eine Verbesserung der Retrieval Effektivität erzielt werden kann.

Die Kollektion:

Der verwendete Hypertext setzt sich aus 962 englischsprachigen *Berkeley-UNIX online manual pages* zusammen (ohne die *X-Windows manual pages*). Die Verweise zwischen den *manual pages* werden durch die in ihnen enthaltenen 'SEE_ALSO'-Referenzen gebildet. Dadurch werden die 962 Knoten durch 4341 Kanten miteinander verbunden (927 Kanten weisen eine inverse 'Gegenkante' auf).

Die in formatierter Form vorliegenden Knoten wurden ihrer Format-Information entledigt, so dass nur noch ein reiner Text vorlag. Dieser wurde in einzelne Wörter zerlegt. Nach Anwendung einer Stoppwort-Liste mit 329 Einträgen (es wurden neben generellen Stoppwörtern auch Wörter eliminiert, welche in mehr als 80% der Knoten vorkamen) und einer Wortreduktion [POR 80] blieben 10'787 verschiedene Indexierungsterme übrig. Die Terme wurde mit Hilfe der Funktion *Termhäufigkeit × inverse Knotenhäufigkeit* gewichtet. Es wurde auf eine initiale Deskribierung der Kanten verzichtet, d.h. die Kantendeskribate waren zu Beginn der Experimente *leer*.

Die Relevanzrückkoppelung:

Die Relevanzrückkoppelung wird analog zu der im Kapitel 4 erwähnten Methode vorgenommen. Die Relevanzklasse ++ wird mit einem Faktor $\beta = 4$ bewertet.

Die Aehnlichkeitsfunktionen:

Der initiale $RSV_0^{q,n}$ des Knotens n wird für alle folgenden Experimente durch das Kosinus-Mass ausgedrückt: $\rho\,(\vec{q},\,\vec{n}) := \cos(\vec{q},\,\vec{n})$. Für die Aehnlichkeitsfunktion σ wurde das Skalarprodukt verwendet: $\sigma\,(\vec{q},\,\vec{\lambda}) := \vec{q}\cdot\vec{\lambda}$. Das Prädikat e lautet $\sigma\,(\vec{q},\,\vec{\lambda}) \geq 0$.

Die Modifikation des initialen $RSV_0^{q,n}$ wird in allen hier beschriebenen Experimenten durch die folgende Funktion vorgenommen:

$$RSV_{korr}^{q,n} := RSV_0^{q,n} + \frac{1}{|n_i|}\cdot\sum_i\left(\left(1+\log_{100}\left(1+\sigma\left(\vec{q},\vec{\lambda}(n,n_i)\right)\right)\right)\cdot RSV_0^{q,n_i}\right)$$

Diese Funktion stellt im wesentlichen eine Korrektur des RSVs des Quellknoten um das arithmetische Mittel aus den RSVs seiner Zielknoten dar. Ferner wird eine zusätzliche, sehr kleine (positive) Korrektur vorgenommen. Dies geschieht mit der Absicht, Zielknoten, welche über vielversprechende Kanten erreicht werden, etwas stärker zu gewichten. Damit erreicht man auch, dass nach einer positiven Beurteilung eines Knotens, dessen danach höher gewichtete ausgehende Kanten sich auch mit einem positiven Effekt auf den RSV bemerkbar machen.

Zur Ermittlung der Effektivität der Methode:

Das implementierte System *hyperman* liefert in einem normalen Betriebsmodus auf jede Anfrage parallel drei gewichtete Ranglisten von Knoten (d.h. es werden bei jeder Anfrage gleichzeitig die Resultate unter Verwendung von drei Retrieval Methoden bestimmt):

- Resultat ohne jegliche Verwendung von Kanten
- Resultat unter Verwendung von Kanten, aber mit leerer Kantenbeschreibung
- Resultat unter Ausnützung der Kantenbeschreibung

Beispiel (Anfrage = "COMPATIBILITY SUN WITH MS DOS"):

```
rank   without links          with 'see also' links     with user feedback
----   -------------          ---------------------     ------------------
( 1)   0.39734  ms            0.70878  dos              0.90215  dos
( 2)   0.39610  dos           0.62785  dos2unix         0.86329  dos2unix
( 3)   0.32859  as            0.62597  unix2dos         0.86271  unix2dos
( 4)   0.28779  dos2unix      0.50733  ms               0.56331  fdformat
( 5)   0.28403  unix2dos      0.44441  fdformat         0.49702  pcfs
( 6)   0.22519  pcfs          0.38581  pcfs             0.39734  ms
( 7)   0.21616  fdformat      0.37139  as               0.32859  as
( 8)   0.20686  msync         0.22939  i386             0.22939  machid
( 9)   0.19815  i386          0.22939  iAPX286          0.22939  mc68010
(10)   0.19815  iAPX286       0.22939  m68k             0.22939  mc68020
```

Dieser Betriebsmodus eignet sich zur Gewinnung eines Ueberblicks. Zudem lassen sich hier gewisse Effekte gut illustrieren. Zur fairen Ermittlung der Relevanzinformation in Experimenten werden vom System jeweils zwei dieser Listen (Retrieval Methode A und Methode B) miteinander verschmolzen, alphabetisch sortiert und ohne Angabe der RSV dem Anwender präsentiert. Dabei wird darauf geachtet, dass von jeder Methode jeweils die ersten r Knoten verwendet werden. In allen Experimenten wurde r=10 verwendet, ausser, wenn mindestens eine der beiden Methoden weniger als 10 Knoten lieferte. In diesem Fall wurde für r das Minimum der beiden Kardinalitäten der Resultatmengen verwendet.

Der Anwender beurteilt die gelieferten Knoten und ordnet sie den bereits erwähnten vier Relevanzklassen zu (++, +, ~, -). Daraus resultieren einerseits modifizierte Kantenbeschreibungen und andererseits Präferenzrelationen zwischen allen beurteilten Knoten. Das Nützlichkeitsmass [FRE 91b] bestimmt anhand der vollständigen RSV-Listen zur Methode A und Methode B und anhand der gemeinsamen Präferenzrelationen, welche Methode besser ist. Neben dieser Aussage *u* (*in wievielen Fällen die Methode B besser ist als A*) bestimmt das Nützlichkeit ein Mass u^* *um wieviel* B besser ist als A und eine *Fehlerwahrscheinlichkeit* P_k.

Schwach überlappende Anfragen

In einem ersten Experiment wurden 30 Fragen formuliert (siehe Anhang), so dass nur wenige gemeinsame Anfrageterme resultierten. Die Fragen wurden vom System ausgewertet und zwar einmal ohne jegliche Verwendung von Kanten (Methode A) und einmal *mit* Berücksichtigung der Kanten, jedoch ohne Kantenbeschreibung; d.h. die Kanten wurden als eine Art referentielle Kanten interpretiert.

In einem nächsten Schritt musste zu allen Fragen die Relevanzinformation gegeben werden. Diese Relevanzinformation wurde vollumfänglich vom Autor gegeben. Der Aufwand dafür ist beträchtlich. Im Schnitt wurden pro Anfrage 14 Dokumente geliefert, d.h. für die 30 Anfragen wurden etwa 420 *manual pages* beurteilt. Die Bewertung eines Knotens bezüglich einer Anfrage blieb über alle Experimente konstant (d.h. es war keine widersprüchliche Relevanzinformation vorhanden).

Mit dieser Information konnte einerseits eine erste Auswertung vorgenommen werden zur Beantwortung der Frage "was bringt die Verwendung von referentiellen

Kanten?" und andererseits resultierte eine Kantenbeschreibung. Das Resultat der Auswertung bestätigt, dass referentielle Kanten etwas zur besseren Effektivität beitragen können:

$$u_{A,B} = 0.740741$$
$$u^*_{A,B} = 0.088291$$
$$P_k \leq 0.000385$$

Von den 30 Anfragen konnten nur 27 für die Auswertung verwendet werden (Anfragen 3, 22 und 23 lieferten Resultate, in welchen bei beiden Methoden genau gleich viele Präferenzen erfüllt und nicht erfüllt waren). Die Anfragen 13, 24, 10, 27, 9, 30 und 17 (sortiert nach absteigender Effektivität der Methode B, d.h. Anfrage 13 wurde von B nur wenig schlechter beantwortet, Anfrage 17 massiv schlechter) wurden von der Methode B schlechter beantwortet als von A, für alle anderen Anfragen war Methode B stets besser oder gleich gut. Der Wert von u^* signalisiert eine Verbesserung.

Die mit Hilfe der Relevanzinformation generierte Kantenbeschreibung konnte nun für eine weitere Auswertung verwendet werden. Wiederum sollte die Referenz die Auswertung ohne Verwendung von Kanten sein (Methode A), diese wurde nun mit der Methode unter Ausnutzung der Kantenbeschreibung verglichen (Methode B).

$$u_{A,B} = 0.916256$$
$$u^*_{A,B} = 0.205717$$
$$P_k \leq 0.000011$$

Diesmal waren (in beiden Fällen) 28 Anfragen gültig (Anfragen 23 und 27 waren ungültig), Methode B zeigte bei zwei Fragen (24 und 3) leichte Schwächen. Mit grosser Wahrscheinlichkeit ist die Methode B signifikant besser als Methode A.

Die Resultate zeigen, dass es möglich ist, mit Hilfe des hier gezeigten Verfahrens eine Verbesserung der Retrieval Resultate zu erreichen. Im folgenden wird versucht aufzuzeigen, wie sich das System verhält, wenn die Anfragen überlappen (d.h. gemeinsame Anfrageterme aufweisen) und wenn die Auswertung nicht mit jenen Fragen vorgenommen wird, mit denen das System 'trainiert' wurde.

Ueberlappende Fragen, Kontrolle mit weiteren Fragen

Da die Auswertungen sehr viel Zeit in Anspruch nehmen, wurde hier mit kleineren Mengen von Anfragen gearbeitet. Konkret wurde mit fünf Fragen 'trainiert' und mit fünf weiteren Fragen in drei Experimenten verifiziert. Damit dennoch genügend Präferenzen gewonnen werden konnten, wurde für dieses Experiment eine fünfte Relevanzklasse (--) eingeführt mit der Bedeutung: "Für die Fragestellung völlig irrelevant". Die Gewichtung wurde symmetrisch zum Fall (++) auf $\beta = -4$ festgesetzt. Das Szenario ist in der folgenden Uebersicht festgehalten:

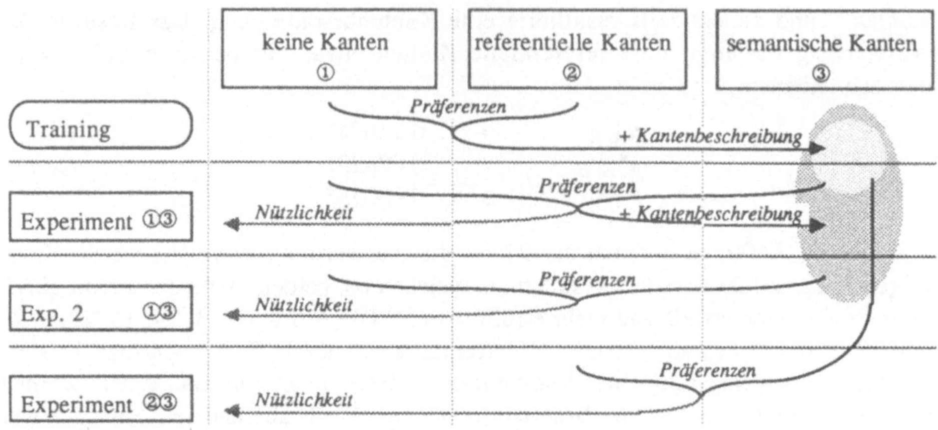

Fig. 1: Szenario zu den Experimenten mit Ueberlappung

Trainingsfragen: *encrypt decrypt* Testfragen: *text editors with data encryption*
NBS encryption *line editor ex*
create encryption key *simple text editors*
decrypt text *public key encryption methods*
line counting in files *editor for texts drawings images*

In einem ersten Schritt wurden die Relevanzwerte für die fünf Trainingsfragen gegeben; dadurch wurde eine erste Kantenbeschreibung generiert. Die unmittelbar nach dem Training gefundene Effektivität für die Testfragen wurde ermittelt, indem die Präferenzen zwischen der Methode ohne Verwendung von Kanten und derjenigen unter Ausnutzung der semantischen Kanten gegeben wurden. Dies führte einerseits zur Auswertung des 'Experiments ①③' und auch zu einer neuen, verbesserten Kantenbeschreibung. Das 'Experiment 2 ①③' zeigt, dass die Kantenbeschreibung tatsächlich besser geworden ist. Das 'Experiment ②③' überprüft (anhand der *ersten* Kantenbeschreibung bereits unmittelbar nach dem Training), was die Kantenbeschreibung an Verbesserung bringt, gegenüber der Verwendung von einfachen Referenzen (referentielle Kanten). In den Auswertungen waren jeweils alle Anfragen gültig ($k=k_0=5$):

Experiment ①③		Experiment 2 ①③		Experiment ②③	
$u_{A,B}$	= 1.000000	$u_{A,B}$	= 1.000000	$u_{A,B}$	= 0.600000
$u^*_{A,B}$	= 0.181150	$u^*_{A,B}$	= 0.261054	$u^*_{A,B}$	= 0.038373
P_k	≤ 0.033945	P_k	≤ 0.021557	P_k	≤ 0.112458
μ	= 5.0	μ	= 7.5	μ	= 5.0
w^+	= 10	w^+	= 15	w^+	= 12

Die Resultate zeigen, dass die Kantenbeschreibungen sowohl durch die Relevanzrückkoppelung auf die Trainingsfragen, als auch durch die Relevanzrückkoppelung auf die nachfolgenden Testfragen an Qualität gewonnen haben. Der Betrag der *Verbesserung* nimmt bei weiteren Relevanzangaben ab und stagniert mit der Zeit. Das Niveau der Verbesserung ist jedoch in praktisch allen bisher durchgeführten Tests recht hoch. Die Motivation zur *Verwendung von semantischen Kanten* wird durch das 'Experiment ②③' nur wenig unterstützt (im gezeigten Beispiel sind zuwenige Anfragen vorhanden um einen eindeutigen Schluss zu ziehen, die Nützlichkeit konnte inzwischen aber auch an repräsentativeren Beispielen gezeigt werden). Eine Wiederholung dieses Experiments *nach* dem 'Experiment ①③' ergibt übrigens bereits eine recht signifikante Differenz zur Methode ohne Verwendung der Kantenbeschreibung ($u_{A, B} = 1.00$, $u^*_{A, B} = 0.13$ und $P_k = 0.02$, bei $k=k_0=5$).

Alle in diesem Abschnitt gezeigten Resultate weisen eine relativ hohe Fehlerwahrscheinlichkeit auf, welche auf die kleine Menge von Anfragen zurückzuführen ist. Repräsentativere Resultate könnten erst mit 20 oder mehr Anfragen gewonnen werden. Dies führt jedoch zu einem extrem hohen Aufwand in der Auswertung.

6. Zusammenfassung, Ausblick

Es wurde gezeigt, dass eine initiale Kantenbeschreibung automatisch bestimmt und diese Beschreibung bei einer automatischen Suche genutzt werden kann. Automatisch generierte Kantenbeschreibungen haben den Vorteil, dass sie ohne intellektuellen Aufwand entstehen und frei sind von subjektiven Bewertungen. Experimente zeigten, dass Retrieval Algorithmen, welche Kantenbeschreibungen berücksichtigten, bessere Resultate liefern als bei Vernachlässigung der semantischen Kanten.

Kantenbeschreibungen können durch die Relevanzangaben von Benutzern verbessert werden. Sie werden allerdings dadurch anwenderspezifisch, was die Anwendbarkeit der Relevanzrückkoppelung auf gewisse Benutzer oder Benutzergruppen einschränkt. Wir konnten zeigen, dass sich in diesem Fall die Retrieval Resultate stark verbessern, was wiederum einen Anreiz für den Anwender darstellt, die vom System angeforderte Relevanzinformation zur Verfügung zu stellen

Die gefundenen Ergebnisse sollten an weiteren Hyper-Kollektionen verifiziert werden. Die präsentierte Methode lässt sich *ohne Modifikationen* auch auf multimediale Kollektionen anwenden, wobei allerdings das Problem der automatischen Kantendeskribierung gelöst sein muss.

Literatur

[BOY 91]   Boy, G.A.: Indexing Hypertext Documents in Context. *Proc. Hypertext '91*, Dec. 1991, pp. 1-11.

[COH 87]   Cohen, P.R., Kjeldsen, R.: Information Retrieval by Constrained Spreading Activation in Semantic Networks. *Inf. Proc. & Management*, Vol. 23, No. 4, 1987, pp. 255-268.

[CON 87]   Conklin, J.: Hypertext: An Introduction and Survey. *IEEE Computer*, Vol. 20, No. 9, Sept. 1987, pp. 17-41.

[CRO 89]   Croft, W.B., Turtle, H.: A Retrieval Model for Incorporating Hypertext Links. *Proc. Hypertext '89*, Pittsburgh, PA, Nov. 1989, pp. 213-224.

[FRE 91a] Frei, H.P., Schäuble, P.: Designing a Hypermedia Information System. *Proc. DEXA 91, Springer Verlag*, Wien, 1991, pp. 449-454.

[FRE 91b] Frei, H.P., Schäuble, P.: Determining the Effectiveness of Retrieval Algorithms. *Inf. Proc. & Management*, Vol. 27, Nos. 2/3, 1991, pp. 153-164.

[FRE 92] Frei, H.P., Stieger, D.: Making Use of Hypertext Links when Retrieving Information. *4th ACM Conference on Hypertext and Hypermedia, Proc. ECHT '92*, Milano, Nov. 30 - Dec. 4, 1992, to appear.

[FRI 88] Frisse, M.E.: Searching for Information in a Hypertext Medical Handbook. *Comm. of the ACM*, Vol. 31, No. 7, July 1988, pp. 880-886.

[HAA 91] Haake, J.M., Hannemann J., Thüring, M.: Ein Ansatz zur Organisation von Hyperdokumenten. *Proc. Hypertext/Hypermedia '91, Informatik Fachberichte 276*, Springer Verlag, Graz, Mai 1991, S. 119-134.

[KWO 88] Kwok, K.L.: On the Use of Bibliographically Related Titles for the Enhancement of Document Representations. *Inf. Proc. & Management*, Vol. 24, No. 2, 1988, pp. 123-131.

[MAR 89] Marshall, C.C., Irish, P.M.: Guided Tours and On-Line Presentations: How Authors Make Existing Hypertext Intelligible for Readers. *Proc. Hypertext '89*, Pittsburgh, PA, Nov. 1989, pp. 15-26.

[POR 80] Porter, M.F.: An Algorithm for Suffix Stripping. *Program*, Vol. 14, No. 3, 1980, pp. 130-137.

[SAL 86] Salton G., Zhang, Y.: Enhancement of Text Representations using Related Document Titles. *Inf. Proc. & Management*, Vol. 22, 1986, pp. 385-394.

[SAL 90] Salton, G., Buckley, C.: Improving Retrieval Performance by Relevance Feedback. *J. of the American Soc. for Information Science*, Vol. 41, No. 4, 1990, pp. 288-297.

[SAV 92] Savoy, J.: Ranking Schemes in a Hypertext Retrieval System, *Publ. 811, Dépt. d'informatique et de recherche operationelle Univ. de Montréal*, Fev. 1992, (see also Publ. 794, 799, 804 (1991, same author).

Anhang

30 schwach überlappende Fragen

1 create symbolic link	17 play music or sounds
2 change password	18 screendump
3 data encryption	19 painting tool
4 replace single characters	20 keyboard
5 display active users	21 sort file alphabetically
6 compatibility with ms dos pc	22 dynamic linker
7 debugging tools	23 ndbm
8 remove files from directories and subdirectories recursively	24 rlogin
9 data compression	25 determine processor family
10 font catalog	26 floppy drive
11 text editors	27 games
12 compilers	28 tell actual time
13 running jobs in background	29 display printer status information
14 electronic mail tools	30 kill running job
15 adding new user	
16 producing large core dumps	

D. Reiter

D. Roller

Hewlett Packard GmbH
Herrenbergerstr. 130
D-7030 Böblingen

Universität Stuttgart
Institut für Informatik
Breitwiesenstr. 20-22
D-7000 Stuttgart 80

Kurzfassung

Gegenwärtig werden die ersten rechnergestützten technischen Informationssysteme im Servicebereich der Automobilhersteller (Händler und Reparaturbetriebe) eingeführt, die bereits die Grundelemente von Hypermedianwendungen (verschiedene Datentypen - Text, Graphik, Video, Audio - und Verknüpfungen) bereitstellen.

Dieser Beitrag konzentriert sich auf die Darstellung von Methoden, die eine anwendungsgerechte Strukturierung und Präsentation von verknüpften Informationseinheiten erlauben und damit einen wesentlichen Mangel der heutigen Systeme beheben sollen. Ziel ist es, durch die Realisierung dieser Konzepte für die nächste Generation von technischen Informationssystemen im Servicebereich nicht nur ein passives "Information-Backbone" zu schaffen, sondern vielmehr eine den Anwender bei den täglich durchzuführenden Arbeiten aktiv unterstützende Hypermedia-Wissensdatenbank. Grundlage hierfür ist eine Datenaufbereitung, die den Anforderungen von elektronischen Systemen i.a. und Hypermediaanwendungen im besonderen Rechnung trägt.

Die grundlegenden Gedanken hinsichtlich Literaturorganisation, -strukturierung, -präsentation und -navigation werden im folgenden vorgestellt und anhand von Beispielen aus der Anwendungsbereich erläutert.

Schlüsselwörter:

Technische Information, Hypertext, Hypermedia, Hyperraum, Information Retrieval, Browsing, Exploration, Kontext, Assoziation, Serendipity, Hypertrail, Kohärenz

1. Einleitung - Technische Informationssysteme in der Automobilindustrie

Aufgrund der wachsenden Komplexität der modernen Kraftfahrzeuge, hervorgerufen insbesondere durch den vielfältigen Einsatz elektronischer Komponenten und Baugruppen, erlangt der Bereich *Service und Wartung* immer größere Bedeutung - umsomehr, als sich hier, in der *Qualität* der Wartung, ein wesentliches Unterscheidungsmerkmal zwischen verschiedenen Fahrzeugherstellern und damit ein Wettbewerbsvorteil herauskristallisiert.

Dem gestiegenen Informationsbedarf wird durch eine immer größere und in kürzeren Zyklen bereitgestellte Menge von Service- und Wartungsliteratur Rechnung getragen, die heute in erster Linie in Papierform oder auf Microfiches vorliegt. Allerdings können die Forderungen nach hoher Aktualität der Information und nach kurzen Suchzeiten kaum befriedigend erfüllt werden, da die zum Einsatz kommenden Medien Papier und Microfiche systembedingt nur die *sequentielle* Erarbeitung von Wissen auf Basis von großen, monolithischen Informationseinheiten unterstützen, die keine rasche Aktualisierung von Teilinformationen erlauben. Der Suchvorgang wird i.d.R. lediglich durch hierarchische Inhaltsverzeichnisse und bestenfalls durch einen Index unterstützt.

Den Konsequenzen - länger dauernde Arbeitsvorgänge, Reparaturen nach dem "trial and error" Verfahren - kann durch den Einsatz *computergestützter (technischer) Informationssysteme (CAI-Systemen)* begegnet werden, mit dem Ziel die Kundenzufriedenheit zu steigern [Roll91][1]. Wesentlicher Bestandteil dieser Informationssysteme sind kombinierte Information Retrieval (IR)/Hypermedia Komponenten[2]. Sie erlauben einerseits den effektiven, auf hohe Leistungsfähigkeit ausgerichteten Zugriff auf (unstrukturierte) Dokumente bzw. Informationseinheiten beliebiger Art (Text, Graphik, Video oder Audio), andererseits aber auch eine Berücksichtigung der *Beziehungen* der Informationseinheiten untereinander. Somit können die erwähnten monolithischen Dokumentstrukturen zugunsten kleinerer "atomarer"[3] Einheiten aufgebrochen werden, auf die mittels leistungsfähiger, klassischer Retrieval-Methoden zugegriffen werden kann. Gleichzeitig ist jedoch eine dynamische, situationsbezogene Gruppierung und Präsentation der gefundenen Informationseinheiten durch die Hypermediakomponente möglich. Auf diese Weise wird dem Anwender Information in einer hinsichtlich seiner Intention und dem Anwendungskontext optimierten Struktur zugänglich gemacht, die auch den transparenten Austausch einzelner Bestandteile durch neue, modifizierte Teile gestattet (Aktualisierung). Der Benutzer erhält die Möglichkeit, selbständig oder unter Anleitung des Informationssystems das Retrievalergebnis zu "erforschen" (Exploration) und den durch die Hypermediakomponente verwalteten Verknüpfungen zu folgen (Navigation).

Gegenwärtig werden die ersten CAI-Systeme im Servicebereich der Automobilhersteller (Händler und Reparaturbetriebe) eingeführt, die bereits die Grundelemente von Hypermediaanwendungen (verschiedene Datentypen - Text, Graphik, Video, Audio - und Verknüpfungen) bereitstellen.

Dieser Beitrag konzentriert sich auf die Darstellung von Methoden, die eine anwendungsgerechte Strukturierung und Präsentation von verknüpften Informationseinheiten erlauben und damit einen wesentlichen Mangel der heute im Bereich "Service und Wartung von Kraftfahrzeugen" eingesetzten Systeme beheben sollen. Ziel ist, durch die Realisierung dieser Konzepte für die zweite Generation der CAI-Systeme im Servicebereich, basierend auf einer den Anforderungen von Elektronischen Systemen i.a. und Hypermediaanwendungen im besonderen entsprechenden Datenaufbereitung, nicht nur ein passives "Information-Backbone" zu schaffen, sondern vielmehr eine den Anwender bei den täglich durchzuführenden Arbeiten aktiv unterstützende Hypermedia-Wissensdatenbank.

Die grundlegenden Gedanken hinsichtlich Literaturorganisation, -strukturierung, -präsentation und -navigation werden im folgenden vorgestellt und anhand von Beispielen aus dem Anwendungsbereich (Service und Wartung von Fahrzeugen) erläutert.

---

[1] Das Konzept eines *integrierten technischen Informationssystems* wird hier ausführlich diskutiert und dient als Grundlage für die in diesem Beitrag erläuterte Betrachtung von Hypertext/-mediastrukturen.

[2] Eine vergleichende Darstellung von Retrieval- und Hypertextkonzepten ist in [Fuhr90] enthalten.

[3] kleinste, unstrukturierte Informationseinheit.

2. Spezielle Anforderungen an Hypermediasysteme

Entscheidend für die erfolgreiche Anwendung von Hypermediasystemen im Umfeld von technischen Informationssystemen für die Automobilindustrie ist die Berücksichtigung des besonderen Anwendungskontextes, der in vorstehendem Abschnitt kurz skizziert wurde (eine ausführlichere Darstellung enthält [Roll91]). Die wesentlichen direkt aus dem Anwendungskontext abzuleitenden Anforderungen sind:

(1) Signifikante Verbesserung der Wartungsqualität durch Bereitstellung *umfassender* und *vollständiger* Information mit weitgehender automatischer Auflösung von Referenzen: z.B. Serviceinformation, Reparaturhandbuch, Anleitung Spezialwerkzeuge, Teilekatalog etc., entsprechend der logischen Sequenz der Arbeitsschritte. All diese Dokumente sind mannigfach (manuell) verknüpft.

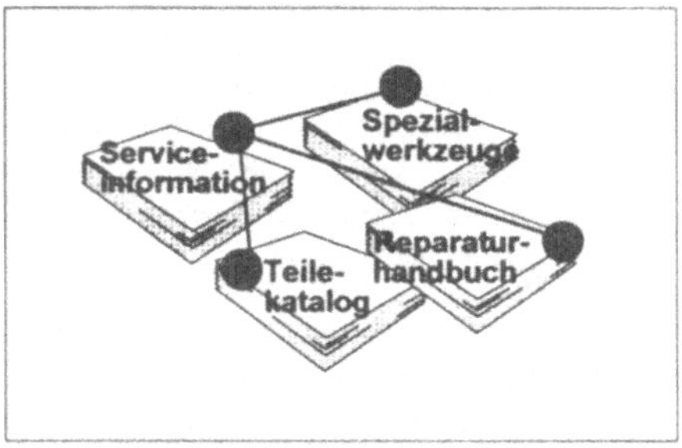

Abb. 1: Serviceliteratur für die Kfz-Wartung

(2) Beschleunigung des Zugriffsprozesses auf Information bei erhöhter Treffsicherheit - (automatische) Auswertung sämtlicher zur Verfügung stehender Konextinformation.

(3) Erhöhung der Aktualität der Wartungsdokumentation durch Bereitstellung kleiner, permanent aktualisierter Einheiten.

(4) Verbesserung der inhaltlichen Struktur durch Vermeidung von redundanter Information[4], um den kognitiven Verarbeitungsprozeß zu unterstützen.

Das Anwenderprofil ist charakterisiert durch fehlende Erfahrung im Umgang mit EDV und eine reservierte, kritische Haltung gegenüber Computersystemen, was zu entsprechendem Akzeptanzvorbehalt führt. Zusammenfassend können aus der kurzen Darstellung von Anwenderprofil und Anwendungskontext die folgenden Forderungen für ein Hypermediasystem abgeleitet werden:

(1) Browsingmechanismen für Hypermediasysteme müssen einerseits kreative Mitnahmeeffekte, die zur Lösung einer Aufgabe (z.B. einer Wartungsarbeit: Zündungseinstellung) beitragen, zulassen, andererseits aber dem kontraproduktiven *Serendipityeffekt* (das Überangebot an Information führt zur Desorientierung und Ablenkung von der anfänglichen Intention) [Kuhl91] entgegenwirken, der sich gerade bei einem nicht mit den "Reizen" der modernen EDV vertrauten Anwenderkreis besonders fatal auswirken kann.

---

[4] Bedingt durch das lineare Lesen (sequentielle Rezeption) von Buchinhalten (Medium Papier) werden bestimmte Informationsteile mehrfach in z.B. verschiedenen Kapiteln wiederholt, um einen Gesamtzusammenhang herzustellen - ausgehend davon, daß i.d.R. kein Quereinsprung stattfindet. Der Leser jedoch tut sich gerade in diesem Fall schwer, den neuen Informationsgehalt aus dem bereits bekannten auszufiltern.

Hyperlinks erlauben die direkte Verknüpfung von kohärenten[5] Informationsinhalten und stellen somit eine wesentliche Verbesserung hinsichtlich Zugriffsgeschwindigkeit und -qualität dar (im Gegensatz zum "manuellen" Verfolgen von textuellen Verzweigungen wie z.B. "siehe Wartungshandbuch Motronic 1.5., Kapitel Einstellwerte für BMW 316i"). Jedoch dürfen Browsingmechanismen, die die Exploration eines Kohärenzfeldes erlauben, nicht zum Eintreten des Serendipityeffektes führen, bei dem das ursprüngliche Informationsziel aus den Augen verloren wird. Ein Kohärenzfeld könnte z.B. durch die Gesamtheit aller Informationsgehalte zum Thema "Zündungseinstellung bei BMW 316i, Baujahr 92" definiert werden.

(2) Das Hypermediasystem als ("ungeliebtes") *Werkzeug* zur effizienten Abfrage von Information muß in seiner durch den Anwender erlebten Präsenz (Gestaltung der Benutzeroberfläche, bereitgestellte Funktionalität) in den Hintergrund treten (Vermeidung von *Systemdominanz* [Kuhl91]) und eine intuitive Integration in den Arbeitsablauf ermöglichen.

(3) Die Einfachheit und Effizienz sowie die Qualität des Abfrageergebnisses sind für die Akzeptanz und den Erfolg (der vorwiegend durch wirtschaftliche Erwägungen bestimmt wird) letztendlich von entscheidender Bedeutung.

3. Lösungsbeschreibung

Der Serendipityeffekt stellt die größte Gefahr für den erfolgreichen Einsatz von Hypermediasystemen in dem vorgestellten Umfeld dar. Bei einer Dokumentbasis in der Größenordung von mehreren zehntausend Dokumenten[6] haben bereits die üblicherweise auftretenden Kohärenzfelder eine derartige Ausdehnung, daß das eigentlich gesuchte Informationsziel bei extensivem Browsing leicht aus den Augen verloren werden und somit potentiell eine Konterkarierung des beabsichtigten Effekts, eines qualitativ verbesserten und beschleunigten Zugriffs mittels Verknüpfungen, eintreten kann [Conk87][Roue90].

Daher müssen Verfahren eingesetzt werden, die einerseits eine effektive *Exploration* des Hyperraums bzw. des darin durch den aktuellen Kontext definierten Kohärenzraumes erlauben und unterstützen, aber andererseits dem Serendipityeffekt entgegenwirken.

Nachfolgend werden Konzepte auf Basis von *Hypertrails*, *Kontextstrukturen* und *Assoziativen Verknüpfungen* dargestellt, um eine anwendungsgerechte Erschließung des Hyperraums durch leistungsfähige Browsingmechanismen zu ermöglichen.

---

[5] semantisch und thematisch stimmige Informationsobjekte.

[6] Eigentlich stellen Dokumente sogenannte *Mikrokontexte* dar, die nicht monolithisch aufgebaut sind, sondern ihrerseits ein eng begrenztes Kohärenzfeld abbilden - Mikrokontexte werden später ausführlich vorgestellt.

3.1. Hyperräume und Hypertrails

Der hier beschriebene Ansatz basiert auf dem Konzept der sogenannten *Hypertrails*[7,8] [Zell89], also der Bereitstellung von definierten (entweder durch den Autor während der Dokumentationserstellung vorinstantiierten oder erst zur Laufzeit dynamisch besetzten) Pfaden, die Informationseinheiten aus der Hyperbasis miteinander verbinden und dem Anwender entlang dieser Kanten eine Exploration des Hyperraums[9] gestatten.

Unter Hyperraum wird hierbei die Gesamteinheit aller (atomisierten) Informationseinheiten und ihrer Beziehungen untereinander verstanden, aus denen dem Anwender während des Zugriffs auf die Information (Dokumentation) eine Auswahl in Form von Dokumenteinheiten präsentiert wird (Abb. 2). Bestandteil des Hyperraums sind auch Metainformationen, die in statischer oder dynamischer Weise eine Segmentierung des Informationsbestandes entsprechend bestimmter Kohärenzkriterien unterstützen.

3.1.1. Segmentierung des Hyperraums

Metainformationen werden aus der Sitzungshistorie des Systems oder aus Antworten des Anwenders auf konkrete Fragen des Systems abgeleitet. Die hierbei gewonnenen Kohärenzinformationen (z.B. die Anwendung "Große Inspektion" oder "Kupplungsaustausch am 3er BMW") werden nun zur Segmentierung des Hyperraums eingesetzt.

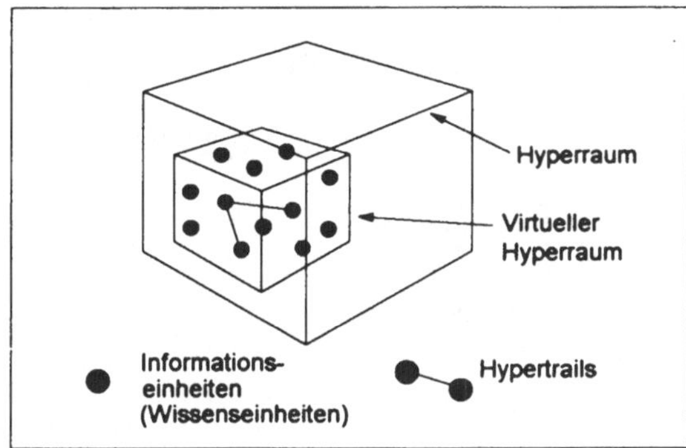

Abb. 2: Virtuelle (Hyper-)teilräume

Dabei wird nicht einfach eine Teilmenge bereits existenter *Hyperknoten* und *Hypertrails* herausgelöst, sondern vielmehr ein dem aktuellen Kontext angepaßter individueller *virtueller Hyperraum*[10] erzeugt. Teils werden bestehende Hypertrails übernommen, teils neue hinzugefügt, als auch Mikrokontexte (vgl. Abschnitt "Mikro- und Makrokontexte") modifiziert.

---

[7] vgl. die "Memex"-Vision in Bush V.: "As we may think." Atlantic Monthly 176, July 1945, 101-108

[8] Eine Unterscheidung der einzelnen Hypertrail-Typen in z.B. *Prerequisite, Classification, Definition*, etc. wird hier nicht vorgenommen, da eine allgemeine Darstellung des Konzepts angestrebt wird.

[9] "Einen Raum kann man nicht suchen, sondern nur Dinge in einem Raum. In diesem Sinne bedeutet 'Raum' alles, dessen man gewiß sein muß, um eine Frage stellen zu können." [Witt84]

[10] Der virtuelle Hyperraum stellt den durch den Anwender explorierbaren Teil des gesamten Hyperraums dar. Die Gesamtheit aller Information wird für den Benutzer nie "sichtbar", vielmehr nur je nach Kontext wechselnde Teilräume.

3.1.2. Konstruktion virtueller Informationsräume

Der resultierende virtuelle Hyperraum präsentiert sich dem Anwender als seine *individuelle Sicht* auf den für seine Intention optimal aufbereiteten Informationsbestand, der vom Ballast irrelevanter Daten befreit ist. Innerhalb dieses Teilraums ist entlang der erzeugten Hypertrails die Exploration auch auf Basis von Assoziationen (vgl. Abschnitt "Einsatz assoziativer Verknüpfungen") möglich.

Nachfolgend wird anhand eines Beispiels das vorgestellte Konzept erläutert. In Abbildung 3 sind die Pfade (Trails) dargestellt, entlang denen der Hyperraum zum Kontext von "Probleme mit der Kupplung" exploriert werden kann, *bevor* die Reduktion auf einen virtuellen Teilraum anhand von Kontextwissen durchgeführt worden ist. Ein Einstiegspunkt ist (noch) nicht definiert, so daß mit unterschiedlichen Informationseinheiten begonnen werden kann, wobei die Pfeilrichtungen jeweils die möglichen Verzweigungen angeben. Dabei ist auch semantisches Kontextwissen abgebildet: Bei Vierradantrieb kann sich die Ursache für Kupplungsprobleme durch zwei Symptome bemerkbar machen (Kante 1→2, 1→3), bei herkömmlichem Zweiradantrieb nur durch ein Symptom (2→4).

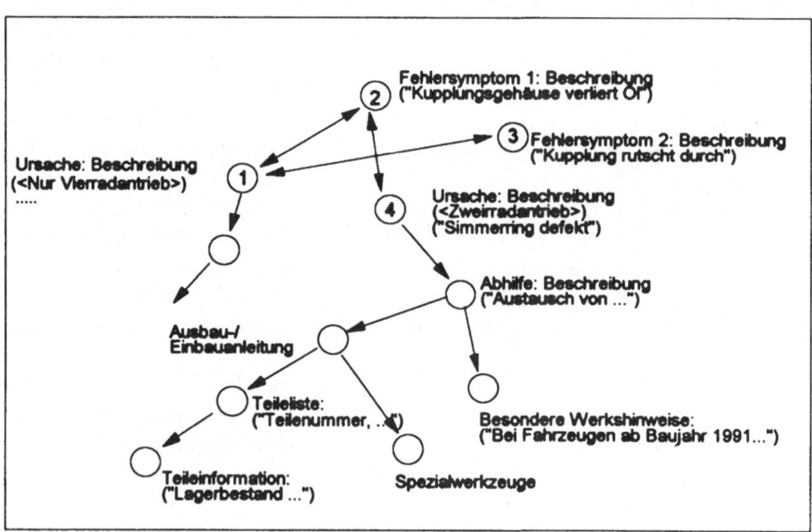

Abb. 3: Teilansicht des nicht durch Kohärenz segmentierten Hyperraums mit vordefinierten (Standard-)Trails

Abbildung 4 stellt nun den virtuellen Teilraum des vollständigen Hyperraums dar, der auf Grund der individuellen Intention des Anwenders erzeugt wurde, unter Berücksichtigung von Kontextwissen, wie z.B. Daten über das betroffene Fahrzeug (Typ, Modell, Baujahr). In diesem Beispiel weiß der Anwender bereits über die Ursache Bescheid ("Kupplungs-Simmerring defekt") und möchte für ein bestimmtes Fahrzeug, Baujahr 92, sämtliche verfügbare Information über mögliche Abhilfsmaßnahmen erfragen. Zu diesem Kontext werden *dynamisch* bestimmte Trails entfernt (im Vergleich zum originären Hyperraum, Abb. 3, grau dargestellt), die nicht relevant sind (z.B. da keine Information verfügbar ist). Die Orientierung der Trails wird modifiziert (der Einstiegspunkt wurde aus dem Kontext abgeleitet), und in diesem Fall wurde eine vollständig neue Verbindung durch den Trail zur *Einbauanleitung Getriebe* mit *Instruktionsvideo* geschaffen.

Die dynamische Segmentierung des Hyperraums zur Laufzeit stellt somit dem Anwender die gewünschte Information in einer Form bereit, die logisch entsprechend der Intention strukturiert ist, eine einfache und intuitive Exploration innerhalb des konstruierten, virtuellen Informationsraumes erlaubt und damit der in Abschnitt "Spezielle Anforderungen an Hypermediasysteme" formulierten Forderung nach einer Fokussierung auf das wesentliche - nämlich das schnelle Auffinden von kohärenter Information, unter Vermeidung des Serendipityeffektes - gerecht wird.

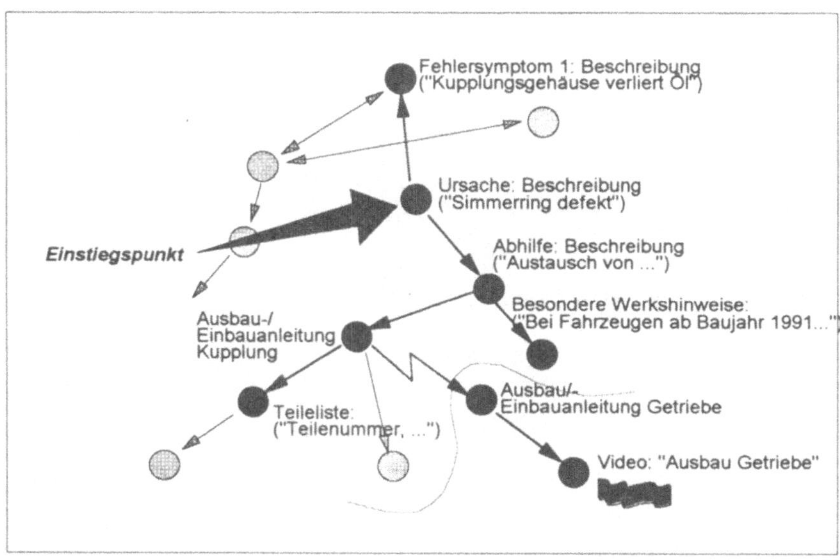

Abb. 4: Virtueller Teilraum mit dynamisch modifizierten Trails

3.2. Kontextorganisation und Verknüpfungstypen

In vorstehend erläutertem Beispiel wurde noch keine Aussage darüber gemacht, *wie* die innerhalb des dynamisch erzeugten virtuellen Informationsraums vorhandenen Informationseinheiten dem Anwender präsentiert werden. Prinziell können hierbei zwei Verfahren eingesetzt werden:

- *implizite* Verknüpfung von Informationseinheiten zu *Mikrokontexten*,

- *explizite* Verknüpfung von Informationseinheiten zu *Makrokontexten*

3.2.1. Mikro- und Makrokontexte

Mikrokontexte können als *virtuelle Dokumente* beschrieben werden, denn die einzelnen im Mikrokontext enthaltenen Informationseinheiten werden zur Systemlaufzeit in eine (virtuelle) Dokumentstruktur zusammengefügt und so dem Anwender visuell dargestellt. Das somit erzeugte "konventionelle" Dokument präsentiert sich dem Benutzer als konsistente, geschlossene Einheit (die Unterteilung ist nicht sichtbar), analog der ihm z.B. aus den traditionellen Papierhandbüchern vertrauten Form. Implizit wird der Anwender der Verantwortung enthoben, *aktiv* durch Anwahl von Verknüpfungen, z.B. über *Hotpsots* oder *Icons*, den Hypertrails folgen zu müssen. Der damit verbundene Verlust an Freiheitsgraden hinsichtlich Exploration kann in bestimmten Fällen durch eine Verbesserung der intuitiven Handbarkeit des Systems (z.B. weniger Benutzerinteraktionen, Anlehnung an vertraute Informationspräsentationsformen) gerechtfertigt werden.

Weitere zum Kontext eines Informationsobjekts gehörende Informationseinheiten, die jedoch nicht in einen Mikrokontext überführt werden sollen, werden als Makrokontext definiert, der direkt durch Aktivierung von Verknüpfungen vom Ursprungsobjekt aus erreichbar ist.

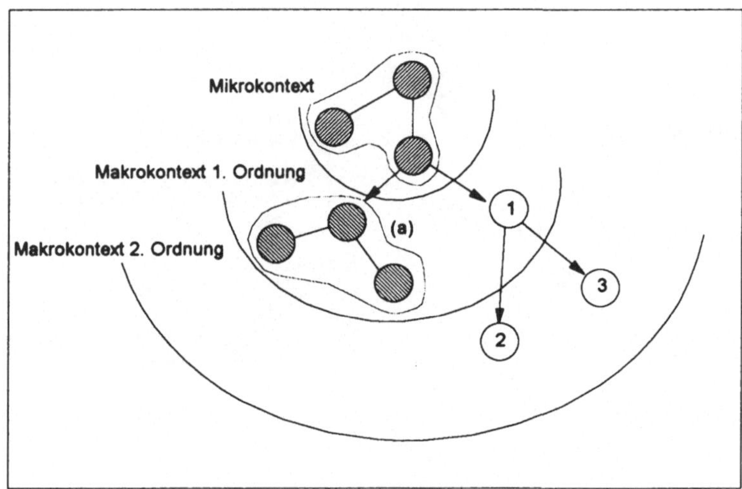

Abb. 5: Mikro- und Makrokontexte n-ter Ordnung

Abbildung 5 zeigt als "Quelle" einen aus drei Objekten organisierten Mikrokontext, der (bezogen auf das "Ursprungsobjekt") als Makrokontext ein Objekt ① sowie wiederum einen weiteren Mikrokontext (a) referenziert. Die Verknüpfungskette reicht hier bis in den Makrokontext zweiter Ordnung (Objekte ② und ③), der vom Gesichtspunkt der inhaltlichen Interpretation bezüglich Kohärenz nur noch einen peripheren Informationsgehalt aufweist. Der Anwender erhält also hochkohärente Information unmittelbar in der verdichteten Form von Mikrokontexten präsentiert, während Makrokontexte die Exploration thematisch und semantisch nicht direkt betroffener Informationsobjekte erlauben.

Als Beispiel für die Anwendung von Mikro- und Makrokontexten sei an dieser Stelle die Präsentation bestimmter Bereiche des in Abbildung 3 vorgestellten Hypertrails beschrieben (Abbildung 6).

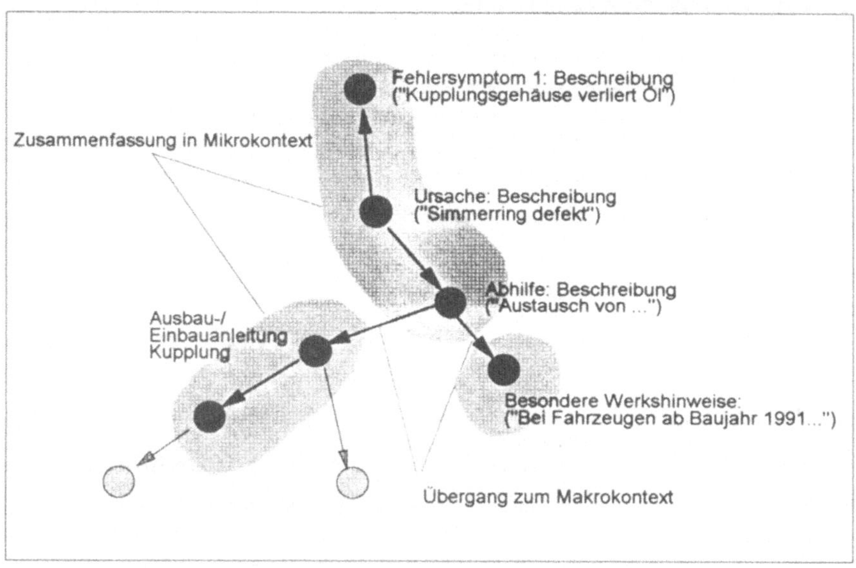

Abb. 6: Präsentation von Kontextstrukturen

Die Angaben über *Ursache*, *Symptom* und *Abhilfemaßnahmen* werden zu einem Dokument zusammengezogen und als geschlossene Einheit dargestellt. Layout und Formatangaben für die Darstellung sind in einem sogenannten *Virtual Document Frame (VDF)* mittels einer Struktur- und Seitenbeschreibungssprache abgelegt[11] [Stie90]. Die Informationseinheiten *Besondere Werkshinweise* und *Einbauanleitung* werden als Makrokontext strukturiert und daher über explizite Verknüpfungen (z.B. mittels *Icons*) zugänglich gemacht.

3.3. Einsatz assoziativer Verknüpfungen

Sämtliche bisher vorgestellten Verfahren zur dynamischen Instantiierung von Links basieren auf *Systementscheidungen* und berücksichtigen nur implizit Wünsche des Anwenders, indem bei der Konstruktion des virtuellen Teilraums der durch den Anwender definierte thematische Kontext (z.B. Angaben über *Fahrzeugtyp*, *Modell* und *Baujahr*) berücksichtigt wird.
Ein durch den Anwender angestoßenes Browsing, gleichwohl systemkontrolliert und in sinnvolle Bahnen gelenkt, setzt andere Konzepte voraus, die im folgenden kurz vorgestellt werden. Dabei wird diese Klasse von Explorationsmethoden unter dem Begriff *Assoziation*

---

11 Gegenwärtig werden RTF (Microsoft Rich Text Format) sowie SGML (Standard Generalized Mark Up Language) eingesetzt.

zusammengefaßt, da sie dem Benutzer das Verfolgen seiner eigenen, *individuellen* kognitiven Assoziation erlauben sollen.

3.3.1. Deterministische Assoziationen

In dem hier beschriebenen Systemkonzept werden Informationseinheiten durch sogenannte *Subjects* semantisch und thematisch beschrieben. Subjects enthalten ein hochverdichtetes, inhaltliches Kondensat der referenzierten Informationseinheit[12] und werden als Schlüsselelement für den Zugriff verwendet. Die Speicherung der Subjects erfolgt in einer normierten Form, die durch folgenden Prozeß erzeugt wird:

(1)   Strukturierung des Subjects in eine Nominalphrase mit (optionaler) adverbialer Erweiterung:

    Beispiel: *"Tür quietscht beim Schließen"*

(2)   Reduktion von "Füllwörtern" und grammatikalischen Wortformen durch einen Noise Reduction Parser

(3)   Überführung der Phrase in eine lautsprachliche Repräsentation

(4)   Begriffsklassenbildung auf Basis eines themenbezogenen hierarchischen Thesaurus

Dieser Prozeß wird bei der Datenbasiserzeugung auf sämtliche Informationseinheiten angewandt. Beim Retrieval kann der Anwender durch Eingabe einer Formulierung in Subject-Syntax (z.B. "Ölwanne verliert Öl"), die gemäß der Prozeßschritte (1) bis (4) verarbeitet wird, auf die entsprechende Informationseinheit zugreifen. Das System kann zusätzlich den Kontext zu dieser Anfrage erschließen (als weiterführende Information oder als Alternativangebot, falls zu der formulierten Anfrage keine direkte Information verfügbar ist), indem die hierarchischen Beziehungen des Thesaurus (sowohl inhaltlicher[13] als auch funktionaler[14] Art) ausgewertet werden.

In unserem Konzept werden deterministische[15] Assoziationen als Unterstützung zur Exploration der virtuellen Informationsräume eingesetzt. Sie erlauben den direkten Sprung zwischen Informationseinheiten, ohne daß sie notwendigerweise durch Hypertrails miteinander verbunden sein müssen. Beispielsweise kann durch Anwahl (etwa mittels Maus) des Satzfragments "... Beim Kupplungseinbau ist zu beachten ..." automatisch durch das System zur Laufzeit die Assoziation zu dem Dokument, das durch das Subject "Einbauanleitung Kupplung" thematisiert ist, erzeugt werden.

Diese Möglichkeit wird allerdings auf den definierten virtuellen Teilraum limitiert, um dem Serendipityeffekt vorzubeugen.

---

[12] Beispiel: Eine Serviceinformation könnte durch das Subject "Ölundichtigkeit am Lenkgetriebe" beschrieben werden.

[13] Durch Verwendung der vom Thesaurus bereitgestellten, relationierten Synonymfelder.

[14] Dies kann auf der Grundlage einer vollständigen Fahrzeugmodellierung auf Baugruppen- oder Teileebene geschehen. So können z.B. *Zündkerze* und *Zündspule* dem *Zündsystem* zugeordnet werden. Zukünftig sind auch wissensbasierte Zusammenhänge hier denkbar, die auch nicht zusammenhängende Baugruppen bezüglich einer bestimmten Problemstellung in einen Kontext bringen.

[15] Assoziationen, die algorithmisch erzeugt werden und jederzeit reproduzierbar sind (im Gegensatz zur wissensbasierten bzw. kognitiven Assoziation)

3.3.2. Freie (kognitive) Assoziation

Gegenwärtig werden neue Konzepte entwickelt, um die deterministische durch eine kognitive Assoziation zu ergänzen[16]. Dies dürfte sinnvoll zu sein, um dem Anwender einen informativen, vielstufigen Makrokontext zur Verfügung zu stellen (vgl. Abschnitt "Mikro- und Makrokontexte"), der *nicht* ausschließlich durch inhaltliche und strukturelle Abbildungen konstruiert ist [17], sondern auch Raum für logische Entdeckungen gibt[18].

4.   Zusammenfassung und Ausblick

Es wurden Konzepte im Rahmen eines CAI-Systems für den Einsatz im Kfz-Servicebereich vorgestellt, die eine dynamische Strukturierung und Präsentation des Informationsraums, entsprechend den Anforderungen der Anwender, erlauben. Dabei wurde besonderer Wert auf Verfahren gelegt, die einerseits zielgerichtet, unter Vermeidung des Abschweifens durch ein zu vielfältiges Wissensangebot, zu den relevanten Informationseinheiten führen, andererseits aber auch, falls notwendig, eine Ausdehnung des Kontextes mit Hilfe von assoziativen Verknüpfungen erlauben.
Neue Verfahren im Autorenbereich (Publishing und Indexierung von Informationseinheiten) müssen hierbei der starken Zergliederung der Information in atomare Einheiten und der Informationsverknüpfung Rechnung tragen, unter besonderer Berücksichtigung von Aspekten der Datenintegrität, Konsistenz und Performanceoptimierung für das Retrieval.

---

[16] Projekt *HyDRA*("Hypermediasystem mit dynamischem Retrieval durch Assoziation") an der Universität Stuttgart, Institut für Informatik, Prof. Dr. D. Roller).

[17] entsprechend der vorgestellten Verfahren: Segmentierung des Hyperraums durch (vordefinierte) Hypertrails, deterministische Assoziationen

[18] "Eine logische Entdeckung ist etwas ganz anderes als das Finden von etwas in einem Raum. Bei der logischen Entdeckung ist es so: Wenn wir das Gesuchte beschreiben könnten, hätten wir es schon gefunden." [Witt84]

Literaturhinweise

[Borm91]   Bormann U., Bormann C.: Offene Bearbeitung multimedialer Dokumente. In: Informatik Spektrum 14/5/1991, Themenheft Multimediale System, Springer-Verlag (1991)

[Broc90]   Brockmann R.J.: Writing better Computer Documentation: From Paper to Hypertext. John Wiley&Sons (1990)

[Camp89]   Campagnoni F.R., Ehrlich K.: Information Retrieval using a Hypertext-Based Help System. ACM Trans. Off. Inf. Syst. 7,3 (July 1989), pp. 271ff

[Conk87]   Conklin J.: Hypertext - An introduction and a survey. IEEE Computer 20, (1987), 9

[Fuhr90]   Fuhr N.: Hypertext und Information Retrieval. In: Gloor, Streitz (eds): Hypertext und Hypermedia. Springer-Verlag (1990) pp. 101ff

[Jone91]   Jones S.: Text and Context - Document Processing and Storage. Springer-Verlag (1991)

[Kuhl91]   Kuhlen R.: Hypertext. Springer-Verlag (1991)

[Mühl91]   Mühlhäuser M.: Hypermedia-Konzepte zur Verarbeitung multimedialer Information. In: Informatik Spektrum 14/5/1991, Themenheft Multimediale System. Springer-Verlag (1991)

[Niel90]   Nielsen J.: The art of navigating through hypertext. Commun. ACM 33, Np. 3, March 1990, pp. 296ff.

[Roll91]   Roller D.: Technisches Informationssystem für computergestützten Fahrzeugservice. In Maurer H. (ed.): Proceedings of Hypertext/Hypermedia Symposium, Graz, May 26-28, 1991. Springer-Verlag (1991), pp. 229-237

[Ropi87]   Ropiequet S. (ed.): CD ROM Vol. II, Optical Publishing. Microsoft Press (1987)

[Roue90]   Rouet, J.F.: Interactive text processing by inexperienced (hyper-) readers. In: Rizk, Streitz, André:Hypertext: Concepts, Systems and Applications. Cambridge (1990), pp. 250ff

[Rumel86]   Rumelhart D, McClelland J.: Parallel Distributed Processing. The MIT Press (1986)

[Stie90]   Stieger D.: Zur Integration von klassischen und hypermedialen Dokumenten und dem Retrieval in Datenbanken. In: Gloor, Streitz (eds): Hypertext und Hypermedia. Springer-Verlag (1990) pp. 162ff

[Stre91]   Streitz N.A.: Hypertext: Bestandsaufnahme, Trends und Perspektiven. In: Encarnação (ed.): Telekommunikation und multimediale Anwendungen der Informatik. Springer-Verlag (1991), 543ff

[Witt84]   Wittgenstein L.: Vorlesungen 1939-35, Frankfurt/M. (1984), pp.39

[Paul91]   Paulousek, P.: Das Projekt "Zentrum fuer multimediale Telekommunikation". In: Informatik Spektrum. Springer-Verlag (1991), pp. 91/14/291

[Zell89]   Zellweger P.T.: Scripted Documents: A hypermedia path mechanism. In: ACM-Hypertext (1989)

Hypermedia als Zwischenrepräsentation bei der Expertensystementwicklung[1]

Frank Maurer & Gerd Pews
Universität Kaiserslautern
AG Expertensysteme Prof. Richter
Postfach 3049
D-6750 Kaiserslautern
e-Mail: {maurer, pews}@informatik.uni-kl.de

In diesem Papier vergleichen wir Hypermedia- und Expertensystemansätze zur Wissensverarbeitung. Wir zeigen, wie ein integrierter Ansatz die Erstellung von Expertensystemen erleichtert. Das von uns entwickelte und implementierte System ermöglicht einen "sanften" Entwicklungsprozeß ausgehend von initialen Protokollen zu einer semi-formale Strukturierung in Form eines getypten Hypertextes. Dem Hypertext ist eine aufgabenorientierte Struktur aufgeprägt, so daß eine anschließende Operationalisierung in Form eines Expertsystems vereinfacht wird. Die in diesem Prozeß erzeugte Zwischenrepräsentation (der Hypertext) wird von einem Interpreter direkt zur interaktiven Lösung von Problemen benutzt, wobei die einzelnen Aufgaben auf die verschiedenen Sachbearbeiter verteilt werden. Abschließend erläutern wir, daß Hypertext und Expertensysteme nur die Ränder eines Kontinuums einer allgemeinen Wissensverarbeitung sind.

1.0 Einleitung und Überblick

Die Integration von Hypermedia- und Expertensystemtechniken erscheint vielen Autoren erfolgversprechend ([2], [3], [11], [14]). Beide Techniken erlauben die Verwaltung von und den effektiven Zugriff auf Wissen mit Hilfe des Rechners.

Atomare Wissenseinheiten (Knoten) in Hypermediasystemen werden typischerweise in einer vom Rechner nicht interpretierbaren Form (z. B. Videosequenzen, Bilder, natürlichsprachlicher Text) gespeichert. Das Wissen kann vom Benutzer kontextabhängig, d.h. mit Hilfe seines "gesunden Menschenverstandes", interpretiert und so zur Lösung eines Problems herangezogen werden. Zusätzlich sind an die einzelnen Knoten Verweise auf weitere Knoten gekettet, denen der Benutzer folgen kann um weitere Informationen zu erhalten. Die Suche nach dem für die Lösung des aktuellen Problems benötigten Wissen wird in erster Linie vom Benutzer gesteuert[2].

---

1. Diese Arbeit wurde teilweise unterstützt vom Ministerium für Wirtschaft und Verkehr des Landes Rheinland-Pfalz im Rahmen des Projektes "Integration von Hypermedia und Expertensystemen"

Expertensysteme hingegen basieren auf einer Formalisierung des Wissens, die von einem Interpreter dann verarbeitet wird. D.h. der Interpreter benutzt das gespeicherte Wissen, um den Benutzer bei der Lösung des Problems anzuleiten. In diesem Sinne liegt die Initiative bei Expertensystemen eher bei der Maschine.

Beide Ansätze haben ihre Stärken und Schwächen:

- Expertensysteme stellen *weniger Anforderungen an den Benutzer*, da dieser sehr stark durch das System bei der Problemlösung angeleitet wird. Das "lost-in-hyperspace"-Problem kommt aus diesem Grund auch weniger zum Tragen, da der Benutzer seinen Weg im Informationsraum nicht selbst sucht und von daher auch nicht verlieren kann.

- Expertensysteme ermöglichen die *weitgehende Automatisierung* der Bearbeitung wissensintensiver Probleme, da Inferenzen durch ein Programm, den Interpreter, gezogen werden.

- Expertensysteme verlangen eine *Dekontextualisierung von Wissen*, da Inferenzen nur aufgrund des formalisierten Wissens gezogen werden können und dabei die Einbettung in den natürlichen Kontext verloren geht.

- Hypermediasysteme erfordern *weniger Aufwand bei der Entwicklung*, da Wissen nicht formalisiert werden muß: Die Interpretation der Knoteninhalte wird vom Benutzer vorgenommen, der dazu sein gesamtes Wissen über die Domäne benutzen kann. D.h. über den Benutzer kann auf den natürlichen Kontext, die Welt, zurückgegriffen werden.

- Die *Kommunikation* mit dem Benutzer wird durch die multimediale Schnittstelle von Hypertextsystemen stark verbessert.

Eine Frage, die sich stellt, ist: Wie kann man die Ansätze miteinander integrieren, so daß die jeweiligen Vorteile übernommen und die entsprechenden Nachteile zurückgedrängt werden? In [13] haben wir uns mit der Integration der beiden Ansätze auseinandergesetzt. Die für dieses Papier relevanten Aspekte fassen wir zusammen und beleuchten sie aus der Sicht der Hypermediasysteme. Im zweiten Kapitel beschreiben wir, wie wir das Wissen über eine neue Anwendung in Form eines Hypertextes strukturieren. Die resultierende Zwischenrepräsentation bildet die Basis des im dritten Kapitel vorgestellten Interpreters, der die verteilte Problemlösung ermöglicht. Im vierten Kapitel erläutern wir dann, warum Hypertexte und Expertensysteme nur die Ränder eines Spektrums von wissensverarbeitenden Systemen sind. Im fünften Kapitel stellen wir kurz die KADS-Methodik vor, die ein Ausgangspunkt unserer Arbeit war, und vergleichen unseren Ansatz damit. Das letzte Kapitel beschreibt den Stand der Realisierung und gibt einen Überblick über weitere Arbeiten.

---

2. "guided tours" verlagern die Initiative stärker auf das System und sind von daher die Ausnahme zu obiger Beschreibung.

2.0 Strukturierung von Wissen

Die Strukturierung von Wissen, mit dem Ziel einer Operationalisierung, ist seit langen Jahren Gegenstand der Forschungen im Knowledge Engineering. Die dabei gewonnenen Erkenntnisse übertragen wir auf die Strukturierung von Hypertexten[3]:

Ausgehend von initialen Daten (wie z.B. Mitschriften von Expertenbefragungen, Schaubildern über die Domäne, etc.) erstellen wir ein Hypermedianetzwerk als Zwischenrepräsentation, dessen Knoten und Kanten typisiert sind. Die vom System bereitgestellten Typen werden in Anlehnung an Ergebnisse der Wissensakquisitions-Forschung definiert, um dadurch einen guten Anknüpfungspunkt für eine spätere Formalisierung des Wissens zu erhalten. Die Hypertext-Zwischenrepräsentation ist die Eingabe eines interaktiven Interpreters, der eine Gruppe von Anwendern bei der Problemlösung unterstützt. Einzelne Unteraufgaben werden über ein lokales Netz (LAN) den jeweiligen "Sachbearbeitern"[4] zugewiesen, d.h. wir unterstützen eine verteilte Problemlösung.

Zur Unterstützung der Wissensingenieure bei der Strukturierung und Formalisierung einer Domäne entwickeln wir das System CoMo-Kit[5], das in Abschnitt 2.1 vorgestellt wird. Abschnitt 2.2 erläutert, wie wir mit CoMo-Kit ausgehend von initialen Daten die Zwischenrepräsentation entwickeln.

2.1 CoMo-Kit: Conceptual Model Construction Kit

Die Erstellung von Expertensystemen der 1. Generation erfolgte im wesentlichen nach dem Prototyp-Ansatz. Die dabei zutage tretenden Schwächen führten zur Entwicklung von modellbasierten Methodiken. Eine in Europa vorrangige ist KADS (vgl. Abschnitt 5.0). In KADS wird das Ergebnis der Analyse einer Domäne *konzeptuelles Modell* genannt.

CoMo-Kit basiert auf dem HyperCAKE-System [12] und Ideen von [14]. HyperCAKE nutzt eine erweiterte Hypertext Abstract Machine [7] für die Verwaltung multimedialer Informationen. HyperCAKE[6] ermöglicht die Definition von anwendungsspezifischen Sichten auf einen globalen Hypertext. Hypermedianetze sind in einer globalen Datenbank gespeichert und von allen Workstations in einem lokalen Netz zugänglich.

---

3. Die hier vorgestellte Arbeit beruht auf [13]. Wir fassen hier die relevanten Ergebnisse zusammen und diskutieren sie aus dem Blickwinkel der Hypertext/Hypermedia-Systeme.
4. "Sachbearbeiter" sind dabei entweder Menschen oder Programme.
5. CoMo-Kit wurde in Zusammenarbeit mit Susanne Neubert, Uni Karlsruhe, entwickelt, die eine Beispielapplikation (Zusammenstellen von Versicherungspaketen) zur Verfügung stellte.
6. HyperCAKE: Hypermedia-Based Computer Aided Knowledge Engineering

CoMo-Kit nutzt das HyperCAKE-System zur Verwaltung *aller* im Verlauf des Knowledge Engineering Prozesses anfallenden Daten. Dazu wurden folgende Knotenklassen definiert (wir beschränken unsere Darstellung auf im folgenden relevante Klassen):

- **Protokoll:** Ein Protokoll enthält initiale, unstrukturierte Daten, die vom Experten oder aus sonstigen Wissenquellen erhoben wurden.

- **Konzept:** Konzepte beschreiben für die Lösung des Problems notwendige Informationseinheiten in textueller, natürlichsprachlicher Form. Wir unterscheiden, wie beim objektorientierten Design üblich, zwischen Klassenbeschreibungen und Instanzen. Konzeptklassen werden in eine IS-A-Hierarchie eingeordnet[7].

- **Aufgabe (Task):** Eine Task beschreibt (in textueller, natürlichsprachlicher Form) eine Aufgabe, die durchgeführt werden muß, um ein gegebenes Problem zu lösen. Jede Task kann aus mehreren Unteraufgaben bestehen, die dann in Form eines Datenfluß-Diagramms beschrieben werden. Aufgaben sind also hierarchisch organisiert. Für jede Aufgabe werden ihre Ein- und Ausgaben definiert.

- **Bearbeiter (Agent[8]):** Agenten werden eindeutig über ihren Namen angesprochen. Jeder Agent kann zu verschiedenen Gruppen gehören. In der Spezifikation wird für jede Aufgabe festgelegt, welcher Agent oder welche Gruppe von Agenten sie potentiell bearbeiten kann.

Da der im Entwicklungsprozeß entstehende Hypertext sehr umfangreich ist, wodurch die Gefahr des "lost-in-hyperspace" wächst, werden in CoMo-Kit verschiedene Sichten auf das Netzwerk definiert[9]:

- **Protokoll-Kontext:** Diese Sicht umfaßt alle Protokolle für ein Projekt.

- **Konzept-Kontext:** Diese Sicht zeigt alle Konzepte und Relationen zwischen Konzepten[10].

- **Aufgaben-Kontext:** Der Aufgaben-Kontext zeigt alle definierten Tasks in einer Verfeinerungshierarchie.

- **Aufgabenstruktur-Kontext:** Diese Sicht zeigt die innere Struktur, d.h. den Datenfluß, einer Aufgabe.

---

7. Die durch die IS-A-Relation gebildete Hierarchie wird durch den später beschriebenen Interpreter nicht direkt ausgenutzt. Dieser arbeitet mit Instanzen der einzelnen Klassen. Die Hierarchie dient nur der Strukturierung der Begriffswelt der Domäne.

8. Der Begriff des Agenten wird bei uns nicht in dem umfassenden Sinn wie in der verteilten KI benutzt, sondern bezeichnet nur den Bearbeiter einer Aufgabe.

9. Technisch unterscheiden wir zwischen statischen Sichten, den *Contexts* der HAM, und dynamischen Sichten, die durch eine Bedingung an die in ihnen enthaltenen Objekte spezifiziert werden. Das Benutzerinterface für beide Arten ist identisch. Deshalb sprechen wir im folgenden nur noch von Kontexten.

10. CoMo-Kit unterstützt weitere Relationen zwischen Konzepten, wie PART-Of, CAUSES etc. Wir gehen auf diese nicht ein, da sie außerhalb des Fokus dieses Papiers liegen.

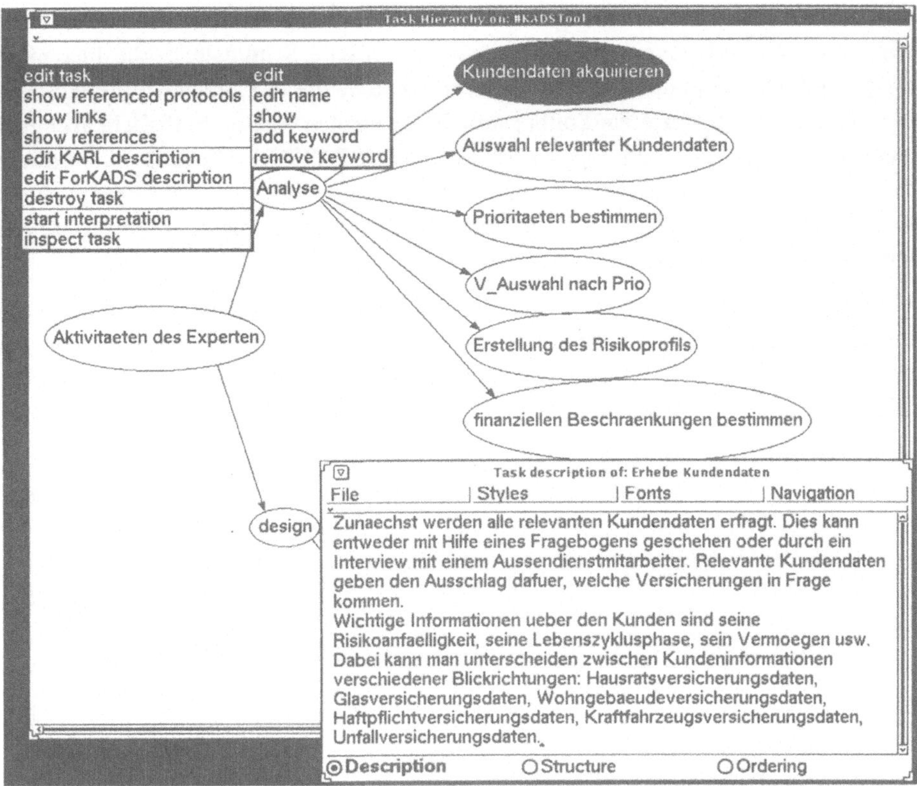

Abbildung 1: Die Aufgaben-Hierarchie und eine Aufgabenbeschreibung

Für jeden Kontext ist ein graphisches Interface implementiert, daß dem Benutzer ermöglicht, den Kontext zu manipulieren. Desweiteren kann der Benutzer jederzeit durch Angabe von Knoten- und Kantenbedingungen eine spezielle Sicht auf das Netz spezifizieren, die ihm dann über ein graphisches Interface präsentiert wird.

2.2 Benutzung von CoMo-Kit

Ausgangspunkt der konzeptuellen Modellierung ist das Protokoll eines Gesprächs mit einem Experten. Dieser soll die zu lösende Aufgabe umgangssprachlich beschreiben. In einem Protokoll kann der Wissensingenieur[11] einen Teil des Textes selektieren, der eine zu bearbeitende Teilaufgabe beschreibt. Anschließend wählt er in einem Menü den Eintrag "create task", um einen entsprechenden Aufgabenknoten zu erzeugen. Analog kön-

---

11. In einer Beispielanwendung (Baunutzungsverordnung) von CoMo-Kit wird die Strukturierung der Domäne direkt von Raumplanern, d.h. den Experten, vorgenommen. Wir denken, daß sich das auch auf andere Domänen übertragen läßt, da keine Programmierung im eigentlichen Sinne durchgeführt werden muß.

nen Konzepte und Agenten erzeugt werden. Die Zuordnung eines Bearbeiters zu einer Gruppe und zu Aufgaben erfolgt über eine graphische Schnittstelle, die hier nicht gezeigt wird. Die Terminologie einer Anwendung, d. h. die relevanten Konzeptklassen, kann mit Hilfe eines speziellen Editors strukturiert werden. Dieser ermöglicht über eine graphische Schnittstelle den Aufbau von IS-A- und PART-OF-Hierarchien. Attribute einer Klasse werden typisiert. Aus der so erstellten Spezifikation der Konzepte kann eine maskenorientierte Benutzerschnittstelle generiert werden, die nur die Eingabe von Werten aus dem Wertebereich erlaubt.

Abbildung 1 zeigt eine Aufgabenstruktur. Desweiteren ist die Beschreibung einer Aufgabe zu sehen. Der in einem Protokoll angewählte Text wurde in den neu erzeugten Knoten kopiert. Der Wissensingenieur kann die Beschreibung dann editieren, um die Aufgabe genauer zu spezifizieren.

Ein Datenfluß-Diagramm stellt die innere Struktur einer Aufgabe dar (vgl. Abbildung 2). Konzepte werden als Rechteck gezeigt, wohingegen Ellipsen Aufgaben repräsentieren. Die Hierarchie der Datenfluß-Diagramme eines zu lösenden Problems ist die Basis des im folgenden Kapitel beschriebenen Interpreters.

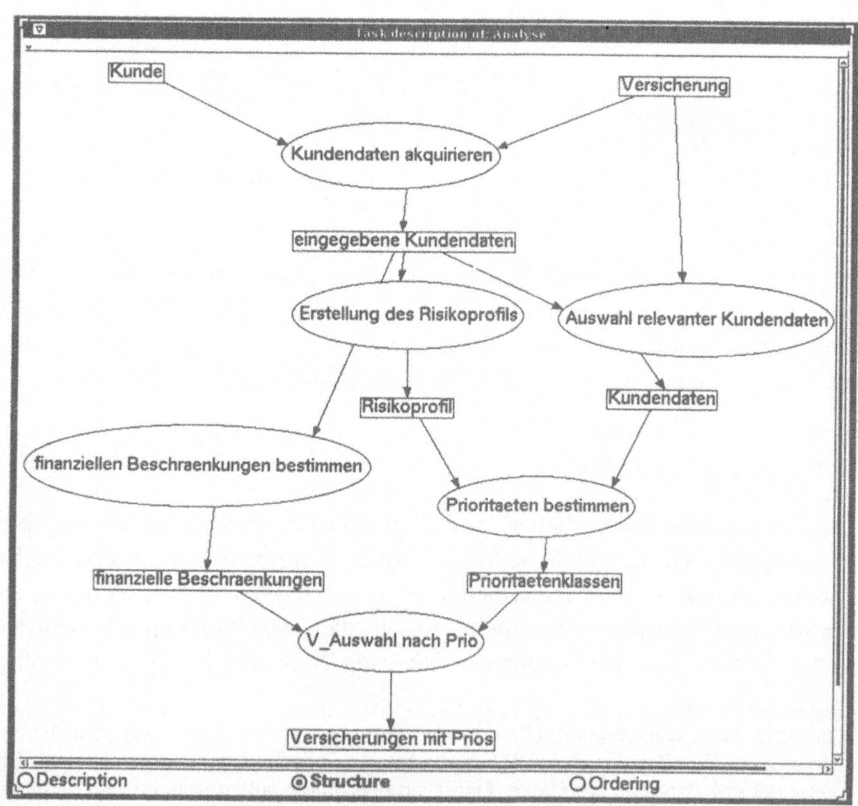

Abbildung 2: Eine Aufgabenstruktur

Jeder Aufgabe kann eine formale, ausführbare Annotation beigefügt werden. D. h. man ersetzt die natürlichsprachliche Beschreibung durch Programmcode. Daran interessierte Leser möchten wir auf [13] verweisen.

3.0 Der Interpreter für Aufgabenstrukturen

CoMo-Kit umfaßt einen Interpreter, der eine semi-formale[12] Aufgabenstruktur in Interaktion mit den Benutzern verarbeiten kann. D.h. schon die Strukturierung der Domäne in Form eines Hypertextes führt zu einem verwertbaren Ergebnis: Komplexe Aufgaben werden in kleinere Teile zerlegt, die dann von (weniger qualifizierten) Sachbearbeitern[13] bearbeitet werden können. Diese haben nur Zugriff auf für die Aufgabe relevante Information; die anderen werden vom System weggefiltert.

Ein Manager initiiert die verteilte Bearbeitung einer Aufgabe (Task), indem er sie an einen oder mehrere andere Benutzer delegiert und zur Ausführung freigibt. Er startet dadurch einen Scheduler-Prozeß. Dieser sorgt dafür, daß nur Aufgaben bearbeitet werden, für die zum jeweiligen Zeitpunkt auch alle benötigten Eingaben vorhanden sind. Ein Benutzer kann dann aus allen von ihm bearbeitbaren Tasks diejenige auswählen, die er als nächstes bearbeiten möchte. Die Aufgaben lassen sich in zwei Gruppen einteilen: komplexe und atomare.

Komplexe Aufgaben bestehen aus mehreren Unteraufgaben. Sie sind die inneren Knoten des in Abbildung 1 gezeigten Baumes. Wenn ein Benutzer eine komplexe Aufgabe bearbeiten will, übernimmt er die Rolle eines Managers. Ein Manager muß Aufgaben auf Sachbearbeiter verteilen und die Durchführung der Aufgaben überwachen.

Dabei wird er vom Rechner unterstützt. Dieser leitet Aufgaben, die nur einen möglichen Bearbeiter haben, direkt an diesen weiter. Desweiteren kann der Manager interaktiv Aufgaben delegieren und den Stand der Bearbeitung überprüfen[14]. Abbildung 3 zeigt ein Verwaltungsfenster. Das Fenster enthält vier Listen mit:

- Aufgaben, die noch unbearbeitet sind (links oben),

- Aufgaben, die schon an einen oder mehrere Benutzer delegiert sind, von diesen aber noch nicht bearbeitet wurden (links unten),

- Aufgaben, die gerade bearbeitet werden (rechts unten),

- Aufgaben, die schon bearbeitet sind (rechts oben)

---

12. Vgl. Abschnitt 4.0, "Informale, semi-formale und formale Wissensrepräsentation"

13. Durch die Strukturierung des Wissens findet indirekt eine *Qualifikation* der Sachbearbeiter statt, die nun neue Aufgabengebiete bearbeiten können. Desweiteren werden "echte Experten" von Routinetätigkeiten entlastet und können sich somit intensiv schwierigen Problemen widmen.

14. Im Moment erweitern wir, auf Anregung eines ungenannten Gutachters, den Interpreter im Sinne der Vorgangsbearbeitung um Möglichkeiten der Terminverfolgung.

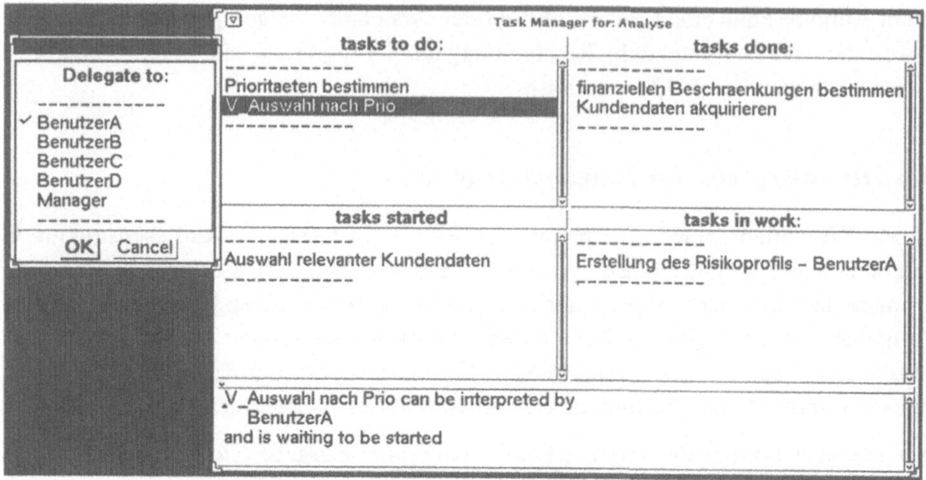

Abbildung 3: Verteilung der Aufgaben auf einzelne Agenten

Unter den Listen befindet sich ein Textfeld, in dem Informationen über den Stand der Bearbeitung jeder Aufgabe dargestellt werden. In der Überschrift ist die auszuführende Aufgabe zu sehen (hier: Analyse). Links oben werden alle noch zu verteilenden Aufgaben gezeigt. Diese können mit Hilfe eines Menüs an einen der möglichen Sachbearbeiter delegiert werden (hier: Benutzer A - Benutzer D, Manager). Sobald dies geschehen ist, erscheint die Aufgabe in der Liste links unten. Das Fenster rechts unten wiederum enthält eine Liste der Tasks, die gerade von dem Sachbearbeiter ausgeführt werden, dessen Namen hinter der Aufgabe gezeigt wird (hier: Benutzer A). Die Liste rechts oben umfaßt alle Aufgaben, die bereits abgeschlossen sind. D.h. im Verlauf der Zeit wandern die einzelnen Aufgaben (entgegen dem Uhrzeigersinn) von links oben nach rechts oben. Der Manager kann den Bearbeitungsvorgang verfolgen, bei Stockungen nach der Ursache forschen und evtl. eingreifen.

Atomare Aufgaben werden mit Hilfe des in Abbildung 4 gezeigten Fensters bearbeitet Der Editor enthält auf der linken Seite dynamisch erzeugte Buttons, die den Zugriff auf für die Aufgabe relevante[15] Informationen ermöglichen. In der Mitte findet der Benutzer eine Beschreibung der Aufgabe. Rechts befindet sich der Editor für die Eingabe des Resultats[16]. Sobald der Propagate-Button gedrückt wird, werden die Ergebnisse an den Scheduler propagiert. Anschließend können in dem Datenfluß-Diagramm nachfolgende Aufgaben von den dafür zuständigen Benutzern durchgeführt werden.

---

15. Was für eine Aufgabe relevant ist, wird bei der Strukturierung der Domäne festgelegt: Die Eingaben einer Aufgabe sind relevant für deren Lösung.

16. Falls die Aufgabe mehrere Resultate erzeugen soll, sind mehrere Editoren zu sehen. Sind die Ausgaben strukturiert, dann wird kein Texteditor (wie in der Abbildung oben) sondern eine entsprechende Maske gezeigt werden. Die Struktur der Daten muß nicht vorab definiert werden, sondern kann inkrementell entwickelt werden. Jedes Zwischenstadium kann in der Problemlösung eingesetzt werden, wodurch ein sanfter Übergang erreicht wird.

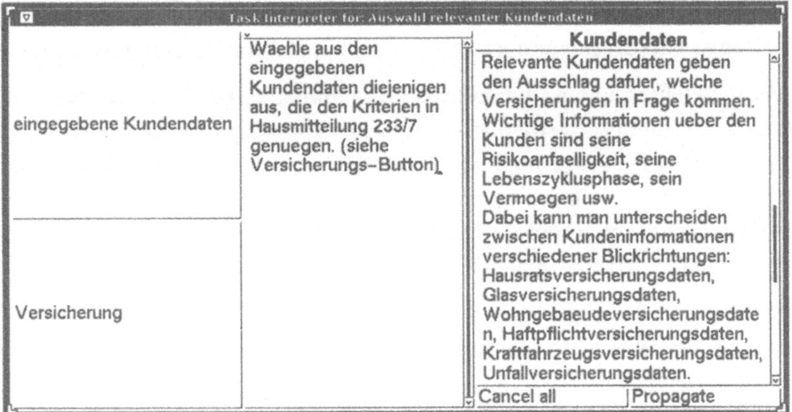

Abbildung 4: Editor für die Bearbeitung einer atomaren Aufgabe durch den Benutzer

Der beschriebene Interpreter hat im wesentlichen zwei interessante Eigenschaften:

1. Das Wissen muß nicht vollständig formalisiert werden, sondern liegt in Form eines Hypermedia-Netzwerks vor. Der Interpreter argumentiert nur über die Struktur des Netzes (d.h. Knoten- und Kantentypen haben eine operationale Semantik), nicht aber über die Knoteninhalte, deren Interpretation dem Benutzer überlassen bleibt.

2. Die Lösung des Problems wird auf mehrere Agenten, d.h. Sachbearbeiter oder Rechner, verteilt. Von daher bestehen Querbezüge zum Computer Supported Cooperative Work (CSCW) und zur verteilten KI, die wir aber hier nicht ausarbeiten können.

4.0 Informale, semi-formale und formale Wissensrepräsentation

Ausgangspunkt der Entwicklung mit Hilfe von CoMo-Kit sind textuelle Beschreibungen von Aufgaben. Diese sind *informal* im Sinne von "nicht durch einen maschinellen Interpreter verarbeitbar". Unter *formalisiertem Wissen* verstehen wir hingegen, eine Menge von Informationen, die von einem Rechner zur selbständigen Lösung von Problemen herangezogen werden können, ohne daß ein Mensch involviert ist. Das damit beschriebene Modell ist formal: Die Syntax *und* die Semantik der Sprache kann im Sinne formal-logischer Kalküle und Funktionen festgelegt werden. D. h. ein Programm ist im Prinzip in der Lage, Eingabedaten durch eine Menge von syntaktischen Umformungen in die gewünschten Ausgabedaten zu verwandeln, ohne das dabei ein Mensch involviert ist.

Ein *semi-formales Modell* ist eine Mischung der beiden anderen Arten: Die Transformation der Eingabe in die Ausgabe geschieht nicht vollautomatisch, sondern der Rechner und der Mensch teilen sich die Arbeit. *Semi-formal* bedeutet für uns, daß die Topologie des Netzes formal ist (jeder Knotentyp und jeder Kantentyp hat eine durch den Interpreter festgelegte Bedeutung für die Lösung der Aufgabe), die Inhalte der Knoten können allerdings nur durch den menschlichen Benutzer interpretiert werden.

Nach unserer Definition sind interaktive Programme, deren Verhalten durch Eingaben des Benutzers beeinflußt werden kann, keine (vollständig) formalen Modelle sondern nur semi-formal. Jede Frage muß von einem Benutzer interpretiert werden. Wenn sein Verständnis der Frage nicht mit dem im Rechner festgelegtem übereinstimmt, dann liefert der Rechner in der Regel ein vom Benutzer nicht erwartetes Ergebnis, das dann üblicherweise als Programmfehler bezeichnet wird.

Daß dem Rechner ein Verständnis der von ihm interaktiv manipulierten Symbole fehlt, läßt sich an einem Beispiel verdeutlichen: Bei der Diagnose eines Ottomotor stellt der Rechner dem Benutzer die Frage "Ist der Vergaser nicht vereist?". Der Benutzer kann nun über ein Menü mit "ja" oder "nein" antworten. Aus dieser Antwort werden dann weitere Fakten abgeleitet. Überliest der Benutzer nun das Wort "nicht" in der Frage, so verdreht sich die Bedeutung der Antwort ins Gegenteil. Und die vom System hergeleiteten Antworten werden falsch. D.h. das System kann nicht *über* das Frage-Antwort-Paar argumentieren, sondern muß davon ausgehen, daß der Benutzer unter den Symbolen dasgleiche versteht, was in ihm festgelegt wurde.

Hypermedianetze strukturieren Wissen auf der informellen Ebene. Die Semantik der Knoten und Kanten ist nicht formal definiert. Typisiert man nun die Knoten und Kanten, so kann für diese Typen eine operationale Semantik festgelegt werden. Genau dies ist die Basis unseres Interpreters, der somit ein Hypermedianetz zum semantischen Netz erweitert. Aus diesen Überlegungen folgt, daß zwischen (getypten) Hypermedianetzen und den im Expertensystembereich üblichen Wissensrepräsentationsmechanismen nur ein gradueller Unterschied besteht und somit ein sanfter Übergang erreicht werden kann.

5.0 Die KADS-Methodik

Eine in Europa vorrangige Wissensakquisitionsmethodik ist KADS ([19], [20], [5]). Diese ist eine Basis unseres Ansatzes und soll im folgenden kurz geschildert werden, wobei wir unsere speziellen Sichtweisen hervorheben.

5.1 Das 4-Ebenen-Modell

Die Spezifikation einer neuen Applikation wird in KADS *konzeptuelles Modell* genannt. Das konzeptuelle Modell besteht aus der Beschreibung der Benutzerschnittstelle (Model of Cooperation) und dem Wissensmodell (Model of Expertise). Das Model of Expertise unterscheidet verschiedene Wissensarten, die vier verschiedenen Ebenen zugerechnet werden:

- Die Domänen-Ebene umfaßt das anwendungsabhängige Wissen über Konzepte, deren Attribute und Beziehungen. Wir unterscheiden dabei zwischen der Struktur der Domäne (die Definition der Klassen) und den konkreten Objekten (den Instanzen).

- Die Inferenzebene enthält das Wissen über die verwendete Problemlösemethode. KADS unterscheidet dabei zwischen den Rollen (roles), die Konzepte in einem Problemlöseprozeß spielen, und den Aktivitäten (knowledge sources), die zu gegebenen Eingaben eine entsprechenden Ausgabe erzeugen.

- Die Task-Ebene beschreibt den Kontrollfluß einer Problemlösemethode, d.h. diese Ebene beschreibt *wann* eine Aktivität ausgeführt werden soll.

- Die Strategie-Ebene soll Meta-Wissen über die Auswahl und Kombination von verschiedenen Tasks enthalten. Sie ist bis jetzt noch nicht vernünftig beschrieben und wird deshalb in unserem Tool nicht unterstützt.

5.2 Vergleich mit unserem Ansatz

Unser Ansatz baut auf KADS auf, unterscheidet sich aber durch die folgenden Punkte davon:

- **hierarchische Aufgabenstrukturen**: Im Gegensatz zu KADS beschreiben wir eine Aufgabe auf verschiedenen Ebenen der Abstraktion.

- **Toolentwicklung**: Wir versuchen, unsere Methodik direkt durch ein Computer-Aided Knowledge Engineering Tool zu unterstützen; dies ist nicht der Schwerpunkt von KADS.

- **Hypermedia**: Unser Ansatz versucht, Hypermedia-Netze als Zwischenrepräsentation einzusetzen.

- **Model of Cooperation**: Wir planen, Multimedia-Schnittstellen im Model of Cooperation zu definieren. Dies wird durch unsere Basis, ein Hypermediasystem, erleichtert.

6.0 Stand der Realisierung und Ausblick

Das HyperCAKE-System ist vollständig implementiert und an die objektorientierte Datenbank GemStone von Servio Cooperation angekoppelt. CoMo-Kit ist ebenfalls implementiert. Der Interpreter für Aktivitätsstrukturen ist als Single-User-System implementiert, die Erweiterung auf den Multi-User-Betrieb ist in Arbeit.

HyperCAKE/CoMo-Kit bilden die Basis der Entwicklung mehrerer Expertensystem-Shells: SAFRaN koppelt ein geographisches Informationssystem mit einem Expertensystem, um eine wissensbasierte Auswertung von Karten zu ermöglichen (vgl. [6], [8] und [10]). HyDi unterstützt die Entwicklung von hypermediabasierten Diagnosesystemen und wird Ende 1992 fertiggestellt (vgl. [17] und [18]).

7. Literatur

[1] Angele, J.; Fensel, D.; Landes, D.; and Studer, R: KARL: An Executable Language for the Conceptual Model. In: Proceedings of the Knowledge Acquisition for Knowledge-Based Systems Workshop KAW'91, October 6-11, Banff, 1991

[2] Bielawski, L., Lewand, R.: Intelligent Systems Design, Wiley 1991

[3] Biethahn, J.; Bogaschewsky, R.; Hoppe, U. (Hrsg.): Expertensysteme in der Wirtschaft 1992 - Anwendungen und Integration mit Hypermedia, Gabler Verlag, 1992

[4] Boehm, B. W.: A Spiral Model of Software Development and Enhancemant, Computer, 21, 5 (May 1988), p. 61-72

[5] Breuker, J.; Wielinga, B.; Someren, M.v.; de Hoog, R.; Schreiber, G.; de Greef, P.; Bredeweg, B.; Wielemaker, J.; and Billault, J.-P.: Model-Driven Knowledge Acquisition: Interpretation Models. Esprit Project P1098, University of Amsterdam (The Netherlands), 1987

[6] Burde, M.: Die langfristige Sicherung von Grundwasservorkommen - durch die Ausweisung von Grundwasservorranggebieten - als gemeinsame Aufgabe von Raumplanung und Fachplanung, Unveröffentliches Manuskript; Dissertation im Fachbereich ARUBI, Universität Kaiserslautern, 1992

[7] Campbell, B., Goodman, J. M.: HAM: A General Purpose Hypertext Abstract Machine, Communications of the ACM, July 1988, Vol. 31, No. 7

[8] Hemker, H..: Entwurf und Implementierung eines Expertensystems mit GIS-Kopplung, Diplomarbeit Uni Kaiserslautern, 1992

[9] Hoppe, U.: Einsatz von Hypertext/Hypermedia zur Verbesserung der Erklärungsfähigkeit Wissensbasierter Systeme. In [3]

[10] Jäckel, Th.: Entwurf und Implementierung einer Benutzeroberfläche für ein Expertensystem unter Berücksichtigung planerischer Vorgehensweisen, Diplomarbeit Uni Kaiserslautern, 1992

[11] Maurer, F. (Hrsg.): Proc. Workshop "Expertensysteme und Hypermedia", Seki-Working-Paper , 7.11.1991, Kaiserslautern

[12] Maurer, F.: HyperCAKE: Ein Wissensakquisitionssystem für hypermediabasierte Expertensysteme. In [3]

[13] Maurer, F., Pews, G.: Validierung von konzeptuellen Modellen, Proc. XPS-93, Springer, 1993

[14] Neubert, S.: Einsatz von Hypermedia im Bereich der modellbasierten Wissensakquisition. In [3]

[15] Neubert, S., Maurer, F.: The Conceptual Model Construction Kit, to appear

[16] Nielsen, J.: Hypertext & Hypermedia. Academic Press, San Diego, London, 1990

[17] Traphöner, R., Maurer, F.: Integrating Hypermedia and Expert System Technology for Technical Diagnosis, Proc. Expersys 92, Paris, 21.-22. Okt. 1992

[18] Traphöner, R., Maurer, F.: HyDi: Integration of Hypermedia and Expert System Technology for Technical Diagnosis, Proc. Gesellschaft für Klassifikation 92

[19] Wielinga, B.J.; Schreiber, A.Th.; Breuker, J.A.: KADS: A Modelling Approach to Knowledge Engineering. ESPRIT Project P5248 KADS-II, An Advanced and Comprehensive Methodolgy for Integrated KBS Development, Amsterdam, 1991

[20] Wielinga, B.J.; Schreiber, A.Th.; Breuker, J.A.: KADS a modelling approach to knowledge engineering. In: Knowledge Acquisition (1992) 4, 5-53, Academic Press Limited, 1992

A Knowledge-Based Hypermedia System for Molecular Spectroscopy

Marc Cadisch, Andreas Gloor, Tamàs Kocsis, Renate Bürgin, and Ernö Pretsch
Swiss Federal Institute of Technology (ETH)
Department of Organic Chemistry
CH - 8092 Zürich

The hypermedia system SpecTool for the structure elucidation of organic compounds by spectroscopic methods is presented. In addition to alphanumerical and graphical data, it also contains nodes with arithmetic tools as information units. The data structure and navigation tools allow to browse through the system according to different aspects. The danger of getting "lost in hyperspace" due to the enormous flexibility and navigation possibilities was eliminated by superimposing a hierarchical table of contents on the data organization. For future versions, the use of different navigation structures within the same system is conceivable.

Introduction

The elucidation and confirmation of structures or constitutions of organic compounds is mainly achieved by spectroscopic methods. Despite their widely different physical basis, the various spectroscopic techniques have certain formal properties in common, in that the spectrum of a compound is always a function of its structure:

$$spectrum = F(structure)$$

Formally, the spectrometer may be regarded as an analogous computer executing this transformation. Although the function F is definite, it is never exactly known. The chemist's actual target in structure elucidation is the inverse of F:

$$structure = F^{-1}(spectrum)$$

and is an unknown too. Yet in practice,[1,2] a huge amount of empirical correlations has been found between partial structures and parts of the spectrum:

$$partial\ spectrum = f(partial\ structure)$$

Normally, the inverse of this function is also known:

$$partial\ structure = f^{-1}(partial\ spectrum)$$

These relationships are recorded in correlation tables and data collections[3] which enable the user to derive heuristic rules fitting his specific problem or, less favourably, to consult generalized rules. This part of spectra interpretation is difficult to formalize. As a consequence, none of the hitherto existing attempts to develop expert systems for automatic spectrum interpretation, including the extensive Dendral project,[4] has ever attained any practical relevance.[5]

Aside from the task of recognizing connections between parts of a spectrum and partial structures, there are certain steps in structure elucidation that can be exactly formalized as, for example, the calculation of possible molecular formulas agreeing with a specific mass range (with constraints in respect of kind, number and percentage of elements),[6] the combination of molecular fragments to whole molecules[7,8,9] or the application of empirical correlations for predicting spectra.[10]

The combined application of various spectroscopic techniques leads to partly overlapping and partly complementary pieces of information. Thus, hints based on a spectrum of one method may be confirmed or disproved by the corresponding data from another. Therefore, when examining a certain substructure, the user of a structure elucidation system must be able to switch both between different spectroscopic methods and substructures within the same method. Thus, for the interpretation of molecular spectra, documentations with non-linear structures allowing versatile navigation procedures are especially attractive.

This work presents SpecTool, a hypermedia system developed to support spectra interpretation.[11,12] It contains reference data and spectra, heuristic rules and arithmetic tools for the five most relevant spectroscopic methods, namely mass spectrometry (MS), ^{13}C and ^{1}H nuclear magnetic resonance spectroscopy (^{13}C NMR, ^{1}H NMR) as well as infrared (IR) and ultraviolet/visible (UV/Vis) spectroscopy. The system was created in HyperCard™ on Macintosh™ computers.

Contents of the System

Currently, the system consists of 34 stacks with a total of 1400 cards (nodes) requiring a 7 MByte disk space. Approximately 850 cards are provided with data and rules, 200 with spectra, 50 with arithmetic tools, and about 300 are used exclusively for navigation purposes. The navigation structure is finished and the data material for the first version is almost completed, but further additions are planned.

A typical data card is shown in Figure 1. In order to avoid overloaded cards, additional information (e.g., literature, citations or comments) is displayed only after clicking at certain buttons. Further data is recorded in invisible fields (e.g., names of compounds) which, in a later version, will allow to search through entire stacks. Other pieces of information (such as spectrum recording conditions) are displayed in specific fields as soon as the cursor enters a certain area of the card.

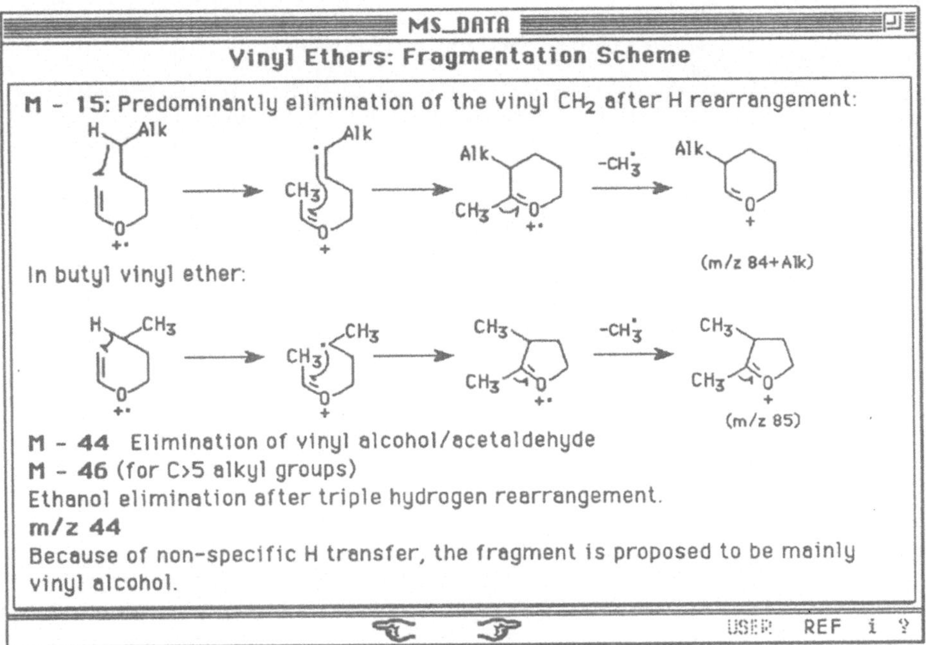

Figure 1: Example for a data card in SpecTool

The data is logically divided into different stacks in such a way that browsing within a stack permits easy orientation. In addition, the organisation allows for a straightforward data update procedure. Although the user cannot modify the data stacks, he has the option of entering his own data. It is saved on new cards in special user data stacks, but each card logically connected with the starting node of the original stack. This organization uses two types of button-icons when opening a data stack card, namely a dark or dim "USER" button depending on whether there exits a related user card or not. Due to this strategy, all data stacks may be put on a CD-ROM, but the user still has the possibility of entering his own related data and remarks.

Data Representation

Larger tables are stored in scrollable fields. They are always accompanied by an index field which allows a quick search. Complex tables may be sorted according to the numerical values of a selected column by clicking at it.

Whenever useful, the numerical information can also be displayed graphically. This is illustrated in Figure 2. The card shows the relative isotope abundances of all naturally occurring elements. A particular element may be found either by scrolling the table or with the help of the numerical or alphabetical index. The latter is accompanied by an additional index field on the very left. As the numerical representation of isotope

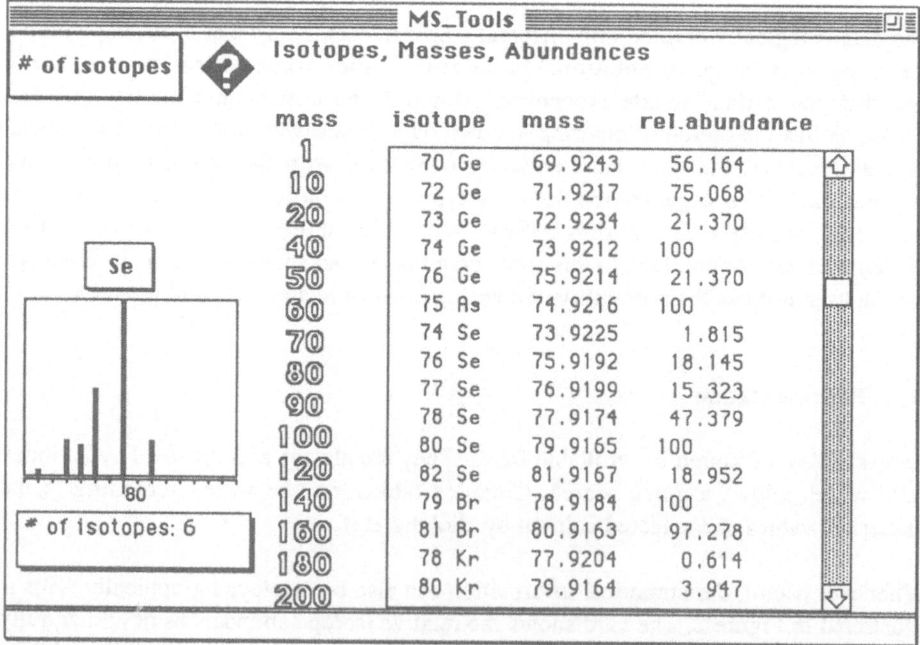

Figure 2a: Masses and relative abundances of naturally occurring isotopes: Numerical data

Figure 2b: Masses and relative abundances of naturally occurring isotopes: Graphical representation

abundances, in spite of its precision, is more difficult to interpret, reference data is also displayed graphically (cf. Fig. 2b) by clicking at the desired element.

Navigation

The reference material is allocated on 15 stacks, 3 for each of the 5 spectroscopic methods covered. The information for each method is arranged in one stack with reference data, another with reference spectra and the third with computational tools. In data and spectra stacks, the reference material is distributed in 25 compound classes. Browsing within one stack is performed by using HyperCard commands for reaching the next or the previous card. Whenever reasonable, additional HyperText links between cards have been implemented.

The real power of a hypermedia system is its flexible navigation system. Too many possibilities, however, entail the danger of losing one's orientation. This is avoided by superimposing a tree structure on the complex network of cards and stacks (cf. Fig. 3), so that high flexibility and easy orientation is achieved. This tree structure is implemented on 6 so-called navigation stacks. Each node of the tree represents the table of contents of the next lower level. Information on links to hierarchically lower cards is collected in buttons or fields. Furthermore, every card in SpecTool has an invisible field with the addresses of all cards higher up in hierarchy. In this way, upward navigation along the tree is also possible. In both, the purely navigational and the data stacks, corresponding cards bear the same name. This allows easy switching between the different spectroscopic methods and information types (data, spectra, tools), i.e. a horizontal navigation.

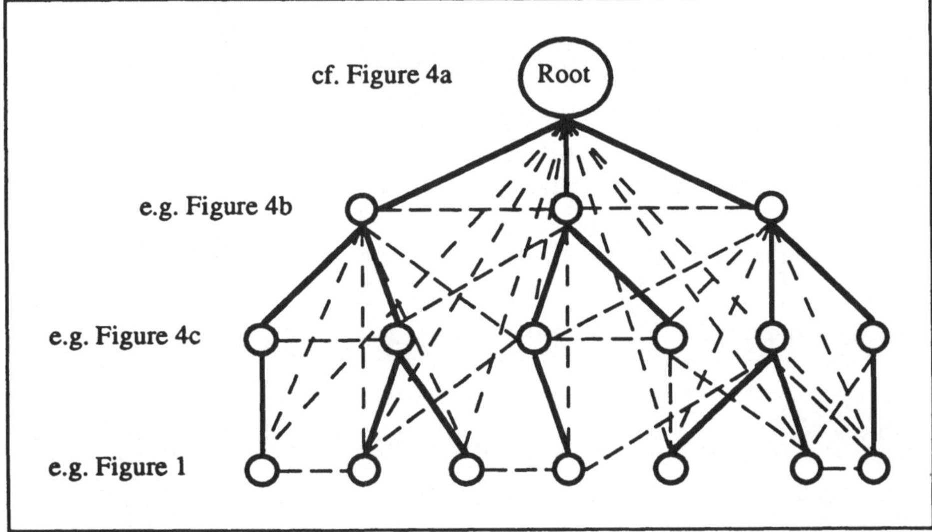

Figure 3: Superposition of tree structure on network

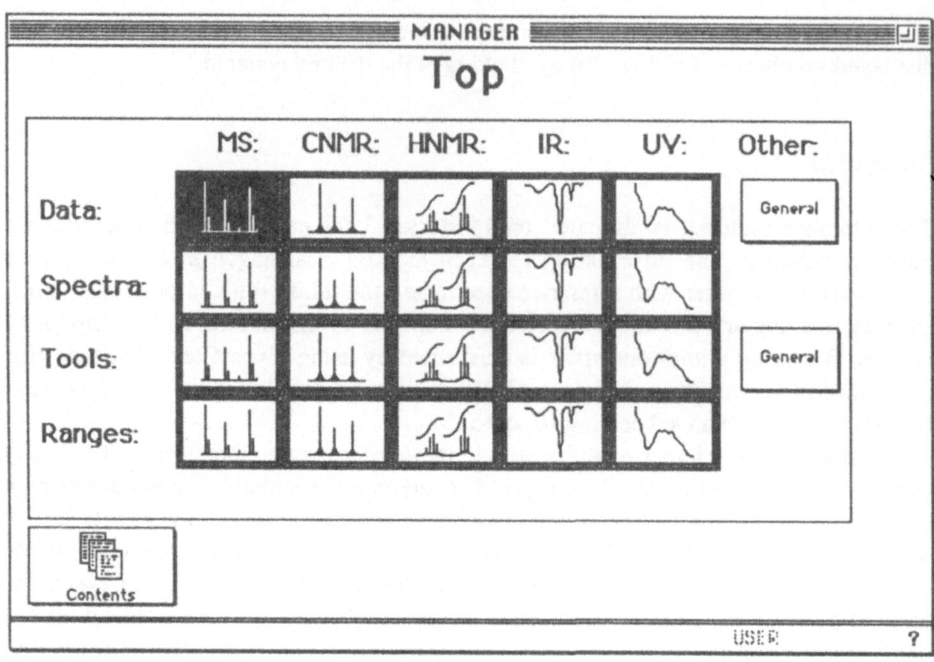

Figure 4a: TOP card

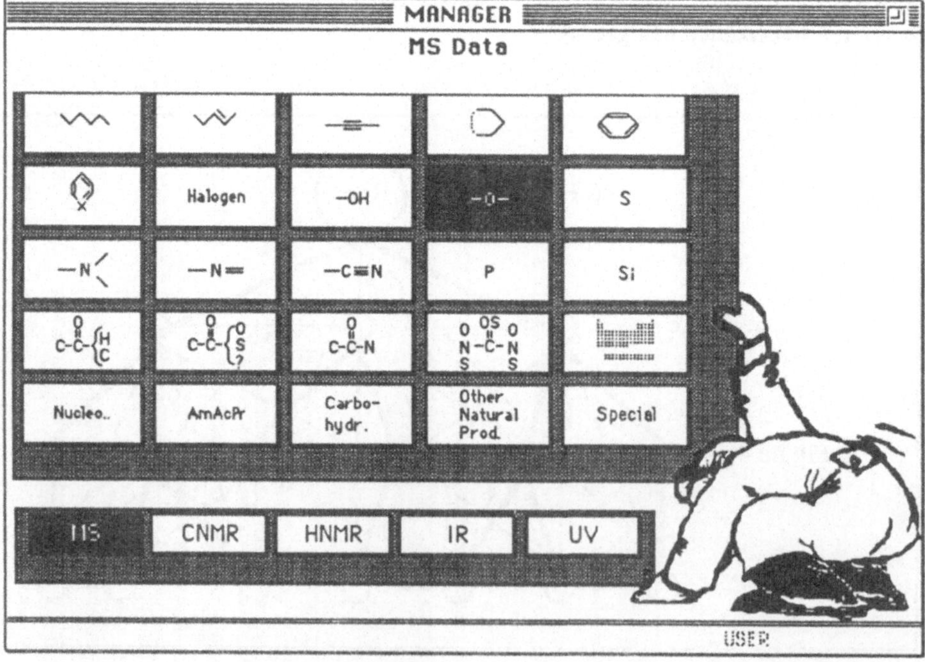

Figure 4b: Table of contents of "MS Data"

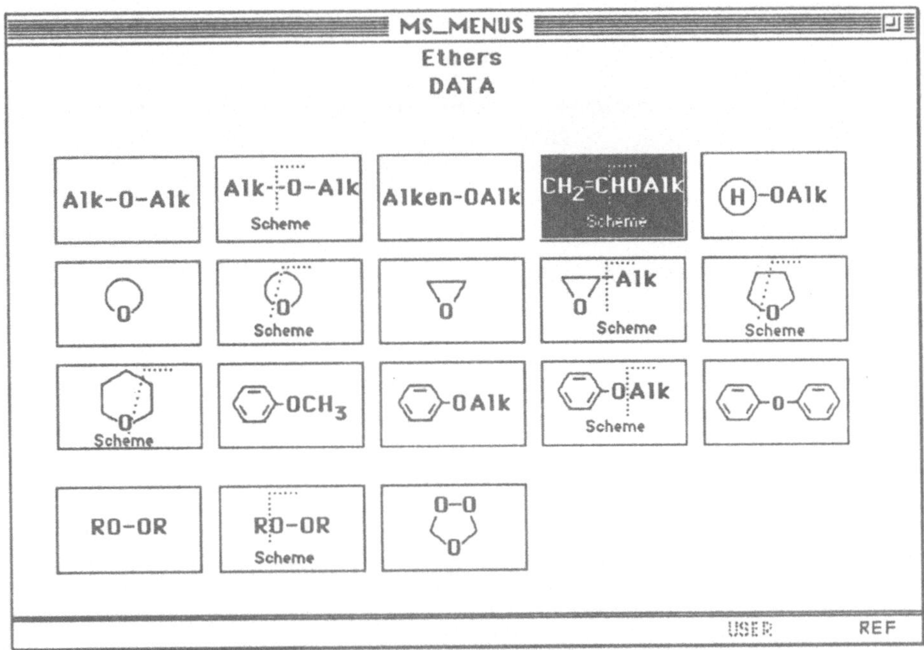

Figure 4c: Table of contents of the compound class "Ethers"

Figure 4 shows a sequence (one pathway selected along the tree) leading to mass spectroscopic reference data of vinyl ether derivatives. The root of this tree (the so-called TOP card, Fig. 4a) is accessible in one step from any point of the system. It gives an overview of the tables of contents of the next lower level. As the reference material is divided into the same 25 compound classes for all 5 methods (for MS data cf. Fig. 4b), these tables of contents for data and spectra look alike. Thus, horizontal links are always obvious and definite. For this reason, also the next lower level for spectra and data is organized in the same way (cf. Fig. 4c). However, the contents of these cards may differ from one method to another, because the data cards on the next level may vary according to the specific method.

Apart from entering the system through this tree structure, there are additional possibilities of access, e.g. by searching for compound names or numerical data values. The latter case is illustrated by the IR "Ranges" card in Fig. 5, but is analogous for the other methods. By clicking at a frequency on the scale displayed on the top, a list of all cards containing the selected value is generated, each of which may be reached by clicking at the corresponding line. As the search for matching values on hundreds of data cards is very slow, a special search list is stored in a hidden field. It contains all the information necessary for reaching the desired data card. A procedure allows updating of these lists with corrections and additional data from the authors of SpecTool.

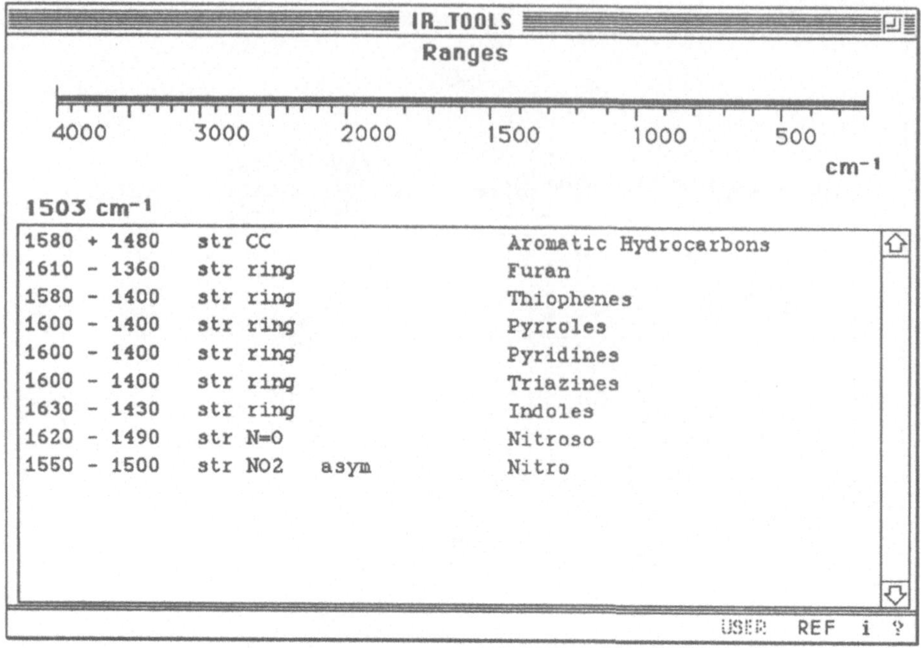

Figure 5: Entry according to frequency ranges

Most of the horizontal links are globally defined (scripts high up in hierarchy). When switching from a data or spectra card of method A to the corresponding information from method B, the system looks for a card with the same name in the analogous stack of the latter. If there is no such card, the table of contents of the next higher level is presented (cf. Fig. 4c). Thus, the user immediately sees which related data is available. This organisation, among others, enables the automatic generation of new links after updates.

The implementation of the navigation tools is highly redundant. Not only navigation cards (cf. Fig. 4) may be used, but also pull-down and pop-up menus as well as corresponding palettes (see Fig. 6).

Typically, it is possible to reach about 50 other cards within one jump from any point of the system. This tight, but clearly structured network guarantees that each card is accessible from any position within 4 steps at the most, even after enlarging the system to more than 10,000 cards. The maximum number of steps necessary to reach any other card of the system could be designated as its diameter.

The user has the possibility of expanding the system not only with his own cards, but also with individual means of navigation in the form of bookmarks. Any card can be marked, whereupon it is immediately available in a pull-down menu. Sets of bookmarks may be saved as files and loaded again.

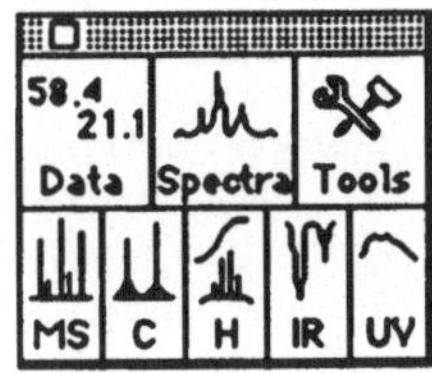

Figure 6: The switch palette. A mouse click in one of the fields causes the system to switch to the selected method, at the same time maintaining the relevant parameters

In contrast to many other hypermedia systems, the image of the cursor in HyperCard™ is not altered when moving over hot areas, i.e. over regions of a card where actions can be triggered by a mouse click. Since the presence of hot areas is not always obvious to the user, HyperCard™ has been provided with external commands (XCMDs) for altering the cursor. In addition, possible cross connections in text fields are indicated by underlining.

Arithmetic tools

In the course of structure elucidations, the chemist must have the possibility of carrying out certain calculations. For simpler tasks, the necessary programs have been implemented on so-called tool cards. When a calculation procedure is so demanding that it cannot be reasonably accomplished even by external commands (XCMDs), an external stand-alone application is launched from within HyperCard™. Strictly speaking, arithmetic tools are just another type of information within SpecTool.

Figure 7 illustrates the user interface for doing a simple calculation. In this example, a spectroscopic property (^{1}H-NMR chemical shift) of a basic skeleton (benzene ring) is estimated as a function of its substituents. These can be selected by means of hierarchical pop-up menus appearing at each substitution location when clicking at it (see centre in Figure 7). The chemical group chosen is then placed in the correct position and its contribution directly added to the estimated parameters. The arithmetic tools will be described in detail elsewhere.[13]

Implementation

The biggest part of SpecTool consists of HyperCard™ stacks. External applications, commands, and functions increase the versatility and performance of the system, and special fonts allow chemical formulas to be represented in pop-up menus. For easy maintenance and in order to have the possibility of expanding, all major HyperTalk™ scripts are centralized in 5 common stacks inserted into the message-passing hierarchy of HyperCard™. Cards which are created by the user are stored in special stacks.

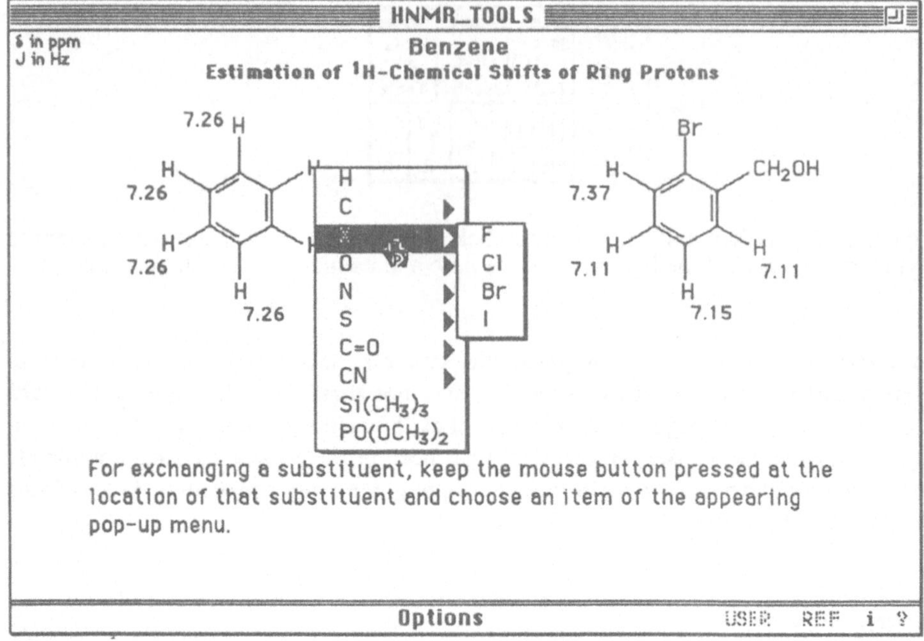

Figure 7: ¹H-NMR tool for estimating chemical shifts

Acknowledgement

This work was partly supported by the Swiss National Foundation.

References

1   Silverstein, R.M.; Bassler, G.C.; Morrill, T.C. Spectrometric Identification of Organic Compounds, 5th edn., *Wiley*, New York, 1991.

2   Clerc, J.T.; Pretsch, E.; Seibl, J. Structural Analysis of Organic Compounds by Combined Application of Spectroscopic Methods, *Elsevier*, Amsterdam, 1981.

3   Pretsch, E.; Clerc, J.T.; Seibl, J.; Simon, W. Tables of Spectral Data for Structure Elucidation of Organic Compounds, *Springer-Verlag*, Berlin, 1981, 2nd edn., 1989.

4   Lindsay, R.K.; Buchanan, B.G.; Feigenbaum, E.A.; Ledeberg, J. Applications of Artificial Intelligence for Organic Chemistry: The DENDRAL Project, *McGraw-Hill*, New York, 1980.

5   Gray, N.A.B. Dendral and Meta-Dendral - The Myth and the Reality, *Chemom. Intell. Lab. Syst.*, 1988, 5, 11-32.

6   Fürst, A.; Clerc, J.T.; Pretsch, E. A Computer Program for the Computation of the Molecular Formula, *Chemom. Intell. Lab. Syst.* 1989, 5, 329-334.

7   Gray, N.A.B. Computer-Assisted Structure Elucidation, *Wiley*, New York, 1986.

8   Shelley, C.A.; Munk, M.E. CASE, a Computer Model of the Structure Elucidation Process, *Anal. Chim. Acta* 1981, 133, 507-516.

9   Kerber A.; Laue R.; Moser D. Ein Strukturgenerator für molekulare Graphen, *Anal. Chim. Acta* 1990, 235, 221-228.

10 Fürst, A.; Pretsch E. A Computer Program for the Prediction of ^{13}C-NMR Chemical Shifts of Organic Compounds, *Anal. Chim. Acta*, 1990, 229, 17-25.

11 Farkas, M.; Cadisch, M.; Pretsch E. Hypermedia Tools for Structure Elucidation Based on Spectroscopic Methods, in: *Scientific Computing and Automation (Europe)*, E.J. Karjalainnen (Ed.), *Elsevier*, Amsterdam, 1990.

12 Cadisch, M.; Farkas, M.; Clerc, J.T.; Pretsch, E. SPECTOOL: A Hypermedia Toolkit for Structure Elucidation, *J. Chem. Inf. Comput. Sci.* 1992, 32, 286-290.

13 Brodmeier, T.; Gloor, A.; Cadisch, M.; Bürgin, R.; Pretsch, E. Hypermedia Tools for the Interpretation of Mass Spectra. *Anal. Chim. Acta*, in preparation.

Navigation in hypertext by browsing in survey objects

Users' searches and travels as a source for their orientation

Peter Purgathofer   Thomas Grechenig
University of Technology Vienna
Dep. Design of Technology   Dep. Software Engineering
A-1040   Möllwaldplatz 4/187   A-1040   Resselgasse 3/2/188
Vienna, Austria
Email: Grechenig@eimoni.tuwien.ac.at
              Purgi@iguwnext.tuwien.ac.at

Abstract: The following paper deals with an approach supporting users while navigating in complex information spaces structured by objects. The concept presented is based on survey objects, which are titled lists of references to information objects. Conventional survey entities like the *list of contents*, the *list of bookmarked cards* or a *guided tour* are survey objects. Useful survey objects can be extracted by analyzing users' work. E.g. *today's history* or a specific *search request*. Moreover, survey objects can be connected by operations similar to operations on sets what will result in new survey objects themselves. Some of these "calculated" objects seem artificial in practice, others are matching typical survey interests of users well, though, e.g. the request *"those cards which I was looking for but I have not yet seen"* corresponds to the object *"the latest search selection"* minus *"the cards in today's history"*. We suggest including survey objects in a browser for information objects, handling them like normal objects. We have implemented the presented concept for user's orientation in a HyperCard facility called Navigåtor. This application provides the creation of survey objects, operations on survey objects and browsing in objects plus survey objects.

Keywords: navigation in hypertext, user's orientation, survey objects, overview in large information spaces, browsing

1) Introduction

There is a certain consensus within the scientific community of hypermedia that navigation may be a serious difficulty for the users of hypertext. Omitting the "linear" structure of paper makes it more likely for users to get lost. Meanwhile the problem has been discussed extensively (see e.g. [Conk87], [Hala88], [vanD88], [Aksc88], [Brow89], [Nils92]). Therefore today's hypertext systems can offer a variety of approaches helping the reader
  - in not getting lost
  - in gaining an overview about the material
  - in finding some specific piece of information.

There are various ways of classifying navigation support. With respect to the ideas presented in this paper we distinguish between *implicit* and *explicit* types of navigation support. An implicit facility is built in the internal structure of a hypertext system. It is information on orientation integrated as a part of the hypertext objects' contents.
E.g. the idea of *structured nodes* discussed in [Aksc88] suggests a standardized layout and data model of nodes, from which users can expect orientation information of similar characteristics and location in every node. *Typed links* (see e.g. [Conk87]) are considered to give users an idea of what type of information they can expect in a subsequent node referenced by a corresponding type of link. *Hierarchical structures* have been suggested as a principle design skeleton for hypertext systems. This kind of structure can support users in developing a mental model of the system. Some systems provide *special nodes* which act as landmarks ([Niel90]), thus being a navigational aid corresponding to human psychology of orientation in physical environment (see also introduction of part 2).

Explicit navigation support on the other hand is any technique that provides survey information separated from domain information. Navigation tools are members of that sort of navigation support. A number of hypertext systems [Garr86], [Deli86], [Hala87], [Conk87] provide *browsers* to give overview information. Another frequently used concept are *maps* which help users develop a mental map of the system. In larger systems the viewing of maps may require special techniques, such as *zooming* [BeWa90], *flying over* it [Fair88] or *fish eye views* [Furn86]. Giving the user the possibility to make use of *bookmarks* [Niel90] and *history lists* [Foss89] will help them to locate nodes they visited before. *Guided tours* [Niel90] - being the most hypertext-unlike method - can give the user a domain-oriented overview of a hypertext system. [Hann92] developed a widely ranging model for a browsing semantic including navigation-effective entities like *structure nodes, composite nodes,* or *structure links.* A part of these concepts and implementations is related to the concepts of the paper at hand.

Browsing is a frequently applied technique for orientation in hierarchically structured objects[1]. Our concept suggests including *survey objects* into this browsing procedure, handling them like normal objects. Survey objects are a named list of references to information objects. E.g., conventional survey entities like the *list of contents*, the *list of bookmarked cards* or a *guided tour* are survey objects. Useful survey objects can be found by analyzing users' cognitive world. E.g. *today's history* or a specific *search request.*
Moreover, survey objects can be connected by operations similar to operations on sets. According to the above taxonomy, browsing in survey objects is an explicit method for orientation.

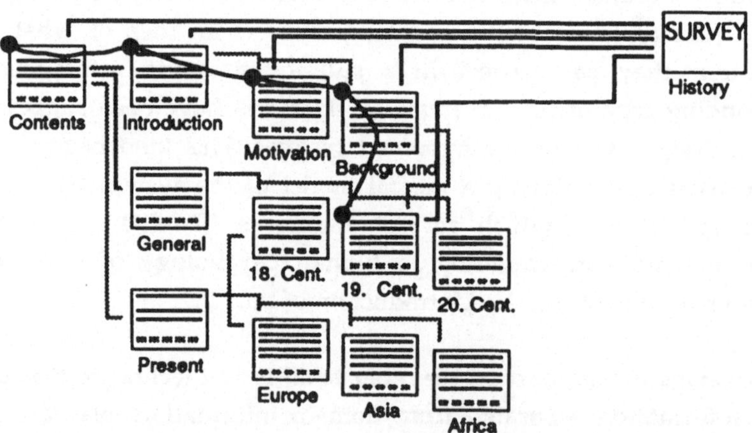

Figure 1: Creating a survey object from user's path

---

[1] The words object, node and card are used nearly synonymously in this article. *Object* is the term according to the concept of visual units in HCI. *Node* refers to the link and node metaphor in the hypermedia field. The word *card* is sometimes used for the reason that presented implementation was made in HyperCard, which uses cards as its object oriented data model.

In part 2 of this paper survey objects are defined from the user's point of view. A formal definition is presented. Part 3 shows the practical application of survey objects within a hierarchical browser . In part 4 the benefit from creating new survey objects by applying operations to existing survey objects is outlined. Finally we discuss open questions.

2) Informal and formal definition of survey objects

Some research on the way people gather navigational knowledge about an unknown surrounding has proved to be of a practical use for the visualization of complex information in computer systems (see e.g. in [Ande80], [ThHa82], [Wick84]), too. This model of cognitive psychology suggests three stages which may but need not necessarily be constructed successively:

- *salient landmarks*: allowing people to recognize their position in relation to these objects such as attractions, building, hills, etc..
- *routes*: describing the navigation from one point to another and back
- *survey knowledge*: allowing people to plan travels between points that have not been visited before. Actually, this last stage presumes a sort of cognitive map.

There is no obvious analogy between these model stages of human mind and the various attempts to support user's navigation in hypertext systems as described in part 1. But all of them support the building of the above mentioned cognitive stages in one way or the other. E.g., *special objects* are kind of a *landmark*. *Typed links* and *structured nodes* will ease the building of *routes*. *Maps* and *browsers* support the acquisition of survey knowledge. [Dill89] reported on using psychological research for hypertext navigation.

The concept presented in this paper relates to the third stage of orientation knowledge. Survey objects are named lists of references to information objects. E.g., frequently used entities like *a list of contents, a list of bookmarked pages* or *a guided tour* are survey objects within the notion of the concept at hand. There are also other lists of references to objects which turn up very naturally in the cognitive world of users working with hypertext systems. E.g. "today's history", which is a list of all objects that have been visited since a certain span of time. Another common candidate to be selected as a survey object is the list of all objects in the hypertext information system that match a given search request for some piece of text. Further examples and reasonable applications are mentioned in part 3 and 4.

$IO = \{N_1,N_2,N_3,.....,N_k\}$	is the set of all objects N_i containing original information in S, where k is the number of these objects in S.
$IS = \{S_1,S_2,S_3,.....,S_l\}$	is the set of all objects S_i containing survey information about IO, where l is the number of these objects in S. Therefore the information system S can be written as a set of objects O_i
$S = IO \cup IS = \{O_1,O_2,O_3,.....,O_n\}$	where $n = k + l$ and $\{O_1,O_2,O_3,.....,O_k\} = \{N_1,N_2,N_3,.....,N_k\}$ $\{O_{k+1},O_2,O_3,.....,O_n\} = \{S_1,S_2,S_3,.....,S_l\}$. Let
L_{ij}	be defined as a link between nodes that allows the user to move from object O_i to O_j. Then an object
O_i	can be defined as an entity consisting of
$Name(O_i),$	a unique identifier in S,
$Info(O_i),$	the actual information of the object including its visual presentation,
$LinkL(O_i) = [L_{ix_1},L_{ix_2},.....,L_{ix_r}],$	a list of links of all outgoing connections from object O_i to other objects in S, where
$LinkO(O_i) = \{O_{x_1},O_{x_2},.....,O_{x_r}\}$	is the set of objects that can be reached from O_i. For reasons of simplicity we first of all assume $\mid LinkO(O_i)\mid$ is equal to # of elements in $LinkL(O_i)^2$. $LinkL(O_i)$ is a list and not a set. In some cases the order of elements is not significant. It is useful then to work with sets only:
$LinkS(O_i) = \{L_{ix_1},L_{ix_2},.....,L_{ix_r}\},$	the set of links listed in $LinkL(O_i)$

Definition 1: A quasi-formal view of objects, links and survey objects

---

[2] This restriction is not absolute (see also conclusion).

The above quasi-formal definition will help to outline the concept. The model presumes some large information system S which is object-oriented in structure. Its objects can be obvious visual representations like cards in a HyperCard application. They could also be any underlying object-oriented data model, which is visible or at least known to the user.

Any object S_i and N_j must have a name by definition. The objects N_i always have an information part $Info(N_i)$, but not necessarily a non-empty list $Link(N_i)$. Survey objects very often will have no information part $Info(S_i)$ and usually a non-empty list $LinkL(S_i)$[3]. Survey objects have links to information objects as well as to other survey objects. Usually $LinkO(N_i) \cap IS = \emptyset$ although some exceptions like general links (e.g. *"back to overview"*) can make sense.

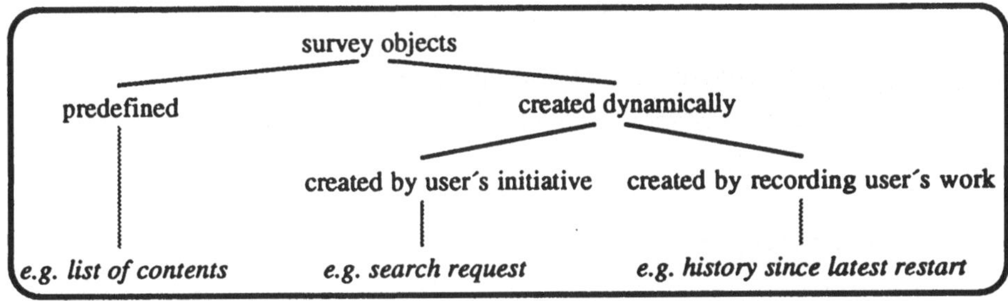

Figure 2: Distinguishing survey objects
according to the initiative of their creation

Survey objects can be predefined. Some of them are already well known. The concept presented, though, is based on the idea of triggering and creating survey objects during user's work and travel through the information system. Survey objects can either be created by user's initiative (e.g. a search request) or by autonomous selection of the system (e.g. recording of the seen objects). Figure 3 illustrates two examples of dynamic creation of survey objects. The user's path from object "Inhalt" to object "Brass Bands" was recorded by the system. The survey object "History" contains the objects

---

[3] Apart from their formal treatment survey objects will have many links to other objects as they are meant to provide an overview on other objects.

visited in the list LinkL("History"). In the second example the user initiated a search for the year "1938". A survey object S was created containing 5 cards as LinkO(S) and Name(S) = "Suche 1938".

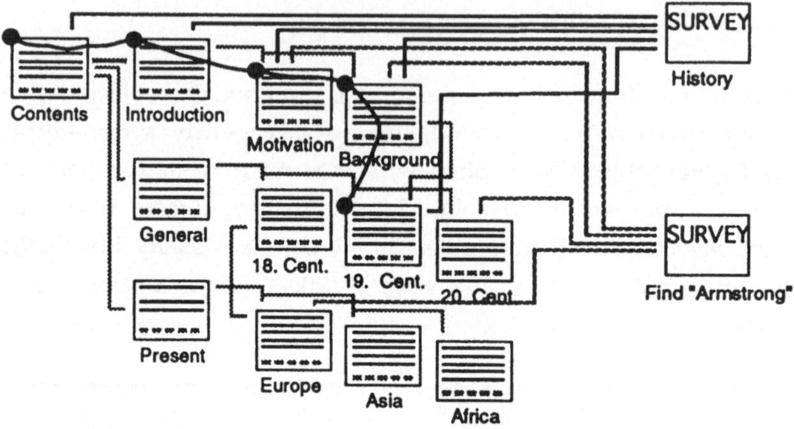

Figure 3: Illustration of two survey objects: *latest history*
and *search request "1938"* in a jazz information system

3) Browsing in survey objects and in objects

In the previous section survey objects were introduced as a concept of selecting, grouping and titling available pieces of information. In the following the use of these objects as means of orientation will be outlined. The suggested activity - providing overview for the user - is browsing in objects and survey objects.

From a general point of view browsing is an exploratory, information-seeking strategy. It is especially appropriate for ill-defined requests or problems and for exploring task domains not sufficiently known (see e.g. [MaSh88]). Browsers are frequently applied for providing an overview on file structures. The most evident benefit from using a browser is the possibility to do fast navigation with a very low cognitive load.

Since hypertext systems have been in use (e.g. the Neptune system, [Conk87]) browsing has been applied. Whenever a user will select a node from a list of node names he/she is shown a list of any link emerging from the node of choice.

By definition survey objects are primarily lists of links. It is therefore evident to introduce them within the browsing of hypertext objects. Survey objects are objects for browsing: in an object that has been created by a search request all found nodes are linked to it. The object *history* is an abstract object linked to all recently visited nodes.

Figure 4 shows a browser using survey objects. It is implemented in a HyperCard application. This facility called Navigåtor is just a conventional browser integrating survey objects in the browser's overview lists. The top list shows objects and survey objects like "Inhalt" (contents), "Heute" (today's history), two search requests and others. The highlighted survey object "Heute" was selected by the user, opening the list of linked objects in the second column which shows all the visited nodes (object "Inhalt" to "Brass Bands"). From these nodes the user selected the object "Motivation". This action opened the list of two objects connected to it.

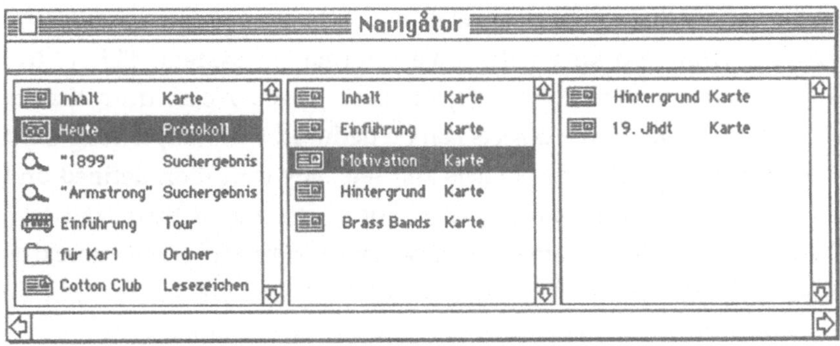

Figure 4: Orientation support by browsing in survey objects

Browsing a survey object S_i in Navigåtor shows the list of names $Name(O_{x_1})$, $Name(O_{x_2}),......,Name(O_{x_r})$ to the user. Together with the name of a survey object type, information is provided in the form of a text and an illustrating icon expressing the object's type of creation. Any object typed as "Karte" (card) can be visualized by pressing a button while browsing. The attempt of visualizing survey objects is ignored by the Navigåtor facility as they do not contain more information than their title and the list of linked objects which is all visual within the browser. Survey objects can be provided with extra information (e.g. a picture), but will then be regarded as conventional information objects, too. As a consequence their type will be changed to "Karte".

According to our experience, users who are familiar with hypertext systems and the idea of browsing can easily grab the extension of survey objects. There are no problems with a "virtuality" of survey objects compared to real information nodes. The objects providing overview are accepted as "natural" entities. In fact this is mainly caused by the fact that they are tightly connected to an action of the user. *Dynamically created* survey objects take their name and contents from user's work. Since *predefined* survey objects are already frequently used objects in hypertext systems, no special introduction will be necessary as these objects relate to familiar metaphors such as the *list of contents*, the *list of bookmarked nodes* or a *guided tour*.[4]

4) Operations on survey objects

A previous part of this article dealt with the deduction of survey objects from user's actions while working with some information system. This is in fact the original source where survey objects come from. Apart from that basic form of creation, new survey objects can be deduced by manipulating existing ones. Due to their acquaintance to lists and sets, any operation defined on lists or sets can be defined on survey objects. For sure some of them will be *l´art pour l´art*. Nevertheless, some are associated directly with typical user intentions (e.g. *the nodes of the request "1938" I have not yet visited.*) some come out from the formal approach only but are of use at least for a group of advanced users.

<table>
<tr><td>

$\lozenge$

$T = S_i \lozenge S_j$

$LinkL(T) = LinkL(S_i) \lozenge LinkL(S_j)$

</td><td>

According to definition 1 we may say that given the binary infix operation on lists, the survey object can be defined by

</td></tr>
</table>

---

[4] It is somehow a matter of academic purity to include the so-called predefined survey objects. The authors never tried to create the impression of having invented the idea of providing overview.

<table>
<tr><td>

$\emptyset$

$T = S_i \; \emptyset \; S_j$

$LinkO(T) = LinkO(S_i) \; \emptyset \; LinkO(S_j)$

</td><td>

Correspondingly we may say that given a binary infix operation

on sets, the survey object can be defined by

Additionally some definition must be given about the order of elements $LinkO(T)$ in $LinkL(T)$.[5]

</td></tr>
</table>

Definition 2: Binary operations on survey objects

For sets and lists it is appropriate to define $Name(T)$ gets the value of a string concatenation $Name(S_i)$, " $\emptyset$ " and $Name(S_j)$, unless a more user-oriented title can be found.

<table>
<tr><td>

S_1

$Name(S_1)$ = "yesterday´s record"

S_2

$Name(S_2)$ = "today´s record"

$\cap$

$T = S_1 \cap S_2$

$Name(T)$ = "yesterday´s record $\cap$ today´s record"[6]

$LinkO(T) = LinkO(S_1) \cap LinkO(S_2)$

</td><td>

For example let

be a survey object with linked to all nodes a user has visited the day before today. Let

be a survey object with linked to all nodes the same user has visited today.

be the operation of intersection on sets, then

is a survey object with

T is a new survey object referencing all nodes a user has seen yesterday as well as today.

</td></tr>
</table>

Definition 3: Intersecting survey objects

The intentional background of the example in definition 3 might be some hazy notion of *"I look for a piece of information in a node whose title and*

---

[5] A reasonable default ordering is to take over the sequence of elements in S_i and S_j. If an element of T is in S_i and S_j then it shall take over its relative position from S_i.

[6] In fact a name like "seen yesterday and today" would be a more userfriendly identification. More appropriate object titles can be produced for standardized operations only. Or they must be entered by the user him-/herself.

location I have forgotten. But I know, I have been there yesterday and today already".

Figure 5 shows the implementation of survey object operations in Navigåtor. 4 basic set operations are provided to the user in a pull-down menu. The actual example shows a scene in which the user has selected today's protocol and the search request "1899". These two objects are connected by the operation of difference between sets. The user's underlying intention in this case is to get a list of all objects contained in his/her request which he/she has not yet looked at. Navigåtor provides the resulting survey objects with the according icon shown in the pull-down menu (see entry before last in fig. 5).

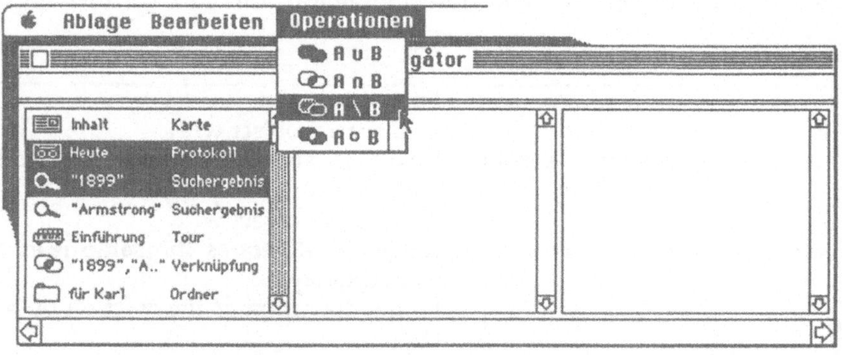

Figure 5: Illustration of an operation on survey objects
"All objects concerning "1899" which I have not yet seen"

Moreover there is the possibility of applying results from survey object operations as operants for operations. Two simple unary operations on lists obviously are of use. One is a cut from a given survey object link list from a certain object (e.g. from/to a certain object). The other one is chronologic cuts like "all objects since a certain time span". The more general facility of editing a link list is useful and reasonable. It can be used e.g. for defining a private tour or a personal guided tour for a special user group.

In any case mathematical or highly abstract operations on sets or lists will not be of use for casual users of hypertext systems. For this group of users the facility of combining survey objects should be presented as an extra suitable only for advanced users. Or it should be available as a limited number of standardized commands, predefined operations which correspond directly to common needs of users (the examples in figure 5 show operations of that kind).

5) Conclusion

The idea of the presented paper is close to a common concept in computer science: The transforming of procedural information into declarative information[7]. Survey objects are a declarative form of information. They represent a titled selection of objects in a hypertext system. These selections have an evident meaning to the user as they are mainly derived from his/her actions.

We are currently working on an evaluation within two different domains testing the effectiveness, acceptance and performance of the concepts presented as means of.navigation support.

In this paper we described the structure and creation of survey objects, showed their use for overview in a browser, discussed a reasonable application of manipulating them and implemented a prototype in a HyperCard application. The concept of survey objects fits best but is not limited to information systems with a homogeneous object-oriented structure. In fact, implementing and working with the prototype brought to mind a variety of interesting questions to be investigated upon:

- In part 2 we defined survey objects to contain a Link L_{ij} only once in $LinkL(S_i)$ for reasons of simplicity. There are scenarios for which this limitation is too restrictive, e.g., in chronologic recording of objects visited. Thus, allowing cycles in survey objects will need a clear solution to the problem of presentation.
- By definition survey objects can have links to other survey objects. Reasonable structures can be defined in which cycles appear in object hierarchy. Therefore, while browsing deeper, the user might come back to his/her start. The obvious restriction is to prohibit further browsing into depth at this point. Nevertheless, the more extras are provided in the browser, the more it becomes a travelling

---

[7] compare e.g. procedure vs. data driven programming, or the procedural vs. declarative knowledge paradigm in AI.

tool in itself or even a data retrieval tool (see part 4). In that case a prohibition in browsing cycles might become inconvenient.

- There are cases in which it is unclear whether a survey object shall become a member of an actually recorded history list or not. E.g., if the user starts some search request, it will be convenient to add the resulting survey object to the record. If he/she is browsing through yesterday's record, it might be convenient not to add nodes visited as the user might have done it just to find a specific piece of information. It is necessary to find reasonable limitations for recording to history lists, such as cards being by default not added if they are looked at during a browsing session. Or such as cards being added only, if they are visited for a certain span of time. As another possibility of limitation recording could be parametrized by the user. Obviously survey objects must be editable.

- Survey objects have to provide overview and must not be endless lists of rubbish, they shall not provide an information overkill. Not all the actions, not all the search requests should lead to a permanent survey object. In a practical application user's decisions and domain-specific characteristics have to be applied to reduce a list of objects to valuable survey knowledge.

- We had a strange feeling in the beginning caused by the fact that entities being cognitively as different as intersections of *search requests, daily histories* and *guided tours* are covered by one and only one object type. Having made first evaluations, though, we are confident about the basic principle in the approach as all the evaluated examples have one thing in common: they are primarily lists of references to information objects. However, information on the origin of a survey object is important. The examples in this paper refer to survey object types whose type is somehow generic. Apart from that, defining types of survey objects as well as their detailed semantic description is a domain specific task.

The concept implemented in Navigåtor is for sure not the ultimate solution to the *"lost-in-hyperspace" problem*. It is, though, a promising facility of very simple and natural structure for users' navigation which can be easily attached to a variety of hypertext systems.

Bibliography

[Aksc88]   R. Akscyn, D.L. McCracken, and E. Yoder, "KMS: A Distributed Hypermedia System for Managing Knowledge in Organisations", Commun. ACM, vol. 31, no. 7, July 1988, pp. 820-835.

[BeWa90]   D. V. Beard, J. Q. Walker II, "Navigational techniques to improve the display of large two-dimensional spaces." In Behavior & Information Technology, 1990, vol. 9, no. 6, pp. 451-466.

[Brow89]   P.J. Brown, "Hypertext: Dreams and reality", Proc. of the Hypermedia/ Hypertext and Object Oriented Databases Seminar, Brunel University, London 1989

[Conk87]   J. Conklin, "Hypertext: A survey and introduction." IEEE Computer, vol. 20, no. 9, September 1987, pp. 17-40.

[CoSt92]   R. Cordes, N. Streitz (eds.), "Hypertext und Hypermedia 1992 - Konzepte und Anwendungen auf dem Weg in die Praxis", Springer Berlin 1992

[Deli86]   N. Delisle, M. Schwartz, "Neptune: A hypertext system for CAD applications." In Proceedings ACM SIGMOD '86, May 1986, pp. 132-142.

[Dill90]   A. Dillon, C. McKnight, J. Richardson, "Navigation in hypertext: A critical review of the concept", Proc. Interact 90 3rd IFIP HCI Conference, Cambridge U.K. 1990

[Fair88]   K. Fairchild, S. Poltrock, and G. Furnas. "Semnet: Three- dimensional graphic representetions of large knowledge bases." In Cognitive Science and its Applications for Human-Computer Interaction, R. Guindon, Ed. Lawrence Erlbaum Associates, Hillsdale, N.J., 1988.

[Foss89]   C. L. Foss, "Tools for reading and browsing hypertext", Information Processing and Management, vol. 25, no. 4, 1989, pp. 407-418.

[Furn86]   G. Furnas. "Generalized fish-eye views." In Proceedings of the 1986 ACM Conference of Human Factors in Computing Systems, CHI '86, April 1986, pp. 16-23.

[Garr86]   N. Garrett, K. Smith, N. Merowitz, "Intermedia: Issues, strategies, and tactics in the design of a hypermedia documenr system." In Proceedings of the Conference on Computer Supported Cooperative Work, December 1986, pp. 163-174.

[Hala87]   F. Halasz, T. Moran, R. Trigg, "Notecards in a Nutshell." In Proceedings of the 1987 ACM Conference of Human Factors in Computer Systems, CHI+GI '87, April 1987, pp. 45-52.

[HaAl88]   N. Hammond, L. Allison, "Travels around a learning support environment: Rambling, orienteering or touring?", Proc. of ACM CHI'88, Washington DC, pp. 269-273

[Hann92]   J. Hannemann, M. Thüring, N. Friedrich, "Hyperdocuments as user interfaces: Exploring a browsing semantic for coherent hyperdocuments", in [CoSt92], pp. 87-102

[McKn91]   C. McKnight, A. Dillon, J. Richardson, "Hypertext in Context", Cambridge University Press 1991

[MaSh88]   Marchionini G., Shneiderman B., "Finding Facts vs. Browsing Knowledge in Hypertext Systems", IEEE Computer, vol. 15, no. 6, 1988, pp. 70-80.

[Niel90]   J. Nielson, "Hypertext and Hypermedia", Academic Press, New York 1990

[ThHa82]   Thorndyke P., Hayes-Roth B., "Differences in Spatial Knowledge Acquired from Maps and Navigation", Journal for Cognitive Psychology, Nr. 14, 1982, pp. 560-589

[vanD88]   A. van Dam, "Hypertext '87 Keynote Address." In Commun. ACM, vol. 31, no. 7, July 1988, pp. 887-895.

Strait-Jacketing Authors:
User Interface Consistency in Large-Scale Hypermedia Systems

Keith Andrews and Frank Kappe

Institute for Information Processing and Computer Supported New Media (IICM),
Graz University of Technology,
Austria.

Abstract. This paper examines the issue of user interface consistency in large-scale, multi-author hypermedia systems. Many existing systems allow the author full control of both information content and the user interface. Previous experience uncovered consistency problems when a large number of different authors were given such control. The solution proposed is to "strait-jacket" authors: to restrict their role to the provision of information only. The flexibility taken away from the author can be granted to the user by offering a choice of configurable user interface metaphors.

A short survey of the approaches taken by existing systems is followed by a proposal for a multi-metaphor distributed system where information content and user interface policy are strictly separated. The paper concludes with an outline of its implementation as part of the Hyper-G project, a general-purpose, large-scale, multi-user hypermedia system currently under development at Graz University of Technology. To our knowledge, this is the only system designed to support such multi-metaphor use.

1   Introduction

As hypermedia systems become larger, more dynamic, and possibly distributed, it becomes impossible for a single author to create and maintain the entire hyperweb of information. Provision for multiple authors necessitates some kind of consistent user interface policy.

Previous experience with a large database of instructional material[1] created by a large number of different authors revealed the difficulty of providing consistent "look-and-feel" across a large multi-author system. Authors were given a powerful editing tool that would let them exploit the full flexibility of the execution system in designing their lessons. As a consequence, many authors created lessons with complicated structure, confusing and inconsistent user interfaces,

---

[1] About 500 one-hour COSTOC[10] lessons covering topics ranging from medicine, ecology, and natural sciences to computer science were prepared by experts in the field in the years 1986-90. They are now used by some 25 universities throughout the world, mainly on PCs, but other execution platforms are also available.

and strange colour combinations that were unreadable on some monitors. We drew the following conclusions from that project:

- Authors should be experts in the field of the lesson to be authored. They can not generally be considered good at designing user interfaces.
- With 100 authors there would exist about 110 slightly different user interfaces (some authors will even change their metaphor in the middle of a lesson), some of them excellent, some of them poor. From the user's point of view it would be better to have a good or only average user interface, if at least it were *consistent* across all lessons.
- Authoring tools should allow the author to edit the information content (i.e. *what* is presented) and not the user interface (*how* it is presented). Also, the structure of information (the web in hypermedia terms) should be restricted to a certain set of layouts in order not to confuse the user.
- On the other hand, the flexibility taken away from the author can be granted to the user. The user can be given control of how information is presented, for example by being able to choose from a set of different user interface metaphors.

The above observations apply to more general hypermedia systems, especially large-scale systems, where there will be a large number of authors. They suggest that authors should be restricted in their freedom to influence the user interface and forced to concentrate on providing information content — hence the analogy of a strait-jacket for authors.

2 Existing Systems

The most successful systems for creating small, stand-alone hypermedia applications, such as HyperCard[4], ToolBook[3], and their relatives use the "frame-based" approach, where information is presented in chunks ("frames") that consist of several layers with active areas ("buttons") on them. Figure 1 shows a screen dump from ToolBook explaining the construction of ToolBook pages; a similar example of a HyperCard frame can be found in Nielsen's book[12].

Activating a button executes a script which has to be provided by the author. The script may just invoke another frame or do something more complex (e.g. execute an animation sequence). In general, the author has full control of both the information content and the user interface of a frame (actually of almost every pixel on the screen), which leads to the problems identified before. Also, the frame-based nature makes it difficult to change the information content of the frame at a later date (e.g. to insert a sentence or an image). These systems not only allow authors to customise the user interface, they *require* them to do so. The result is that there is no agreed standard approach on how to write and use a HyperCard stack or a ToolBook book.

The trend away from absolute author control can be observed in the HyTime [11] standardisation effort, where generic tagging allows formatting according to style sheets read by the application.

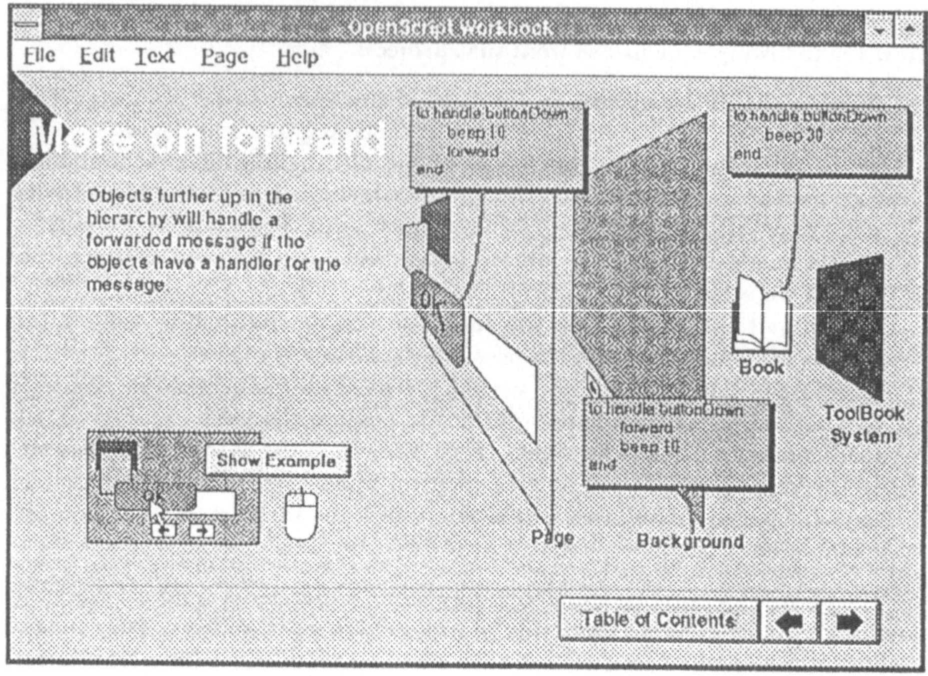

Fig. 1. Frame-Based Approach in ToolBook

On the other side of the spectrum, systems such as NoteCards[5], Guide[15], and Hyperties[13] allow the author little or no direct influence over the user interface. Having seen one document of a particular type, users know how to interact with any document of that type. These systems conform to our notion of a strait-jacket for authors, but unfortunately also strait-jacket users, who are tied to a single "hard-wired" user interface metaphor.

3 A Multi-Metaphor, Distributed Hypermedia System

As is apparent from the preceding discussion, we advocate the strict separation of information content from user interface policy, with provision for user configuration. The author's role is restricted to that of information provider: he/she provides pieces of text, drawings, images, sound clips, film clips, etc. from his/her knowledge domain (in one of an agreed set of formats or structures) and specifies anchoring and linkage between them. The issues of whether anchor and link information should be embedded within a document or stored separately, and how much markup should be allowed within documents generally, go beyond the scope of this paper. The main point here is that user interface decisions (such as choice of colours and fonts for text, placement of buttons, how and when to display anchors, etc.) should be moved out of the realm of the author. Such decisions are properly made by user interface specialists and by user configuration settings[2].

The use of an agreed set of standard formats, free of user interface specifications, makes the sharing of hypermedia data across computer networks much easier. One or more hypermedia databases can be accessed by one or more user interfaces in a transparent way. Whether the information is stored in a local database or fetched from the other side of the world, it looks the same to any particular user interface. Many different user interface metaphors can be implemented, all of them using the same database functionality.

This leads intuitively to the notion of partitioning a distributed hypermedia system into servers that provide access methods to information (which we will call *hypermedia engines*) and clients that manage the user interface (called *viewers*). Typically, hypermedia engines and viewers are connected by a local area network, as shown in Fig. 2.

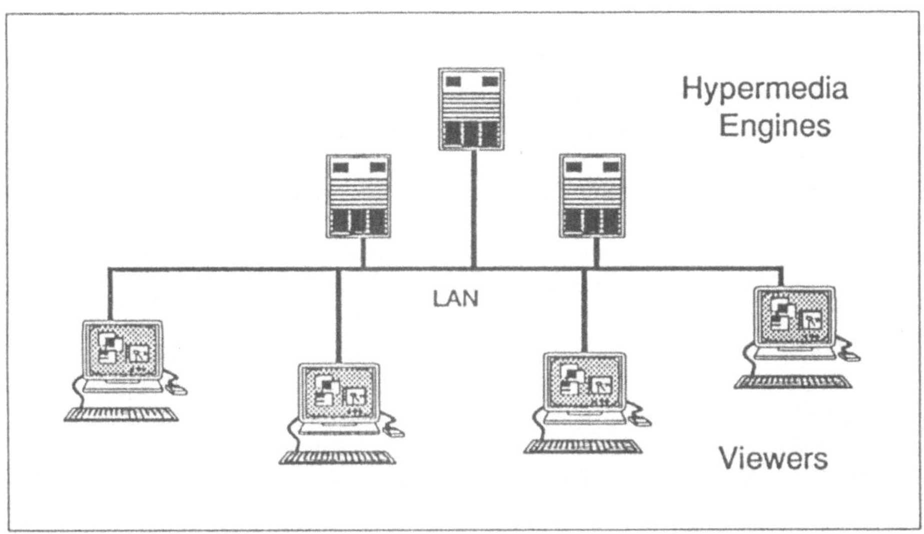

Fig. 2. Hypermedia Engines and Viewers

From a user interface designer's point of view, the concept of hypermedia engines and viewers also offers advantages:

- The local intelligence of the end user's terminal can be utilised for things like cursor movement, scrolling, entering keywords and searching through a document. This spreads processing load more widely, unburdening the server and allowing multi-user access with reasonable performance.

---

[2] Clearly, this approach means authors will have less control over how users finally perceive their data. However, we believe the benefits of consistency in large, multi-author hypermedia systems outweigh the loss in creative freedom for authors.

- Viewers make use of all the features of the user's hardware and software environment (such as windows, icons, pointing devices, bitmapped graphics, sound, ...).
- Viewers can be implemented for a number of platforms (e.g. PC, MacIntosh, NeXT, UNIX/X-Windows), using the typical look-and-feel of that platform (e.g. MS Windows, Mac Finder, NeXTStep, Motif).
- It is easy to export data from a viewer to other software (e.g. text processor) by means of a clipboard.
- Multiple viewers offer a range of user interface metaphors, such as the well-known *desktop* metaphor first seen on the Xerox Star [7] and the Apple Macintosh, HyperCard's *stack* metaphor[16], or the *book*[1], *holiday travel*[6] and *library*[2] metaphors.
- User interface metaphors can be adapted to the needs and preferences of different users. In addition, the users themselves might be allowed to choose from a set of user interface metaphors and to configure some of the parameters of the user interface, such as:
  - The system entry point.
  - A language preference.
  - Preference of short, medium or long versions of semantically equivalent text documents.
  - Preference of digitised voice documents or semantically equivalent text documents.
  - A list of preferred document viewers for each document type.
  - Parameters describing the visual appearance of the user interface (e.g. window positions and sizes, colours, window manager behaviour etc.).
- Different types of user may require not only different metaphors, but also different user interface devices. For example, a museum visitor will probably be best served with touch screens and speech output, while a scientist will probably prefer a computer keyboard and a mouse.
- Different viewers can be implemented independently of each other.

4   The Engine/Viewer Concept in Hyper-G

Hyper-G[8] is an ambitious, general-purpose, large-scale, multi-user hypermedia system currently under development at Graz University of Technology. In Hyper-G, information nodes and links are stored in separate, distinct databases. *Link servers* and *file servers* accessing these databases take the role of hypermedia engines. The role of a viewer is embodied by a session manager, which provides core functionality (user preferences, undo/redo, annotation, navigation aids, etc.) and a set of *document viewers*, which display individual documents of a specific type (e.g. text, 2D drawing, raster image, sound, etc.). This architecture is illustrated in Fig. 3.

Multiple document viewers may be provided for a single document type, allowing the user a choice of which document viewer to use. This preference is stored in a configuration file and read by the session manager on start-up.

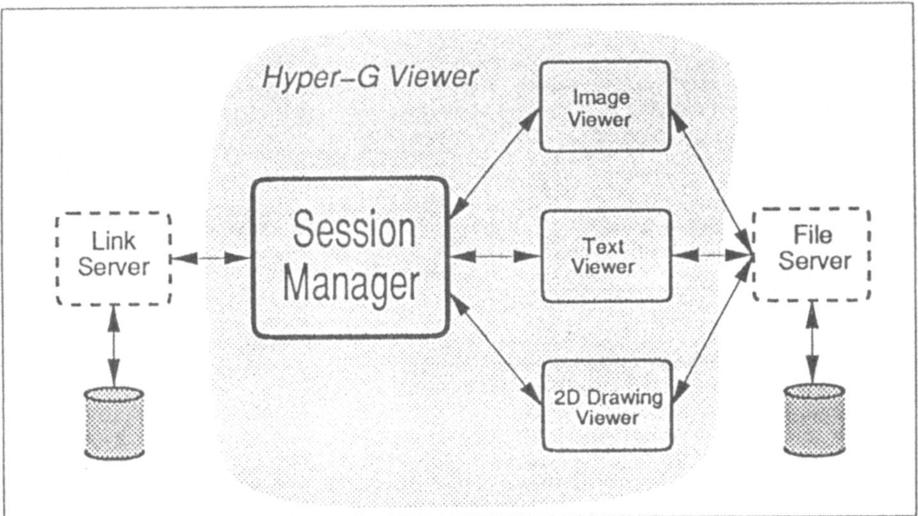

Fig. 3. Hyper-G Architecture

Both the session manager and the various document viewers enforce an internal boundary between functionality and user interface, as shown in Fig. 4. A number of differing user interfaces can be "bolted" onto the same base functionality. The net result is a multi-metaphor, user-configurable, distributed hypermedia system. To our knowledge, Hyper-G is the only system designed to support multi-metaphor use.

Hyper-G's hypermedia engine was developed in C++ [14] on UNIX workstations. In addition, there exists a sophisticated text-only interface for VT100-like terminals. Currently, user interfaces are under development for PC-compatibles under MS-Windows, UNIX workstations under X Windows (using the Inter-Views [9] toolkit) and NeXT machines under NeXTstep. We intend to use these as a base to implement and evaluate a variety of user interface metaphors.

5 Summary

We have looked at some of the consistency problems which arise in a large-scale multi-author hypermedia system, when authors are given control over the user interface as well as information content. Many existing hypermedia systems grant the author such control.

We advocate the strict separation of information content from user interface, in order to achieve consistency. Authors should be responsible for information content, user interface specialists for the user interface. We also propose the provision of a number of exchangeable, configurable user interface metaphors, thus transferring the power of choice from the author to the user.

The multi-metaphor, distributed hypermedia system proposed here offers an

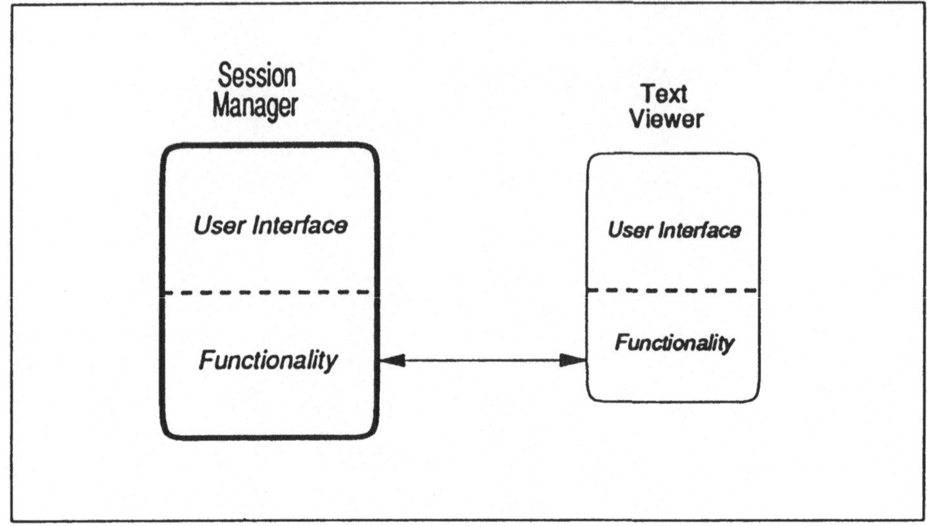

Fig. 4. The Separation of Functionality from User Interface in Hyper-G

elegant solution. Such a system, Hyper-G, is now under development at Graz University of Technology.

References

1. BENEST I. D.: "A Hypertext System with Controlled Hype". In *Proc. of the Hypertext II Conference, York*, 1989.

2. DAVIES G., MAURER H., and PREECE J.: "Presentation Metaphors for Very Large Hypermedia Systems". *Journal of Microcomputer Applications*, 14(2):105–116, April 1991.

3. DUNCAN R.: "An introduction to building applications with ToolBook". *PC Magazine*, 9(21):493–497, December 1990.

4. GOODMAN D.: *The Complete HyperCard Handbook*. Bantam, New York, 1987.

5. HALASZ F. G.: "Reflections on NoteCards: Seven Issues for the Next Generation of Hypermedia Systems". *Communications of the ACM*, 31(7):836–852, July 1988.

6. HAMMOND N. and ALLISON L.: "The Travel Metaphor as Design Principle and Training Aid for Navigating Around Complex Systems". In DIAPER D. and WINDER R. (editors), *People and Computers III*, Cambridge University Press, 1987.

7. JOHNSON J., ROBERTS T. L., VERPLANK W., SMITH D. C., IRBY C., BEARD M., and MACKEY K.: "The Xerox Star: A Retrospective". *IEEE Computer*, 22(9):11–26, September 1989.

8. KAPPE F., MAURER H., and SHERBAKOV N.: "Hyper-G – A Universal Hypermedia System". *To appear in: Journal of Educational Multimedia and Hypermedia*.

9. LINTON M. A., VLISSIDES J. M., and CALDER P. R.: "Composing User Interfaces with InterViews". *IEEE Computer*, 22(2):8–22, February 1989.

10. MAKEDON F. and MAURER H.: "COSTOC – Computer Supported Teaching of Computer Science". In *Proc. IFIP Conference on Teleteaching, Budapest*, pages 107–119, North Holland Publ. Co., Amsterdam, 1988.

11. NEWCOMB S. R., KIPP N. A., and NEWCOMB V. T.: "The HyTime Hypermedia/Time-based Document Structuring Language". *Communications of the ACM*, 34(11):67–83, November 1991.

12. NIELSEN J.: *Hypertext & Hypermedia*. Academic Press, San Diego, CA, 1990.

13. SHNEIDERMAN B.: "User Interface Design for the Hyperties Electronic Encyclopedia". In *Proc. of Hypertext '87, TR88-013*, pages 199–205, University of North Carolina, Dept. of Computer Science, March 1988.

14. STROUSTRUP B.: *The C++ Programming Language*. Addison-Wesley, Reading, Massachusetts, second edition, 1991.

15. WEISS-FERSKO H.: "Guide. (OWL International Inc.'s Guide 3.01 – Software Review)". *PC Magazine*, 10(10):257–259, May 1991.

16. WILLIAMS G.: "HyperCard". *Byte*, 12(14):109–117, December 1987.

Audiodokumente in Hypermedia-Informationssystemen

Ulrike Glavitsch, Daniel Knaus, Jörg Rentsch
Eidgenössische Technische Hochschule (ETH)
Institut für Informationssysteme
CH-8092 Zürich

Audiodokumente werden in zukünftige Hypermedia-Informationssysteme integriert sein. In diesem Artikel stellen wir zwei neue Operationen auf Sprachdokumenten vor: Positionieren und Retrieval von Sprachdokumenten. Beim Positionieren gibt der Benutzer ein beliebiges Suchmuster als Text- oder Sprachsequenz an. Das Positionierverfahren liefert darauf eine Liste derjeniger Positionen im Sprachdokument, die am besten mit dem Suchmuster übereinstimmen. Das Information Retrieval System ermittelt zu einer gegebenen Anfrage und einer gegebenen Dokumentenkollektion die zur Anfrage ähnlichen Dokumente. Die Dokumentenkollektion kann sowohl Text- als auch Sprachdokumente enthalten. Die den beiden Operationen zugrunde liegende Indexierungsmethode ist imstande, sowohl Texte als auch Sprachdokumente zu indexieren.

1. Einleitung

In zukünftigen *Hypermedia-Informationssystemen* werden die Daten in Form von Texten, Bildern und Audiodokumenten abgelegt sein. Ein Benutzer eines solchen Systems spezifiziert eine Anfrage, worauf ihm das Informationssystem eine Reihe von Dokumenten zurückgibt, die die Anfrage befriedigen sollen. Die Antwortmenge kann dabei Dokumente der verschiedenen Medientypen enthalten.

Audio ist eine Medienklasse, welche alles hörbare wie Geräusche, gesprochene Sprache, Musik usw. umfasst. *Audiodokumente* sind Sequenzen abgetasteter und quantisierter analoger Signale im hörbaren Bereich. Wir befassen uns in diesem Artikel mit einer speziellen Klasse von Audiodokumenten, nämlich mit solchen, die *gesprochene Sprache* enthalten. Solche Audiodokumente nennen wir künftig *Sprachdokumente (speech documents)*.

Sprachdokumente werden bis heute vorwiegend als digitalisierte Tonbandaufnahmen betrachtet und funktionell entsprechend behandelt, z.B. (Schmandt & McKenna, 1988). Das heisst, die einzigen Operationen sind Aufnehmen, Abspielen, Löschen und Kopieren von Sprachdokumenten. Oft stehen einige Editiermöglichkeiten zur Verfügung, die in Analogie zum Schneiden von Tonbändern stehen. Schliesslich werden Sprachdokumente wie gewöhnliche Dateien verwaltet.

Mit den obigen Operationen lässt sich nichts über den Inhalt von Sprachdokumenten aussagen. Suchoperationen und Information Retrieval auf Sprachdokumenten sind somit nicht möglich. Die Verfügbarkeit dieser Operationen würde jedoch die Brauchbarkeit von Sprachdokumenten in Hypermedia-Informationssystemen erhöhen.

Suchmethoden sind vorallem für Texte entwickelt worden. Bekannt sind der Algorithmus von Boyer und Moore (1977) und der Algorithmus von Aho und Corasick (1975), die nach bestimmten Zeichenfolgen in einem Text suchen. Neben den Suchmethoden, wo nach eindeutig bestimmten Zeichenketten gesucht wird, sind einige Algorithmen mit vagen Suchkriterien bekannt. Willett (1992) hat Methoden beschrieben, wie in englischen Texten aus dem 17. Jahrhundert nach Wörtern, die ähnlich zu einem Wort in modernem Englisch sind, gesucht werden kann. Gonnet und Baeza-Yates (1992) haben mit ihrem "All-Against-All Matching" eine Methode präsentiert, mit der man zu einem gegebenen Suchmuster alle ähnlichen Sequenzen innerhalb eines Texts findet. Der Befehl "agrep" (approximate grep) - ein Software Paket für Unix - erlaubt dem Benutzer, die möglichen Abweichungen zwischen Suchmuster und Textstelle selbst anzugeben (Wu & Manber, 1992).

Das Suchen auf Sprachdokumenten wurde bisher wenig untersucht. Heute existieren einige "Wordspotting" Systeme, mit denen man nach gewissen Stellen in Sprachdokumenten suchen kann. Mit den Systemen von Rose and Paul (1990) und von Wilpon, Rabiner, Lee und Goldrain (1990) ist es möglich, verschiedene Schlüsselwörter in einem Sprachdokument zu finden. Im "Wordspotting" System von Wilcox und Bush (1990) kann man eine beliebige Sequenz aus einem Sprachdokument als Suchmuster angeben.

Die Methoden des Text-Retrievals sind seit längerem bekannt (Salton & Buckley, 1988) (Salton & Buckley, 1990). Unseres Wissens gibt es keine Forschungsgruppe, die sich mit Information Retrieval auf Sprachdokumenten befasst. Es existieren jedoch Systeme, welche Sprachdokumente gegebenen Themenklassen zuordnen (Rose, 1991) (Rose, Chang, Lippmann, 1991).

In diesem Artikel präsentieren wir eine neue Suchmethode für Sprachdokumente, die wir als *Positionieren* von Sprachdokumenten bezeichnen. Unter *Positionieren* verstehen wir das rasche Auffinden und Anzeigen einer beliebigen Stelle in einem Sprachdokument. Die gesuchte Stelle kann dabei als Text oder als Sprachsequenz eingegeben werden. Ausserdem stellen wir ein *Retrieval System* für Sprach- und Textdokumente vor. Sowohl das Positionierverfahren als auch das Retrieval System basieren auf einer speziellen *Indexierungsmethode*. Diese Indexierungsmethode ist auch auf Texte übertragbar.

Im folgenden Abschnitt werden automatische Spracherkennungsmethoden vorgestellt. In Abschnitt 3 präsentieren wir die Indexierungsmethode für Sprachdokumente. Der neue Ansatz des Positionierens wird in Abschnitt 4 vorgestellt. Abschnitt 5 beschreibt einen Prototypen des Retrieval Systems auf Sprachdokumenten. Schliesslich ziehen wir in Abschnitt 6 die Schlussfolgerungen.

2. Spracherkennungsmethoden

Suchmethoden und Information Retrieval auf Sprachdokumenten erfordern eine Spracherkennungskomponente. In diesem Abschnitt geben wir eine Zusammefassung von automatischer Spracherkennung, um das Verständnis des Abschnitts über die automatische Indexierung von Sprachdokumenten zu erleichtern.

Eine Spracherkennungskomponente setzt sich aus zwei Teilen zusammen, aus der Verarbeitung des Sprachsignals und der Komponente zur Modellierung der zu erkennenden Einheiten (Worte, Phrasen, Unterworteinheiten). Für beide Teile gibt es standardisierte Verfahren.

Durch die Signalverarbeitung wird das digitalisierte Sprachsignal in eine Serie von Vektor Codes transformiert. Grob gesagt, entspricht ein Vektor Code einer Stellung des Vokaltrakts, der während einer kurzen Zeitdauer (ca. 10 ms) stabil ist. Ferner führt die Signalverarbeitung zu einer Kompression der Daten um einen Faktor 160 - 600.

Bei der Modellierung von Spracheinheiten (Worten, Phrasen, Unterworteinheiten) sind Hidden Markov Modelle (HMM) (Rabiner, 1988) zu einem Standard geworden. Hidden Markov Modelle sind stochastische Modelle. Sie sind durch eine Menge von Zuständen, einem Ausgabealphabet, einer Menge von Übergangswahrscheinlichkeiten und einer Menge von Ausgabewahrscheinlichkeiten definiert. In der Spracherkennung entspricht das Ausgabealphabet der Menge verschiedener Vektor Codes. Für jedes Paar von Zuständen ist eine Übergangswahrscheinlichkeit und ein Vektor von Ausgabewahrscheinlichkeiten definiert. Fig. 1 zeigt das Hidden Markov Modell eines Phonems (Laut), wie es im Spracherkennungssystem SPHINX (Lee, 1989) verwendet wurde. Die Zustände sind durch Kreise gekennzeichnet. Ein Pfeil zwischen zwei Zuständen gibt eine positive Übergangswahrscheinlichkeit an.

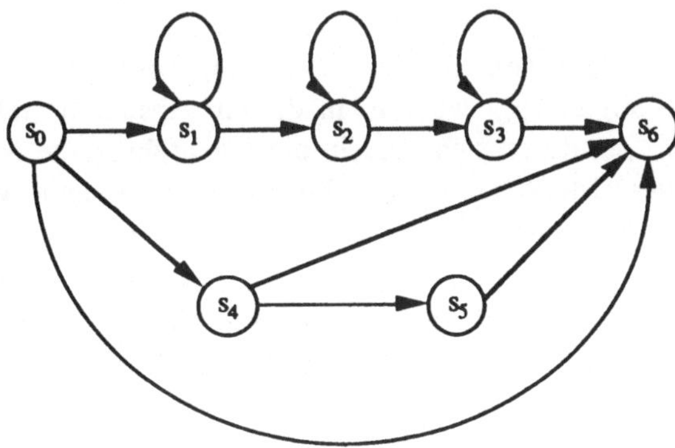

Fig. 1: Hidden Markov Modell eines Phonems (ohne Übergangs- und
Ausgabewahrscheinlichkeiten)

Die Parameter der Hidden Markov Modelle (Übergangswahrscheinlichkeiten, Ausgabewahrscheinlichkeiten) werden durch ein Trainingsverfahren (Baum-Welch
Algorithmus) (Rabiner, 1988) bestimmt. Dazu benötigt das Verfahren Trainingsse-
quenzen, in denen die zu erkennende Spracheinheit gesprochen ist. Je mehr Trainingsdaten vorhanden sind, umso besser können die Parameter des Modells bestimmt
werden.

Für die Erkennung von Spracheinheiten stehen verschiedene Algorithmen zur Verfügung. Der Vorwärts-Algorithmus (Rabiner, 1988) wird für isolierte Worterkennung
verwendet. Der Viterbi-Algorithmus (Rabiner, 1988) eignet sich für die Erkennung
von Spracheinheiten in fliessend gesprochenem Text. Der Viterbi Algorithmus
berechnet für eine gegebene Ausgabesequenz die wahrscheinlichste Zustandssequenz
durch ein gegebenes Markov Modell. In (Wilcox & Bush, 1991) ist ausserdem eine
Variante des Vorwärts-Algorithmus beschrieben, mit der man ebenfalls Spracheinheiten in fliessend gesprochenem Text erkennt.

Mit den heutigen Spracherkennungsmethoden ist es möglich, kleine, einsilbige oder
zweisilbige Worte in fliessend gesprochenem Text zu erkennen (Wilcox & Bush,
1991).

3. Indexierung von Sprach- und Textdokumenten

Sowohl das neuartige Positionierverfahren für Sprachdokumente als auch das
Retrieval System für Sprach- und Textdokumente verwenden indexierte Dokumente.
Indexierungsmethoden für Texte sind aus dem Gebiet Information Retrieval bekannt.
Eine Indexierungsmethode liefert eine automatische Beschreibung eines Dokuments

mittels geeigneter Merkmale (Indexierungsmerkmale). Indexierungsmerkmale für Texte bestehen meist aus Termen, die durch Anwendung eines Reduktionsalgorithmus (Porter, 1980) erzeugt wurden. In diesem Abschnitt stellen wir Indexierungsmerkmale vor, mit denen sich Sprach- und Textdokumente beschreiben lassen. Wir zeigen, wie diese Merkmale in Sprachdokumenten erkannt werden und geben die Form indexierter Dokumente für beide Medientypen an.

An Indexierungsmerkmale für Sprachdokumente stellen wir die folgenden vier Bedingungen, die bereits in (Glavitsch & Schäuble, 1992) beschrieben wurden:

1. Indexierungsmerkmale für Sprachdokumente sollen phonetische Einheiten sein, welche durch Spracherkennungsmethoden leicht zu erkennen sind.
2. Die Anzahl veschiedener Merkmale soll möglichst klein sein, denn die Spracherkennungsmethode benötigt für jedes Merkmal ein Hidden Markov Modell, welches vorgängig trainiert werden muss. Die Aufbereitung der Trainingsdaten ist ein manueller Prozess und deswegen sehr zeitaufwendig.
3. Die Merkmale sollen gut diskriminieren, d.h. sie sollen die Fähigkeit, Dokumente voneinander zu unterscheiden möglichst erhöhen.
4. Die Kollektionshäufigkeit der Indexierungsmerkmale sollte nicht zu klein sein, damit genügend Trainingsdaten zur Verfügung stehen.

Unter den Merkmalskandidaten befinden sich beispielsweise Phoneme, Biphone, Triphone, Wörter und Phrasen. Worte und Phrasen erfüllen zwar die erste Bedingung ganz und die dritte und vierte teilweise, aber die zweite Bedingung überhaupt nicht. Phoneme hingegen genügen Bedingungen 2 und 4, nicht aber 1 und 3. Wörter scheinen also zu grosse, Phoneme zu kleine Einheiten zu sein. Teufels (1989) Experimente mit Unterworteinheiten (genau: Trigramme) zeigten, dass von den 26^3 = 17576 möglichen Trigrammen in der INSPEC-Kollektion bloss 26% auftreten, und erst noch 60% davon in weniger als 1% aller Dokumente. Dies bewog uns zur folgenden Auswahl von Indexierungsmerkmalen für Sprachdokumente.

Wir wählen die Indexierungsmerkmale aus der Menge aller Unterworteinheiten, die mit einer Vokalgruppe (V) beginnen, von einer Konsonantengruppe (C) gefolgt sind und mit einer weiteren Vokalgruppe (V) aufhören. Wir bezeichnen mit einer Vokalgruppe eine maximale Folge von Vokalen und mit einer Konsonantengruppe eine maximale Folge von Konsonanten innerhalb desselben Wortes. Wir verlangen zudem, dass die Merkmalskandidaten VCV im gleichen Wort vorkommen. Beispiel 1 zeigt einen Satz einer Radionachricht mit allen in ihm enthaltenen Merkmalskandidaten. Aus dem Beispiel geht hervor, dass die gewählten Merkmale auch auf Texte anwendbar sind.

Beispiel 1:

Die neue französische Premierministerin Edith Cresson hat in ihrer Regierungser-
klärung ...

anzö | ösi | ische | emie | iermi | ini | iste | eri | edi | esso | ihre | egie | ieru | ungse |
erklä | äru ...

Ein Indexierungsmerkmal ϕ_i für Sprachdokumente ist nun eine Gruppierung VCV,
dessen Diskriminationswert grösser als ein gewisser Schwellwert ist und dessen Kollektionshäufigkeit einen Mindestbetrag aufweist. Der Schwellwert für die Kollektionshäufigkeit ist von der Spracherkennungskomponente her gegeben und ist auf 30
festgelegt. Der Schwellwert für den Diskriminationswert wurde so gewählt, dass die
Grösse m des Indexierungsvokabular $\Phi = \{\phi_0, ..., \phi_{m-1}\}$ auf wenige hundert beschränkt werden konnte.

Für die Erkennung von Indexierungsmerkmalen in Sprachdokumenten wird für
jedes Indexierungsmerkmal ϕ_i ein Hidden Markov Modell erstellt und trainiert. Ausserdem wird derjenige Anteil der Sprache modelliert, in der kein Indexierungsmerkmal gesprochen wird. Dieses Modell wird Hintergrundmodell genannt. Für die
Erkennung des Merkmals ϕ_i in einem Sprachdokument werden Merkmalsmodell und
Hintergrundmodell zu einem Erkennungsmodell ρ_i parallel verknüpft, wie in Fig. 2
gezeigt ist.

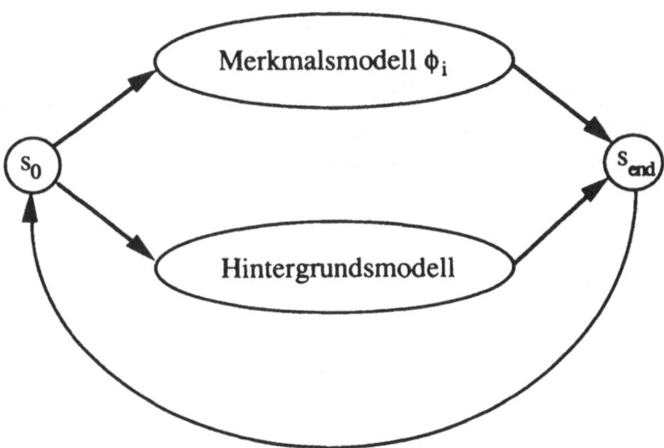

Fig. 2: Erkennungsmodell ρ_i

Der Viterbi-Algorithmus liefert nun für jedes Sprachdokument d_j und jedes Erkennungsmodell die wahrscheinlichste Zustandssequenz durch das Erkennungsmodell. Aus dieser Zustandssequnz lassen sich die zeitlichen Auftreten der Indexierungsmerkmale im Sprachdokument berechnen. Ein indexiertes Sprachdokument $\underline{d}_j$ hat dabei folgende Form:

$$\underline{d}_j = ((\phi_{g(0)}, t_0, l_0), \ldots, (\phi_{g(q-1)}, t_{q-1}, l_{q-1})),$$

wobei die Funktion $g: \{0,\ldots,q\text{-}1\} \to \{0,\ldots,m\text{-}1\}$ angibt, um welches Indexierungsmerkmal es sich handelt. Das Tripel $(\phi_{g(k)}, t_k, l_k)$ bezeichnet dann, dass das Merkmal $\phi_{g(k)}$ zum Zeitpunkt t_k während l_k Zeiteinheiten als solches erkannt wurde. Bei der Erkennung von Indexierungsmerkmalen in Sprachdokumenten können Fehler auftreten. Die typischen Fehler sind Nichterkennungen und Falscherkennungen. Bei einer Nichterkennung übersieht der Spracherkennungsprozess das Vorkommen eines Merkmals, während bei einer Falscherkennung ein Merkmal an einer Stelle erkannt wird, wo es nicht auftritt. Sowohl bei Nichterkennungen und Falscherkennungen kann es sich um Verwechslungen handeln. Bei einer Verwechslung wird ein Merkmal anstelle eines anderen erkannt.

Die Erkennung der oben beschriebenen Indexierungsmerkmalen in Texten erfolgt durch einfache Textverarbeitungsroutinen. Ein indexiertes Textdokument $\underline{d}_k$ wird folgendermassen repräsentiert:

$$\underline{d}_k = ((\phi_{h(0)}, p_0), \ldots, (\phi_{h(r-1)}, p_{r-1})),$$

wobei die Funktion $h: \{0,\ldots,r\text{-}1\} \to \{0,\ldots,m\text{-}1\}$ ähnlich wie g bezeichnet, um welches Merkmal es sich handelt. Das Tupel $(\phi_{h(k)}, p_k)$ bezeichnet ein Vorkommen des Merkmals $\phi_{h(k)}$ bei Position p_k im Textdokument. Die Länge eines Indexierungsmerkmals muss bei den indexierten Texten nicht angegeben werden, da dessen Schreibweise eindeutig ist.

4. Positionieren

Im folgenden stellen wir unseren neuen Ansatz zum *Positionieren* von Sprachdokumenten vor. Wie bereits erwähnt, verstehen wir unter dem Positionieren von Sprachdokumenten das rasche Auffinden und Darstellen einer Stelle innerhalb eines Dokuments. Wir nehmen an, dass die betrachteten Sprachdokumente lang sind, so dass das Suchen nach einer Stelle durch Abhören zuviel Zeit in Anspruch nehmen würde.

Die Problemstellung für das Positionieren von Sprachdokumenten ist die folgende: Gegeben sei ein Sprachdokument d_j und ein Suchmuster q als kurze Sprachsequenz oder als Text. Gesucht ist eine Rangliste von Positionen in d_j, an welchen q am wahrscheinlichsten ausgesprochen wurde.

Wir nehmen an, dass das Dokument d_j bereits als indexiertes Dokument $\underline{d}_j$ vorliegt. Das indexierte Dokument $\underline{q}$ wird nach der Eingabe von q berechnet.

$$\underline{d}_j = ((\phi_{g(0)}, t_0, l_0), ..., (\phi_{g(w-1)}, t_{w-1}, l_{w-1}))$$

$$\underline{q} = \begin{cases} ((\phi_{h(0)}, t_0, l_0), ..., (\phi_{h(r-1)}, t_{r-1}, l_{r-1})), & \text{falls q eine Sprachsequenz} \\ ((\phi_{i(0)}, p_0), ..., (\phi_{i(s-1)}, p_{s-1})), & \text{falls q ein Text} \end{cases}$$

Um Positionen in d_j zu finden, wo das Suchmuster gesprochen wird, werden nun Subsequenzen $u_{x,y}$ aus $\underline{d}_j$ mit der Folge von auftretenden Indexierungsmerkmalen v_z in $\underline{q}$ verglichen. Eine Subsequenz $u_{x,y}$ ist eine Folge von hintereinander auftretenden Indexierungsmerkmalen in d_j, die mit dem an x-ter Stelle erkannten Merkmal $\phi_{g(x)}$ beginnt und y Merkmale enthält.

$$u_{x,y} = (\phi_{g(x)}, ..., \phi_{g(x+y-1)}), \quad \text{wobei x, y} \geq 0 \text{ und x+y-1} < w$$

$$v_z = (\phi_{k(0)}, ..., \phi_{k(z-1)}), \quad \text{wobei}$$

$$k = \begin{cases} h, & \text{falls q eine Sprachsequenz} \\ i, & \text{falls q ein Text} \end{cases}$$

Da bei der Erkennung von Indexierungsmerkmalen in Sprachdokumenten Fehler auftreten, kann nicht auf Gleichheit der Sequenzen $u_{x,y}$ und v_z geprüft werden, sondern es muss die *Ähnlichkeit* der beiden Sequenzen bestimmt werden. Als Ähnlichkeitsmass verwenden wir die Rekursionsformel des "All-Against-All Matching" Algorithmus (Gonnet & Baeza-Yates, 1991).

$$sim(u_{j,x,0}, v_z) = - z * D$$

$$sim(u_{x,y}, v_0) = - y * D$$

$$sim(u_{x,y}, v_z) = \max (sim(u_{x,y}, v_{z-1}) - D, sim(u_{x,y-1}, v_z) - D,$$
$$sim(u_{x,y-1}, v_{z-1}) + M[g(x+y-1), k(z-1)]),$$

    wobei D : positive Kosten für die Nichterkennung eines Indexierungs-
                merkmals

    $M[i, j]$: Ähnlichkeit der Indexierungsmerkmale ϕ_i und ϕ_j

Die Grössen D und $M[i, j]$ werden empirisch aus den Auftretenshäufigkeiten der entsprechenden Erkennungsfehler ermittelt. Für jede mögliche Folge $u_{x,y}$ wird ein Ähnlichkeitswert $sim(u_{x,y},v_r)$ bzw. $sim(u_{x,y},v_s)$ berechnet. Die Folgen $u_{x,y}$ werden nach absteigendem Ähnlichkeitswert sortiert und ein Anfangsstück der resultierenden Rangliste wird dem Benutzer präsentiert. Die Darstellung der gefundenen Subsequenzen in einer Rangliste ist bezüglich der Ausbeute optimal (Robertson, 1977). Die Ausbeute ist ein Begriff aus dem Information Retrieval und bezeichnet - auf dieses Problem angewandt - den Prozentsatz richtig gefundener Subsequenzen $u_{x,y}$ bezüglich aller richtigen Subsequenzen $u_{x,y}$. Bei einer richtigen Subsequenz $u_{x,y}$ wird das Suchmuster q tatsächlich zwischen den Zeitpunkten t_x und t_{x+y-1} im Dokument d_j ausgesprochen. Die Zeiten t_x und t_{x+y-1} können dem indexierten Dokument $\underline{d}_j$ entnommen werden.

In diesem Abschnitt wurde gezeigt, wie man zu einem gegebenen Suchmuster alle ähnliche Stellen in einem gegebenen Dokument findet. Die Eingabe des Suchmusters als Text erlaubt dem Benutzer auch, via Modem auf Sprachdokumente zuzugreifen.

5. Retrieval von Sprach- und Textdokumenten

Wie in der Einleitung erwähnt wurde, sind Methoden für das Information Retrieval auf Texten bekannt. Ein Retrieval System findet für eine gegebene Dokumentenkollektion und eine gegebene Anfrage diejenigen Dokumente, welche die Anfrage am ehesten befriedigen. Es wird meist eine Rangliste der gefundenen Dokumente erstellt, wobei das Dokument am Anfang der Liste am ähnlichsten zur Anfrage ist.

Wir stellen im folgenden ein Retrieval System für Sprach- und Textdokumente vor. Die Dokumentenkollektion besteht aus Dokumenten beider Medientypen, ebenso kann die Anfrage als Text oder als Sprachsequenz spezifiziert werden. Unseres Wissens ist dieses Retrieval System das einzige, das textähnliches Retrieval auf Sprachdokumenten möglich macht.

Die Dokumente d_j der Dokumentenkollektion sowie die Anfrage q werden mit der in Abschnitt 3 beschriebenen Methode indexiert. Wie in (Glavitsch und Schäuble, 1992) gezeigt wird, werden aus den indexierten Dokumenten $\underline{d}_j$ und $\underline{q}$ Dokumentenvektoren $\vec{d_j}$ und $\vec{q}$ erzeugt. Die Komponenten der Vektoren $\vec{d_j}$ und $\vec{q}$ werden gemäss dem Gewichtungsschema *tf * idf* (Salton & Buckley, 1988) des Text Retrievals berechnet.

Die Ähnlichkeit zwischen einem Dokumenten- und einem Anfragevektor wird mit einer Retrieval Funktion bestimmt. Wir verwenden als Retrieval Funktion das Skalarprodukt. Der resultierende Ähnlichkeitswert wird Retrieval Status Value (RSV) genannt.

$$RSV(q, d_j) = \vec{q} \ * \ \vec{d_j}$$

Der Retrieval Status Value wird zu einer gegebenen Anfrage q für jedes Dokument d_j der Kollektion berechnet. Dem Benutzer wird ein Anfangsstück der nach absteigendem Retrieval Status Value sortierten Dokumentenliste präsentiert.

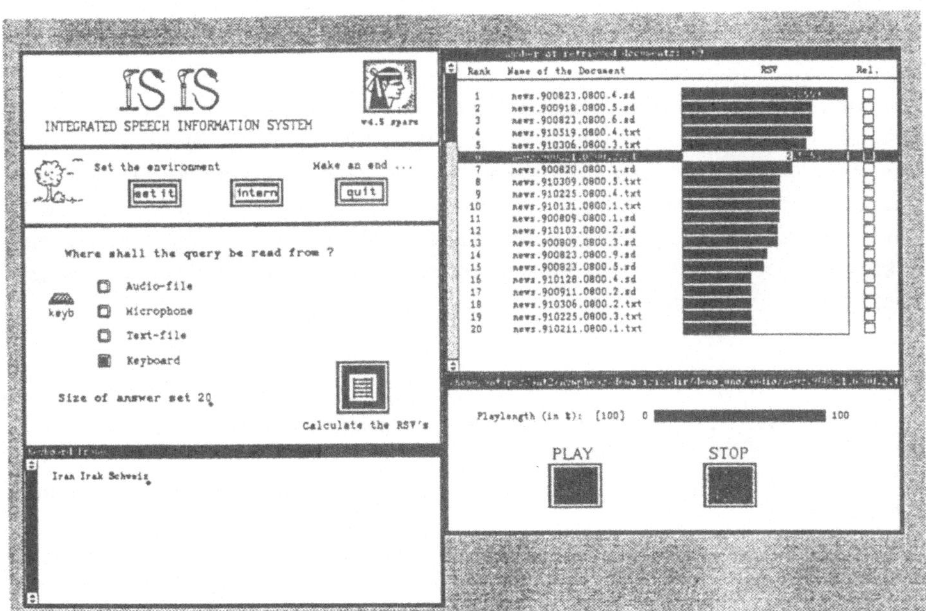

Figur 3: Prototyp eines Information Retrieval Systems für Radionachrichten und Agenturmeldungen

Figur 3 zeigt einen eben erstellten Prototypen eines Sprach-Retrieval-Systems für Radionachrichten (Radio DRS) und Agenturmeldungen (Schweizerische Depeschen Agentur, SDA). Die Sprachdokumenten-Kollektion besteht aus 200 Sprachdokumenten, welche aus 31 Radionachrichten extrahiert wurden. Radionachrichten wurden deshalb gewählt, weil sie in guter Sprachqualität verfügbar sind und von geschulten Sprechern gesprochen werden. Die verwendeten Sprachdokumente sind alle vom selben Sprecher gesprochen. Wir verwenden 100 Sprachdokumente zum Training des Systems und 100 zur Auswertung. Die Trainings-Dokumente sind momentan noch auf 100 begrenzt, weil sie manuell segmentiert werden müssen, was sehr zeitaufwendig ist. Die ausführliche Evaluation des Retrieval Systems steht noch bevor.

5. Schlussfolgerungen

Wir haben in diesem Artikel zwei neue Operationen auf Sprachdokumenten vorgestellt: ein Positionierverfahren und eine Retrieval Methode. Beide Methoden basieren auf einem Indexierungsverfahren, mit dem sich sowohl Texte als auch Sprachdokumente beschreiben lassen. Während die Indexierung von Texten fehlerfrei ist, treten bei der Identifikation von Indexierungsmerkmalen in Sprachdokumenten Erkennungsfehler auf. Es ist noch nicht bekannt, welchen Einfluss diese Erkennungsfehler auf die Ausbeute des Positionierverfahrens und die Retrieval Effektivität der Retrieval Methode haben.

Sprachdokumente werden in zukünftigen Computersystemen an Bedeutung gewinnen. Neuere Arbeitsstationen und Engeräte sind mit Audio-Hardware ausgerüstet. Immer grösserer Massenspeicher sowie Gigahertz-Netzwerke erlauben es, Sprachdokumente in Mengen und Geschwindigkeiten zu übertragen wie heute Textdokumente. Die dargestellen Erweiterungen der Funktionalität von Sprachdokumenten können dabei eine wichtige Bedeutung erlangen und den Zugang zu grossen Hypermedia-Archiven ermöglichen.

Referenzen

Aho, A.V., & Corasick, M. (1975). Efficient String Matching: An Aid to Bibliographic Search. *Communications of the ACM*, 18(6), pp. 333-340.

Baeza-Yates, R.A., & Gonnet, G.H. (1991). All-Against-All Sequence Matching. Submitted for Publication.

Boyer, R.S., & Moore, J.S. (1977). A Fast String Searching Algorithm. *Communications of the ACM*, 20(10), pp. 762-772.

Glavitsch, U., & Schäuble, P. (1992). A System for Retrieving Speech Documents. *ACM SIGIR*, Copenhagen, pp. 168-176.

Lee, K. F. (1989). *Automatic Speech Recognition: The Development of the SPHINX System*. Kluwer Academic Publishers, Boston.

Porter, M.F. (1980). An Algorithm for Suffix Stripping. *Program*, 14(3), pp. 130-137.

Rabiner, l. R. (1988). A Tutorial on Hidden Markov Models and Selected Applications in Speech Recognition, *Proceeedings of the IEEE*, 77(2), 257 - 286.

Robertson, S.E. (1977). The Probability Ranking Principle in IR. *Journal of Documentation*, 33(4), pp. 294-304.

Rose, R.C., & Paul, D.B (1990). A hidden Markov Model Based Keyword Recognition System. *Proc. of the Int. Conf. on Acoustics, Speech and Signal Processing*, Albuquerque, New Mexico, April 1990, pp. 129 - 132.

Rose, R.C. (1991). Techniques for Information Retrieval from Speech Messages. *Lincoln-Laboratory-Journal*, 4(1), pp. 45-60.

Rose, R.C., & Chang, E.I., Lippmann, R. (1991). Techniques for Information Retrieval from Voice Messages. *International Conference on Acoustics, Speech, and Signal Processing*, pp.317-320.

Salton, G., & Buckley, C. (1988). Term Weighting Approaches in Automatic Text Retrieval, *Information Processing & Management*, 24(5), pp. 513-523.

Salton, G., & Buckley, C. (1990). Improving Retrieval Performance by Relevance Feedback, *Journal of the ASIS*, 41(4), pp. 288-297.

Schmandt, C., & McKenna, M.A. (1988). An Audio and Telephone Server for Multi-Media Workstations. *Proceedings of the 2nd IEEE Conference on Computer Workstations*, Santa Clara, 7-10, pp.150-159.

Teufel, B. (1989). Informationsspuren zum numerischen und graphischen Vergleich von reduzierten natürlichsprachlichen Texten. *Doktorarbeit, ETH Zürich*, VdF-Verlag Zürich.

Wilcox, L.D., & Bush, M.A. (1991). HMM-Based Wordspotting for Voice Editing and Audio Indexing. *European Conference on Speech Communication and Technology*, pp. 25-28.

Willet, P., & Robertson, A.M. (1992). Searching for Historical Word-forms in a Database of 17th-Century English Text Using Spelling-Correction Methods. *ACM SIGIR*, Copenhagen, pp. 256-265.

Wilpon, J.G., Rabiner, L.R., Lee, C.H., Goldman, E.R. (1990). Automatic Recognition of Keywords in Unconstrained Speech Using Hidden Markov Models. *IEEE Transactions on Acoustics, Speech and Signal Processing*, 38(11), pp. 1870-1878.

Wu, S., & Manber, U. (1992). Fast Text Searching Allowing Errors. *Communications of the ACM*, October 1992, Vol. 35, No.10.

Ein Stufenindex als Navigationshilfe für Hypertextdokumente

Werner Herold und Matthias Müller
Universität-Gesamthochschule Paderborn
Fachbereich Wirtschaftswissenschaft
Schwerpunkt Wirtschaftsinformatik & OR
Warburger Straße 100
D-4790 Paderborn

Zusammenfassung

Es wird eine textuelle Navigationshilfe für Hypertextdokumente vorgestellt. Ein automatisch erstellbarer Stufenindex stellt in der ersten Stufe den unmittelbaren Kontext eines Knotens durch die Angabe der mit ihm verbundenen Vater- und Sohnknoten dar. Durch die Navigationsmöglichkeit in dem Stufenindex kann in weiteren Stufen der erweiterte Kontext des Knotens erkundet werden. Insbesondere wird diskutiert, wie ein Hypertextgraph effizient gespeichert werden kann.

Ein Prototyp des Stufenindex wurde mit dem Hypertextsystem ToolBook realisiert. Dabei wurde besonders Wert auf eine wirksame Erweiterung von ToolBook gelegt. Diese wurde mit dem DLL-Konzept von MS-Windows erreicht. Das DDE-Konzept wird als alternatives Konzept angesprochen.

1. Problem der Disorientierung

In Hypertextdokumenten wird das darzustellende Wissen in Informationseinheiten (*Knoten*) angeboten, die aus Text, Grafik oder anderen visuellen oder akustischen Abbildungen bestehen. Die Knoten sind durch Verbindungen (*Kanten*) miteinander verknüpft. Über die Kanten erschließen sich dem Benutzer Wege durch das Hypertextdokument. Im Gegensatz zu linearen Dokumenten, in denen einer Informationseinheit (Seite) jeweils maximal eine weitere folgt, können in Hypertextdokumenten von einem Knoten mehrere Kanten zu unterschiedlichen Knoten führen. Je nach Interesse und Ziel des Benutzers kann er einer der Kanten folgen.

Damit bietet Hypertext geeignete Konzepte, um dem Benutzer einen flexiblen Zugriff auf das Wissen zu ermöglichen. Die Knoten und die Kanten zwischen den Knoten bilden eine Verbindungsstruktur, die als *Hypertextgraph* bezeichnet wird. Der Benutzer durchläuft beim Lesen des Hypertextdokumentes diesen Graphen. Die Vielfalt der Verzweigungsmöglichkeiten kann zu einer großen Komplexität des Hypertextgraphen führen. Der Benutzer hat nur die Informationen eines Knotens vor Augen und läuft Gefahr, die Orientierung in dem Hypertextdokument zu verlieren - "lost in hyperspace" [CON 87]. Das kann bedeuten, daß er nicht weiß,

- *wo* er sich innerhalb des Hypertextdokumentes befindet,
- *welche* für ihn relevanten Informationen in dem Hypertextdokument noch vorhanden sind,
- *wie* er zu ihn interessierenden Informationen gelangen kann,
- *welche* Knoten er bisher besucht hat.

Es sind also Orientierungsinformationen notwendig, die dem Benutzer die Struktur des Hypertextgraphen sowie die Einbettung des gerade angezeigten Knotens in dem Graphen verdeutlichen - eine Navigationshilfe. Nahe liegt eine grafische Übersicht. Hier treten aber Probleme hinsichtlich der durch die Monitorgröße begrenzten Darstellungsfläche auf. Mit wachsender Zahl der Knoten und Kanten bringt es kaum Sinn, das Netz auf die Fläche eines Monitors "zusammenzupressen" [UTT 89].

Es gibt zahlreiche Lösungsansätze zu diesem Problem. In dem Hypertextsystem Intermedia wird dem Benutzer neben einer globalen Übersicht, die das gesamte Hypertextdokument als Graph darstellt, auch eine lokale Übersicht zur Verfügung gestellt, die zu dem aktuellen Knoten die umliegenden Knoten anzeigt [SMI 88]. Nielsen [NIE 89] stellt eine ähnliche Lösung für das Hypertextsystem HyperCard vor. Er stellt allerdings in Frage, ob bei einer sehr großen Anzahl von Knoten (größer 100) zwei Übersichtsebenen ausreichen. Neben Übersichtsdiagrammen und Backtracking mißt er der Anzeige von schon besuchten Knoten eine große Bedeutung zu. Grafische Übersichten der schon besuchten Knoten, werden von Foss [FOS 88] vorgeschlagen. Furnas [FUR 86] beschreibt die Möglichkeit, eine sogenannte "Fischaugen-Sicht" zu verwenden, die die naheliegende Umgebung eines Knotens in allen Details, aber den weiteren Kontext nur andeutungsweise darstellt.

2. Stufenindex

2.1 Arbeitsweise

Der von uns gewählte Stufenindex stellt die Verbindungsstruktur textuell dar. In dem Stufenindex wird die Bezeichnung eines bestimmten Knotens, sowie die Bezeichnungen der Knoten angegeben, die mit diesem Knoten über Kanten verknüpft sind. Dies sind die *Nachbarknoten* des bestimmten Knotens. Wie in der Abbildung 1 verdeutlicht, werden die Nachbarknoten unterteilt in

- *Väter:* Knoten, von denen eine Kante zu dem betrachteten Knoten führt,
- *Söhne:* Knoten, zu denen eine Kante von dem betrachteten Knoten führt.

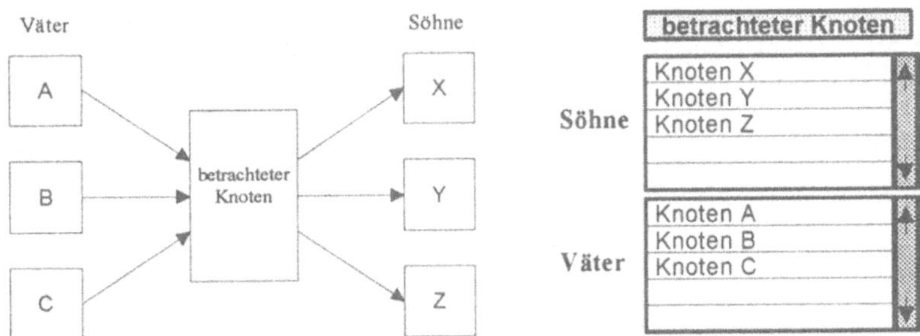

Abbildung 1: Knoten im Graphen und im Stufenindex

Die Bezeichnung Stufenindex deutet darauf hin, daß der Index in Stufen aufgebaut ist. In der ersten Stufe werden die Nachbarknoten des Knotens angegeben, von dem der Stufenindex aufgerufen wurde (dem Ausgangsknoten). Zu den weiteren Stufen gelangt man durch das Aktivieren eines Nachbarknoten (z.B. durch Mausklick) in dem Stufenindex. Daraufhin werden jeweils die Bezeichnungen der Nachbarknoten dieses Knoten angezeigt. So kann innerhalb des

Stufenindex navigiert werden, um den Kontext des Ausgangsknotens zu erkunden. Falls während des Navigierens in dem Stufenindex ein Knoten gefunden wird, der aufgrund seiner Bezeichnung interessant erscheint, kann dieser aus dem Stufenindex aktiviert werden. In dem Stufenindex werden außerdem schon besuchte Knoten markiert. Dies zeigt dem Benutzer an, daß er die Informationen eines Knotens schon gelesen hat.

Die folgende Abbildung (Abb. 2) gibt einen relativ einfachen Hypertextgraphen wieder.

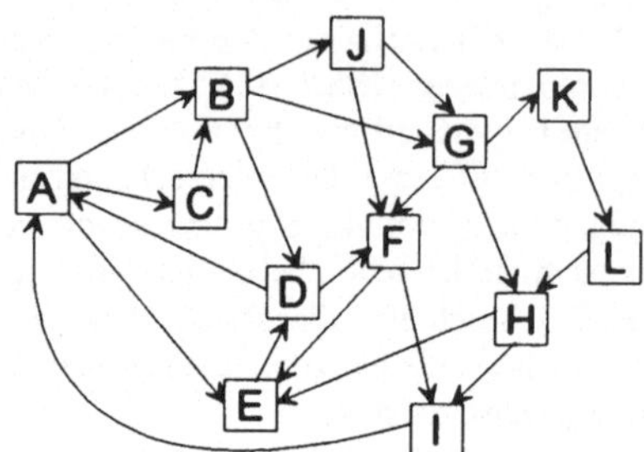

Abbildung 2: ein Hypertextgraph

Mit Hilfe des Stufenindex ist es möglich, durch diesen Hypertextgraphen zu navigieren (Abb. 3). Beispielsweise könnte der Stufenindex von dem Knoten D aufgerufen werden. Dementsprechend werden die Söhne und Väter dieses Knoten angezeigt. Dann wird innerhalb des Stufenindex zu dem Knoten F navigiert. Der vorher besuchte Knoten D wird mit einem "*" als schon besucht markiert. Danach wird nach Knoten G, einem Vater von Knoten F, navigiert und dessen Söhne und Väter angezeigt.

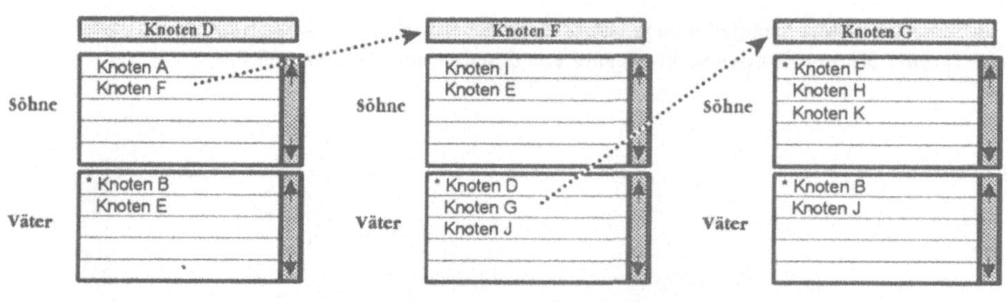

Abbildung 3: Navigation im Stufenindex

2.2 Darstellung

Im Hinblick auf das Antwortverhalten stellt sich die Frage, wie die Daten, die für den Stufenindex benötigt werden, so effizient gespeichert werden können, daß ein schneller Zugriff darauf möglich ist.

Da mit dem Stufenindex die Verbindungsstruktur des Hypertextdokumentes, ein Graph, dargestellt wird, kommen folgende zwei Darstellungsweisen in Betracht:

- *Adjazenz-Matrix*
  Bei *n* Knoten wird eine *nxn*-Matrix gebildet. Eine Kante zwischen zwei Knoten *i* und *j* wird durch die Kennzeichnung des Matrixeintrages *i,j* dargestellt.
- *Adjazenz-Listen*
  Für jeden Knoten wird eine Liste geführt, in der alle Knoten enthalten sind, die von dem Knoten direkt erreichbar sind. Es gibt also *n* Listen.

Die beiden folgenden Abbildungen verdeutlichen den Aufbau beider Darstellungsarten:

	1	2	3	4	5	6	7	8
1		x		x			x	
2								
3	x						x	
4		x						
5				x				
6							x	
7								x
8	x							

```
1->2->4->7->nil
2->nil
3->1->7->nil
4->2->nil
5->4->nil
6->7->nil
7->8->nil
8->1->nil
```

Abbildung 4: Adjazenz-Matrix   Abbildung 5: Adjazenz-Listen

Adjazenz-Listen sind wesentlich einfacher in Dateien zu speichern, da sie eindimensional sind. Außerdem ist der benötigte Speicherbedarf für Adjazenz-Matrixen größer, da auch die leeren Einträge gespeichert werden. Um zu wissen, ob eine Verknüpfung zwischen zwei Knoten besteht, liefert die Adjazenz-Matrix auf Anhieb das Ergebnis. Dieser direkte Zugriff wird aber für den Stufenindex nicht benötigt.

Da in den Adjazenz-Listen nur die Söhne eines Knotens gespeichert sind, ist es notwendig, auch noch Adjazenz-Listen für die Väter zu erstellen. Sie können leicht mit den Adjazenz-Listen der Söhne erstellt werden, indem diese durchsucht werden.

In der Implementierung des Stufenindex werden also ausschließlich Datenstrukturen verwendet, die auf Adjazenz-Listen basieren.

3. Implementierung eines Prototyps

Das Hypertextsystem ToolBook 1.5 [ASY 91], welches unter der Benutzeroberfläche MS-Windows 3.0 arbeitet, eignet sich für eine einfache Erstellung von Hypertextdokumenten. Es fehlt ihm aber die Möglichkeit, die Verbindungsstruktur anzuzeigen. Dieses Defizit haben wir durch den Stufenindex, der unter Benutzung der in ToolBook integrierten, ansatzweise objektorientierten Programmiersprache *OpenScript* prototyphaft implementiert wurde, beseitigt.

In ToolBook entspricht einem Knoten eine Seite. Jeder Seite wird ein eindeutiger Name zugewiesen. Auf einer Seite können verschiedene Objekte (Texte, Grafiken oder Buttons) angeordnet werden. Verknüpfungen werden in ToolBook durch die, den Objekten zugeordneten, Befehle in OpenScript realisiert. Die Befehle werden zu sogenannten Handlern zusammengefaßt, die den Objekten zugeordnet werden und auf bestimmte Ereignisse (z.B. einem Mausklick auf ein Objekt) reagieren. Ein Handler, der eine Verknüpfung beschreibt, könnte beispielsweise wie folgt aussehen (Abb. 6):

```
to handle buttonUp                          -- bei Mausklick ausführen
   go to page "icons zum navigieren"        -- gehe zu Seite "..."
end
```

Abbildung 6: Handler in ToolBook, der durch einen Mausklick aktiviert wird

Durch das Aktivieren eines Handlers wird zu dem verknüpften Knoten verzweigt. Eine Verknüpfung von zwei Knoten wird durch eine Referenzierung auf eine andere Seite realisiert. Die einfachste Form ist

   go to page <Seitenname>.

Diese Art der Verknüpfung ist statisch. Wir betrachten im folgenden nur statische Verknüpfungen. Wie dynamische Verknüpfungen, deren Zielseiten erst zur Laufzeit des Hypertextdokumentes bestimmt werden, zu handhaben sind, wird im Ausblick (Kapitel 4) angedeutet.

In ToolBook werden die Verknüpfungen zusammen mit den Knoteninformationen in einer gemeinsamen Datei gespeichert. Im Gegensatz zu großen Hypertextsystemen, in denen die Verknüpfungen in einer Datenbank gespeichert werden, ist daher in ToolBook kein direkter Zugriff auf die Verknüpfungen möglich. Dieser ist aber für die Implementierung des Stufenindex notwendig. Aus diesem Grund ist in ToolBook zunächst das Hypertextdokument nach Referenzierungen zu durchsuchen, um sie in eine separate Datei zu speichern.

Da ein Hypertextdokument in der Regel aus einer großen Anzahl von Seiten besteht, kann der Stufenindex nur maschinell erstellt werden. Der Aufwand eines manuellen Vorgehens wäre zu umfangreich und fehlerträchtig, zumal leicht einzelne Referenzierungen übersehen werden könnten. Die automatische Erstellung erfolgt in zwei Schritten:

1. Mit einem Programm der Programmiersprache OpenScript werden die Handler aller Objekte nach Referenzierungen (also nach "go to page <Seitenname>") durchsucht und die Zielseiten (<Seitenname>) in eine Datei gespeichert.
2. Über die gefundenen Referenzierungen werden zu jeder Seite sowohl Väter als auch die Söhne bestimmt. Die Namen der Seiten mit den entsprechenden Vätern und Söhnen werden in Adjazenz-Listen gespeichert.

Ziel des weiteren Vorgehens ist es, das Ergebnis von Schritt 2 so zu gestalten, daß der Stufenindex, wie in Abschnitt 2 beschrieben, realisiert werden kann. Dabei wird für den Stufenindex eine Seite des Hypertextdokumentes verwendet, die von jeder anderen Seite aktiviert werden kann. Den Aufbau der Seite mit dem Stufenindex zeigt die Abbildung 7. An ihr wird auch deutlich, daß ein Knoten sowohl Sohn als auch Vater des gleichen Knotens sein kann. Dies ist der Fall, wenn Verknüpfungen zwischen zwei Knoten in beiden Richtungen existieren.

Im Hinblick auf die Implementierung des Stufenindex sind zwei wichtige Kriterien zu beachten:

1. Der Benutzer soll den Stufenindex effizient benutzen können, wobei kurze Antwortzeiten bei der Navigation innerhalb des Stufenindex von großer Bedeutung sind.
2. Das Hypertextdokument und damit die Anzahl der Kanten kann beliebig groß werden. Die Größe der Adjazenz-Listen darf also nicht beschränkt sein.

Im folgenden werden unter Berücksichtigung der genannten Kriterien drei Möglichkeiten untersucht, den Stufenindex zu implementieren.

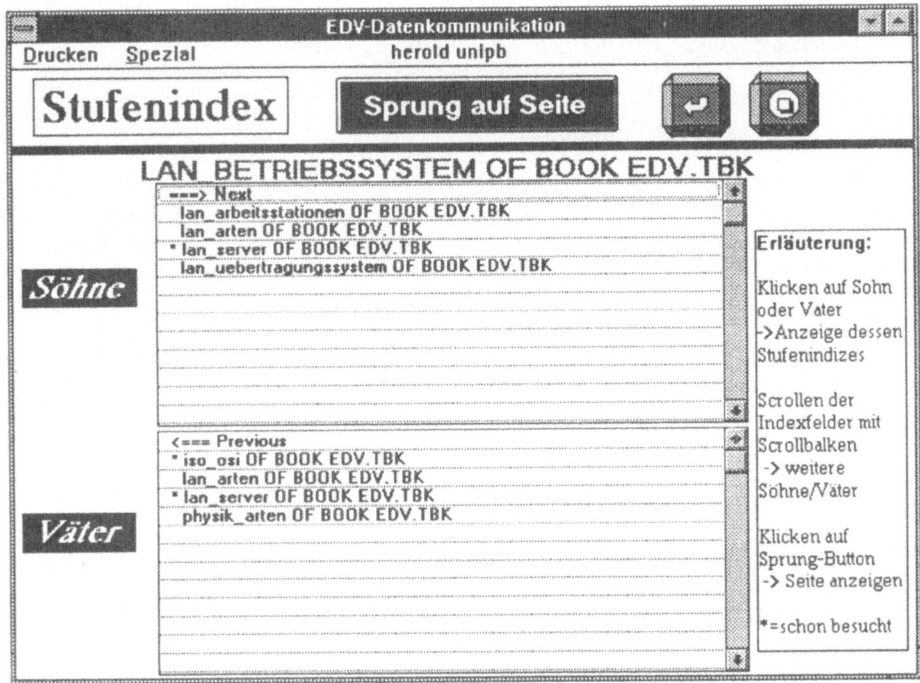

Abbildung 7: Stufenindex in ToolBook

3.1 Speichern in ein ToolBook-Objekt

Es ist naheliegend, die Adjazenz-Listen in eine mit ToolBook erstellte Datenstruktur zu speichern und diese einem Objekt in ToolBook zuzuordnen. Dies scheitert aber an der Tatsache, daß die Anzahl der Zeichen aller Objekte pro ToolBook-Seite auf ca. 32.000 (also ca. 1000 Seitennamen bzw. Verknüpfungen bei einer Länge von 15 Zeichen pro Seitennamen) beschränkt ist und damit auch die Anzahl der verwaltbaren Kanten begrenzt wäre. Eine Verkürzung der Seitennamen schafft keine wesentliche Abhilfe und vermindert nur das treffende Benennen von Seiten. Außerdem ist zu bemerken, daß bei einer in ToolBook implementierten Datenstruktur die Zugriffsgeschwindigkeit und damit die Navigationsgeschwindigkeit im Stufenindex mit wachsender Anzahl von Seiten und Kanten erheblich abnimmt.

3.2 Speichern in eine Datei

Das Speichern der Adjazenz-Listen in eine Datei löst das Problem der begrenzten Anzahl von verwaltbaren Kanten für den Stufenindex. Es müssen nur die Daten geladen werden, die für die Darstellung der jeweiligen Seite im Stufenindex benötigt werden: die Namen der Väter und Söhne der betreffenden Seite. Da ToolBook nur den sequentiellen Dateizugriff unterstützt, muß eine sequentielle Datei verwendet werden (Abb. 8). Um die Daten für den Stufenindex einer Seite zu erhalten, muß im schlechtesten Fall die gesamte Datei nach dem Dateinamen durchsucht werden. Diese Tatsache und zusätzlich

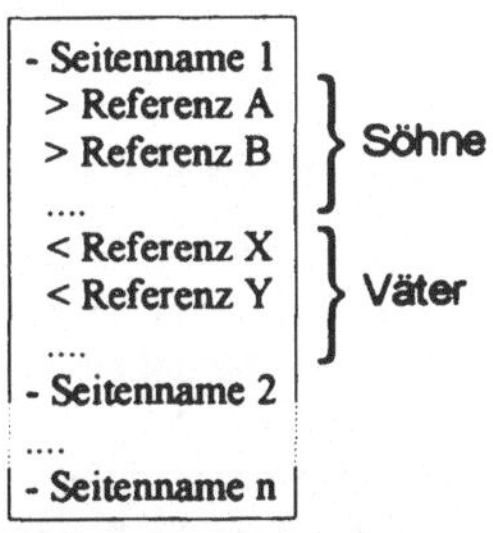

Abbildung 8: mögliche Datenstruktur

die langsamen Dateioperationen von ToolBook führen zu nicht hinnehmbaren Antwortzeiten im Stufenindex, die sogar schlechter als die in Abschnitt 3.1 sind.

3.3 Verwenden externer Funktionen

Die schlechte Effizienz von ToolBook führte zu der Überlegung, ToolBook selbst nicht für das Auffinden der benötigten Daten zu benutzen, sondern dieses von einer externen Funktion durchführen zu lassen. Unter MS-Windows empfiehlt sich hierfür das dynamische Linken von Funktionen (DLL = dynamic link library) mit Hilfe des Entwicklungssystems Turbo Pascal für Windows 1.0 (TPW) [BOR 91]. Gegenüber ToolBook ist der Zugriff auf Dateien wesentlich effektiver, da mit den Dateioperationen von TPW direkt auf die Dateielemente zugegriffen werden kann. Die Dateioperationen sind außerdem schneller als die von ToolBook. Eine ähnliche Lösungsmöglichkeit besteht in der Verwendung des DDE-Konzeptes (DDE = dynamic data exchange) von MS-Windows, wobei der Stufenindex durch ein mit TPW entwickeltes autarkes Programm realisiert wird.

3.3.1 Linken von externen Funktionen mit DLL

ToolBook ist in der Lage, per DLL externe Funktionen in der Programmiersprache OpenScript so zu benutzen wie die eigenen Funktionen. Die Funktionen werden für die Zeit der Benutzung mit ToolBook verbunden. Das Linken eines DLL mit ToolBook erfolgt mit Befehlen in OpenScript.

Für die Verwaltung des Stufenindex haben wir mehrere Funktionen entwickelt und in einem DLL zusammengefaßt. Diese Funktionen greifen auf drei Dateien zu, in denen die Adjazenz-Listen gespeichert sind. Der Aufbau dieser Dateien ist der Abbildung 9 zu entnehmen.

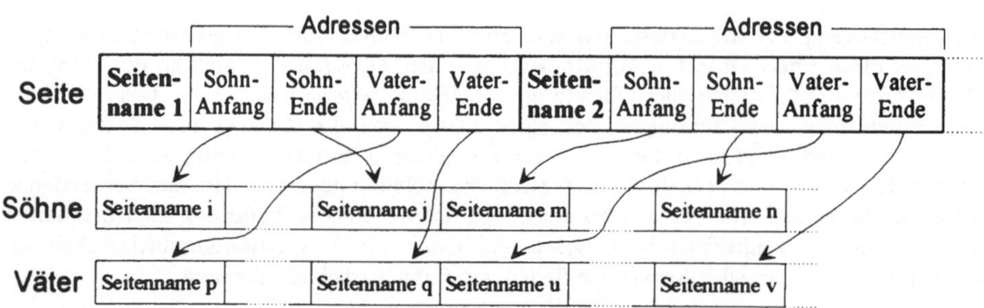

Abbildung 9: Organisation der Adjazenz-Dateien

Die folgenden drei Funktionen werden in dem DLL zu Verfügung gestellt:

- *Datenholen:* Sie liefert je Seite die Anfangs- und Ende-Adressen der Söhne und Väter in den Dateien "Söhne" und "Väter". Dazu wird der Seitenname von ToolBook an die Funktion übergeben und die Datei "Seite" mittels binärer Suche nach dem Seitennamen durchsucht.
- *Sohnholen:* Diese Funktion liefert die Seitennamen der Söhne aus der Datei "Söhne", nachdem die Adresse des ersten und des letzten Namens übergeben wurde.
- *Vaterholen:* Sie liefert die Seitennamen der Väter aus der Datei "Väter", nachdem die Adresse des ersten und des letzten Namens übergeben wurde.

Diese Funktionen werden von einem Handler in OpenScript nacheinander aufgerufen. Die zurückgegebenen Seitennamen werden in die scrollbaren Fenster auf der Seite mit dem Stufenindex geschrieben (vgl. Abb. 7). Den genauen Ablauf gibt die folgende Abbildung (Abb. 10) wieder:

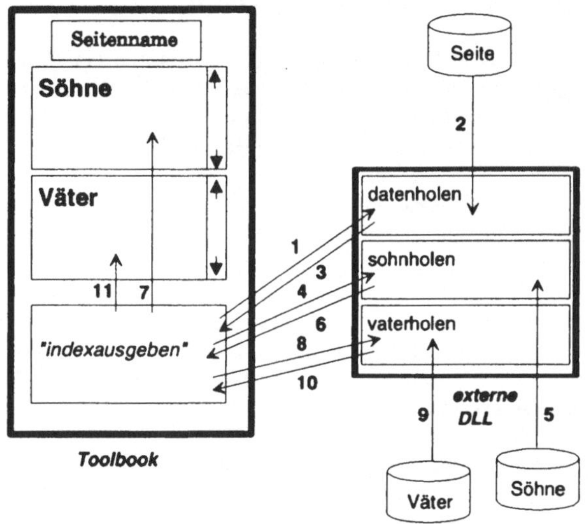

Abbildung 10: Bestimmung der Nachbarknoten zu einem Knoten

Nachdem die externen Funktionen mit ToolBook gelinkt wurden, werden die Söhne und Väter einer Seite bestimmt. Der Ablauf ist dabei wie folgt:

1. Für die Seite, deren Stufenindex dargestellt werden soll, werden die Daten (Anfangs-/Endadresse von Vätern und Söhnen) benötigt. Hierfür wird die Funktion "datenholen" aufgerufen.
2. Die Daten der gewählten Seite werden aus der Datei "Seite" gelesen. Dazu wird diese Datei binär nach dem Namen der Seite durchsucht.
3. Die erhaltenen Daten werden ToolBook übergeben.
4. Falls es Söhne zu der Seite gibt, wird die Funktion "sohnholen" aufgerufen. Dabei wird die Adresse des Sohnes übergeben.
5. Der Seitenname des Sohnes wird aus der Datei "Söhne" gelesen.
6. Er wird an ToolBook übergeben.
7. Der Seitenname des Sohnes wird in das Fenster "Söhne" geschrieben.
   Falls noch mehr Söhne existieren, geht es bei Schritt 4 weiter, sonst bei Schritt 8.
8. Falls es Väter zu der Seite gibt, wird die Funktion "vaterholen" aufgerufen. Dabei wird die Adresse des Vaters übergeben.
9. Der Seitennamen des Vaters wird aus der Datei "Väter" gelesen.
10. Der Seitenname wird an ToolBook übergeben.
11. Der Seitenname des Vaters wird in das Fenster "Väter" geschrieben.
    Falls noch mehr Väter existieren, geht es bei Schritt 8 weiter.

In Schritt 7 und Schritt 11 werden die Seitennamen zusätzlich auf das Vorkommen in der intern von ToolBook geführten Liste von schon besuchten Knoten (Historyliste) überprüft. Falls sie dort enthalten sind, werden sie mit einem "*" - als schon besucht - markiert.

Bei der Betrachtung der Laufzeiten für die Ausgabe der Väter und Söhne sind kaum Verzögerungen festzustellen. Gegenüber den in den Abschnitten 3.1 und 3.2 beschriebenen Methoden ist dieses Verfahren wesentlich schneller. Mit dem DLL-Konzept kann die Verwaltung des Stufenindex also effizient implementiert werden.

3.3.2 Kommunikation mit einem Programm über DDE

Das Kommunikationsprotokoll DDE ermöglicht den Austausch von Nachrichten und Daten zwischen zwei Programmen, die unter der Benutzeroberfläche Windows ausgeführt werden. Voraussetzung ist die Unterstützung von DDE durch die jeweiligen Programme. ToolBook und mit TPW entwickelte Programme unterstützen das DDE-Konzept.

Der Ablauf einer DDE-Kommunikation zwischen zwei Programmen sieht prinzipiell wie folgt aus: Ein Programm möchte mit einem anderen Programm kommunizieren, um Daten oder Nachrichten auszutauschen. Das anfordernde Programm wird als *Client* bezeichnet, das antwortende als *Server*. Falls der Server noch nicht gestartet wurde, wird er durch den Client gestartet. Der Client beginnt die Kommunikation, indem er eine Nachricht zu dem Server schickt. Der Server bestätigt die Kommunikationsanforderung. Danach ist ein beliebiger Nachrichten-/Datenaustausch zwischen Client und Server möglich. Nach Übergabe der Daten wird die Kommunikation beendet.

Mit diesem Konzept könnte eine von ToolBook unabhängig programmierte Navigationshilfe realisiert werden, die in einem eigenen Fenster läuft und ToolBook als Server dient. Damit entfallen Unzulänglichkeiten von ToolBook, wie langsamer Dateizugriff und fehlende Fenstertechnik in der ToolBook-Umgebung.

4. Beurteilung und Ausblick

Die textuelle Darstellung des Stufenindex besitzt gegenüber einer grafischen Übersicht den Vorteil, daß eine nahezu unbegrenzte Anzahl von Nachbarknoten zu einem bestimmten Knoten dargestellt werden kann, ohne daß der Benutzer den Überblick verliert. Dabei beschränkt sich der Stufenindex nicht nur auf die Nachbarknoten, sondern stellt in weiteren Stufen auch einen größeren Kontext zur Verfügung. Zusätzlich enthält er Informationen über schon besuchte Knoten.

Mit dem Stufenindex werden elementare Eigenschaften einer Navigationshilfe realisiert. Der Basisansatz ist auf Erweiterungen angelegt, wie

- Zurückverfolgen des Weges im Stufenindex,
- Einführen eines globalen Stufenindex, der nur Verknüpfungen zwischen wichtigen Knoten anzeigt (gewichteter Stufenindex).

Das Konzept des Stufenindex wurde zunächst auf statische Verknüpfungen begrenzt. Um dynamische Verknüpfungen, die von dem Zustand des Hypertextdokumentes abhängen, mit in den Stufenindex einzubeziehen, ist es notwendig, dynamische Verknüpfungen zur Laufzeit auszuwerten. Dies erfordert eine Datenhaltung der dynamischen Ausdrücke und die Möglichkeit, diese Ausdrücke zu interpretieren. Hierbei kann vor allem die Bestimmung der Väter eines Knotens zu Laufzeitproblemen führen, da dazu alle dynamischen Verknüpfungen eines Hypertextdokumentes auf deren Übereinstimmung mit dem Zielknoten überprüft werden müssen.

Ferner läge die Anwendung des DDE-Konzeptes nahe, wenn - trotz der o.a. Probleme der Beschränkungen durch die Monitorgröße - eine grafische Form des Stufenindex zu entwickeln wäre.

Für die Entwicklung unseres Prototyps haben wir ein Hypertextsystem gewählt, welches kommerziell für PCs vertrieben wird. In dieser Kategorie von Hypertextsystemen erfolgt oft keine Trennung von Knoten- und Verknüpfungs-Daten. Dies ist auch bei Guide [BRO 87] und Hyperties [SHN 89] zu beobachten. Für die Implementierung des Stufenindex ist es daher notwendig, solche Hypertextsysteme entsprechend zu erweitern. Falls ein Hypertextsystem die Verknüpfungen in einer Datenbank verwaltet, wie es im allgemeinen bei großen, vor allem in der Forschung verwendeten Hypertextsystemen der Fall ist (z.B. bei Intermedia [YAN 88]), kann das Konzept des Stufenindex unmittelbar diese Daten und die entsprechenden Operationen für die Implementierung des Stufenindex nutzen. Ein Durchsuchen des Hypertextdokumentes nach Referenzierungen würde entfallen und die notwendigen Zugriffsoperationen ständen schon zur Verfügung.

Literatur

[ASY 91]   Asymetrix Corporation: ToolBook, Version 1.5, Asymetrix Corporation, Bellevue, 1991

[BOR 91]   Borland International Inc.: Turbo Pascal für Windows, Borland International Inc., 1991

[BRO 87]   Brown, P.J.: Turning ideas into products: the Guide system, *ACM-Hypertext*, 1987/89, S. 33-40

[CON 87]   Conklin, J.: Hypertext - An introduction and a survey, *IEEE Computer*, Vol. 20 (1987), 9, S. 17-41

[FOS 88]   Foss, C.L.: Tools for reading and browsing hypertext, *Information Processing & Management*, Vol. 24 (1989), 4, S. 407-418

[FUR 86]   Furnas, G.W.: Generalized fisheye views, *Proc. of the ACM CHI '86*, Boston (MA), April 1986, S. 16-23

[NIE 90]   Nielsen, J.: The Art of Navigationg through Hypertext, *Communications of the ACM*, Vol. 33 (1987), 3, S. 296-310

[SHN 89]   Shneiderman, B.; Kearsley, G.: Hypertext hands-on! An introduction to a new way of organizing and accessing information, Reading, MA, Addison-Wesley, 1989

[SMI 88]   Smith, K.E.: Hypertext- Linking to the future, *Online*, Vol. 12 (1988), 3, S. 32-40

[UTT 89]   Utting, K.; Yankelovich, N.: Context and orientation in hypermedia networks, *ACM Transactions on Information Systems*, Vol. 7 (1989), 1, S. 58-84

[YAN 88]   Yankelovich, N.; Haan, B.J.; Meyrowitz, N.K.; Drucker, S.M.: Intermedia: the concept and the construction of a seamless information environment, *IEEE Computer*, Vol. 21 (1988), 1, S. 81-96

Orientierung und Navigation in strukturierten Hyperdokumenten

K.Meusel, B.Schröcksnadl, J.Schiff

Siemens AG, ZFE BT SE 22

Otto-Hahn-Ring 6, 8000 München 83

e-mail: meusel@ztivax.zfe.siemens.de

Abstract

Im Projekt HYTEA (HYperTExt Authoring) wird die Entwicklung komplexer, systematisch strukturierter Hyperdokumente unterstützt.

Grundlage ist das Hypertext Design Modell HDM. Mit HDM wurden die Online-Version eines Benutzermanuals zum Formularbearbeitungsprogramm SIFORM sowie ein Hilfetext zur Dokumentation der Hardware- und Software-Infrastruktur unserer Gruppe modelliert.

In diesem Papier wird exemplarisch das Übertragen der HDM-Spezifikation der SIFORM-Anwendung in das Zielsystem FrameMaster beschrieben. Die explizit visualisierte HDM-Struktur soll dem Benutzer Orientierungs- und Navigationsvorteile liefern.

Die Layout-Überlegungen wurden verallgemeinert und in einem weiteren Zielsystem (Tool-Book) anhand beider Anwendungen evaluiert.

1   Einleitung

> The answer on 'gotos' was not to produce
> elaborate maps off all the gotos in a program. . . .
> A hypertext link is a goto.   Peter Brown

In [SMS 92] wurden die ersten Ergebnisse des Projektes HYTEA (HYperTExt Authoring) vorgestellt. Durch einen Strukturierungsansatz sollen sowohl dem Autor beim Erstellen als auch dem Leser beim Bearbeiten großer Hyperdokumente Vorteile entstehen.

In HYTEA werden Autorenwerkzeuge sowie konkrete Hypertext-Anwendungen erstellt. Das theoretische Fundament von HYTEA, ein Hypertext Design Modell (HDM), die HYTEA Autorenwerkzeuge sowie eine mit HDM modellierte Anwendung sind in [SMS 92] ausführlich beschrieben. Bei der Anwendung handelt es sich um ein Benutzerhandbuch zum Formularbearbeitungsprogramm SIFORM, das als Online-Dokument zur Verfügung gestellt werden soll. Zur Erinnerung werden im Kapitel 2 zunächst das Projekt HYTEA, HDM und die SIFORM-Anwendung knapp dargestellt.

In [SMS 92] stand die (abstrakte) HDM-Modellierung der SIFORM-Applikation im Mittelpunkt. Im Kapitel 3 dieses Papiers wird nun beschrieben, wie die HDM-Spezifikation konkret in das Zielsystem FrameMaster übertragen wurde und welche Orientierungs- und Navigationsvorteile dem Benutzer durch die HDM-Struktur entstehen.

Die Ergebnisse aus dem SIFORM-Prototypen und deren mögliche Nutzung werden im Kapitel 4 zusammengefaßt. Kapitel 4 enthält außerdem zwei Hardcopies unserer Anwendungen im Zielsystem ToolBook.

2 Das Umfeld der SIFORM-Anwendung

Das Projekt HYTEA

Im EG-geförderten Projekt HYTEA (HYperTExt Authoring, ESPRIT P 5252) werden Methoden und Werkzeuge für die systematische Strukturierung von Hypertext entwickelt [SMS 92].
Bei großen, komplexen Anwendungen besteht ein erheblicher Aufwand für das Erzeugen und Warten von Node-Link Verknüpfungen. Spaghetti-Strukturen können entstehen mit der Gefahr, daß der Leser die Orientierung verliert. Derzeitige Hypertext/Hypermedia-Systeme sind auf das direkte Bearbeiten von Knoten und Links ausgerichtet, von uns mit 'authoring-in-the-small' bezeichnet. Ein Arbeiten im größeren Maßstab wird meistens nicht unterstützt. Deswegen werden im Projekt HYTEA Autorenwerkzeuge entwickelt, um große Hyperdokumente systematisch und effizient aufbauen und warten zu können. Die Autorenproduktivität wird durch die Verwendung von Werkzeugen erheblich verbessert.
Wesentlicher Kern von HYTEA ist HDM, ein Hypertext Design Modell [GPSb 91]. Mit HDM können Hypertexte systemunabhängig auf einem abstrakteren Niveau modelliert und beschrieben werden: Der Autor geht von der Node-Link Ebene über zum Arbeiten mit höheren, selbstdefinierten Strukturen ('authoring-in-the-large', s.u. sowie [GPSa 91]).
Neben den Werkzeugen werden in HYTEA auch Anwendungen erstellt, die bereits die geforderten strukturellen Regularitäten aufweisen. Anhand dieser Anwendungen sollen sowohl die wichtigsten Ideen von HDM verdeutlicht als auch der Entwurf der HYTEA Werkzeuge überprüft und beeinflußt werden. Eine dieser Anwendungen ist die in [SMT 92] ausführlich beschriebene SIFORM-Applikation.

Das Hypertext Design Modell (HDM)

Das Hypertext-Design-Modell HDM ist ein erweitertes, modifiziertes Entity-Relationship-Modell. Grundprimitive sind definiert, um Objekte, deren Eigenschaften sowie Beziehungen zwischen den Objekten einfach zu modellieren. Diese Grundprimitive sollen hier anhand eines kleinen Beispiels kurz erläutert werden.
Beim Arbeiten mit HDM wird zwischen Schema-Level und Instanz-Level unterschieden. Auf dem Schema-Level werden Klassen von Objekten gebildet sowie die interne Struktur der Elemente einer solchen Klasse definiert. In der HDM-Sprechweise werden die Klassen mit 'Entity-Typ' bezeichnet, die Substrukturen mit 'Aggregaten', die sich aus weiteren Aggregaten oder 'Komponenten' zusammensetzen können. Beispielsweise könnten auf Schema-Level die beiden Entity-Typen 'Maler' und 'Kunstwerk' definiert werden, die sich aus den Komponenten 'Persönliche Daten', 'Lebenslauf' und 'Werke' bzw. 'Kurzbeschreibung' und 'Abbildung' zusammensetzen. Dadurch ist die Struktur der Beschreibungen aller Maler und aller Kunstwerke allgemein definiert. Auf Instanz-Ebene würde man dann konkrete Instanzen -sogenannte 'Entities'- angeben, z.B. den Maler 'Kandinsky' mit seinen konkreten Daten, seinem Lebenslauf und eine Liste seiner Werke. Analog können mit HDM Link-Typen sowie konkrete Links definiert werden. Dabei unterscheidet HDM zwischen strukturellen und applikativen Links. Strukturelle Links verbinden Komponenten innerhalb einer Entity, applikative Links führen zu einer anderen Entity des gleichen oder eines anderen Entity-Typs.
Durch das Instantiieren eines HDM-Schemas entsteht eine Hypertext-Basis aus Entities und Links. Um direkten Zugriff auf die Informationen der Hypertext-Basis zu ermöglichen, bietet HDM zusätzlich zwei Arten von Zugriffsstrukturen an: Guided Tours und Indexe. Diese alternativen Zugriffsstrukturen ermöglichen es, den Benutzer-spezifischen Bedürfnissen entsprechend unterschiedliche Lesestrategien zu unterstützen.

Zur HDM-Modellierung der SIFORM-Anwendung

SIFORM (SINIX) V2.0 ist ein von der Siemens Nixdorf Informationssysteme AG entwickeltes komfortables Programm zur Formularbearbeitung. SIFORM basiert auf dem DTP-Programm FrameMaster und läuft unter SINIX, der von SNI vertriebenen UNIX-Version.
Figur 1 zeigt einen Bildschirmausschnitt, in dem rechts Dialogboxen und Fenster der SIFORM-Arbeitsumgebung in einer typischen Weise angeordnet sind. Links daneben ist das Deckblatt der Online-Version des dazugehörigen Benutzerhandbuches zu sehen.

SIFORM unterscheidet bei der Formularbearbeitung zwischen dem Erstellmodus und dem Ausfüllmodus. Im Erstellmodus können Formulare neu erstellt, modifiziert und gespeichert werden. Im Ausfüllmodus können mit SIFORM erstellte Formulare am Bildschirm schnell und einfach ausgefüllt werden. Sowohl für Anwender, die Formulare erstellen als auch für Anwender, die Formulare ausfüllen, existieren entsprechende Manuale. Mit HDM modelliert wurde das Benutzerhandbuch zum Erstellen von Formularen, das 136 Seiten umfaßt. Als prototypales Online-Dokument wurden wiederum Teile der HDM-Spezifikation mit FrameMaster implementiert. Dieser Teil der Anwendung steht im Blickpunkt des vorliegenden Papiers. Nachfolgend werden die relevanten Teile der HDM-Spezifikation angegeben. Zur vollständigen Beschreibung der Anwendungsmodellierung verweisen wir auf [SMT 92].

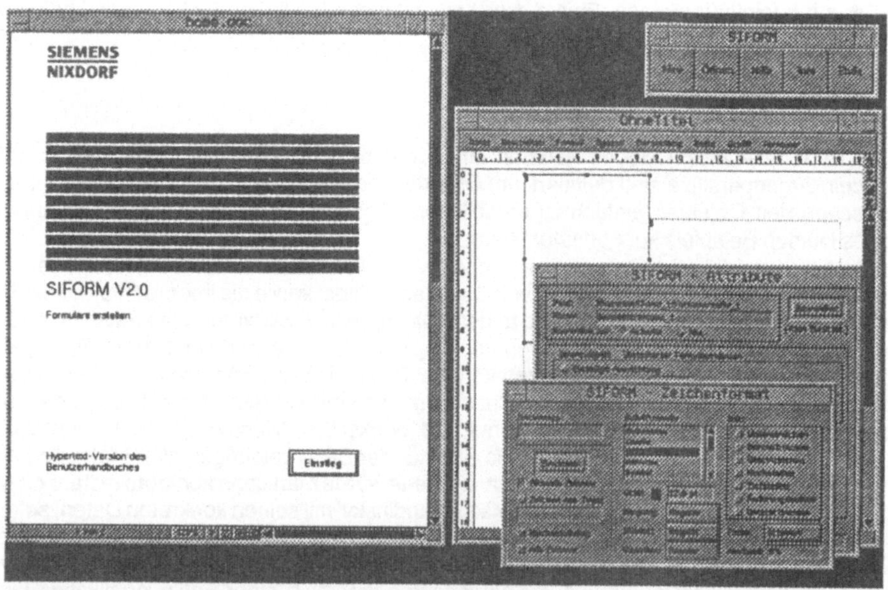

Figur 1

Der in FrameMaster implementierte Prototyp umfaßt die vier Entity-Typen 'Formular', 'Prozedur', 'Dialogbox' und 'Fehler'.
Bei den Instanzen des Entity-Typen 'Formular' handelt es sich um Beschreibungen von SIFORM-spezifischen Formularkomponenten, wie etwa Formularrahmen oder Feldern.

Diese Beschreibungen können in einen allgemeinen Teil, in Abschnitte über den Aufbau und Verwendungszweck einer Formularkomponente sowie Detailinformationen gegliedert werden. Der Entity-Typ 'Formular' setzt sich also aus den (optionalen) Komponenten 'Allgemeines', 'Aufbau', 'Verwendung' und 'Details' zusammen.
Entsprechend sind die drei weiteren Entity-Typen in Komponenten unterteilt. Prozeduren werden in SIFORM zum Kreieren und Modifizieren von Formularkomponenten benötigt. Mithilfe von Dialogboxen werden die entsprechenden Prozeduren ausgeführt. Zu einer Prozedur gibt es allgemeine Informationen sowie eine Folge von Handlungsanweisungen (Komponenten 'Allgemeines' und 'Aktionen'), zu einer Dialogbox neben dem Allgemeinen noch eine 'Abbildung' und 'Attribute'. Ein Fehler wird durch 'Allgemeines' beschrieben. In der Komponente 'Lösung' wird eine mögliche Fehlerbehandlung angegeben.

3 Die SIFORM-Anwendung im Zielsystem FrameMaster

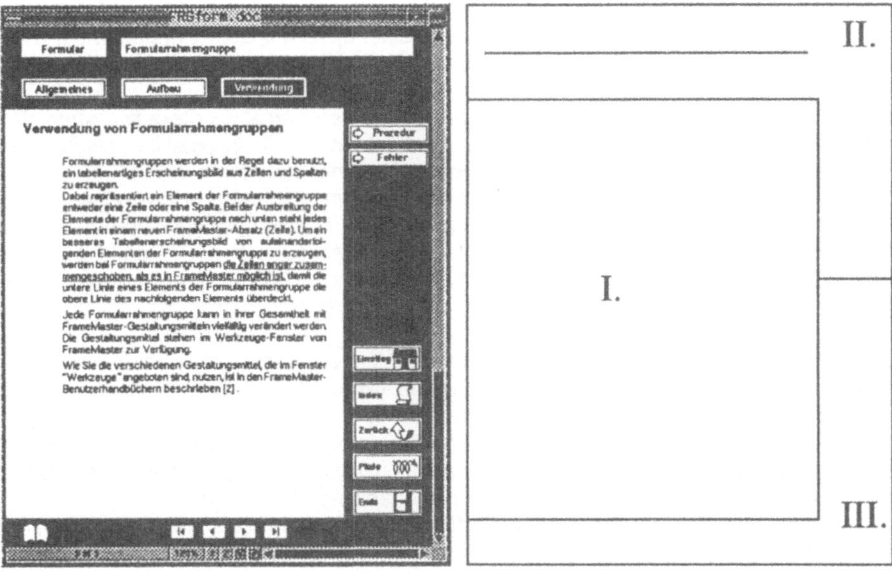

Figur 2

Entwurf eines einheitlichen Layouts für alle Instanzen

Unser Grundgedanke war es, alle Seiten des Hypertextes mit einem einheitlichen Layout zu präsentieren. Der Benutzer soll die jeweiligen Navigations- und Orientierungshilfen stets an gleicher Stelle vorfinden, um sich möglichst einfach im gesamten Hyperdokument zurechtzufinden. Das Hypertext-Fenster ist somit in ff. Teilbereiche untergliedert:

- Inhaltsbereich für Text und Grafik (I.)
- HDM Status- und Navigationsbereich (II.)
- Bereich für Werkzeuge, Features (III.)

Über dem eigentlichen Inhalt (Text, Grafik) wird in zwei Kopfleisten die HDM-Strukturierung der Anwendung explizit hervorgehoben. Die Knöpfe dieses Bereiches dienen sowohl zur Navigation als auch zur Orientierung. Außerdem werden Links auf andere Instanzen im HDM-Bereich verankert, wobei Links gleicher Link-Typen in einem gemeinsamen Anker zusammengefaßt werden.

Streng getrennt vom HDM-Bereich ist der dritte Bereich, über den gängige Hypertext-Möglichkeiten wie etwa die Historie oder ein Index gesteuert werden können. Nachfolgend werden die einzelnen Bereiche genauer betrachtet.

Der Inhaltsbereich (I.)

In der Mitte des Fensters wird im flächenmäßig größten Bereich der eigentliche Inhalt der Anwendung angezeigt. Bei der SIFORM-Anwendung handelt es sich hierbei um Text und Darstellungen diverser Dialogboxen. Der Text lag bereits in FrameMaster-Dateien vor[1]. Da die Textformatierung dieser Dokumente für den Ausdruck auf Papier ausgerichtet war, mußten nach dem Kopieren einzelner Textstücke in das Hyperdokument die Schriftart- und Größe angepaßt werden, so daß der Text am Bildschirm in einer optisch ansprechenden und gut lesbaren Form erscheint. Bei den Grafiken handelt es sich um Screendumps der SIFORM-Dialogboxen, die als Bitmaps in den Inhaltsbereich importiert wurden.

Teile des Textes wurden mit FrameMaster Hypertext-Markern versehen, die optisch durch Unterstreichungen zu erkennen sind. Bei den somit entstandenen 'Hotwords' ist zwischen einfachen Popup-Texten und Menüs sowie eingebetteten Links zu unterscheiden.

Beim Aktivieren von Popups' bleibt die aktuelle Seite im Inhaltsbereich unverändert. Es wird lediglich Zusatzinformation angeboten, beispielsweise in einer kleinen Popup-Box. Im Gegensatz dazu wird bei einer Link-Aktivierung im Inhaltsbereich die Link-Quelle durch das Link-Ziel ersetzt. Um den Leser vor 'unerwarteten' Links zu schützen, sind Popups und eingebettete Links optisch unterscheidbar: Popup-Hotwords sind durch das zusätzlich angehängte Zeichen '❑' gekennzeichnet.

Durch die eingebetteten Links wird dem eiligen Benutzer ein rasches Navigieren ermöglicht. Mit einem Mausklick kann beispielsweise von einer Textstelle wie ' ... Attribute, die in einem entsprechenden Dialogfenster eingetragen werden ... ' zur zughörigen Abbildung navigiert werden. Die in den Text eingebetteten Link-Quellen zeigen dem Leser an, daß es zu einer Zeile, einem Absatz oder einer Seite relevante Zusatzinformationen gibt, verdeutlichen jedoch oftmals nicht, welcher 'Art' diese Informationen sind.

Um dem Benutzer vor der Link-Aktivierung den Zusammenhang zwischen Link-Quelle und Ziel deutlich aufzuzeigen, sind alle zu den Hotwords gehörenden Links zusätzlich im nachfolgend beschriebenen HDM-Bereich verankert.

Der HDM Status- und Navigationsbereich (II.)

In zwei Kopfleisten und im rechten, oberen Seitenbereich des Fensters wird die Strukturierung der SIFORM-Anwendung mit HDM-Primitiven explizit hervorgehoben. Verglichen mit ad hoc erstellten Hypertexten soll dem Benutzer über diesen Mehr-Aufwand (Strukturierungsarbeit, größerer Platzbedarf, ...) ein Nutzen entstehen: Durch das Miteinbeziehen der Struktur sollen Orientierung und Navigation deutlich verbessert werden.

Betrachtet man den Inhaltsbereich des Hypertext-Fensters, so ist der gerade sichtbare Text und/oder die dargestellte Dialogbox Teil einer Instanz. Diese Instanz wird hier mit 'aktuelle Instanz' bezeichnet.

---

1. Aus pragmatischen Gründen sollten keine Veränderungen am Originaltext vorgenommen werden.

Zur globalen und lokalen Einordnung des dargestellten Inhalts werden folgende Orientierungshilfen angeboten: Neben dem Instanznamen wird in der oberen Kopfleiste der Entity-Typ der aktuellen Instanz angezeigt. In der unteren Kopfleiste kann der Benutzer die Struktur der aktuellen Instanz erkennen, d.h. die Anzahl sowie die Bezeichnung der einzelnen Komponenten. Jeder Komponente entspricht ein Knopf, der mit dem Namen der Komponente beschriftet ist. Durch das schwarz Hinterlegen einzelner Knöpfe in der unteren Leiste wird angedeutet, in welchem Teil der internen Struktur der aktuellen Instanz man sich gerade befindet.

Um den expliziten Gebrauch von Entity-Typ, Instanz, Instanznamen und Komponenten als Orientierungshilfen zu verdeutlichen, soll hier beispielhaft der Inhalt des in Figur 2 abgebildeten Fensters eingeordnet werden: Der Textausschnitt ist Teil der Instanz 'Formularrahmengruppe' vom Entity-Typ 'Formular'. Diese Instanz ist aus den Komponenten 'Allgemeines', 'Aufbau' und Verwendung zusammengesetzt. Momentan ist die Komponente 'Verwendung' sichtbar.

Aus Instanzname und Bezeichnung der Komponenten können Sätze wie etwa 'Allgemeine Informationen zu Formularrahmengruppen' gebildet werden. Dies kann hilfreich sein, da nicht alle Textstücke wie im Beispiel mit eigenen Überschriften versehen sind.

Die Komponentenknöpfe können gleichzeitig zur Navigation eingesetzt werden. Will man beispielsweise von der aktuellen Komponente 'Verwendung' zu 'allgemeinen Informationen über Formularrahmengruppen' gelangen (siehe Figur 2), so wird die Komponente 'Allgemeines' durch Anklicken des entsprechend beschrifteten Knopfes angesteuert. Nach dem Aktivieren dieses strukturellen Links (HDM-Terminologie) wird der Komponentenknopf 'Allgemeines' schwarz unterlegt, der Knopf 'Verwendung' erscheint wieder in normaler Darstellung.

In obiger Beschreibung des Inhaltsbereiches wurde bereits erwähnt, daß die in HDM mit applikativen Links bezeichneten Querverweise zu anderen Instanzen (Entities vom gleichen Entity-Typ sowie Entities anderer Entity-Typen) zusätzlich im HDM-Bereich verankert sind. Derartige Anker für applikative Links finden sich im Hypertext-Fenster rechts oben, im zum HDM-Bereich gehörenden Seitenbereich. Die Knöpfe sind durch kleine Pfeile gekennzeichnet.

Außerdem tragen die Knöpfe den Namen des Entity-Typen der Ziel-Instanzen, auf die die im Knopf verankerten Links gerichtet sind: Es können mehrere Links in einem Knopf verankert werden, wobei diese Links vom gleichen Link-Typ sind, d.h. speziell also auch auf Instanzen vom gleichen Entity-Typ verweisen.

Beim Anklicken eines Knopfes erscheint ein Popup-Menü mit den Link-Bezeichnern. Durch das Aneinanderreihen von Entity-Typ und Instanzname der Quelle, Entity-Typ der Ziel-Instanz sowie Link-Bezeichner können wieder -ähnlich wie oben beschrieben- Sätze gebildet werden, die dem Benutzer Aufschluß geben über die Bedeutung eines Links, über Art des Ziels, etc. Damit können wiederum Überraschungseffekte vermieden werden. Ist beispielsweise der Entity-Typ 'Prozedur' als Ziel bekannt, so erwartet der Benutzer bereits beim Aktivieren des Links eine Folge von Handlungsanweisungen in der Ziel-Instanz. Das Problem der Desorientierung (vgl. z.B. [Con 87], [ShM 91]) kann somit a priori verringert werden.

Nachfolgend werden Vorteile und Probleme dieses Ansatzes angesprochen.

Genauer betrachtet sind sowohl von Hotwords ausgehende Links zusätzlich als auch weitere, nicht in den Text eingebettete Links 'einmalig' in den entsprechenden Knöpfen des HDM-Bereiches verankert. Die Zuordnung ist also nicht ein-eindeutig. Oftmals ergeben sich durch die Umstrukturierung des Originaltextes Verzweigungen, die nicht textuell beschrieben sind, wodurch auch keine Basis für Hotwords gegeben ist. Zum Beispiel könnten im linearen Text eine Beschreibung des Objekts XYZ sowie Handlungsanweisungen zum Erzeugen und Modifizieren dieses Objekts direkt aufeinanderfolgen. Bei der Umstrukturierung dieses Text-

Materials in Entities der Typen 'Formular' und 'Prozedur' muß die Instanz 'Objektbeschreibung XYZ' Absprungplätze zu den beiden Prozedur-Instanzen 'Erzeugen XYZ' und 'Modifizieren XYZ' aufweisen. Durch das Aufeinanderfolgen im linearen Text fehlen entsprechende Hinweise, die Links werden somit im HDM-Bereich verankert. Es gäbe auch die Möglichkeit, entsprechenden Text manuell hinzuzufügen, z.B. 'Wählen Sie jetzt eine der beiden nachfolgenden Prozeduren aus: . . . '. Dies widerspricht sich mit unserer Auflage, den Originaltext möglichst unverändert zu lassen. Außerdem sind durch den oben beschriebenen Ansatz stets die SIFORM-Handlungsanweisungen von den Hypertext-Anweisungen getrennt. Dadurch wird die kognitive Belastung (vgl. z.B. [Ber 91], [Con 87], [ShM 91]) des Benutzers bei der Handhabung des Hyperdokumentes verringert.
Daß nicht ganz auf die Hotwords verzichtet wird, hat neben dem Geschwindigkeitsaspekt (für obigen Ansatz sind mehrere Mausklicks- und Bewegungen nötig) noch folgenden Grund: Die applikativen Links können den relevanten Textstellen besser zugeordnet werden. Der Benutzer kann dadurch abschätzen, welchen Teil des Inhaltsbereiches er bereits bearbeitet haben sollte, bevor er einen Link aktiviert und zu welchen Textstellen überhaupt noch weitere Informationen existieren, auf die verwiesen wird.

Der Bereich für Werkzeuge und Features (III.)

Abschließend soll hier noch der dritte Bereich beschrieben werden, über den Werkzeuge und gängige Hypertext-Möglichkeiten (an)gesteuert werden können. Neben einfachen Blättermechanismen werden u.a. alternative Zugriffsstrukturen (Index, Guided Tours) sowie eine Historie angeboten. Als Grundgedanke soll hier hervorgehoben werden, daß die Bedienung dieser Features klar von der Navigation über visualisierte HDM-Primitive getrennt wurde. Eine Mixtur von strukturellen Elementen und Werkzeugen könnte den Benutzer verwirren. Außerdem wäre es somit denkbar, den Werkzeugbereich des Fensters für andere Applikationen erneut zu nutzen und nur im HDM-Bereich neue Primitive einzufügen.
Nachfolgend eine Kurzbeschreibung der Knöpfe. Als alternative Zugriffsstruktur wird exemplarisch der Index diskutiert.

Im unteren Bereich des Fensters befinden sich vier Pfeiltasten, die zum Durchblättern von Komponenten benutzt werden, welche sich über mehrere Seiten erstrecken. Die Knöpfe haben die gebräuchlichen Bedeutungen 'Anfang', 'rückwärts', 'vorwärts' und 'Ende'.
Über die Buch-Ikone in der linken, unteren Ecke kann der Benutzer abfragen, auf welcher Manual-Seite sich der aktuell sichtbare Inhalt befindet. Es wäre beispielsweise ein Scenario denkbar, in dem zunächst im Hypertext zur relevanten Information navigiert wird und dann im Manual weitergearbeitet wird.
Die Knöpfe des rechten Seitenbereiches: Über den Knopf 'Einstieg' gelangt der Benutzer zum Deckblatt (Einstiegspunkt, erste Seite; vgl. Figur 1) des Hyperdokumentes, über 'Ende' kann die Sitzung beendet und das Dokument geschlossen werden. Die Historie wird über den Knopf 'Zurück' gesteuert. Der Benutzer kann sich schrittweise zu den zuletzt besuchten Komponenten bzw. Entities zurückhangeln. Über den Knopf 'Pfade' kann in vordefinierte Pfade (Guided Tours) eingestiegen werden.
Figur 3 zeigt einen Ausschnitt der Fensterfolgen beim alternativen Informationszugriff über einen Index. Beim Anklicken des Knopfes 'Index' wird im Dokumentfenster eine Indexseite angezeigt, die zunächst globale Kontexte anbietet, konkret unsere Entity-Typen der SIFORM-Anwendung. Per Mausklick kann ein Entity-Typ ausgewählt werden, worauf detailliertere Unterteilungen des Kontextes eingeblendet werden, nämlich Unterbereiche und Instanzen. Figur 3 zeigt im linken Fenster die Unterteilung des Entity-Typen 'Prozedur'. Beim Auswählen einer Instanz wird diese im Dokumentfenster angezeigt, mit der gewohnten Unterteilung in drei Bereiche. Im Scenario von Figur 3 hätte der Benutzer die Instanz 'Formularrahmengruppe

- individuelle Attribute festlegen' ausgewählt. Diese Art der Navigation wird in erster Linie für erfahrene SIFORM-Benutzer angeboten, die bereits konkret wissen, zu welcher Formular-komponente, Prozedur oder Dialogbox sie Informationen benötigen.

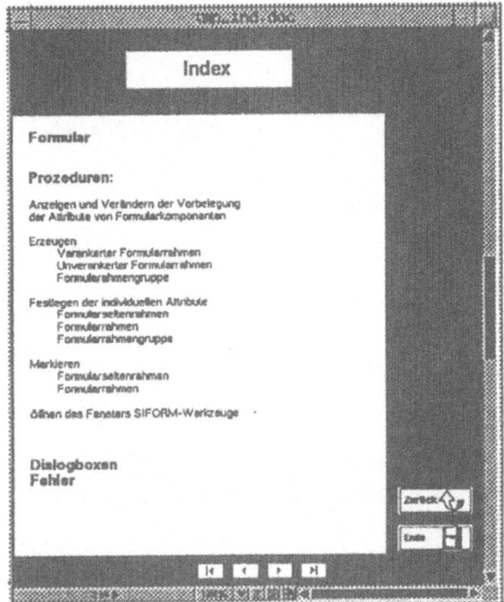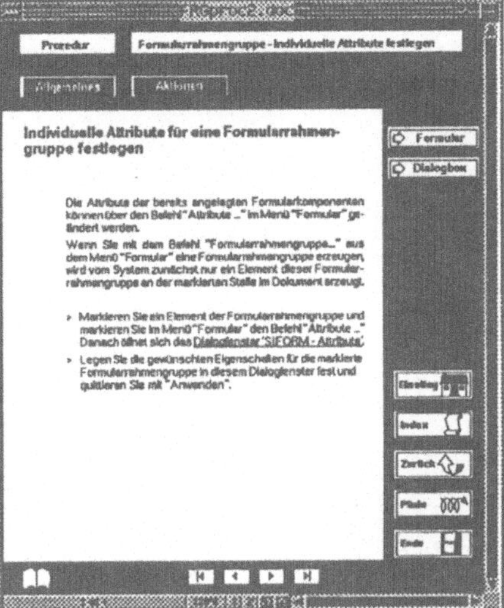

Figur 3

4   Kritische Diskussion, Zusammenfassung, Ausblick

Was kann man aus dem SIFORM-Prototypen lernen ?

Der Übergang von chaotischen Netzen aus Knoten und Links zu strukturierten Netzsystemen, die aus abstrakteren Einheiten gebildet sind, wird immer häufiger gefordert [Ber 91][GPSa 91]. Unsere Erfahrungen zeigen, daß es sinnvoll ist, die Strukturierungselemente explizit zur Orientierung und Navigation in einem Hyperdokument zu visualisieren.
In unserem mit HDM modellierten Hypertext werden Entity-Typen zur Bildung von Teil-systemen sowie zur Definition interner Strukturen einzelner Elemente eines solchen Teil-systems herangezogen. Der Entity-Typ 'Prozedur' umfaßt beispielsweise die Menge aller Prozeduren und definiert gleichzeitig die Struktur einer einzelnen Prozedurbeschreibung (vgl. [SMT 92]). Außerdem werden über einen Index weitere Subsysteme definiert, z.B. die Menge der Prozeduren zum Erzeugen von Objekten. Verallgemeinert kann man feststellen, daß fol-gende zwei Aspekte beim Einbeziehen der Struktur in Orientierungs- und Navigationshilfen wichtig sind:

(1)   Es muß möglich sein, innerhalb einer explizit abgegrenzten Substruktur lokal zu navigieren und

(2)   die lokale Substruktur muß global, im gesamten Hyperdokument einge-ordnet bzw. angesteuert erden können (vgl. [ShM 91]).

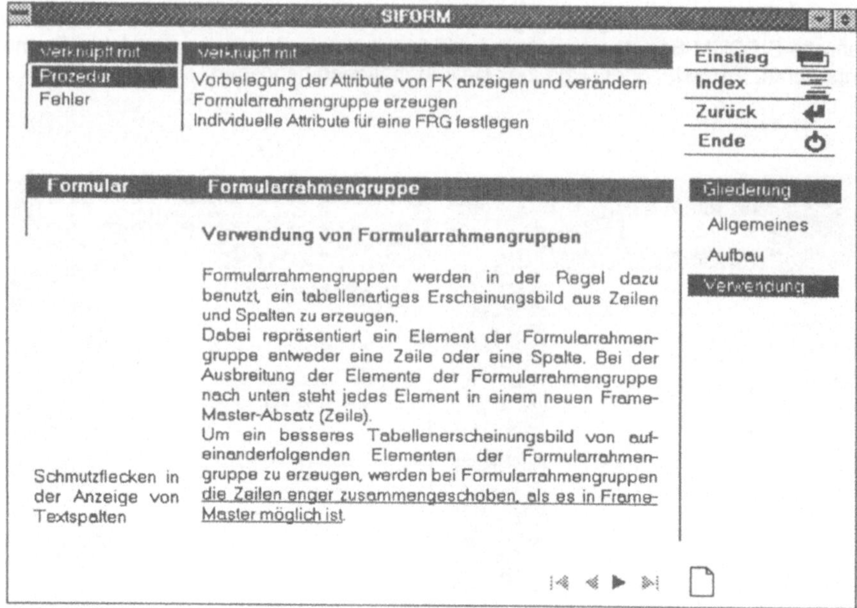

Figur 4

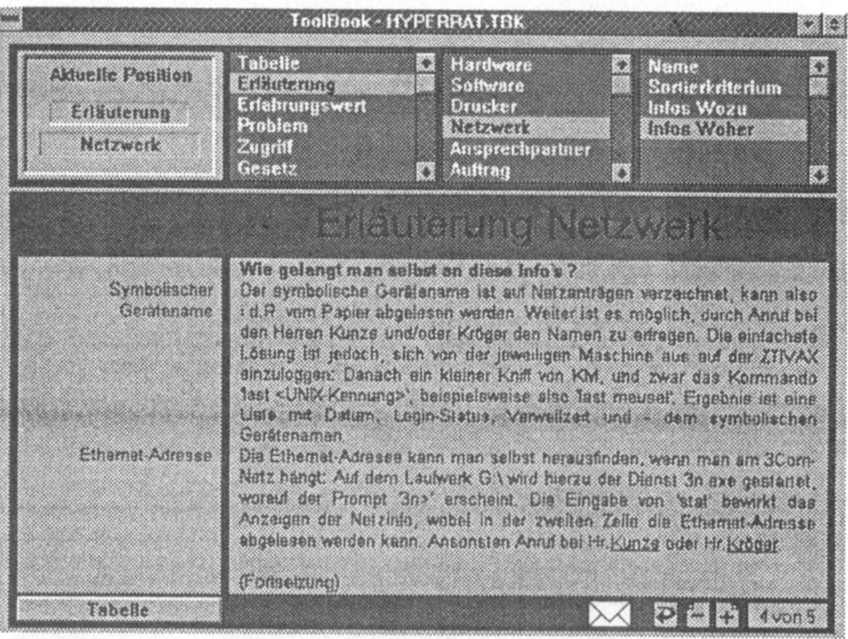

Figur 5

Bei den im SIFORM-Prototypen eingebauten Werkzeugen kommt es uns in erster Linie auf die strikte Trennung von struktureller Orientierung/Navigation und Werkzeugbereich an. Es wurde kein Aufwand für besonders ausgeklügelte Features investiert[1]. Einen unverzichtbaren Grundbaukasten dürften Historie, Index, lineare Pfade [Ber 91] und eventuell grafische Übersichtskarten darstellen. Hier würde es sich anbieten, einen solchen Grundbaukasten gesondert zu entwerfen und wiederverwendbar anzubieten.

Einen hohen Zeitaufwand benötigte das Ausgestalten und Implementieren von FrameMaster-Templates: Neben dem grafischen Entwurf waren Verzeichnishierarchien zu definieren, Hintergrundseiten (Master-Pages) zu implementieren, etc.

Ein weiteres Zielsystem: ToolBook

Die SIFORM-Applikation sowie ein Informationstext, der die Rechnerlandschaft unserer Gruppe beschreibt, wurden auch in ToolBook implementiert. Beim Übergang in dieses weitere Hypertext-Zielsystem wurde das Layout mithilfe eines professionellen Designers überarbeitet. Ziele waren u.a. Erweiterbarkeit und Wiederverwendbarkeit des Entwurfs für beliebige Applikationen. Beispielsweise soll es auch möglich sein, komplexe Strukturen mit mehreren Entity-Typen und Hierarchie-Ebenen anzuzeigen. Die Figuren 4 und 5 zeigen das Bildschirm-Layout beider Anwendungen. Durch ein Raster entstehen wieder Inhalts-Bereich, Navigations- und Orientierungsleiste, Marginalspalte sowie Bereiche zur Steuerung von Hypertext-Werkzeugen.

Wo wurden die Systeme bereits vorgeführt ?

Eine Grundversion der SIFORM-Anwendung wurde auf den Konferenzen 'Hypertext und Hypermedia '92' in München und 'ECHT '92' in Mailand sowie auf der 'ESPRIT Conference Week 1992' in Brüssel vorgestellt.
Die zweite Anwendung, der Informationstext zu unserer Rechnerlandschaft, wurde im November '92 auf einer dreitägigen Informations-Messe der ZFE auf dem Standort München-Perlach präsentiert. Aufgrund der positiven Erfahrungen sind Ausbaustufen beider Anwendungen geplant (beispielsweise Implementierung von Guided Tours).
Der Informationstext wird innerhalb unserer Gruppe als Hilfsmittel bei Hardware- und Software-Bestellungen und in Service-Fällen eingesetzt.

Wofür können die Ergebnisse genutzt werden ?

Konkret im Projekt HYTEA können die Ergebnisse für ein Targeting-Tool [SMS 92] eingesetzt werden. Beim sogenannten Targeting wird das abstrakte, mit HDM spezifizierte Skellett einer Hypertext-Anwendung in ein konkretes Zielsystem übertragen. Es werden Seiten mit einem vorgegebenen Layout automatisch erzeugt. Über aktivierbare Knöpfe und Menüs werden diese Seiten bereits vorverdrahtet. Der Autor muß nur noch den Inhalt in die vorgefertigten Seiten einfügen und kleine Ergänzungen vornehmen, z.B. zusätzliche Hotwords definieren. Konkrete Layouts, Art und Funktionsweise von Knöpfen, zu verwendende Wekzeuge etc. werden in das Targeting-Tool eingespeist. Innerhalb des HYTEA-Teams ist es somit geplant, die Erfahrungen an die Entwickler dieses Tools weiterzuleiten[2].

---

1. In der derzeitigen Version von FrameMaster wäre hierzu ein Hinabsteigen auf die Sprache C nötig gewesen, d.h. es hätten Erweiterungen innerhalb der OSF Motif-Umgebung vorgenommen werden müssen.
2. i.e. Olivetti Systems and Networks, Italy

Allgemein könnte man sich vorstellen, derartige vorstrukturierte und vorverdrahtete Seiten einmalig manuell zu erstellen und in Bibliotheken anzubieten. Dies würde ff. Vorteile bringen:

- Hoher Zeitaufwand beim wiederholten Erstellen von Templates fällt weg

- Einheitliche Oberflächen in verschiedenen Dokumenten und Systemen verbessern die Handhabbarkeit

- Autoren, technische Redakteure etc. müssen/können keine Hypertext-Spezialisten werden/sein

Beim Entwurf von 'General-Purpose' Hypertext-Systemen oder aber beim Definieren von Standards können obige Erfahrungswerte ebenfalls nützlich sein.

Vergleichbare Ansätze

Die Strukturierung von Hypertexten wird beispielsweise auch im Toolkit von SEPIA [THH 91] als wichtige Möglichkeit angesehen. Die Erfahrungen beim Entwurf von Hypertext-Templates werden in [CGL 91] geschildert. Lokale und globale Sichtweisen zur Orientierung und Navigation werden im Hypertextsystem 'SmallCard' angeboten. Eine ausführliche Beschreibung findet sich in [ShM 91]. Ideen zum 'Erweitern' des Hypertext-Systems 'HyperCard' sind in [Nie 90] beschrieben. Ähnliche Erweiterungen für das System 'ToolBook' sind bei uns geplant, ebenso wie die geplante Re-Implementierung der SIFORM-Applikation in 'ToolBook'.

5 Danksagungen

Wir möchten uns bei allen Partnern des HYTEA-Konsortiums für die Unterstützung bei der Entwicklung des SIFORM-Prototypen bedanken. Insbesondere gilt unser Dank Franca Garzotto und Paolo Paolini vom Politecnico di Milano, Manfred Thüring von der GMD sowie den beiden Studenten Iris Rademacher und Thomas Nordmeyer.

6 Literatur

[Ber 91]   M.Bernstein, P.J.Brown, M.Frisse, R.J.Glushko, G.Landow, P.Zellweger: *'Structure, Navigation, and Hypertext: The Status of the Navigation Problem'* Proceedings of the 3rd ACM Conference on Hypertext, pp. 363-366, December 1991

[CGL 91]   K. Smith Catlin, L.N.Garrett, J.A.Launhardt: *'Hypermedia Templates: An Author's Tool'*, Proceedings of the 3rd ACM Conference on Hypertext, pp. 147-160, December 1991

[Con 87]   J.Conklin: *'Hypertext: An Introduction and Survey'*, IEEE Computer, S.17-41, September 1987

[GPSa 91]   F.Garzotto, P.Paolini, D.Schwabe: *'Authoring-in-the-large: Software engineering techniques for hypertext application design'*, Proceedings of the 6th IEEE International Workshop on Software Specification and Design, October 1991

[GPSb 91]   F.Garzotto, P.Paolini, D.Schwabe: *'HDM - A model for the design of hypertext applications'*, Proceedings of the 3rd ACM Conference on Hypertext, pp. 313-328, December 1991

[Nie 90]   J.Nielsen: *'The Art of Navigating through Hypertext'*, auszugsweise enthalten in: *'Hypertext and Hypermedia'*, Academic Press, 1990

[ShM 91]   L.Schmitz, K.Meusel: *'SmallCard - ein Hypertext-System zur Erstellung rechnergestützter Lemeinheiten'*, Diplomarbeit an der TU München, auszugsweise enthalten in: Hypertext/Hypermedia'91, Informatik-Fachberichte 276, Seite 266 ff., Mai 1991

[SMS 92]   B.Schröcksnadl, K.Meusel: *'Benutzerdokumentation von Anwender-Software mit strukturiertem Hypertext'*, 3. Tekom Fachtagung für Online-Dokumentation in Stuttgart/Böblingen, November 1992

[SMS 92]   B.Schröcksnadl, K.Meusel, W.Zucker, J.Schiff, M.Thüring: *'Hypertext Application Design using a Model-Based Approach'*, Kurzvortrag und Systemvorführung auf der Hypertext/Hypermedia'92 in München

[SMT 92]   B.Schröcksnadl, K.Meusel, M.Thüring: *'Technical Documentation: Application requirements; user manual of the forms processing system SIFORM'*, ESPRIT Project 5252, Deliverable 4.1, 1992

[THH 91]   M.Thüring, J.Haake, J.Hannemann: *'What's Eliza doing in the Chinese Room? Incoherent hyperdocuments - and how to avoid them'* Proceedings of the 3rd ACM Conference on Hypertext, pp. 161 -177, December 1991

Hypermedia in der Medizin - Die Gestaltung der digitalen Patientenakte als Hypermedium

Michael Henke
Technische Universität Berlin
Institut für Technische Informatik
Fachgebiet Computer Graphics
Sekr. FR 3-3
Franklinstr. 28/29
D-1000 Berlin 10

Kurzfassung

Die Daten, die von einem Patienten während seiner Aufenthaltsdauer in einer medizinischen Einrichtung anfallen, werden in der Patientenakte abgelegt. Diese Daten entstammen verschiedenen Quellen und sind verschiedenen Typs. War die Patientenakte früher eine Sammlung ausschließlich in analoger Form vorliegender Informationen, so ist heute zu bemerken, daß ein zunehmend großer Anteil als digitale Daten gespeichert wird. Dieses trifft insbesondere auf die Ergebnisse der digitalen bildgebenden Verfahren zu, die den konventionellen Film als Speichermedium immer mehr verdrängen. Das Ergebnis dieses Prozesses ist eine digitale multimediale Patientenakte. Durch die Erweiterung der Krankenhausinfrastrukturen um Hochgeschwindigkeitsnetzwerke für den schnellen Transport extrem hoher Datenmengen, wie sie aus dem Einsatz digitaler bildgebender Verfahren resultieren, besteht die Möglichkeit der multimedia Datenkommunikation zwischen den medizinischen Arbeitsplätzen.
Zwischen den einzelnen Dokumenten einer Patientenakte bestehen enge inhaltliche Zusammenhänge, die einen gemeinsamen Bezugspunkt haben: den Gesundheitszustand des Patienten. So beziehen sich z.B. Befunde auf Bilder vom Patienten, Diagnosen auf Befunde und Therapiepläne auf Diagnosen. Hinzu kommen organisatorische Strukturen, die aus der Logistik der Datenhaltung resultieren. Die Verknüpfung der multimedialen Patientendaten zu einem Hypermedium ergibt sich somit fast zwangsläufig aus der inhaltlichen wie formalen Struktur der Patientenakte.

1. Einleitung

Die Medizin ist ein sensibles Einsatzfeld für Computer. Das medizinische Personal besitzt i.a. nur wenig EDV-Kenntnisse und ist Computertechniken gegenüber oft kritisch eingestellt. Neben dem Einsatz in der Verwaltung (HIS *Hospital Information System*) finden Computer insbesondere in radiologischen Abteilungen Verwendung. Ein Ziel hierbei ist die Ersetzung des Filmmaterials und des konventionellen Lichtkastens durch ein rein digitales System, also einen computergestützten medizinischen Arbeitsplatz (MWS *Medical Workstation*), der über ein hausinternes Netz (LAN *Local Area Network*) mit anderen Arbeitsplätzen, den Scannern der bildgebenden Verfahren und dem Archiv kommunizieren kann. Eine derartige Konfiguration wird PACS (*Picture Archiving and Communication System*) genannt. Hinzu kommt das RIS (*Radiological Information System*), das die Verwaltung der nicht-bildhaften Daten übernimmt. Für die Zukunft wird eine Integration der verschiedenen Systeme angestrebt (für Informationen zu aktuellen Entwicklungen auf diesem Gebiet sei [IMAC 91] empfohlen). Neben den radiologischen Arbeitsplätzen, die mit zweidimensionalen Darstellungen auskommen, gibt es Anwendungen, die Berechnungen und Visualisierung dreidimensionaler Daten benötigen. Diese Anwendungen lassen sich vorzugsweise in der Therapie und deren Planung finden, z.B. in der Strahlentherapie und in der Operationsplanung. Die für die Therapie benötigten Informationen entstammen einer Vielzahl zuvor angelegter Dokumente.

Die Zusammenfasung aller Informationen über einen Patienten geschieht in der Patientenakte. Durch die Vielzahl der darin enthaltenen Datentypen stellt sich die Patientenakte als multimediale Patientenakte (MMMR - *Multi Media Medical Record*) dar.

Dieser Beitrag betrachtet zunächst die digitale Patientenakte, mit den darin vorkommenden Datentypen. Nach einem kurzen Einblick in die Arbeitsabläufe, die zur Behandlung eines Patienten gehören, wird die Gestaltung der digitalen Patientenakte als Hypermedium motiviert. Schließlich wird das Demonstrationssystem HYPAMED (Hypermedia Arbeitsplatz für die Medizin) vorgestellt.

2.   Multimediale Patientendaten

Die Patientenakte, wie sie heute in der überwiegenden Anzahl medizinischer Einrichtungen vorzufinden ist, besteht aus einer Sammlung von Schriftdokumenten, Graphiken und Bildern auf Film. Hinzu kommt ein ständig steigender Anteil digital vorliegender Daten, die überwiegend von den primär digital bildgebenden Verfahren, wie Röntgen-Computer-Tomographie (CT), Magnetresonanz-Tomographie (MR) und digitalen Röntgenaufnahmen (DR) stammen. Tabelle 1 zeigt im Überblick die Vielzahl der Patientendaten. Es ist leicht zu erkennen, daß die meiste Information in Form verschiedener Medien über den Lichtsinn vermittelt wird. Der Gehörsinn leistet für den Arzt zwar nur einen geringen Beitrag zur direkten Gewinnung von

Information über den Patienten, jedoch werden die verbale Kommunikation mit Kollegen (z.B. im Rahmen von Konsultationen) und die Erstellung eines mündlichen Befunds (als Grundlage für eine spätere Niederschrift) schon in den kommenden Jahren wichtige auditive Funktionen eines medizinischen Arbeitsplatzes darstellen. Für zukünftige Entwicklungen ist die Einbeziehung anderer Sinne, als die der bereits genannten, in Erwägung zu ziehen, um möglichst viel Information über den Patienten in seiner Akte zu integrieren. Als Beispiel hierfür ist in Tabelle 1 der Geruchssinn aufgeführt.

Sinn	Medium	Datenquelle
	Festbild	CT, MR, US, DR, SPECT, PET
	Bewegtbild	DSA
	Video	Telekonferenz, Lehrmaterial
	Text	Anamnese, Befund, Diagnose, Therapieplan
	Graphik	Statistiken, EKG, EEG, 2-D / 3-D Vektordarstellungen
	Tabellen	Statistiken, Rechnungen, Zeitreihen
	Sprache	Befunde, Besprechungen, Video-Ton, Sprechart des Patienten
	Töne/ Geräusche	Herztöne, Magen-, Darmgeräusche
	Gerüche	Geruch des Patienten

Tabelle 1: multimediale Patientendaten

Noch liegen Patientendaten in beiden Formen, analog und digital vor. Der Entwicklungstrend vollzieht sich jedoch eindeutig in Richtung auf ein rein digitales Archiv. In Pilotprojekten werden bereits Erfahrungen mit filmlosen medizinischen Einrichtungen gesammelt (siehe z.B [HRUBY 91]).

Speziell in der Bundesrepublik Deutschland werden solche Tendenzen u.a. durch eine restriktive Gesetzgebung (siehe hierzu insbesondere die Röntgenverordnung [RÖV 90]) behindert. So müssen Bilddaten neben der digitalen Archivierung jahrelang auf Film aufbewahrt werden, und für den Transport und die Archivierung digitalen Bildmaterials dürfen keine verlustbehafteten Kompressionsverfahren (z.B. JPEG -*Joint Photographic Experts Group*- Kompression) eingesetzt werden. Bei Datenmengen in der Größenordnung von Gigabyte täglich und Terabyte jährlich ergibt sich ein enorm hoher Bedarf an Langzeitspeicher, zumal das Gesetz eine jahrzehntelange Aufbewahrungsfrist dieser Daten fordert. Für den Transport dieser Datenmengen kommen ausschließlich Hochgeschwindigkeitsglasfasernetze (z.B. FDDI *Fiber Distributed Data Interface*) in Frage. Mit einer erheblichen Verschärfung des Problems des Datenaufkommens ist zu rechnen, wenn solche Dienste, wie Videokonferenzen, in das digitale System integriert werden. Hinzu kommen Tendenzen zum Aufbau verteilter Systeme und zur Einführung der sog. Telemedizin (vergl. [LEMKE 91]).

3.   Befund, Diagnose und Therapie

Während sich ein Patient in einer medizinischen Einrichtung in Behandlung befindet, muß er sich einer Anzahl von Untersuchungen unterziehen. Aus den Ergebnissen, den Befunden, wird eine Diagnose erstellt, die als Grundlage für einen Therapieplan dient. Während und nach der Therapie wird der Patient weiteren Untersuchungen unterzogen, um die Folgen der Therapie zu kontrollieren. Ggf. muß eine Überarbeitung des Therapieplans erfolgen. Abbildung 1 zeigt diesen Kreislauf.
Da die Untersuchungen, die Diagnose und die Therapieplanung i.a. von verschiedenen Ärzten (und anderem medizinischen Personal) vollzogen werden, sind demnach an der Behandlung eines Patienten mehrere Personen beteiligt, die jeweils ihre Aufgabe aufgrund von Informationen lösen, die sie von ihren Kollegen erhalten. Diese Informationen müssen, wie vorher bereits geschildert, heute noch von verschieden Systemen aus abgefragt werden. Durch die Reihenfolge der einzelnen Arbeitsschritte dieses Prozesses ergeben sich die inhaltlichen Abhängigkeiten zwischen den einzelnen Dokumenten, wie sie im nächsten Abschnitt näher vorgestellt werden. Z.Z. geschieht eine Dokumentation dieser Abhängigkeiten lediglich durch eine gemeinsame Aufbewahrung der Dokumente in der (analogen bzw. digitalen) Patientenakte. Beziehungen zu anderen Akten lassen sich nur durch entsprechende Notizen herstellen. Einige digitale Systeme erlauben die Zusammenstellung ausgesuchter Bilder in einer Referenzakte, wobei der Zusammenhang zu den übrigen Patientendaten jedoch für diese Bilder lediglich über den Namen des Patienten besteht.

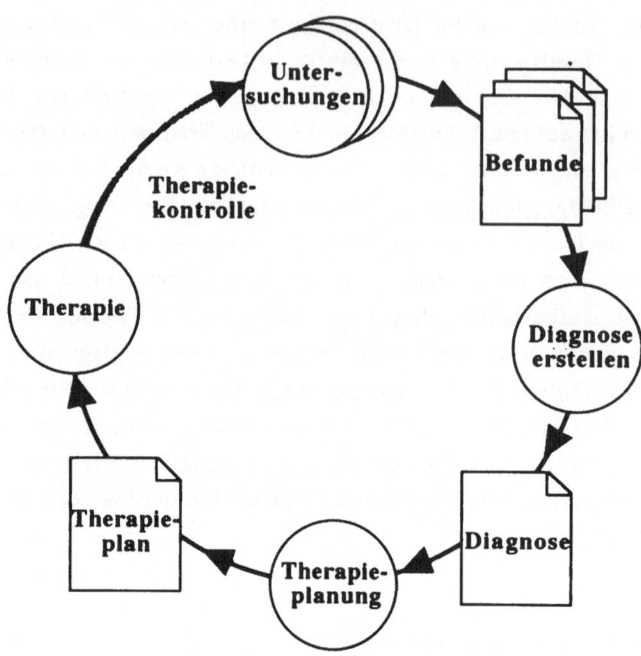

Abbildung 1: Untersuchungs-/Behandlungskreislauf

4. Die Gestaltung der digitalen Patientenakte als Hypermedium

Der entscheidene Punkt bei der Betrachtung der Patientenakte als Hypermedium ist der inhaltliche und formale Zusammenhang der einzelnen Dokumente untereinander. Wie aus dem vorangegangenden Abschnitten ersichtlich wurde, entstehen während der Zeit der Behandlung eines Patienten zahlreiche Dokumente, die z.T. einen inhaltlichen Bezug auf andere Dokumente der selben Akte nehmen. Ebenso können Referenzen zu Dokumenten anderer Patientanakten, z.B. bei einer Bezugnahme auf einen Referenzfall, auftreten.

Abbildung 2 veranschaulicht diese Zusammenhänge. Sie verdeutlicht ebenso das Problem, vor dem der Arzt steht, wenn er die Fähigkeiten eines Arbeitsplatzes ausnutzen möchte, der ihm nicht nur die (Bildverarbeitungs-) Funktionen eines der bereits heute bestehenden medizinischen Arbeitsplätze, sondern zusätzlich auch Hypermedia-Funktionalität bietet: Wie ist es möglich, die gegebenen inhaltlichen Abhängigkeiten zwischen den Dokumenten explizit und nachvollziehbar zu machen? Die Bedeutung einer wohlgestalteten Benutzungsoberfläche zur Lösung des Problems der Handhabung von Bezügen (*links*) und der Navigation durch den Hyperraum kann hierbei nicht hoch genug gewertet werden.

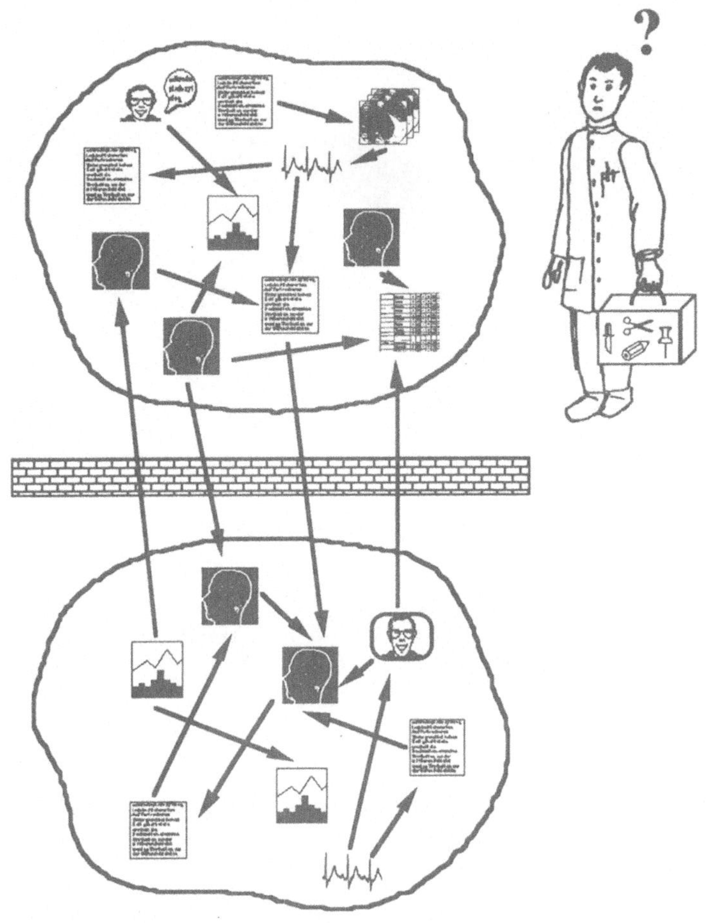

Abbildung 2: Inhaltliche Zusammenhänge von Patientendaten

Durch diese Problemschilderung wird deutlich, daß es sich bei Hypermediasystemen in der Medizin um Autorensysteme handelt. Die beteiligten Ärzte müssen Bezüge eigenständig definieren können (ob aus rechtlichen Gründen eine Löschung von Bezügen überhaupt in Frage kommt ist zumindest fraglich). Diese Bezüge lassen sich nach [CONKLIN 87] als referenzielle Bezüge klassifizieren. Auch die, in der gleichen Quelle erwähnten, organisatorischen Bezüge lassen sich in einer Patientenakte wiederfinden. Organisatorische Bezüge ergeben sich aus der hirarchischen Ordnung der Patientendaten und werden vom System, nicht vom Benutzer, verwaltet.
Abbildung 3 veranschaulicht das Auftreten beider Arten von Bezügen im medizinischen Kontext.

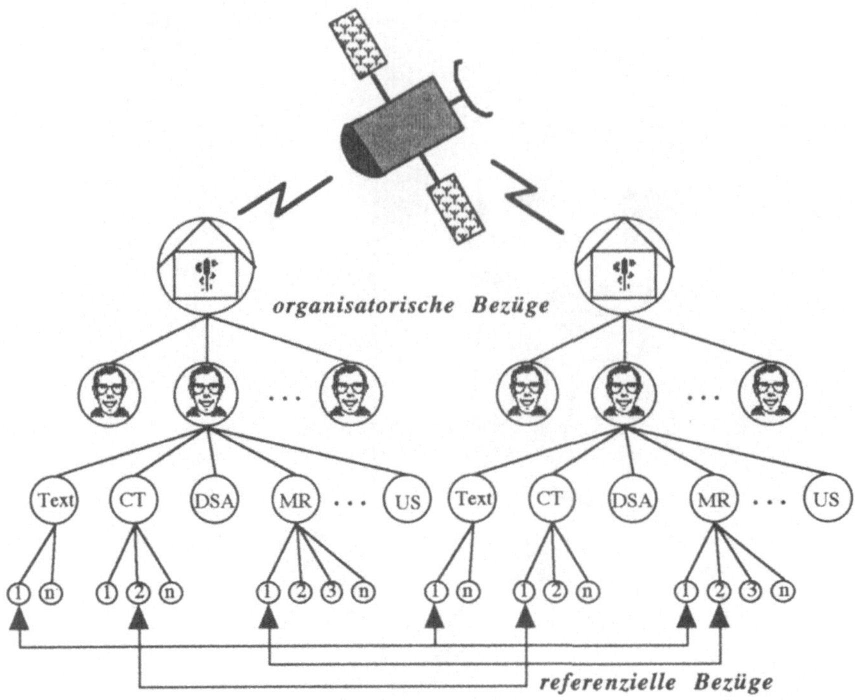

Abbildung 3: Referenzielle und organisatorische Bezüge zwischen Patientendaten

Die oberste Instanz der Hirarchie der Patientendaten bilden die Archive der medizinischen Einrichtungen, die die einzelnen Patientenakten enthalten. Die Anwendung von Verfahren der Telemedizin wird es mit sich bringen, daß es sowohl organisatorische als auch referenzielle Bezüge zwischen den Archiven und den darin enthaltenden Akten geben wird. Eine Patientenakte enthält eine Reihe von Untersuchungen, die wiederum aus einzelnen Dokumenten besteht.

Im Kontext medizinischer Daten spielen Teile von Dokumenten eine spezielle Rolle. Sie dienen vor allem der Hervorhebung besonders interessanter Ausschnitte eines Gesamtdokuments. Eine vom Gesamtinhalt losgelößte Betrachtung des Teilobjekts hat jedoch keine Aussagekraft. Insbesondere bei Bildern spielt die örtliche Lage des Teilobjekts (*region of interest*, z.B. ein Tumor) eine große Rolle, da für eine Therapieplanung auch das gesunde Gewebe berücksichtigt werden muß. Die Interpretation eines Teilobjekts kann also nur im Kontext des gesamten Dokuments erfolgen.

Im Folgenden ist ein Beispiel (Abbildung 4) für den inhaltlichen Zusammenhang von Patientendaten gegeben. In diesem Beispiel leidet ein Patient unter einem Tumor im Kopf.

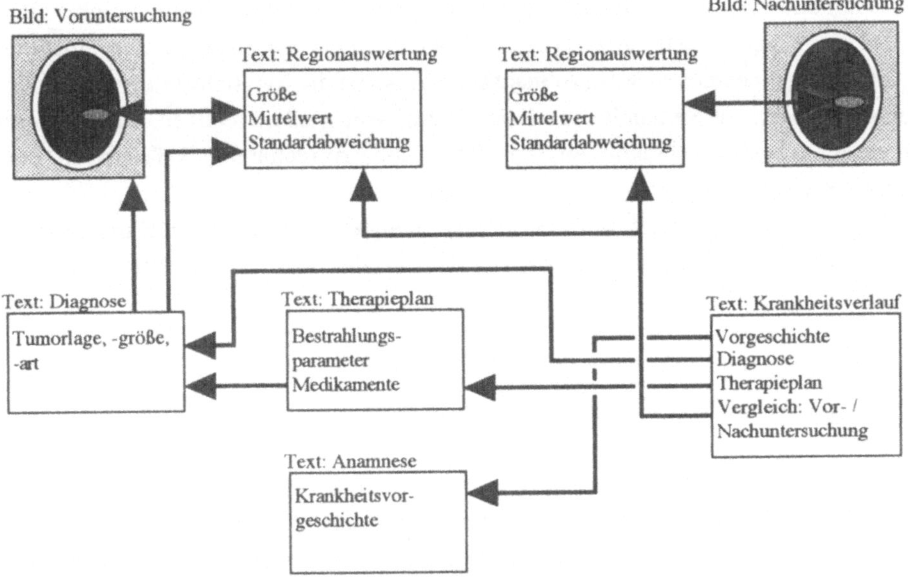

Abbildung 4: Fallbeispiel

Es wurde eine Röntgen-Computer-Tomographie angefertigt. In den **CT-Bildern** wurde der Tumor als **Region** eingezeichnet. Die Region wird statistisch ausgewertet und die **Auswertung** wird für die Diagnose verwendet. Aus der Diagnose wird ein **Therapieplan** abgeleitet, und die Behandlung wird eingeleitet. Nach einer gewissen Zeit wird eine weitere Röntgen-Computer-Tomographie angefertigt. Wieder wird der Tumor als Region markiert und diese statistisch ausgewertet. Der Vergleich der beiden Statistiken dient als Gütekriterium für den Behandlungserfolg. Die **Krankheitsvorgeschichte**, die **Diagnose**, der **Therapieplan** und die **Region-Statistiken** werden im **Krankheitsverlauf** dokumentiert.

Durch die Verknüpfung der inhaltlichen Zusammenhänge der einzelnen Dokumente durch Bezüge erfolgt implizit eine Dokumentation des gesamten Behandlungs-ablaufs. Entscheidungen und ihre Grundlagen können genau nachvollzogen werden. Bei einer späteren Befassung mit einem der Dokumente können die referenzierten Dokumente durch eine einfache Nachverfolgung des jeweiligen Bezugs abgerufen werden.

Hierbei zeigt es sich, daß eine Diversifizierung von Bezügen weitere Vorteile für die Benutzer mit sich bringt. So ist es sinnvoll, Bezüge mit einer Qualität (vergl. [KAPPE 91]) kennzeichnen zu können, um z.B. zu unterscheiden, ob ein Bezug vom Benutzer selbst, von einem Kollegen oder vom System hergestellt wurde. Diese Fähigkeit kann auch in Konferenzsituationen genutzt werden, um die Bezüge der einzelnen Konferenzteilnehmer sichtbar zu machen. Ebenso ist die Möglichkeit der Zuordnung einer bestimmten Semantik zu einem Bezug von großem Nutzen, da hierdurch themenbezogene Kollektionen (z.B. Diagnose, Abrechnung, Referenzfall etc.) gebildet werden können.

Schließlich sind auch dynamische Bezüge denkbar, um z.B. aus Dokumenten der Patientenakte heraus Sensoren zu steuern, die den Zustand des Patienten überwachen.

5. HYPAMED - ein Demonstrationssystem

Von dem Autor dieses Beitrags wurde das Demonstrationssystem HYPAMED (Hypermedia Arbeitsplatz für die Medizin) implementiert (vergl.), das dem Benutzer das Anlegen referenzieller Bezüge zischen einzelnen Dokumenten einer Patientenakte gestattet. Als Entwicklungsumgebung standen SUN Workstations unter Unix, X Windows und dem OSF/Motif Windowmanager zur Verfügung. Als Programmiersprache diente C. Die Funktionalität des Systems beschränkt sich auf wenige ausgewählte Funktionen. Dazu gehört das Einzeichnen und die statistische Auswertung von Regionen in Bildern und die Möglichkeit der Erstellung von Audiodokumenten, also insbesondere der Digitalisierung gesprochener Sprache. Abbildung 5 gibt einen Überblick über das System.

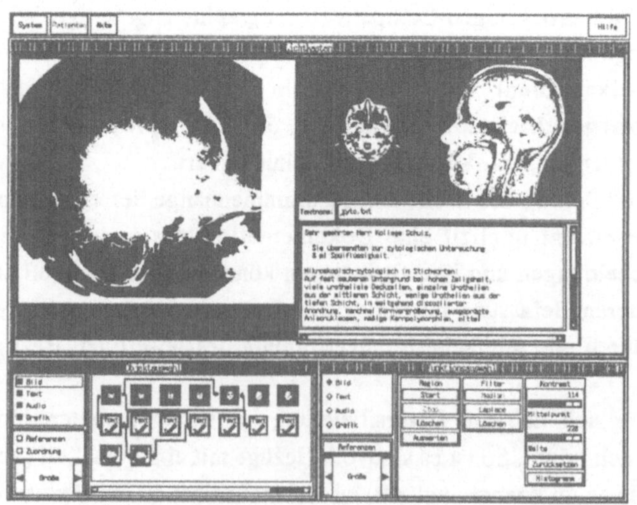

Abbildung 5: Demonstrationssystem HYPAMED

Die Festlegung von Referenzen geschieht in HYPAMED z.Z. über eine Matrix, in der verschiedene Referenztypen zwischen zuvor ausgewählten Dokumenten vergeben werden können. Der Aufruf von Referenzen erfolgt über einen *Referenz-Verfolgungs-Pfeil*.

Abbildung 6 zeigt das Beispiel eines medizinischen Bildes, in dem eine Region eingezeichnet wurde. Für den Benutzer besteht nun die Möglichkeit, die Region, das gesamte Bild oder beide durch Referenzen mit anderen Objekten zu verbinden (z.B. mit einem Text, der die statistische Auswertung der Region enthält, oder einem Grauwerthistogramm, das für dieses Bild berechnet wurde).

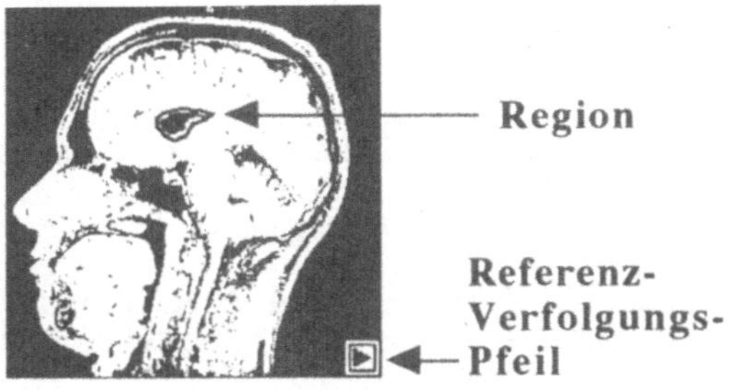

Abbildung 6: Medizinisches Bild mit Referenz-Verfolgungs-Pfeil

Der Referenz-Verfolgungs-Pfeil in der rechten unteren Ecke des Bildes zeigt an, das eine Referenz existiert, die entweder von der Region oder vom Bild oder von beiden ausgeht. Durch Anwählen der Region oder des Bildes als Ganzes, kann der Benutzer feststellen, welches der beiden eine Referenz besitzt, indem sich jeweils die Hintergrundfarbe des Referenz-Verfolgungs-Pfeils entsprechend verändert (ein roter Hintergrund bedeutet, daß es mindestens eine Referenz gibt). Durch einfaches Drücken auf den Pfeil werden alle Dokumente zur Anzeige gebracht, zu denen ein Bezug besteht.

Zusammenfassung

Die Einführung der Hypermediatechnik an medizinischen Arbeitsplätzen darf nicht als ein weiterer Schritt in Richtung Gerätemedizin verstanden werden. Das Ziel ist nicht die Einführung neuer Techniken, die die Endfremdung zwischen medizinischem Personal und Patient vorantreibt, sondern die Integration und Verfeinerung der vorhandenen Informationsquellen (HIS, RIS, PACS), die Unterstützung bestehender Arbeitsabläufe und die explizite Dokumentation inhaltlicher Abhängigkeiten zwischen den Dokumenten von Patientenakten. Diese Form der Dokumentation ist dazu geeignet, den Benutzern medizinischer Arbeitsplätze die gewünschten Informationen umfassender und leichter (und damit schneller) als bisher zugänglich zu machen. Die Folgen hiervon könnten die Vermeidung von Doppeluntersuchungen, fundiertere Diagnosen und Therapiepläne und letzlich gesteigerte Heilungschancen für den Patienten sein.

Literatur

[CONKLIN 87]   Conklin J.: **Hypertext: An Introduction and Survey**, IEEE Computer, September 1987, S. 17-41

[HENKE 91]   Henke M., Voigt G.v.: **A First Approach to a Hyper-Media Radiological Workstation**, Proceedings of the International Symposium CAR'91, Hrsg. H.U. Lemke, M.L. Rhodes, C.C. Jaffe, R. Felix, Berlin, Heidelberg [usw.]: Springer, 1991, S. 876

[HRUBY 91]   Hruby W., Mosser H., Urban M., Rüger W.: **The Vienna SMZO-PACS-Project: The Totally Digital Hospital**, Proceedings of the International Symposium CAR'91, Hrsg. H.U. Lemke, M.L. Rhodes, C.C. Jaffe, R. Felix, Berlin, Heidelberg [usw.]: Springer, 1991, S. 436-441

[IMAC 91]   Proceedings: **The Second International Conference on Image Management and Communication (IMAC) in Patient Care: New Technologies for Better Patient Care**, Hrsg. A. Heshiki, A.K. Mun, Washington, Brussels, Tokyo: IEEE Computer Society Press Los Alamitos, California, 1991

[KAPPE 91]   Kappe F.: **Spezielle Eigenschaften großer Hypermedia-Systeme**, Hypertext/Hypermedia '91, Hrsg. H. Maurer, Berlin, Heidelberg [usw.]: Springer, 1991, S. 164-173

[LEMKE 91]   Lemke H.U.: **Medical Imaging and Computer Assisted Radiology**, CAR'91 Tutorial Notes, Berlin, 1991, S. 9-68

[RÖV 90]   Röntgenverordnung: **Verordnung über den Schutz vor Schäden durch Röntgenstrahlen**, Stand: 1.5.1990, München: König Verlags-GmbH, 1990

Designing Multimedia Presentations

Helmut Eirund[+] , Martin Hofmann[*]

In this paper we focus on the design of multimedia applications. The applications we have in mind can be classified by the criteria: system controlled presentation of multimedia information with predefined user interaction and complex dialogues. Applications of this class can be found e.g. in information kiosks, tutorial systems or in the medical environment.

We describe mechanisms needed to control multimedia presentation. This, we believe, can not be managed by those hypermedia systems that are general purpose information systems. Additional filtering mechanisms help to create draft versions of navigation applications out of larger sets of multimedia objects.

We present our prototype system XMAD (Multimedia Application Developer) that provides direct manipulation to allow interactive design of hypermedia documents and testing of the multimedia presentations described above.

Keywords:
interactive navigation, multimedia application, visual programming, browsing, filter

1. Introduction

The recent years have shown a rapid enhancement of hardware technology for creating and managing multimedia objects (information capturing devices, desktop publishing, and optical mass storage devices). Multimedia objects can be embedded in applications like office automation, entertainment, medical applications, computer based training (CBT) or kiosk applications like product information and ordering systems in sales support.

In most of these applications multimedia information items are sequentially presented, oftenly triggered by user interaction. Interactive access to multimedia objects is addressed in hypermedia systems that permit browsing mechanisms on nets of information objects, interactivly specifying directions for further search. They are multi purpose systems for user controlled information retrieval. In contrast to this we consider customized applications with navigation features that may include

+   Universität Oldenburg - FB 10, Postfach 2503, D-2900 Oldenburg;
      mail: eirund@informatik.uni-oldenburg.de

*   SAP AG - (SAA-C), Max-Planck Str.8, D-6909 Walldorf (Baden); mail: hofmann@sap-ag.de

predefined dialogues, both controlled by the application that are more appropriate to the main application classes mentioned above.

Three simplified examples from the application class mentioned above are given in the sequel. (1) Kiosk information: Customers attend a commercial spot containing sequences of multimedia information. They have restricted control of the presentation (e.g. for choosing different products). (2) Tutorial system: A novice user of a desktop publishing system gets some information portions, interwoven with test inquiries on how to handle special tasks (e.g formatting). The test results determine the succeeding sequence of presentations. (3) Medical application: A physician inspects information of a therapeutics history and new x-rayed and computertomographic pictures in a presorted sequence constructed by his or her assistant, who retrieved the whole bulk of objects.

Examples and experience have shown the need for support of the creation process itself - for both the multimedia presentation and the specification of the dialogues with their graphical user interfaces. These topics, i.e. mechanisms in such applications and their design tools, are focused in this paper.

The paper is structured as the following. In the 2nd section we describe the mechanisms that control the presentation of multimedia information and how to specify interactions. The graphical design tool that is provided to build the multimedia presentation in three levels of refinement is presented in section 3. Section 4 summarizes and describes the current state of the prototype XMAD and further directions of R&D. Throughout the paper we use an example coming from a medical environment - the first testbed of our system.

2.   Multimedia Presentation

In the presentation sequences of the examples given above the user navigates through a set of multimedia objects. At predefined selection points he or she may interact with the system to make a decision on the continuation of the journey. We will consider this kind of application as the class of navigation programs ("NP" in the sequel) for a given set of multimedia objects (the presentation set). An NP implements one or even more alternative traversals through a presentation set. Therefore we regard the functionality of an NP visualized as a directed graph, with the multimedia objects of the presentation set defining the nodes and their presentation ordering its edges. All nodes can be reached from a labeled starting node via a directed path. Throughout the paper we will represent NPs via their graphical representation. A simple example of the visualization and execution of an NP for a presentation set is given in fig. 1.

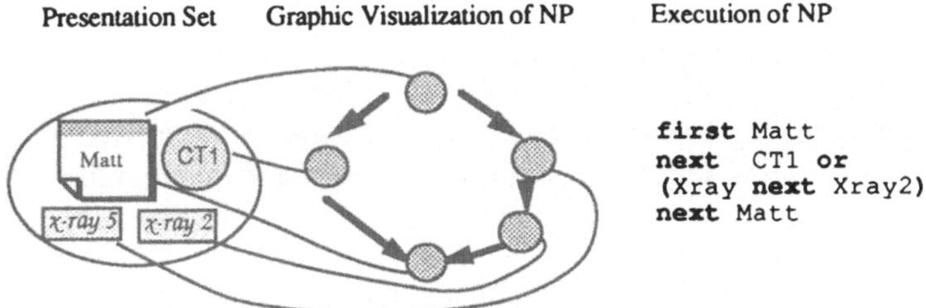

Fig. 1: Presentation set with visualized execution trace of that navigation program NP
(CT: Computer Tomography Picture; X-ray: radiogram; card: patient info.card)

We first want to outline the developments in related systems, mainly coming from hypermedia reseach in the following subsection. With this experience in mind we summarize the concepts of our system thereafter.

2.1   Directions of Development in Related Systems

Hypermedia systems are an approach to structure a set of information and multimedia data. Well known systems are Intermedia, NoteCards, Hyperties, KMS, HyperCard, Guide, Concorde, etc. (see [Conk87], [Hala88], [Hofm90]). Hypermedia systems manage structured multimedia data and offer tools for presentation and manipulation of the database. Various link types can be offered (e.g. generalization, reference, comment, criticism, object-to, etc.). Often, a goal of hypermedia systems is the presentation of all existing references the content of information objects to other objects (respective nodes). This makes these systems *multi-purpose* information systems, where a user can follow links to various nodes, and where the nodes and links can be updated and deleted. This dynamic hypertext structure within a heterogenous group of users can lead to irritations mentioned in [Rask87].

Most systems cited above do not restrict navigation. Some of them (e.g. HyperCard, KMS, Intermedia) do not even use types to taylor the system to a dedicated application. Exceptions are authoring and decision support systems that offer such specialized link types. These types define the only mechanism of system controlled restriction of random navigation.

Standard hypermedia systems (as far as we can call systems of that kind "standard") focus on the support of the user at his or her interaction by filters, history lists, fisheye views, detail views, and presentation algorithms (see [Foss88], [Komo88], [Hofm90], [Niel90], [Hofm91]). These systems do not contain any explicit guide for the user by an automatic navigation aid. Links are not computed interactively but defined as static. The task of the defined network is to support the user in his or her interaction and minimize his or her cognitive overhead from a human factor's point of view. Guiding a user according to the aims of navigation programs is not provided in these systems. Their navigation tools do not interpret the underlaying network of the hypermedia system.

We found only few approaches of automatic navigation in these systems. This is the case when animation is supported. In the multimedia document system MINOS, the creation of so-called "tours" is available to the user of a document. These tours are a *sequence of views* that can be recorded and replayed for other readers [Chri86]. For the hypermedia system Intermedia, links to video disk sequences are described. The user can influence it by setting an attribute that defines the selected sequenze to be played continuously or to be stopped at the first frame of the sequence for further user-driven navigation [Pala90].

While in these applications the navigation commands are embedded into the existing data structure, other approaches gain more flexibility by programming the navigation program using a powerful *formal description language*. ODNA offers various such constructs for the navigation on video disks [Appe87], [Appe91]. The ideas of Zellweger to offer the user an "active path" through the multimedia document are rather similar to that approach. Zellweger's paths are active because interaction and query events changing the presentation of data (a step of navigation) may occure. For the description of such events a script language is supported [Zell88]. In a similar manner all information systems that employ a programming language to develop more complex interactions and applications fit into this category. In HyperCard, an integrated language like HyperTalk can be used to design such interactions and navigation programs [Appl90]. It is important to state that these languages contain elements applicable to time-critical events. Besides HyperTalk, systems embedded into programming environments like Smalltalk-80 [Gold84] offer such facilities.Some extensions based on HyperCard are known. CourseBuilder offers a graphical editor for the definition of navigation programs. It uses interaction templates to compute the possible selections for further navigation [Feld91].

In contrast to such constructs that tend to look rather analogous to control structures well known from programming languages, creation mechanisms for navigation programs exist that try to evaluate and *monitor actions* of the user. The ODNA-system described above provides a monitor to evaluate a manual navigation session of a user and to create a path by this [Appe91]. An implementation of "guided tours" is described for NoteCards which uses special node types of the system. A set of nodes is mapped to a node of a special type (tabletop) to make their fast presentation possible. The nodes of that type can be related by dedicated links; a sequence of these links is called a "guided tour". Any node of the tabletop node is a hardcopy of a system state. The user is enabled to store snapshots of the terminal and to create sequences of them by dragging icons of these snapshots into the tabletop node. This feature can be used for presentation and simulation purposes. A user can directly access and update the objects represented by the bitmaps of the hardcopies. The system is able to automatically create a snapshot, but does not provide any selection facilities [Trig88].

A different creation mode of a "guided tour" through a large set of data is described in [Maye90]. The author of the information (in many cases identical with the end-user) specifies attributes for the objects of an application. A *sequence of these objects is computed* according to given metrics. Other control structures cannot be included. The usage of a metric in this way has similar results to the computation of specially filtered views to a set of information.

The fisheye-view described in [Furn86] realizes no sequence of objects but instead achieves a reduction of the visible (and therefore interactively accessible) data set. Similar issues on *filtering* mechanisms are discussed in [Komo88] and [Kern91]. [Pint88] introduce a browser of a hypermedia system that also uses a metrics to compute the presentation of a given set of objects according to their relationship.

2.2   Control Structures in a Navigation Program

Our primary aim was to provide only a few concepts for structuring navigation programms that offer a maximum of expressive power. According to this paradigm we studied the features in the systems discussed above and we found four types of system specific control objects useful. Their "presentation call" results in the defined control activities described below. During the design phase these objects can be placed like the given multimedia objects within the presentation flow. They define a node in the graphical visualization as sketched in fig. 1. Throughout this subsection the concepts are stepwise introduced in an *example* [1]: multimedia information of a therapeutics history is presented and visualized by the patient card and a computer tomography image or two x-ray images, as he or she preferes. Thereafter, a dialogue for diagnosis specification is added that is defined in a selfcontained application outside of XMAD (for details of this part of the project refer to [Götz91], who presents the system ODIS for dialogue specification). The result of the dialogue defines the successing sequence in the multimedia presentation.

Selection object:

A selection object that evaluates the successor node to be presented next is automaticly created and linked to a node that is followed by multiple alternatives of the presentation flow. Fig. 2a shows an example of its usage. A selection object may have different extensions for manual or automatic evaluation.

---

[1]   The comlete representation of the NP is given in fig. 5 in section 3.

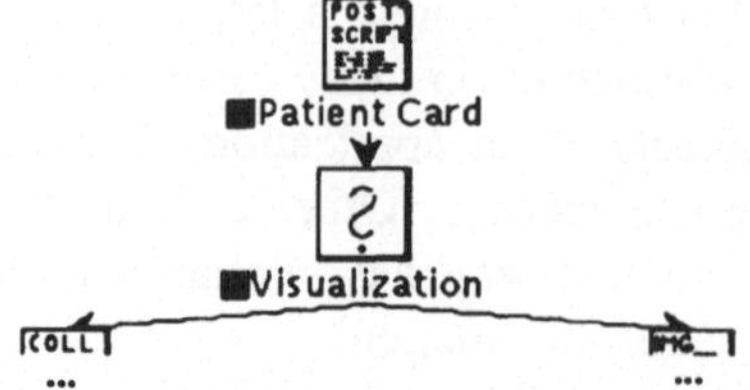

Fig. 2a: Selection object labeled "Visualization" in a navigation program

The default is *manual* evaluation, i.e. user interaction through a pop-up interaction box, where the user has to point to the identifier of the successor node that is included in the set of all possible successors. Differently to this *full-mode* with all alternatives selectable, a *restricted-mode* is available, where the set of possible successors is reduced by those nodes that have been selected in any previous decision made for this choice object. Within the *history-mode* the decision may be even reduced by decisions made for any other choice object (it interpretes a rule like: "if decision d was made for choice object c then successor s is not available"). Thus, the designer can model situations like: "if the user does not want to see a sequence of x-ray images, he or she will not be ask again for a similar decision some steps later in the NP. Fig. 3a shows an example of the editor screen of the selection object visualized in fig. 2a.

In contrast to the manual selection of a successor node the selection decision can be specified as automatic. Again, two modes are available: In the *iteration-mode* the successor nodes are visited in a predefined order, each time the choice object is visited again (within a cycle in the graph). But no successor is visited twice. Like in manual-mode, a *history-mode* is available. It works analogue to this mode but selects a successor (in spite of restricting candidates). The *application-mode* makes it possible to link any predefined program to the selection node. Such a program takes as its arguments the list of successors and returns one of them. The way this decision is produced is totaly left to the implementation of the program, e.g. by checking the system state or as a result of an attached application. Fig. 2b gives an example of a selection object in automatic mode. Fig. 3b shows the editor screen of this selection object.

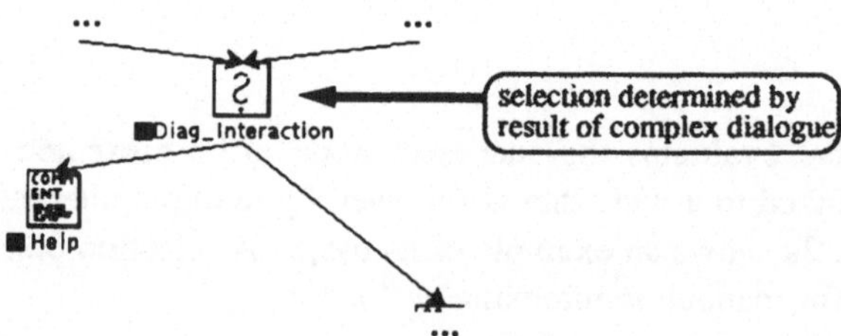

Fig. 2b: Selection object with linked application

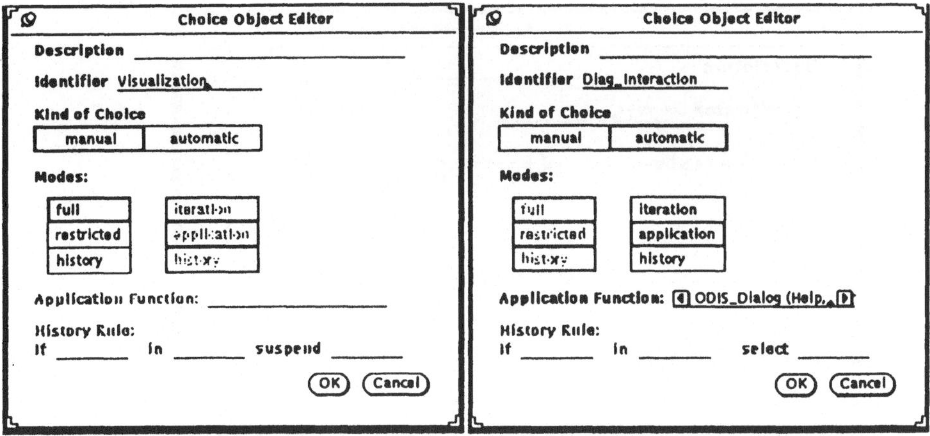

Fig. 3a,b: Manual and automatic modes of a selection object (object editor screendump)

Collection object:

The system developed here supports a simple mechanism for parallel presentation of objects. Several objects of whatever type can join a collection object. Fig. 4a shows a scenario of two x-ray images show side by side. An other example is playing audio information during the evaluation of a selection object in the same collection. The specific object editor for the x-ray collection object is shown in fig.4b. The activation of a collection object results in an immediate activation (i.e. presentation) of its contained objects - a possibly recursive process. Thus, e.g. a picture object can be presented (nearly) at the same time as an object containing audio information. Certainly the sophisticated problems of realtime synchronization in multimedia systems, as figured out e.g. in [Stei89] are not solved by this.

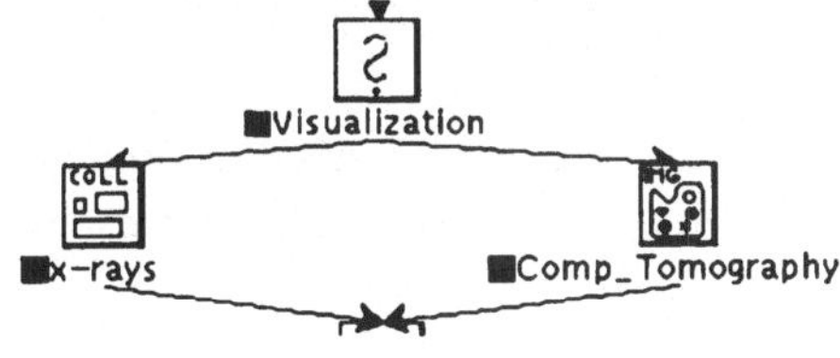

Fig. 4a: Collection object (left most) for side-by-side presentation of two x-ray pictures

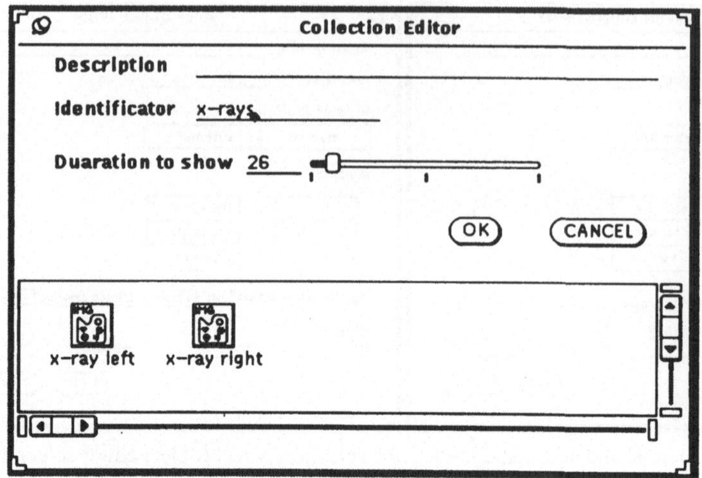

Fig. 4b: Object editor of the x-ray collection object

Comment objects and recursive NP-objects:

Apart from these two object types for controlling the flow of representation, two other system specific object types exist. A comment object takes a text content and can be placed anywhere in a NP. With this system specific type, those information objects that are additionally created for a special role in one NP only (in contrast to the objects of the underlaying set of multimedia objects to be presented), are labeled by a special object type.

An object can even be a sub-NP itself, with a "presentation function" that actually is the execution of this NP. After this sub-NP object has been executed, the presentation continues with the object following the sub-NP object. An NP object also be included in a collection object that presents e.g. a video object while executing this NP.

The tools for designing navigation programs are described in section 3. There we present the NP-workbench from which we take the snapshots presented in the figures fig.2a, 2b, 4a.

3.   Design Tools for Multimedia Presentations

In the application class we have specified earlier, large sets of customized applications must be designed. In section 2 we have shown, how these applications can be specified. The challenging task is to provide easy-to-use tools to make the design as easy as the execution of these applications.

In our system multimedia applications are designed interactively through a graphical user interface. For the navigation programs we provide a design tool with direct manipulation capabilities and, in case, special purpose editors for the different types of objects that specify the presentation or dialogue sequences. The *net editor* and its workbench provides the modification of the NP via its graphical representation. Objects can be arranged according to their desired presentation sequence. The definition of more than one outgoing edge automatically creates a choice object with a default user interaction to inquire the successor (see section 2). Objects of all system specific types can be created here. Fig. 5 shows a snapshot of the complete example introduced in section 2.

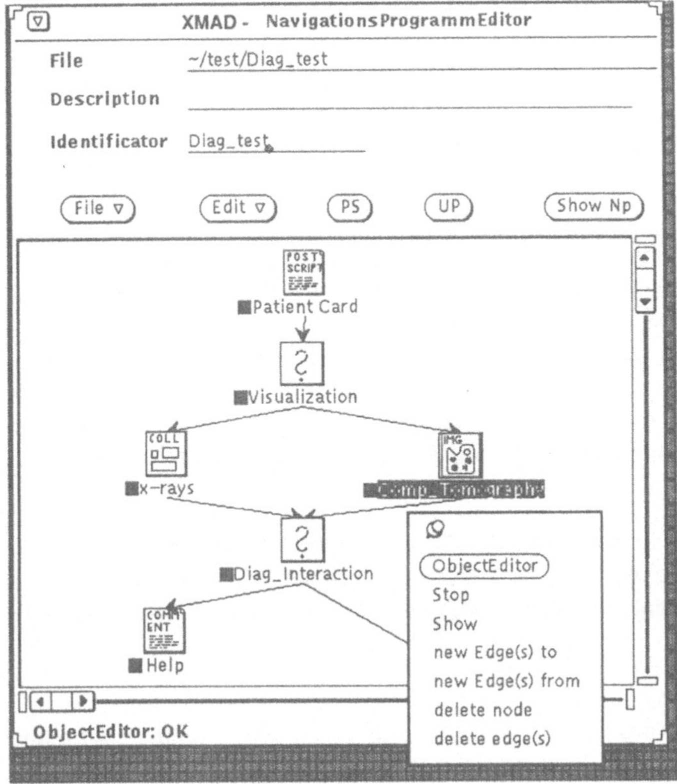

Fig. 5: Workbench with the net editor and pop-up menue for a node

Further specialized editors for manipulating multimedia objects or specific objects like control objects and interaction can be called from the editor environment to adjust parameters (we have shown screen dumps of object editors for control objects in section 2). To verify (parts of) the produced NP, an alternating use of both design and execution system of NPs is provided.

Beside the net-editor for a final detailed elaboration of a NP, two other mechanisms are provided for the top-down design that should be mentioned in this paper: automatic construction of a first draft by filters and development of presentation sequences by user monitoring.

The filter tool can be called within the browser of a presentation set. It evaluates expressions on object descriptors (if provided), object type and membership in presentation set. As we assume the information units as flat and non-complex we see no need for a more advanced query mechanismn that include object structure specification or context information like provided by multimedia archive system (e.g. in MARS [Eiru92]) or mechanismns supporting structure search in a hypertext system (e.g. in Concorde [Hofm92]). With the given expression the filter tool generates an appropriate NP by sequentializing the result sets in a random order. The resulting sequence can be modified by monitoring the manual execution sequence of the presentation of objects.

4.   Current Status and Future Work

We have presented our design system XMAD with a rather small set of mechanisms that can be manifoldly combined to build a large class of multimedia applications. A first prototype of the navigation system was described in [Siem91]. It takes full advantage of object-oriented implementation that makes extensions by new object types easy to perform. Enhancements made by [Wiec92] provide both graphical design and predefined interaction within choice objects and allow switching between the design tools and execution processes.

The prototype is implemented in C++ under the UNIX™ operating system. The user interface is mainly realized with XView [Hell90]. The GUIDE graphical user interface development environment was used for creating parts of the user interface.

We plan to integrate the ODIS dialogue specification and run time system [Götz91] into our system to model more elaborated scenarios like those given in section 1. With this we hope to achieve a full visual programming environment for an even larger class of multimedia applications.

Acknowledgement

E. Wiechmann and H.-H. Siemers implemented main parts of the prototyp. R. Götze, D. Boles, D. Rode and H.-J. Appelrath added helpful discussions and practical advice.

References

Appe87   H.-J. Appelrath, *ODIR and ODNA: Retrieval and Navigation on Laser-disks* , Report 75, ETH Zürich (in German), March 1987

Appe91   H.-J. Appelrath, H. Eirund, *ODIN and MARS: Basic mechanisms for Archiving Multimedia Documents*, Proc. 21st GI-Jahrestagung, IFB 293 (in German), Springer Verlag, 1991

Appl90   *Apple Macintosh Hypercard*, Apple Inc., 1990

Chri86   S. Christodoulakis, F. Ho, M. Theodoridou, *The Multimedia Object Presentation Manager of MINOS*, Proc. ACM SIGMOD, Washington (DC), May 1986

Conk87   J. Conklin, *Hypertext: An Introduction and Survey* , IEEE Computer, 20 / 9, Sep. 1987

Feld91   M. Feldmann, *CourseBuilder, Die Autoren-Software*, M.Feldmann Film-& Videoproduktion, D-8500 Nürnberg 20 (in German), 1991

Foss88   C. Foss, *Effective Browsing in Hypertext Systems*, Proc. RIAO 88, Cambridge (MA), March 1988

Furn86   G.W. Furnas, *Generalized Fisheye Views*, Proc. CHI 86, Boston (MA), April 1986

Gold84   A. Goldberg, *Smalltalk-80: The Interactive Programming Environment*, Addison-Wesley, Reading, Mass., 1984

Götz91   R. Götze, *Object-Oriented User Interface Specification*, Proc. Eurographics Workshop Formal Methods in Computer Graphics, Marina die Carrara, Italy, 1991

Hala88   F.G. Halasz, *Reflections on NoteCards: seven issues for the next generation of hypermedia systems*, CACM 31/7, July 1988

Hell90   D. Heller, *The X Window System Series*, O´Reilly&Ass. Inc., 1990

Hofm90   M. Hofmann, H. Langendörfer, *Browsing as Incremental Access of Information in the Hypertext System CONCORDE*, Proc. Interactive Communications, Paris, May 1990

Hofm91   M. Hofmann et al., *The Principle of Locality Used for Hypertext Presentation*, in: *People and Computers VI,* D. Diaper, N. Hammond (eds.), Cambridge Univ. Press, 1991 (pp. 435-452)

Hofm92   M. Hofmann, S. Schmezko, *Graphical Structure-oriented Search in a Hypertext System* , Proc. DEXA 92, Springer Verlag, Sep. 1992

Jona90   D.H. Jonassen, H. Mandl, *Designing Hypertext for Learning*, Springer Verlag, 1990

Komo88   H.J. Komorowski et al., *Browsing and Authoring Tools for a Unified Medical Language System*, Proc. RIAO 88, Cambridge (MA), March 1988

Maye90   T. Mayes, M. Kibby, T. Anderson, *Learning about Learning From Hypertext*, in: [Jona90]

Niel90   J. Nielsen, *The Art of Navigating through Hypertext*, CACM 33/3, March 1990

Pala90   M. Palaniappan, N. Yankelovich, M. Sawtelle, *Using active anchors: a stage in the evolution of hypermedia*, Hypermedia 2/1, 1990

Pint88   X. Pintado, D. Tsichritzis, *An Affinity Browser, in: Active Object Environments*, D. Tsichritzis (ed.), Tech. Report, Univ. Geneve, May 1988 (pp. 51-60)

Rask88   J. Raskin, *The Hype in Hypertext: A Critique*, Proc. Hypertext '87, Univ. N.-Carolina, Chapel Hill NC, March 1988

Shne83   B. Shneiderman, *Direct Manipulation: A Step Beyond Programming Languages*, IEEE Computer 16/8, Aug. 1983

Siem91   H.-H. Siemers, *Structured Access to Multimedia Object Sets through Navigation*, Diploma thesis, Universität Oldenburg FB 10 (in German), 1991

Stei89   R. Steinmetz, *Synchronization Properties in Multimedia Systems*, Technical Report 43.8906, IBM ENC, Heidelberg, 1989

Trig88   R.H. Trigg, *Guided Tours and Tabletops: Tools for Communication in a Hypertext Environment*, ACM ToOIS, 6 / 4, Oct. 1988

Wiec92   E. Wiechmann, *Graphical Design Tools for Multimedia Applications*, Diploma thesis, Universität Oldenburg FB 10 (in German), 1992

Zell88   P.T. Zellweger, *Active Paths Through Multimedia Documents*, in: J.C. van Vliet (ed.), *Document Manipulation and Typography*, Cambridge University Press, 1988

Implementation und Evaluation computerunterstützter Aus- und Weiterbildung mit dem Hypermedia-System MEM

Ulrich Glowalla, Joachim Hasebrook und Gudrun Häfele

Fachbereich Psychologie
Justus-Liebig-Universität Gießen
Otto-Behaghel-Str. 10/F
D-6300 Gießen

Zusammenfassung

In dieser Arbeit stellen wir das Hypermedia-System MEM vor, das wir zur Durchführung und Evaluation computerunterstützter Aus- und Weiterbildung entwickelt haben. Zunächst werden einige grundlegende Anforderungen an die Evaluation und Durchführung von Lern- und Wiederlernkursen erläutert. Danach stellen wir kurz die in unserem Lernlabor durchgeführten Lern- und Wiederlernkurse vor, an denen mittlerweile über 1.300 Studenten teilgenommen haben. Anschließend schildern wir die Umsetzung dieser Forderungen im Hypermedia-System MEM. MEM zeichnet sich dadurch aus, daß es eine Reihe verschiedener Möglichkeiten der Informationsdarbietung und -aufarbeitung bietet, die schnelle Anpassung eines Kurses an unterschiedliche Benutzergruppen und Forschungsfragen ermöglicht und den Studierverlauf und die Bearbeitungszeiten automatisch protokolliert. Eine integrierte Entwicklungsumgebung für MEM ermöglicht schließlich das automatische Erstellen von Hypermedia-Dokumenten aus Fließtexten. Die Möglichkeiten von MEM erlauben einen sinnvollen Einsatz des Programms in Forschung und Lehre.

1   Einleitung

Ein breiter Einsatz computerunterstützter Bildungsmaßnahmen in Betrieben, besonders aber in Hochschulen und Schulen, steht noch aus. Vornehmlich größere Firmen setzen moderne elektronische Medien bei Schulungsmaßnahmen ein, die mit vielen Teilnehmern durchgeführt werden und deren Schwerpunkt auf der Vermittlung von Grundwissen über technische Vorgänge oder elektronische Datenverarbeitung liegt (a.i.m., 1990). Ein Grund für den begrenzten Einsatz ist einmal ein Mangel an der notwendigen Hardware-Ausstattung in kleineren Betrieben und den verschiedenen Bildungseinrichtungen. Auch fehlt es an Software, die ein wirtschaftliches Erstellen von Kursen gerade in kleinerem Maßstab begünstigt. Schließlich ist ein Mangel an fundierten wissenschaftlichen Erkenntnissen über geeignete Formen multimedialer Wissensvermittlung bzw. deren unzureichende Anwendung zu beklagen (vgl. Glowalla, 1991).

Eine sytematische Evaluation moderner Informationstechnologien ist unerläßlich, wenn die damit durchgeführten Bildungsmaßnahmen verbessert werden sollen. Das Ziel aller Verbesserungen ist es, das Verstehen zu erleichtern und die Behaltensleistungen zu steigern. Forschungsarbeiten, die zur Effizienzsteigerung von Bildungsmaßnahmen beitragen sollen, müssen eine Reihe von Kriterien zur Beurteilung der Effizienz berücksichtigen: Die Akzeptanz der Maßnahme bei den Benutzern muß auf geeignete Weise erfaßt werden, der Umfang des erworbenen Wissens und die benötigte Studierzeit muß ebenso erhoben werden wie ein ausführliches Protokoll von Studierverlauf und Wissensdiagnose. Um an Hand dieser Daten den Einsatz moderner

Informationstechnologien in der Aus- und Weiterbildung optimal zu gestalten, müssen alternative Kursangebote in kontrollierten Untersuchungen miteinander verglichen werden (vgl. Glowalla & Schoop, 1992).

Akzeptanz bei den Teilnehmern und Wissensdiagnose. Während Akzeptanzdaten bereits häufig berücksichtigt werden, werden Behaltensleistungen zumeist nicht ausreichend erhoben. Von einer hohen Akzeptanz kann jedoch keineswegs unmittelbar auf gute Lerneffekte geschlossen werden. Zum einen sind mit Hilfe von Interviews oder Fragebögen erhobene Akzeptanzangaben einer ganzen Reihe von Urteilsfehlern unterworfen (Wilde, 1977). Zum anderen sind Lerner nicht in der Lage, ein differenziertes Urteil über Wissenslücken in einem Sachgebiet abzugeben. Es kann sogar sein, daß bestimmte Varianten von Kursmaterial behaltensfördernde Effekte erzielen, ohne daß den Teilnehmern die Unterschiede zwischen den Varianten überhaupt auffallen (vgl. Glowalla, Rinck & Fezzardi, 1993), so daß in solchen Fällen Akzeptanzdaten gar nicht erst erhoben werden werden sollten. Sie könnten keine Unterschiede zwischen den Kursvarianten aufzeigen und somit nicht aussagekräftig sein. Daher ist neben der Erhebung sinnvoller Akzeptanzdaten auch eine differenzierte Wissensdiagnose erforderlich, die alle relevanten Teile des Lehrstoffs abdeckt.

Arbeitsaufwand und Protokollierung des Studierverlaufs. Der Gesamtaufwand beim Lernen oder Wiederlernen von Wissen, etwa vor Prüfungen oder vor dem Einsatz am Arbeitsplatz, ist von großer praktischer Bedeutung. Dennoch wird etwa der Arbeitszeit, die zum Erlernen der Bedienung eines Systems und zum Studium eines Kurses benötigt wird, nur wenig Aufmerksamkeit geschenkt (Kulik & Kulik, 1991). Häufig unterscheiden sich Bildungsmaßnahmen eben nicht in der Akzeptanz oder bei den Behaltensleistungen, wohl aber bei der Gesamtarbeitszeit (vgl. Glowalla, Häfele, Hasebrook, Rinck & Fezzardi, 1992).

Für viele Forschungsfragen sind aber auch solche summativen Evaluationsergebnisse nicht ausreichend. Wenn beispielsweise zu bestimmten Textpassagen überdurchschnittlich viele Erläuterungen aufgerufen werden oder einzelne Testaufgaben auffällig häufig falsch bearbeitet werden, so läßt dies in der Regel auf mangelhaftes Kursmaterial schließen. Erst ein exaktes Protokoll des Studierverlaufs ermöglicht gezielte Verbesserungen des Kursangebots (Glowalla, 1991). Ein anderer wesentlicher Aspekt ist die Verbesserung der verwendeten Software: Protokolle aller relevanten Benutzeraktivitäten erlauben eine genaue Funktionsanalyse und so die Verminderung überflüssiger oder hinderlicher Handlungsabläufe (vgl. Card, Moran & Newell, 1983; Johnson, 1992).

Umfang und Inhalt von Evaluationsstudien. All diese Daten können jedoch nicht auf informelle Weise mit einigen wenigen Benutzern an Software-Prototypen erhoben werden. Zum einen reicht die so gewonnene Datenbasis für statistische Analysen nicht aus (Calfee, 1985). Zum anderen unterscheiden sich die im allgemeinen bei dieser Art von Software-Qualitätssicherung teilnehmenden geübten Computernutzer ganz wesentlich von gelegentlichen Nutzern oder gar Computerneulingen (vgl. Jöns, 1992). Ein wesentliches Kriterium, das bei allen Untersuchungen zu beachten ist, ist also eine ausreichend große Stichprobe von Kursteilnehmern, die zudem der anvisierten Zielgruppe möglichst ähnlich sein sollte. Eine weitere wichtige Vorbedingung zur Durchführung von Evaluationsstudien ist die Verwendung praxisrelevanten Kursmaterials. Das Kursmaterial sollte im Umfang mindestens einem Seminar von 5 - 15 Doppelstunden oder einer Lehrbucheinheit von ca. 50 - 100 Buchseiten entsprechen. Untersuchungen von einem solchen Umfang können nur dann durchgeführt werden, wenn sie für die Teilnehmer eine Bildungsmaßnahme darstellen, die für das Studium oder die Berufstätigkeit von Bedeutung ist, etwa als Prüfungsvorbereitung oder berufsqualifizierende Maßnahme (vgl. Campione & Armbruster, 1985).

Vergleich sinnvoller Alternativen. Aber auch das sorgfältige Durchführen und Evaluieren einer Bildungsmaßnahme kann nur zu lokalen Verbesserungen dieses einen Bildungsangebots führen. Um schrittweise Kursangebote zu optimieren, ist es erforderlich, sinnvolle Alternativen miteinander zu vergleichen. Eine Reihe von Untersuchungen, die wir zum Wiederlernen von Wissen durchgeführt haben, soll dies verdeutlichen: In zwei Wiederlernkursen haben Glowalla, Häfele, Hasebrook, Rinck & Fezzardi (1992) gezeigt, daß diejenigen Studenten effektiver wiederlernten, die gezielt zu individuell diagnostizierten Wissenslücken einzelne Lernkarten erhielten, als solche, die den gesamten Lehrstoff noch einmal bearbeiteten. Zwar war der Wissenszuwachs bei beiden Wiederlerntechniken vergleichbar groß, doch führte das selektive Wiederlernen zu einer um ein Drittel verkürzten Bearbeitungszeit.

In einer Folgeuntersuchung (Glowalla, Hasebrook, Häfele, Fezzardi & Rinck, 1992) wurde das systemgesteuerte, selektive Wiederlernen mit dem selbstgesteuerten Wiederlernen im Hypertext verglichen. Auch hier zeigte sich, daß die Behaltensleistungen nach dem Wiederlernen vergleichbar gut waren. Das Lernen mit dem Hypertext ging aber mit einer verlängerten Arbeitszeit gegenüber der selektiven Wiederlerntechnik einher. Im Vergleich zum umfassenden Wiederlernen war das selbstgesteuerte Vorgehen im Hypertext hingegen schneller. Hätte man nun das übliche, umfassende Vorgehen unmittelbar mit dem Wiederlernen im Hypertext verglichen, wäre man zu der Schlußfolgerung gelangt, daß das selbstgesteuerte Wiederlernen mit Hilfe unseres Hypertext-Systems die effektivste Methode darstellt, obwohl eine effektivere Methode zur Verfügung steht. Der Auswahl sinnvoller Alternativen und deren Vergleich an Hand der oben genannten Effizienzkriterien kommt daher größte Bedeutung zu.

Anforderungen an ein Lehr-/Lernsystem. Im vorliegenden Artikel wollen wir uns auf solche Anforderungen konzentrieren, die ein Lehr-/Lernsystem zu erfüllen hat, das die hier skizzierte Form von Evaluationsforschung unterstützen will. Wir werden zunächst Aufbau und Ablauf unserer computerunterstützten Lern- und Wiederlernkurse darstellen. Anschließend werden wir wesentliche Merkmale des von uns entwickelten Hypermedia-Systems MEM vorstellen. Dabei werden wir besonderes Augenmerk auf diejenigen Eigenschaften legen, die das System nach unserer Ansicht zum Einsatz im Forschungs- und Bildungsbereich besonders geeignet erscheinen lassen.

2 Die computerunterstützte Einführung in die Gedächtnispsychologie

Wir führen seit mehreren Jahren in unserem Lernlabor computerunterstützte Lern- und Wiederlernkurse zur Gedächtnispsychologie mit dem Hypermedia-System MEM durch. Mittlerweile haben acht Lern- und vier Wiederlernkurse stattgefunden, an denen insgesamt über 1.300 Studenten teilgenommen haben. Die Wissensbasis besteht aus einem Hypertext zur Gedächtnispsycholgie und umfaßt den illustrierten Lehrtext, ein Glossar, Inhaltsverzeichnisse sowie Übungen und Demonstrationen (Glowalla, Rinck, Häfele, Fezzardi & Hasebrook, 1993). Die große Zahl von Teilnehmern und Kursen ermöglichte uns eine kontinuierliche Evaluation und Optimierung sowohl der Wissensbasis als auch der Software.

Die Wissensbasis. Der Lehrtext ist in fünf Lektionen gegliedert. In der ersten Lektion wird ein Überblick über das menschliche Gedächtnis gegeben. Eine Vorbemerkung zur ersten Lektion weist die Kursteilnehmer zudem auf die Methoden zur Erkenntnisgewinnung in der Psychologie hin. In der zweiten Lektion wird die Arbeitsweise des Kurzzeitgedächtnisses an Hand experimenteller Ergebnisse geschildert. In der dritten Lektion wird die Enkodierung in das Langzeitgedächtnis vorgestellt und in der vierten das Erinnern und Vergessen aus dem Langzeitgedächtnis. Die fünfte Lektion schließlich leitet verschiedene Verfahren zur Verbesserung der Gedächtnisleistung aus dem zuvor Gelernten ab. Diese Lektion ist auf die Erfordernisse im Studium zugeschnitten und verdeutlicht den Studenten so die Möglichkeiten zur praktischen Anwendung des Lehrstoffs.

Ablauf eines Lernkurses. Die Teilnehmer studieren die fünf Lektionen an aufeinanderfolgenden Tagen. Die Bearbeitung einer Lektion dauert etwa zwei Stunden. Zu Beginn eines Kurses erhalten alle Teilnehmer eine Einweisung in die Bedienung des Rechners und des Hypermedia-Systems MEM sowie Instruktionen zur Bearbeitung der einzelnen Lektionen. Da an den Lernkursen vorwiegend Computeranfänger teilnehmen, umfaßt die Instruktionslektion nicht nur Erläuterungen zu den Funktionen von MEM, sondern auch das Einüben elementarer Fertigkeiten bei der Nutzung graphischer Bedienoberflächen wie etwa die Nutzung der Maus und das Bedienen von Menüs und Fenstern. Hinzu kommen Erläuterungen und praktische Übungen zu den Aufgaben der Wissensdiagnose oder zu speziellen Informationsangeboten wie etwa animierte Strukturübersichten mit über Kopfhörer eingespielten Erläuterungen. Die Bearbeitung der Instruktionslektion benötigt etwa 45 Minuten.

An Hand verschiedener Aufgaben und Übungen wird das erworbene Wissen während des Studiums der Lektionen und zusätzlich zusammenfassend am Ende des Kurses erhoben. Diese Wissensdiagnose umfaßt alle wesentlichen Fakten und strukturellen Bezüge der Wissensbasis. Hinzu kommen Fragebögen und Interviews zur Erfassung der Akzeptanz verschiedener Aspekte der Bildungsmaßnahme und der Software. Darüber hinaus werden von MEM alle Benutzeraktivitäten und die zugehörigen Bearbeitungszeiten automatisch protokolliert.

Ablauf eines Wiederlernkurses. Im Abstand von einem bis zu sechs Monaten haben wir den Kursteilnehmern zusätzlich eintägige Wiederlernkurse angeboten. Diese Wiederlernkurse sind so aufgebaut, daß am Vormittag in einer Eingangsdiagnose der Kenntnisstand der Studierenden erhoben wird. Dadurch sind wir in der Lage, sowohl das langfristige Behalten zu überprüfen als auch gezielte Rückmeldungen zum Schließen von Wissenslücken zu geben. In der anschließenden Wiederlernphase, in der die Wissensbasis mit Hilfe verschiedener Wiederlerntechniken erneut studiert werden kann, bekommen die Studenten die Aufgaben aus der Eingangsdiagnose zur nochmaligen Bearbeitung vorgelegt. Zu jeder Aufgabe erhalten die Teilnehmer eine Rückmeldung über ihre Leistung in der Eingangsdiagnose. Nach einer längeren Mittagspause wird wiederum der Kenntnisstand der Studierenden sowie die Akzeptanz der unterschiedlichen Wiederlerntechniken erhoben (vgl. Glowalla, Häfele, Hasebrook, Rinck & Fezzardi, 1992; Glowalla, Hasebrook, Häfele, Fezzardi & Rinck, 1992). Auch bei diesen Kursen werden Benutzeraktionen und Studierzeiten von der Software aufgezeichnet.

3 Das Hypermedia-System MEM

Um diese Lern- und Wiederlernkurse durchführen zu können und dabei die Möglichkeit zu haben, alle uns interessierenden Daten zu erheben, haben wir eine eigene Lernumgebung entwickelt - das Hypermedia-System MEM (Fezzardi, Hasebrook & Glowalla, 1992). Wir haben den Namen MEM gewählt, weil er an den Ausgangspunkt unserer Forschungsarbeit erinnert: Die Vermittlung von Wissen über die Funktionsweise des menschlichen Gedächtnisses (engl. memory). MEM liegt in unterschiedlichen Versionen für alle ATARI ST- und TT-Computer sowie den FALCON 030 vor. MEM ist auch auf dem neuen Multitasking-Betriebssystem MultiTOS von ATARI lauffähig. Damit steht unser Hypermedia-System auf einer sehr preisgünstigen und leistungsfähigen Rechnerplattform zur Verfügung. Weitere Programmversionen für WINDOWS 3.1 und OS/2 auf IBM-kompatiblen Computern sind in Vorbereitung.

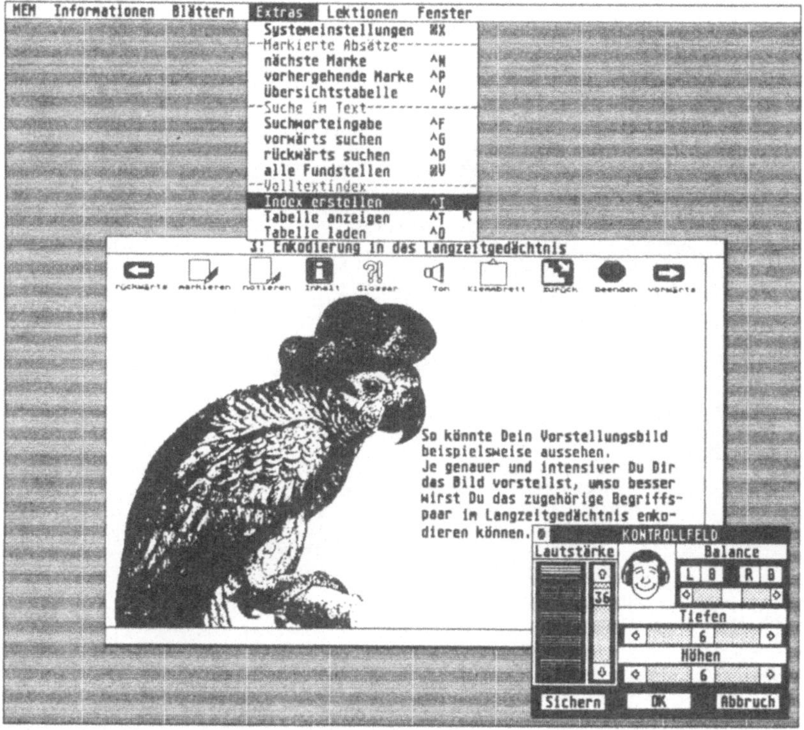

Abbildung 1:   Studierkarte mit Kommandozeile, Systemmenü und Kontrollfeld

Multimediale Informationsdarbietung. MEM stellt Texte, Bilder und Animationen in dynamischen Fenstern dar. Zusätzlich können Töne, ganze Musikstücke oder gesprochene Erklärungen dargeboten werden. Dem Benutzer steht jederzeit ein Systemmenü in Form eines Drop-Down-Menüs zur Verfügung, in dem auch alle Tastenkürzel zum Aufruf von Funktionen aufgeführt sind. Zudem kann bei der Erstellung des Hypertextes zu den einzelnen Informationsfenstern, den sogenannten Studierkarten, eine Kommandozeile angezeigt werden. Diese Kommandozeile enthält eine Reihe von Bildsymbolen (Icons) zum Aufruf häufig gebrauchter Funktionen. Der Autor eines Hypertexts muß daher nicht stets aufs neue Tasten für Vor- oder Zurückblättern vorsehen, sondern kann einfach seine Auswahl von Icons zu Beginn der Hypertexterstellung festlegen. Durch diese Vorgaben ist ähnlich wie bei den Vorschriften zur

Entwicklung von Benutzerschnittstellen bei Apple Computern ein einheitliches Kurs-
design gewährleistet (vgl. Apple, 1989). Der Autor kann im Verlauf eines Kurses jederzeit die Tastenauswahl ändern oder ganz auf die Kommandozeile verzichten.
Selbstverständlich besteht auch die Möglichkeit, eigene Tasten als Verbindung zu anderen Karten oder zum Aufruf von Systemfunktionen festzulegen. Abbildung 1 zeigt
eine Studierkarte mit der Kommandozeile und dem Systemmenü. Die Menüzeile erlaubt zudem jederzeit den Zugriff auf Hilfsprogramme wie etwa das in Abbildung 1
dargestellte Kontrollfeld zur Einstellung der Lautstärke.

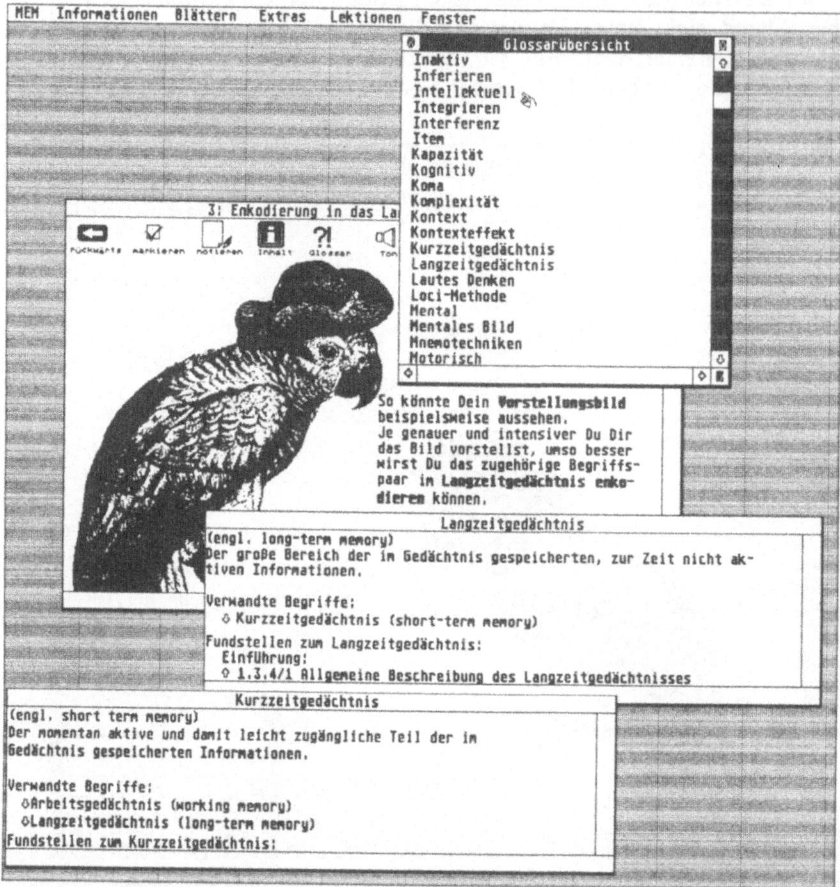

**Abbildung 2: Glossareintrag zum Begriff "Langzeitgedächtnis" mit Verweisen auf eine
weitere Begriffserklärung (↓Kurzzeitgedächtnis) und auf Fundstellen
(↑1.3.4/1 ...) sowie die Glossarübersicht**

Sprachliche Erläuertungen oder Musikstücke von beliebiger Dauer können vom Benutzer aufgerufen oder synchron zum Aufbau der Bildinformation abgespielt werden.
MEM bietet zudem eine Reihe von Signaltönen an, die automatisch abgespielt werden und so auf wichtige Informationen aufmerksam machen können. Außerdem stehen Kursteilnehmern in MEM verschiedene Navigations- und Informationsmöglich-
keiten als On-line-Hilfen zur Verfügung. Diese On-line-Hilfen sind teilweise an die
Angebote angelehnt, wie sie etwa ein gutes Lehrbuch bereithält: Zur Grundausstat-
tung eines Kurses in MEM gehören ein Inhaltsverzeichnis und ein Glossar.

Das Glossar. Die grundlegende Informationshilfe für Hypermedia-Kurse in MEM ist das Glossar. Während in vielen anderen Systemen Begriffserklärungen aus einem Glossar oder einem Lexikon abgerufen werden müssen, erhält der Kursteilnehmer in MEM eine Erläuterung einfach durch Anklicken eines Wortes oder eines Bildausschnitts (z.B. das Wort "Langzeitgedächtnis" in Abb. 2 Mitte). Die Erläuterung erscheint dann in einem weiteren, dynamischen Fenster und erlaubt es somit, die aktuelle Studierkarte und die Begriffserklärung gleichzeitig zu studieren. Neben einem erläuternden Text kann ein Glossareintrag auch Verweise auf andere Erläuterungen oder Fundstellen im Hypertext enthalten (vgl. Abb. 2 unten). Wenn eine Zeile angeklickt wird, in der ein Verweis auf eine andere Begriffserklärung steht, zeigt MEM diese Erklärung in einem weiteren Fenster an (z.B. das Fenster "Kurzzeitgedächtnis" in Abb. 2 unten). Wird eine Zeile mit einer Fundstelle ausgewählt, so springt MEM an die entsprechende Stelle im Hypertext. Somit kann es für eine Textstelle oder einen Bildausschnitt in MEM nicht nur einen einzigen Verweis auf eine andere Studierkarte geben, sondern viele verschiedene Querverweise. Zusätzlich kann eine Tabelle aufgerufen werden, die eine Übersicht über alle im Glossar erläuterten Begriffe gibt (vgl. Abb. 2 oben). Wird eine Zeile in dieser Tabelle angeklickt, so erscheint die betreffende Erläuterung in einem zusätzlichen Fenster.

Das Inhaltsverzeichnis. Als grundlegende Navigationshilfe bietet MEM ein hierarchisch gegliedertes Inhaltsverzeichnis an. Wir favorisieren diese strukturierte Form der Inhaltsübersicht aus zwei Gründen: (1) Die Benutzung eines Inhaltsverzeichnisses kann allgemein als gut geübt vorausgesetzt werden. (2) Psychologische Experimente haben gezeigt, daß hierarchisch gegliederte Informationen weit besser verstanden und behalten werden als nicht klar gegliederte Informationen (Anderson & Bower, 1973). Das Inhaltsverzeichnis zeigt alle Überschriften des aktuellen Kurses und markiert den aktuellen und den zuvor gelesenen Abschnitt des Hypertextes. Zwei Prozentskalen zeigen an, an welcher Position im Lehrtext sich der Lernende befindet und wieviel Prozent der Aufgaben einer Lektion er bereits bearbeitet hat (vgl. Abb. 3 Mitte). Wird eine Überschrift im Inhaltsverzeichnis angeklickt, erscheint unmittelbar die erste Studierkarte des ausgewählten Abschnitts.

Eine Übersichtstabelle über den Lernweg zeigt wahlweise die Überschriften aller bisher bearbeiteten Lektionsabschnitte oder Studierkarten, und zwar in der Reihenfolge wie sie studiert wurden. Auch in dieser Tabelle gibt es die Möglichkeit, an bestimmte Textstellen zu springen. Abbildung 3 zeigt das Inhaltsverzeichnis von Lektion 3 mit einer solchen Übersicht über den Lernweg. Es besteht auch die Möglichkeit, sich eine Tabelle aller noch nicht studierten Textstellen anzeigen zu lassen. In dieser Übersicht werden auch diejenigen Studierkarten aufgeführt, die nur so kurz angezeigt wurden, daß sie nicht ausreichend lange bearbeitet werden konnten. Die Bewertung, ob eine Textstelle hinreichend lange studiert wurde, wird dynamisch errechnet, und zwar auf der Grundlage des auf der Karte dargebotenen Materials, der Anzahl der Darbietungen und der jeweiligen Studierzeiten (vgl. z.B. Carpenter & Just, 1983).

Zusatzinformationen. Im Inhaltsverzeichnis und im Lernweg können Zusatzinformationen zu unbekannten Begriffen oder einzelnen Abschnitten sowie zur aktuellen Lektion und den zugehörigen Aufgaben abgerufen und in weiteren Fenstern angezeigt werden. Beispielsweise können hier kurze Zusammenfassungen eingesetzt werden, die es dem Lerner erlauben, sich vorab einen Überblick über den betreffenden Lektionsabschnitt zu verschaffen (siehe "Zusammenfassung von Abschnitt 3.1" in Abb. 3 unten). Allgemeine Informationen zum Kurs und zur aktuellen Lektion können zudem über das Systemmenü angefordert werden (vgl. das Formluar in Abb. 3 oben). Die in eigenen Fenstern dargestellten Zusatzinformationen können ihrerseits Verweise auf weitere Zusatzinformation oder auf Fundstellen im Hypertext enthalten. Damit können zusätzlich zum hierarchischen Inhaltsverzeichnis beliebig viele weitere Inhaltsübersichten angeboten werden, die nicht hierarchisch geordnet sein müssen. Abbildung 3 zeigt als Beispiele eine Themenliste, die eine Reihe von Begriffserklärungen zum Thema "Langzeitgedächtnis" anbietet, sowie eine Liste von Fundstellen, die verschiedene Stellen im Hypertext zum gleichen Thema zusammenfaßt (Abb. 3 rechts unten).

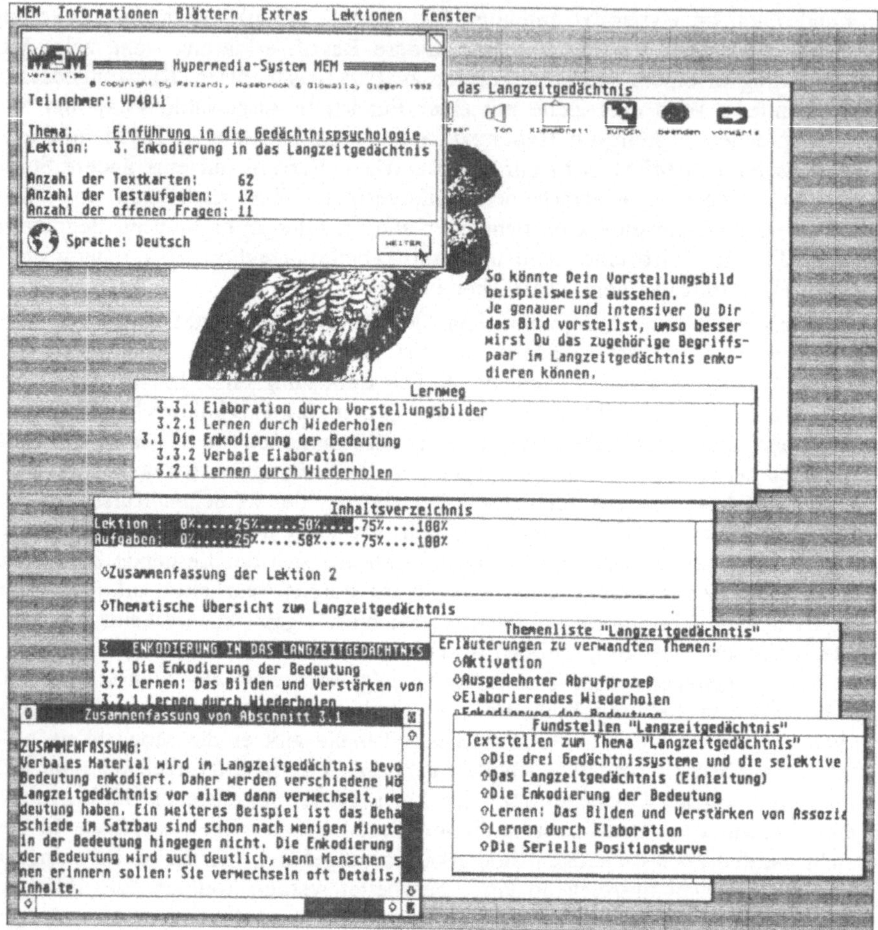

Abbildung 3: Inhaltsverzeichnis von Lektion 3 und Übersicht über den Lernweg mit einer Zusammenfassung von Abschnitt 3.1 sowie Begriffserläuterungen und Fundstellen zum Thema "Langzeitgedächtnis"

Einbindung von Simulationen. Ein wesentlicher Vorteil elektronischer Dokumente im Vergleich zu Printmedien besteht darin, daß jederzeit Simulationen von Vorgängen und Arbeitsabläufen möglich sind. Dies ist insbesondere bei solchen Lehrstoffen von Bedeutung, bei denen es um die Vermittlung von prozeduralem Wissen geht (Gentner & Stevens, 1983; Mayer, 1989). In der Regel sind Simulatoren eigenständige, komplexe Applikationen, die nicht innerhalb eines Hypertextsystems realisiert werden sollten. MEM erlaubt daher von jeder Stelle im Hypertext das Aufrufen externer Programme. So können beispielsweise direkt aus dem Lernkurs heraus mit der Experimentalsteuerung SHOW_IT (Hasebrook, Fezzardi & Glowalla, 1991) Demonstrationsexperimente gestartet werden. Da SHOW_IT mit MEM Daten austauscht, können die Kursteilnehmer direkt nach der Teilnahme an einem Experiment an Hand ihre eigenen Ergebnisse lernen.

Diese Palette von Möglichkeiten zur Informationsdarbietung und -strukturierung bewegt sich durchaus im Rahmen der Möglichkeiten, die auch andere Hypermedia- oder Hypertext-Systeme auf die eine oder andere Weise anzubieten haben. Für den Einsatz als Lernumgebung ist es jedoch von besonderer Bedeutung, daß Möglichkeiten zur individuellen und aktiven Verarbeitung des Lehrstoffs und vielfältige Formen der Wissensdiagnose unterstützt werden.

3.1 Wissensdiagnose und Studiertechniken

Benutzergesteuerte Informationsverarbeitung. In MEM können einzelne Textpassagen mit Hilfe der Maus markiert werden. Der Lerner kann zudem an beliebigen Stellen im Hypertext "Lesemarken" setzen und dann zwischen den markierten Absätzen hin- und herblättern oder eine Tabelle aller markierten Absätze anfordern. Neben diesen beiden Studiertechniken bietet MEM zwei Formen der Suche im Volltext: (1) Der Text kann nach Suchworten, die auch Platzhalter (wildcards) enthalten dürfen, durchsucht werden. Optional können auch ähnliche Begriffe berücksichtigt werden. Der Benutzer kann zwischen den Fundstellen hin- und herblättern oder sich eine Übersicht aller Fundstellen zeigen lassen. (2) Für den aktuellen Kurs kann ein Volltextindex erstellt werden, der alle Begriffe des Textes in einem Gesamtindex zusammenfaßt. Um Funktionswörter wie z.B. "der", "die", "das" aus dem Index auszuschließen, kann eine Stopwortliste angegeben werden. Eine Ersetzungsliste erlaubt zudem das Zusammenfassen aller Flexionen eines Begriffs zu einem einzigen Indexeintrag, etwa indem "Entscheidung" zu "entscheiden" ersetzt wird (Übersicht z.B. in Jones, 1991). Zu jedem Textabsatz gehört ein Notizformular, das mit Hilfe eines einfachen Texteditors bearbeitet werden kann. Notizen werden gespeichert, können ausgedruckt und so etwa beim selbständigen Wiederholen des Lehrstoffs wieder verwendet werden. Auf Grund der vielfältigen Möglichkeiten zum Aufnehmen und Abspielen von Tondaten auf dem FALCON 030 von ATARI unterstützt MEM auf diesem Rechner auch vom Lerner gesprochene Notizen.

Systemgesteuerte Informationsverarbeitung. MEM stellt dem Kursautor eine ganze Reihe von Möglichkeiten zur systemgesteuerten Wissensdiagnose zur Verfügung. So können an beliebiger Stelle im Lehrtext offene Fragen vorgegeben werden, die die Kursteilnehmer mit dem erwähnten Texteditor beantworten können. Der Editor ist auch zum Bearbeiten von Lückentexten geeignet. Dem Kursteilnehmer kann sogar seine eigene, zuvor eingegebene Antwort nach erneuter Bearbeitung des relevanten Stoffes zum Korrigieren vorgegeben werden. Darüber hinaus können JA-NEIN-Fragen und Mehrfachwahlantworten (multiple choice) als Aufgaben gestellt werden. Vom Kursleiter kann vorgegeben werden, wie oft eine Aufgabe richtig beantwortet werden soll, bevor sie nicht mehr dargeboten wird. Zu jeder Antwortalternative kann eine kurze Erläuterung als direkte Rückmeldung gegeben werden, eine Auswahl relevanter Textstellen als Informationsangebot vorgegeben werden oder ein Sprung an eine beliebige Stelle im Hypertext erfolgen. Der Wortlaut der zuletzt bearbeiteten Aufgabe kann jederzeit über eine globale Zwischenablage, dem "Klemmbrett", nachgelesen werden.

Bisher war ausschließlich von der Unterstützung des Lernprozesses die Rede. Der effiziente Einsatz eines Hypermedia-Systems für Bildungsmaßnahmen hängt jedoch nicht allein von den Angeboten an die Lerner, sondern auch ganz entscheidend von der Unterstützung der Autoren ab. Darüber hinaus sollte die Forschungsarbeit durch Systemfunktionen zur Erhebung der Benutzerakzeptanz sowie zur Erfassung des erworbenen Wissens und des Lernverlaufs erleichtert werden. Schießlich müssen plausible Alternativen in ausreichend großen Kursen verglichen werden, um zu schlüssigen Aussagen über die Effizienz von Studiertechniken oder Studierhilfen zu kommen (Glowalla & Schoop, 1992). Während wir in den vorhergehenden Abschnitten eine ganze Reihe von Aufgabentypen vorgestellt haben, die eine umfassende Wissensdiagnose ermöglichen, sollen in den folgenden Abschnitten besondere Fähigkeiten von MEM erläutert werden, die das Erstellen und Evaluieren größerer Hypermedia-Kurse unterstützen.

3.2 Entwicklung und Evaluation von Kursen

Protokoll des Studierverlaufs. Die grundlegende Eigenschaft von MEM für die Durchführung von Evaluationsstudien ist sicherlich die Möglichkeit, Benutzeraktivitäten und Studierzeiten automatisch zu registrieren. Bei vielen Hypertext-Systemen ist die Protokollierung nur möglich, wenn diese vom Autor selbst programmiert wird. Programme zur automatischen Ereignisprotokollierung, wie sie z.B. für einige Betriebssysteme als Debugging-Werkzeug angeboten werden, sind zu Forschungszwekken zumeist nicht geeignet, weil ihre Aufzeichnungseinheit elementare Systemmeldungen und nicht Benutzeraktionen sind. MEM erstellt automatisch und ohne jede Einschränkung für den Benutzer ein vollständiges Protokoll des Studierverlaufs, in dem alle Benutzeraktionen und die zugehörigen Bearbeitungszeiten in chronologischer Reihenfolge enthalten sind. Auch die Eingaben in das Fragen- und das Notizformular werden vollständig protokolliert. Am Ende einer Sitzung wird zudem eine zusammenfassende Tabelle aller relevanten Benutzeraktionen und der zugehörigen Gesamtarbeitszeiten ausgegeben. Das Programm MEM Data erlaubt ausführliche Analysen dieser Benutzerprotokolle hinsichtlich verschiedener Fragestellungen und erzeugt Ergebnislisten, die unmittelbar von Textverarbeitungs- und Statistiksoftware weiterverarbeitet oder auch unmittelbar von Datenbank- und Tabellenkalkulationsprogrammen übernommen werden können. Auf diese Weise stehen umfangreiche Evaluationsdaten unmittelbar im Anschluß an einen Lernkurs zur Verfügung.

Globale Anpassung des Kursdesigns. Hier ergeben sich für die meisten Hypertext-Systeme die größten Probleme: Anpassungen an bestimmte Benutzergruppen oder das Erstellen unterschiedlicher Kursvarianten gehen oft mit arbeitsintensiven Veränderungen im Hypertext selbst einher. MEM hingegen erlaubt globale Anpassungen des Kursablaufs und der Materialdarbietung ohne Änderungen im zugrundeliegenden Hyperdokument. Der Autor kann bei der Erzeugung eines Hypermedia-Kurses sowie für jeden einzelnen Teilnehmer eine Reihe von Programmoptionen festlegen. Dazu gehören Optionen, die den Kursablauf beeinflußen wie etwa das Ein- bzw. Ausschalten des Zurückblätterns oder des Springens im Hypertext. Andere Einstellmöglichkeiten gelten der Informationsdarstellung: Beispielsweise können die On-line-Hilfen in festen anstatt in dynamischen Textfenstern dargeboten werden oder das Abspielen von Tonmaterial für Teile des Kurses abgeschaltet werden. Auf diese Weise kann ein Kurs sowohl an den Kenntnisstand und Übungsgrad verschiedener Benutzergruppen als auch an verschiedene Forschungsfragen angepaßt werden, ohne daß der Hypertext selbst verändert werden muß.

Kurssteuerung und "guided tours". Nach unserer Ansicht sollte ein Autor nicht nur das Layout des Hyperdokuments sondern auch den Kursablauf beeinflussen können. Wie auch bei Veränderungen des Kursdesigns sollten dazu keine großen Änderungen in dem zugrundeliegenden Hyperdokument erforderlich sein. MEM erlaubt aus diesem Grunde die Vorgabe eines Kursablaufs im Sinne einer "guided tour" (vgl. Jonassen & Mandl, 1990) sowie "Drehbücher" oder Skripte für einzelne Studierkarten. In einem solchen Skript können der zeitliche Ablauf der Informationsdarbietung und der Aufruf von On-line Hilfen wie etwa Erläuterungen aus dem Glossar festgelegt werden. Die Ablaufsteuerung beruht auf einer einfachen virtuellen Maschine, so daß eine leichte Handhabung und eine vollständige und exakte Fehleranalyse durch MEM sichergestellt sind (Rechenberg & Mössenböck, 1988).

Erzeugung eines Hypermedia-Kurses. Um überhaupt einer ausreichenden Zahl von Studenten die Teilnahme an unseren Lernkursen zu ermöglichen und ihnen dabei eine Auswahl sinnvoller Kursalternativen anbieten zu können, mußten wir besonders darauf achten, daß zum einen das Erstellen größerer Kurse in mehreren Varianten kurzfristig möglich ist und zum anderen bereits vorhandene Schulungsunterlagen in Form von Texten oder Bildern weiterverwendet werden können. Zu diesem Zweck ist das Lernermodul von MEM in eine integrierte Entwicklungsumgebung eingebunden, die die weitgehend automatische Umsetzung von Fließtexten in ein Hyperdokument erlaubt.

Das Programm MEM Pipe erzeugt aus ASCII- oder RTF-Textdateien MEM Quellcode, indem es den Text in bildschirmgerechte Segmente zerlegt, ein Glossar und ein Inhaltsverzeichnis erstellt sowie Aufrufe für die einzelnen Glossareinträge in den Text einfügt. Mit dem Programmmodul MEM View kann der Autor nachträglich einzelne Studierkarten interaktiv am Bildschirm verändern und diese Änderungen in den Quellcode übernehmen. Der so erzeugte Quellcode wird vom MEM Compiler in einen interaktiven Hypermedia-Kurs umgewandelt. Der Compiler führt während der Bearbeitung des Quellcodes ausführliche Fehleranalysen und eine strikte Versions- und Lizenzkontrolle durch. Eine geschützte Weitergabe von MEM-Kursen ist stets gewährleistet, da Kurse grundsätzlich nur mit einer Lizenz- bzw. Copyrightmeldung weitergegeben werden und zusätzlich komprimiert und verschlüsselt werden können. Das Lernermodul von MEM schließlich führt diese Kurse aus und erlaubt deren interaktive Bearbeitung. Weitreichende Änderungen am Kursmaterial sind auf diese Weise viel schneller zu erreichen als in solchen Hypertext-Systemen, in denen jede Karte des Hypertextes einzeln bearbeitet werden muß (vgl. Hahn, Hammwöhner, Reimer & Thiel, 1990).

4 Diskussion

MEM bietet sicher nicht alle Möglichkeiten, die andere Hypertextsysteme, insbesondere Spezialapplikationen, anzubieten haben. Der Einsatz solcher Hypertext-Systeme, etwa bei technischen Einführungskursen, Reparaturanleitungen oder im mathematischen Bereich, ist an anderer Stelle ausführlich geschildert worden (z.B. Berk & Devlin, 1991; Conklin, 1987). Auch sind im Ausbildungsbereich einige Prototypen entwickelt worden, die den Funktionsumfang von MEM in mancher Hinsicht überschreiten (z.B. Landow, 1989). Für uns ist jedoch nur ein Vergleich mit solchen Hypertextsystemen interessant, die im Hinblick auf den Anschaffungspreis und die Systemeigenschaften einen sinnvollen Einsatz in der Evaluationsforschung und Ausbildungspraxis ermöglichen. Hier zeichnet sich MEM durch spezielle Eigenschaften aus: (1) die flexible Informationsdarbietung, (2) die umfangreiche Unterstützung aktiver Studiertechniken und verschiedener Formen der Wissensdiagnose, (3) die automatische Protokollierung des Studierverlaufes, (4) die schnelle Anpassung des Kursmaterials und des Kursablaufes an unterschiedliche Benutzergruppen und Forschungsfragen, (5) die leichte Übernahme und Bearbeitung von bereits vorhandenen Schulungsunterlagen sowie (6) die Möglichkeit zur kompakten und geschützten Weitergabe von Teachware.

Entwicklungsperspektiven. Derzeit wird eine neue Version von MEM entwickelt, die die Darbietung verschiedener Farbbildformate und unterschiedlicher Schriftarten am Bildschirm erlaubt. Dabei wird das Konzept der Informationsdarbietung in unabhängigen, dynamischen Fenstern erweitert, so daß nun unterschiedliche Stellen im Hyperdokument, beispielsweise unterschiedliche Fundstellen zu einem Stichwort, in mehreren Fenstern angezeigt werden können. Mit dem neuen Multitasking-Betriebsystem MultiTOS werden die Möglichkeiten zur Verwaltung von Netzwerken so erweitert, daß Funktionen zum interaktiven Lernen in der Gruppe implementiert werden können. In der weiteren Entwicklung werden wir MEM an verschiedene Rechnerplattformen anpassen und weitere Schnittstellen zur Ansteuerung von externen Resourcen wie CD-ROM und Video anbieten.

Danksagung

Diese Arbeit wurde von der Deutschen Forschungsgemeinschaft (DFG) im Rahmen des Schwerpunktprogramms *Wissenspsychologie* durch die Sachbeihilfen GL123/2-2 bis /2-4 unterstützt. Die hier erwähnten Untersuchungen wurden an der Justus-Liebig-Universität Gießen durchgeführt. Wir danken der Deutschen Forschungsgemeinschaft und der Universität Gießen für die Unterstützung unserer Forschungsarbeit.

Literatur

a.i.m. GmbH (1990). *Einsatz von Computerlernprogrammen in der betrieblichen Bildung.* München: Ausbildung mit interaktiven Medien, a.i.m. GmbH, München.

Anderson, J.R., & Bower, G.H. (1973). *Human associative memory.* New York: John Wiley & Sons.

Apple Computer GmbH (1989). *Apple Computer in Forschung und Lehre.* München: Apple Computer GmbH.

Berk, E., & Devlin, J. (eds.) (1991). *Hypertext/Hypermedia handbook.* New York: McGraw Hill.

Calfee, R.C. (1985). *Experimental methods in psychology.* New York u.a.: Holt, Rinehart, and Winston.

Campione, J.C., & Armbruster, B.B. (1985). Acquiring information from texts: An analysis of four approaches. In J.W. Segal, S.F. Shipman & R. Glaser (eds), *Thinking and learning skills.* Hillsdale, NJ.: Lawrence Erlbaum.

Card, S.K., Moran, T.P., & Newell, A. (1983). *The psychology of human-computer interaction.* Hillsdale, NJ.: Lawrence Erlbaum.

Carpenter, P.A., & Just, M.E. (1983). What your eyes are doing while your mind is reading. In K. Rayner (Ed), *Eye movements in reading: Perceptual and language processes.* New York: Academic Press.

Conklin, J. (1987). Hypertext: An introduction and survey. *Computer,* 20, 17-41.

Fezzardi, G., Hasebrook, J., & Glowalla, U. (1992). *MEM - Ein Hypermediasystem zur Entwicklung, Evaluation und Durchführung computerunterstützter Aus- und Weiterbildung.* Handbuch, Gießen.

Gentner, D. & Stevens, A.L. (1983). *Mental models.* Hillsdale, NJ.: Lawrence Erlbaum.

Glowalla, U. (1991). *Using computers for learning and relearning of expository text.* Paper presented at the 4th European Conference for Research on Learning and Instruction (EARLI); Turku (Finnland).

Glowalla, U., Rinck, M. & Fezzardi, G. (1993). Integration von Wissen über ein Sachgebiet. *Zeitschrift für Pädadgische Psychologie, 7*.

Glowalla, U., Rinck, M., Häfele, G., Fezzardi, G. & Hasebrook, J. (1993). *Einführung in die Gedächtnispsychologie,* 4. korrigierte und erweiterte Auflage. Gießen: Selbstverlag.

Glowalla, U., & Schoop, E. (1992). Entwicklung und Evaluation computerunterstützter Lehrsysteme. In U. Glowalla & E. Schoop (Hrsg.), *Hypertext und Multimedia. Neue Wege in der computerunterstützter Aus- und Weiterbildung.* Heidelberg: Springer Verlag.

Glowalla, U., Häfele, G., Hasebrook, J., Rinck, M., & Fezzardi, G. (1992). Wiederlernen von Wissen. In U. Glowalla & E. Schoop (Hrsg.), *Hypertext und Multimedia. Neue Wege in der computerunterstützter Aus- und Weiterbildung.* Heidelberg: Springer Verlag.

Glowalla, U., Hasebrook, J., Häfele, G., Fezardi, G., & Rinck, M. (1992). Das gezielte Wiederlernen von Wissen mit Hilfe des Hypermedia-Systems MEM. In R.Cordes & N.Streitz (Hrsg.), *Hypertext/Hypermedia '92: Konzepte und Anwendungen auf dem Weg in die Praxis.* Heidelberg u.a: Springer.

Hahn, U, Hammwöhner, R., Reimer, U., & Thiel, U. (1990). Inhaltsorientierte Navigation in automatisch generierten Hypertext-Basen. In P.A. Gloor & N.A. Streitz (Hrsg.), *Hypertext und Hypermedia. Von theoretischen Konzepten zur praktischen Anwendung.* Berlin u.a.: Springer.

Hasebrook, J., Fezzardi G., & Glowalla, U. (1991). SHOW_IT - Eine Experimentalsteuerung zur Darbietung von Text und Bild. *Software Kurier, 4,* 151-156.

Jöns, I. (1992). Möglichkeiten und Grenzen formativer Evalutaion computerunterstützter Lernsysteme im Rahmen anwendungsorientierter Entwicklungsprojekte. In U. Glowalla & E. Schoop (Hrsg.), *Hypertext und Multimedia. Neue Wege in der computerunterstützter Aus- und Weiterbildung.* Heidelberg: Springer Verlag.

Johnson, P. (1991). *Human computer interaction. Psychology, task analysis and software engineering.* London, New York u.a.: McGraw Hill.

Jonassen, D.H., & Mandl, H. (eds.) (1990). *Designing hypermedia for learning.* NATO Asi Series. New York, Berlin, Heidelberg: Springer.

Jones, S. (1991). Text in context. Document processing and storage. New York u.a.: Springer.

Kulik, C.-L., C., & Kulik, J.A. (1991). Effectiveness of computer-based instruction: An updated analysis. *Computers in Human Behavior, 7,* 75-94.

Landow, G.P. (1989). Hypertext in literary education, criticism, and sholarhip. *Computers and the Humanities, 23,* 173-198.

Mayer, R.E (1989). Models for understanding. *Review of Educational Research,* 59(1), 43-64.

Rechenberg, P., & Mössenböck, H. (1988). *Ein Compiler-Generator für Mikrocomputer. Grundlagen, Anwendung und Programmierung in Modula-2.* München, Wien: Hanser.

Wilde, G.J.S. (1977). Trait description and the measurement by personality questionnaires. In R.B. Cattell & R.M. Dreger (eds), *Handbook of modern personality theory.* Washington: Hemisphere.

Using A Language for Process Specification (ALPS) to Define Hypertext Trails

Bruce Hunter Thomas
School of Computer and Information Science
University of South Australia
The Levels, SA, 5095 Australia
E-Mail: mabht@lux.sait.edu.au

This paper proposes using ALPS to specify a new hypertext trail to an existing hypertext document. In Vannevar Bush's first Hypertext system memex, Bush envisioned memex as having the ability for a user to define a trail in an information space. A trail is a predefined sub-net of an information space. A trail can be used at a later date, be passed on to another user, or be added to existing trails. If trails are to be realized, there needs to be a system independent method of describing them. Trails have two basic primitives, information nodes and links between nodes. Current Hypertext systems provide proprietary linear trail definitions, but a more general definition is needed which includes such features as: sequencing, parallelism, branching, and synchronization.

"Lord, that I'm standin' at the crossroad, babe I believe I'm sinkin' down."

- Robert Johnson, 1936

1. Introduction

This paper proposes and demonstrates the use of a subset of ALPS (A Language for Process Specification) [CAT91] to describe hypertext trails. The premise for this proposal is the observed similarities between process plans in manufacturing and hypertext trails. Process plans describe a temporal relationship between activities in the production of a product.[BRO27] Hypertext trails describe a temporal relationship between processing activities of a reader in an information space. One major problem in describing these reader processing activities is having a proper interchange language external to the information spaces. This paper proposes an interchange language which describes hypertext trails external to a hypertext document.

First, this paper will provide a brief look at some previous work in examining hypertext trails. This paper will then present definitions of hypertext trails and ALPS. Then a description of ALPS in the manufacturing domain will be given. From this description, the subset of ALPS used in defining hypertext trails will be presented. Finally, an implementation of a Hypertext system driven by an ALPS program will be discussed. In the implementation discussion, a description of how current hypertext systems need to be extended to accommodate these trails will be examined.

1.1. Background

In the paper *As We May Think*, Vannevar Bush[BUS45] describes his famous memex hypertext system. He raised many interesting ideas for organizing information; one of those ideas was *trails*. He introduced the idea of associative indexing, or the process of tying two items together, which is referred to today as a link in modern hypertext systems.[NIE90] Bush goes on, *"When numerous items have been thus joined together to form a trail, they can be reviewed in turn, rapidly or slowly."* The ability of the trail author, or as Bush refers to them Trail Blazers, to add their own thoughts to a section of the trail, such as a note, was described. There was also the idea of having side trails off the main trail where a reader might explore further. A very important property of these trails was the ability to pass them to other users and to link them into larger trail systems. The important idea here is that these trails were external to the books and articles which made them up. This external nature of the trails allows for one piece of information from a book or article to be contained in more than one trail. This paper proposes a method for describing Bush's idea of trails in the context of modern hypertext systems.[WOO90]

There has been previous interest in formulating a representation of hypertext documents.[NEU89] Petri-nets have been proposed to overcome deficiencies in a pure directed graph representation of hypertext networks.[STO89] Petri-nets also have the benefit of many elegant mathematical properties.[PET81] Although this past work is similar, the work in this paper is concerned with describing structures which are usable over hypertext documents of different structures.

1.2. Definitions

A *hypertext trail* can be defined as a predetermined sub-net of a hypertext information space. In order to achieve the construction of one of these trails, a trail author needs to specify: where a reader goes through the information space, what is presented from the information space, what order information is presented, what choices the reader can make about the information space, and what additional information not currently in the information space needs to be supplied.

ALPS is a process specification language based on directed graph notation which allows full specification of parallel activities, event synchronization, alternative processes, resource management and task decomposition. The purpose of a directed graph notation is to indicate the temporal relationship between nodes. For this paper, these graph nodes will be referred to as statements, to avoid confusion with hypertext nodes.

2. ALPS

ALPS was developed for describing process plans. The act of process planning produces some form of specification, or a process plan. Some of the activities while specifying a process plan are: determine the tasks to manufacture the part, determine which resources can perform those tasks, and determine the sequence of those tasks. A deeper look into process plans reveals a full specification of processing needs to address the following issues: processing precedence, alternative sequences, parallel actions, synchronization, resource monitoring, post processing and extensibility.

2.1. Process Plans and Hypertext Trails

Hypertext trials and process plans have many goals in common. Both systems need to define processing precedence. In the case of a process plan it is, for example, the order in which a part is assembled, while in a hypertext trail it is the order that information is presented to the reader. Alternative sequences are required in both hypertext trails and process plans for the same reason, there may be a need for a different resource than originally specified. Parallel actions in a process plan allow for two subparts to be made in tandem; whereas in a hypertext trail a parallel action might be a simultaneous displaying of two different portions from an information space. Both systems need some form of synchronization of parallel actions. Both systems need to allow for the end users, process planners or trail authors, to extend or customize a process plan or hypertext trail.

2.2. ALPS Statements

As has been shown, process plans and hypertext trails have similar features. ALPS was developed as a means for transfer of information from a process planning systems to a process controller,[CAT88,THO88] and in the case of hypertext, transfer of information from the trail author to the hypertext system. The general set of classes for ALPS statements are: task, split, join, termination, synchronization, resource monitoring, and information. The hypertext trails will use a subset of these classes.

2.3. ALPS in Hypertext

The classes of ALPS statements used to define hypertext trails are: task, split, join, information, and termination. These classes form two basic groups; the classes which interact with the reader and the classes which control the ALPS programs. There is only one class which interacts with the reader, the task statements. Termination, information, join and split statements are used to control the ALPS programs. The monitoring and synchronization primitives have been removed from this first implementation. The remaining ALPS statements reduce ALPS to a convenient notation for AND/OR graphs.[HOR78] A full implementation of ALPS is a more powerful notation than simple AND/OR graphs, and the full implementation is the ultimate goal of this research. This subset of ALPS is the first step into looking at using a process specification language for specifying a hypertext trail.

This section will present a brief description of each of these ALPS statements. With each of the descriptions, the special attributes for the given statement will be defined. Since processing tasks differ between hypertext and manufacturing, new tasks were defined for the hypertext domain. A special user defined statement for variable declaration was defined for ease of programming.

2.3.1. Termination Statements

The two termination statements are *start* and *end*. Every ALPS program has one start statement and one end statement. There are no special attributes for the *start* and *end* statements.

2.3.2. Information Statements

Information statements provide a means for user-definable operations such as database queries, parameter bindings, and computations. A special information statement has been defined, the *var* statement, to allow an ALPS program to define variables. The var statement allows for a variable to be defined with the statement specific attributes of a label and a type.

2.3.3. Task Class of Statements

The task class of statements in the manufacturing domain specify when actual processing of products is performed. In the hypertext domain, tasks specify when the reader processes information. There are three basic reader tasks the hypertext trail can specify: trail statement, info statement and query statement. Each of these tasks will perform the following sequence of activities: 1) present the reader with information, 2) the reader processes the information, 3) the reader acknowledges they are finished with the information.

An *info* statement is a statement that provides a means for the trail author to present information not originally in the hypertext document to the reader. The info statement has information presented to the reader with some means for the reader to respond with an acknowledgement. This presented information is the only statement specific attribute for the info statement.

The *query* statement is a means for the trail author to specify the need for feedback from the reader. This feedback is to be stored in a variable associated with the returned value from the query statement. The query statement also provides the means for displaying information to the reader the same way as with the info statement; this display information can be in the form a question or query to the reader. The information to be displayed to the reader and the variable name to store the return value are the statement specific attributes for the query statement.

The *trail* statement is a sequential list of node ids from the hypertext document. This list of node ids defines the order that the hypertext nodes are presented to the reader. The trail statement has a node displayed from the hypertext document and allows the reader to traverse forward and backwards displaying previous and next nodes as indicated in the list. The list of hypertext node id's is the only statement specific attribute for the trail statement.

2.3.4. Split Statement

To form two or more parallel paths in an ALPS program, or to make a decision between multiple paths, a split statement is used. This can be achieved by the use of the ALPS *predicted* sub-class split statement. A boolean function is associated with each path of a split statement and can make use of variables defined in the var statement. If the function returns a value of true, then that path is followed. One or more paths can be followed at a time. The list of function/next statement id pairs is the only statement specific attribute for the split statement.

2.3.5. Join Statement

A join statement is used to bring the multiple paths formed from a split statement back to a single path. In ALPS, every split statement is paired with a join statement, and these split/join statement pairs must have symmetric paths, the split statement having the same number of next statements as the join statement has previous statements. The split and join statement pairs may be nested in as many levels as needed. A join statement provides a simple means of synchronizing parallel tasks, in that the join statement will wait until every path followed leaving the paired split statement has passed control on to the join statement. Once all these paths have finished, control is then passed on to the next statement after the join statement. One statement specific attribute for the join statement is the paired split statement's id. As will be shown, this statement id will allow the join statement access to information about how many paths were taken from the paired split statement. The join statement has a list of previous ALPS statement ids and the id of the split statement it is paired with as its two statement specific attributes.

3. Implementation

This section will describe an implementation of a hypertext system using ALPS to describe hypertext trails. A restriction in the implementation is that hypertext nodes will only display static information. Readers can only follow the hypertext trail, and no other links from that node are active. Other limitations will be presented when they arise. Presented first in this section is a general architecture of how an ALPS hypertext trail system will interact with a hypertext display system. Then a definition of messages passed between these two subsystems, the ALPS hypertext trail system and the hypertext display system. The final implementation of the subset of ALPS will be described in terms of these two subsystems.

3.1. The Architectural Model

To simplify the interaction between processing the ALPS program and displaying the hypertext document, the overall system has been partitioned into two main subsystems, the Hypertext Trail System and the Hypertext Display System. The Hypertext Trail System (HTS) is responsible for processing the ALPS program to determine which hypertext nodes are displayed to the reader. The HTS receives a hypertext text trail and while processing the ALPS program makes requests to the Hypertext Display System. The Hypertext Display System (HDS) is responsible for displaying information to the reader in the form of hypertext nodes, and can query the reader for information requested by the HTS. Figure 3.1 gives an overview of the entire system; in this model, the HTS completely drives the HDS as to which hypertext nodes are displayed to the reader. This paper proposes that with the addition of a few high level device independent commands to a hypertext system, a HTS could drive most hypertext systems. A database is attached to HTS for storage, evaluation, and retrieval of variables used in the ALPS program.

There are three basic requests the HTS makes to the HDS display: trails, queries, and static information. The HTS receives two basic responses: acknowledgements and values from a query. The HTS receives a hypertext trail from some external source; this external source could be a library of trails or similar. The next section will give a full description of the messages passed between the HTS and the HDS.

3.2. Messages

The messages passed between the HTS and HDS are in the form of requests from HTS to the HDS, and responses to those requests from the HDS to the HTS, i.e. the messages are in a round-trip protocol.[NYE90] A response from the HDS is always initiated by a reader's acknowledgement. All messages passed between the HTS and HDS use UNIX sockets and the messages themselves are in the form of text strings. Blank spaces act as delimiters where needed.

3.2.1. Requests from the Hypertext Trail System to the Hypertext Display System

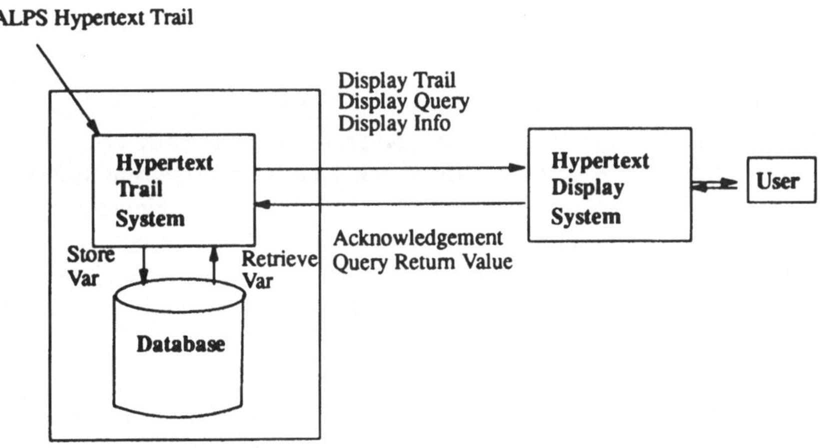

Figure 3.1 Architectural Model of ALPS Trails and a Hypertext System

Requests from the HTS to the HDS are in the form of

type_of_request   next_statement_id   statement_specific_attributes

The types of requests are INFO, TRAIL, and QUERY. The next statement id indicates which statement is to be executed upon completion of the reader's task, and the next statement id is returned to the HTS in the response message. The statement specific attribute for the info message is a text string to be displayed to the reader. The trail message sends a list of hypertext node ids as its statement specific attribute. The list of statement ids first has the total number of nodes in the list followed by the list of node ids. In the case of the query message, the statement specific attributes are the variable name the return value will be stored in and a text string to be displayed to the reader.

3.2.2. Responses from the Hypertext Display System to the Hypertext Trail System

The responses from the HDS to the HTS are also in the form of:

type_of_response   next_statement_id   statement_specific_attributes

The types of responses are also INFO, TRAIL, and QUERY. The INFO and TRAIL message responses do not have statement specific attributes. The type of response and the next statement id form the acknowledgement responses for the INFO and TRAIL requests. The QUERY message has two statement specific attributes, the return value from the query and the variable name for the HTS to determine where to store that value. These statement specific attributes along with the type of response and the next statement id form the acknowledgement response for the QUERY request. The present implementation only supports variables of integer type; therefore the query message can only return an integer value.

3.3. The Hypertext Trail System

The Hypertext Trail System reads the ALPS program in the form of ASCII text file.[THO92] The HTS parses the ALPS program using the LEX and YACC Unix facilities.[SCH85] Perl[WAL90] is used as the database management system by the HTS stores and evaluates variables from the ALPS program. Figure 3.2 shows an ALPS program which includes all the statements defined for use in a hypertext trail. This Figure depicts the program as a directed graph, and the attributes for some of the statements are described in Table 3.1. The program has 19 separate ALPS statements. The remainder of this section will describe the different types of ALPS statements used in this program in terms of how the HTS processes each statement.

In the example, statement 1 is a start statement, and statement 2 is its the next statement, and the end statement is statement 21. Statement 3 in the example is a var statement, and it has **B** as a label for an integer variable. This var statement will create an integer object labeled **B** in the Perl database, and store the value zero in it.

An info statement example is statement 2 with the text string to display to the reader - "Internet Resources Guide". When the info statement is executed, an INFO request is sent to the HDS. The info statement will wait until the response from INFO request is received from the HDS before the ALPS program continues on to the next statement.

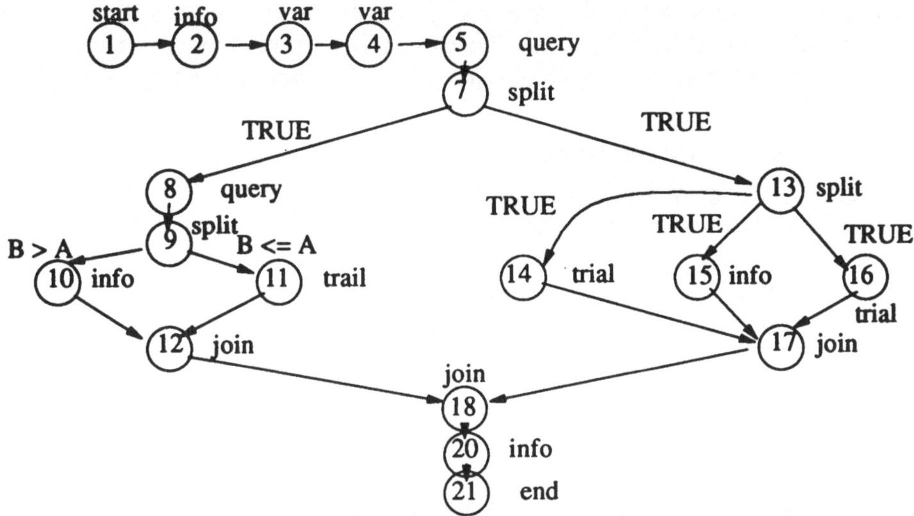

Figure 3.2 Example of a Hypertext Trail ALPS Program

ID	Next ID	Type	Attributes			
1	2	START				
2	3	INFO	'Internet Resources Guide'			
3	4	VAR	B			
5	7	QUERY	'Enter Your ID Number'	A		
9		SPLIT	'B > A' 10	'B <= A ' 11		
14	17	TRAIL	5	23 15 89 90 91		
17	18	JOIN	13	16	15	14
21		END				

Table 3.1 Attributes for the Example ALPS Program

Statement 5 in the example is a query statement with a display text string of - "Enter Your ID Number". The variable label to store the response from the reader is **A**. When a query statement is executed, a QUERY request is sent to HDS, and the query statement waits in the same way as the info statement for a response. On receiving the response, the query statement sends a request to the Perl database to store the integer response value in database object **A**.

Statement 14, in the example, is a trail statement with five hypertext nodes in the trail. Execution of a trail statement has the HTS send a TRAIL request. The trail statement then waits for a TRAIL response from the HDS.

In the example, statement 9 is a split statement with two paths coming out of it. The path going to statement 10 has the associated boolean expression **B > A**. If this expression evaluates to true than that path is followed. The ALPS program has the join statement 17 which has been indicated as being paired with split statement 13, will wait until all three of its previous statements have acknowledged completion.

3.4. The Hypertext Display System

The Hypertext Display System controls the hypertext system which in turn controls all aspects of the user interface of the system. The Hypertext Trail System can make three different types of requests to the HDS, *INFO, QUERY,* and *TRAIL.* Management for the display of these requests is the responsibility of the HDS. This section will give a description of operation of the HDS and the three display windows: query, info, and trail.

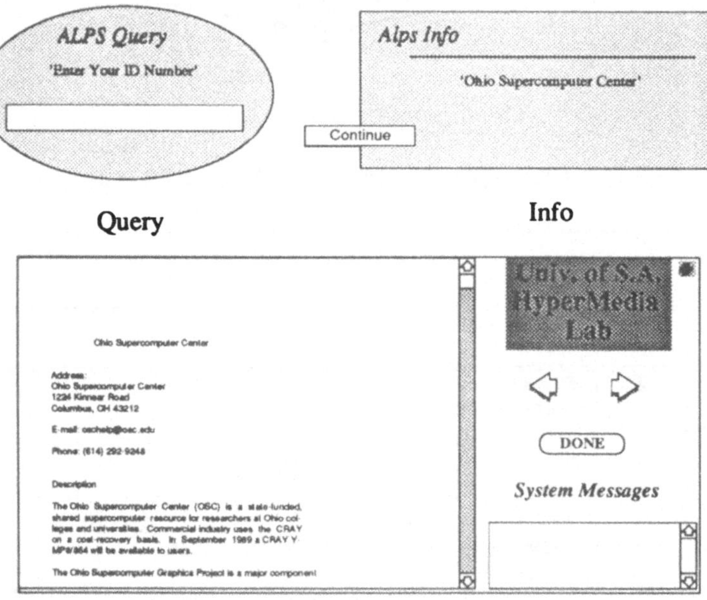

Figure 3.3 Display Windows

3.4.1. Operation

The basic operation of the Hypertext Display System is to process messages from the Hypertext Trail System and process responses from the reader. For a given message there is always a following response initiated by the reader. The processing of a message is to first wait for a request from the Hypertext Trail System, then unpack that request and finally display the proper hypertext interface. The processing of the response is similar, first wait for a acknowledgement from the reader, then return the proper information to the HTS.

3.4.2. Display Windows

There are three types of display windows corresponding to the three type of requests from the HTS, info, query, and trail. Examples of the display for each of these, info, query, and trail display windows, are shown in Figure 3.3. The display windows were developed under the HyperNeWS[NIB90] hypertext system, and this section will describe each of these display windows.

The info display window is designed to present the reader with textual information and a method of acknowledgement. In Figure 3.3, the info window displays the textual information - "Ohio Supercomputer Center". The *Continue* button provides a means for the reader to acknowledge being done with the information.

The query display window provides a text entry field for the user to enter information to HST. In addition to the text entry field, textual information information is presented to the reader. The textual information for the query window in the Figure 3.3 is - "Enter Your ID Number". Termination is signaled by the reader entering a carriage return in the text entry field.

The trail display window functions as means for a reader to view nodes from a hypertext document. The basic control areas of the trail display window in Figure 3.3 are: a scrollable text window, a previous button, a next button, a done button, and a system messages text window. This trail display window was based on the Hyper-Book[THO92] system; where each node of the hypertext document was one page of ASCII text from a conventional document. The scrollable text window holds one node of information. The previous and next buttons are used to move forward and backwards through nodes from the hypertext trail. The done button is for the user to acknowledge being finished with the trail display window. The activation of this button signals the reader has finished with the trail request. The system messages text window is used for displaying error messages to the reader.

3.5 ALPS BNF Grammar

This section presents the BNF grammar for the subset of ALPS used to describe hypertext trails as presented to the Hypertext Trail System. The hypertext trails are defined in an ASCII format using the grammar defined in Table 3.2. The regular expressions describing *Identifier, Constant, String,* and *Delimiter* in the grammar are described in Table 3.3. The Delimiter tokens are not used in the grammar, but are used in the lexical analysiser to delimit the other tokens, as needed.

4. Conclusion

This paper demonstrated the use of a subset of *ALPS (A Language for Process Specification)* to describe hypertext trails. Definitions were given for hypertext trails and ALPS. The subset of ALPS used for hypertext trails was defined, and finally the implementation of a Hypertext system driven by an ALPS program was discussed.

The implementation involved the addition of new hypertext nodes, info, query, and trail to a standard hypertext system to support this form of hypertext trails.

Further investigation into incorporating this use of ALPS with hypertext standards, such as HyTime,[NEW91] needs to be done. The use of a hypertext standard would better expand the usefulness of this specification. The issue of non-static hypertext nodes needs to also be addressed. There needs to be a standard way of defining hypertext trails across different hypertext systems.

References

[BRO88] P. F. Brown and S. R. Ray: NBS AMRF Process Planning System- System Architecture , *NISTIR 88-3828NIST, July 27, 1988*

[BUS45] V. Bush: As We May Think, *The Atlantic Monthly* July, 1945

[CAT91] B. Catron S. Ray ALPS - A Language for Process Specification *International Journal of Computer Integrated Manufacturing* 4 pp. 105-133 (1991).

[CAT88] B.A. Catron and B.H. Thomas, *Generic Manufacturing Controllers* , IEEE Conference on Intelligent Control, (1988).

[HOR78] E. Horowitz and S. Sahni, Fundamentals of Computer Algorithms, Computer Science Press (1978).

[NEU89] C. M. Neuwirth and D. S. Kaufer, *The Role of External Representations in the Writing Process: Implications for the Design of Hypertext-based Writing Tools* , Hypertext '89 Proceedings, pp. 319-341 (Nov. 1989).

[NEW91] S. R. Newcomb, N. A. Kipp, and V. T. Newcomb, *The HyTime Hypermedia/Time-based Document Structuring Language* , Communications of the ACM 34 pp. 67-83 (Nov. 1991).

[NIB90] T. Nibett, D. Pearce, A. van Hoff, and J. Rudolf, *HyperNeWS 1.4 User Guide and Reference Manual* , The Turing Institute Glasgow, UK (1990).

[NIE90] J. Nielsen, *Hypertext & Hypermedia* , Academic Press (1990).

[NYE90] A. Nye, *X Protocol Reference Manual* , O'Reilly & Associates, Inc. (1990).

[PET81] J. L. Peterson, *Petri Net Theory and the Modeling of Systems* , Prentice-Hall (1981).

[SCH85] A. T. Schreiner and H. G. Friedman, Jr., *Introduction to Compiler Construction with Unix* , Prentice-Hall (1985).

[STO89] P. D. Stotts and R. Furuta, *Petri-Net_Based Hypertext: Document Structure with Browsing Semantics* , ACM Transactions on Information Systems 7(1) pp. 3-29 (Jan 1989).

[THO88] B. H. Thomas and C. McLean, *Using Grafcet to Design Generic Controllers* , 1988 International Conference on Computer Integrated Manufacturing, (1988).

[THO92] B. H. Thomas, *An ALPS ASCII Interchange Format for Describing Hypertext Trails*, Univ. of SA School of Computer and Information Science Tech Report 2(1992).

[THO92] B. H. Thomas, *HyperBook* Australian Computer Science Communication 14 pp. 911-926 (29-31 January, 1992).

[WAL90] L. Wall and R. Schwartz, *Programming Perl* , O'Reilly & Associates, Inc. (1990).

[WOO90] N. Woodhead, *Hypertext & Hypermedia Theory and Applications* , Addison Wesley (1990).

<program>	::=	<begin_node> <block> <end_node>
<begin_node>	::=	<statement_id> <next_statement_id> **START_NODE** ;
<end_node>	::=	<statement_id> **END_NODE** ;
<block>	::=	<statement> {<statement>}
<statement>	::=	<statement_id> <next_statement_id> **TRAIL** <trail> ;
			<statement_id> <next_statement_id> **JOIN** <split_statement_id> <list_of_joins> ;
			<statement_id> <next_statement_id> **QUERY** <display_string> <var> ;
			<statement_id> <next_statement_id> **INFO** <display_string> ;
			<statement_id> <next_statement_id> **VAR** <var> ;
			<statement_id> **SPLIT** <path_list> ;
<list_of_joins>	::=	<statement_id> {<statement_id>}
<trail>	::=	<length_of_trail> <fragments>
<fragments>	::=	<fragment> {<fragment>}
<fragment>	::=	<hypertext_node_id>
<path_list>	::=	<path> {<path>}
<path>	::=	<expression> <statement_id>
<var>	::=	<Identifier>
<statement_id>	::=	<Constant>
<split_statement_id>	::=	<statement_id>
<next_statement_id>	::=	<statement_id>
<display_string>	::=	<String>
<hypertext_node_id>	::=	<Constant>
<expression>	::=	<String>
<length_of_trail>	::=	<Constant>

Table 3.2 ALPS BNF Grammar

<Identifier>	::=	(letter)(letter_or_digit)*
<Constant>	::=	(digit)+
<String>	::=	(')(not_quote)*(')
<Delimiter>	::=	(white_space)+

Table 3.3 Identifier, Constant, String, and Delimiter Regular Expressions

Automatically Converting Linear Text to Hypertext: A Case Study

Junzhong Gu   Ulrich Thiel
GMD-IPSI (Integrated Publication and Information Systems Institute)
Dolivostraße 15, D-6100 Darmstadt, FRG
email: {gu,thiel}@darmstadt.gmd.de

Abstract

Automatically converting electronic documents, especially a huge quantity of linear free-text, to a structural non-linear form, e.g. *hypertext*, is more and more important for some applications such as information retrieval (IR)[SM84], office information systems (OIS), etc. We describe an approach to transforming linear textual data from autonomous (free-text based) IR databases to hypertext, and then storing it in a relational DBMS. As an experiment, CORDIS data, a set of IR databases of the *Commission of the European Communities* (CEC) in the form of linear free-text, has been transferred to the relational database system Sybase®[1]. The strategy we have taken, the tools used and the problems encountered are discussed.

1 Introduction

Electronic documents, such as electronic user manuals, electronic mail, electronic user instructions (e.g. README files), are used more and more to replace paper documents. Unfortunately, most of them are in the form of *linear* free-text. In many applications (OIS, IR, AI, etc.), demands are growing to be able to structure large quantities of such linear electronic text into more non-linear forms, which can generally be categorized under the term: *hypertext*.

The two main features of hypertext are: *machine-supported links* (within and between documents); and *use of windows to display a one-to-one correspondence with nodes in the database* [Co87]. In this paper, we stress the first feature, i.e. how to transform linear text to its *node-link* form and store it in a relational database. The second feature is being implemented by the TORI [ZKM92] and MERIT [STT92] projects at GMD-IPSI, which aim to develop cognitive user interfaces for IR.

The problem of converting text to hypertext has only recently received attention in the literature. Most conversion projects are either performed manually or handle only highly-structured text [FPS89–1, FPS89–2, CNVW91, GI89]. The HEFTI model (cf. [CNVW91]) proposes a sequence of six modular steps to achieve conversion in a semi-automated process: (1) text preparation; (2) node preparation; (3) indexing; (4) link creation; (5) organization; (6) link refinement. However, in the case reported here, the textual material extracted from CORDIS is poorly structured, rather than highly structured. Therefore, we use a modelling/converting strategy. For the conversion, a hierarchy-ahead approach is proposed and used, i.e. we integrate the text preparation, node preparation and hierarchy-based link creation in a single step.

The paper is organized as follows:

---

1. Sybase® is a relational database management system of Sybase Inc.

In the next section, features of CORDIS data are discussed. The remodelling of CORDIS data from linear text to hypertext is presented in Section 3. The data conversion is discussed in Section 4. Future work is presented in the last section.

2 CORDIS

CORDIS (Community Research and Development Information Service) provides information about EC Research and Technological Development (RTD) programs and related matters for organizations and individuals. The corresponding databases are named RTD-CORDIS databases, e.g. RTD-Programmes, RTD-Projects, RTD-Acronyms, RTD-Publications, etc. They are isolated and stored as inverted files.

The data transformed by us is supplied by the CEC Brussels, and includes RTD-Acronyms, RTD-Projects, RTD-Programmes, RTD-Publications, RTD-Partners, etc. All data is *linear*, and indexed by document number (preceded by "////<document index>"), and the content indices (preceded by "//<content index>"), as shown in the Example 1.

Example 1: The sample data from RTD–Projects are as follows, where the document index is '1', the content indexes are 'TTL', 'SIC', 'OBJ', etc.

```
////1
//TTL
NETMAN – Functional Specification for IBC Telecommunications Management
//SIC
TEL;ELM;IPS
//OBJ
The successful development of the IBC network demands a Telecommunication Management Network (TMN) addressing the needs of the
operators, their suppliers and the IBC users. The main objective of NETMAN is to produce a set of stable and concise functional specifications for
the TMN, and to submit these specifications to Part II TMN projects, R1053 – TERRACE and to the international standardisation bodies.
//GEN
Technical Approach
The technical approach is based on capturing the TMN functional requirements from the network management methods of existing ISDN, Mobile,
OSI and other networks, from the IBCN Reference Model, from the needs of IBC users and from international standards. These functions will be
structured in a hierarchical manner to form a TMN Reference Model and classified as Core and Optional, Generic and Non–Generic. Using the
methodology developed in Task T.171, a set of functional specifications for Design, Planning, Installation, Fault Management, Accounting
Management, Performance Management, Customer Enquiry and Control and Security (with (R1025) will be produced. It is apparent that to gain
acceptance of the work by PTTs, their direct input to the specifications will be essential to the project. A parallel stream will investigate Quality of
Service parameters, from the viewpoint of the IBC network user and network operator. An original seven–step methodology for the specification of
QoS parameters for IBC will be maintained and enhanced.  The relationship between QoS and TMN will be studied. Key Issues
+ Requirements capture.
+ Methodology.
+ Modelling.
+ Standards.
+ Functional specifications.
+ QoS specification methodology.
Achievements so far
+ Draft Network Management Functional Specifications;
+ Definition of Network Management Functional Areas;
+ Information model of IBCN Managed Objects; Case Studies undertaken with R1023 BEST, FRM and Security projects;
+ Seven–step QoS methodology. Expected Impact
+ Input to the development of TMN Reference Configurations (R1053 TERRACE).
+ Input to the TMN technology projects of a consistent functional approach and terminology to provide a framework for the development of
prototypes.
+ Contribution to the international standards bodies dealing with network management issues.
//SDA
1988–01–01
//EDA
1990–12–31
//DUR
 36
//PGA
RACE 1
//RPG
R1024
//POR
Broadcom Eireann Research Ltd
//PCY
IE
//CPJ
name:       PLAGEMANN, S.    tel:      +353–1–761531    fax:      +353–1–761532
//PAR
BRITISH TELECOMMUNICATIONS PLC, GB; (CENTRO DE ESTUDOS DE TELECOMMUNICACES) CORREIOS & TELECOMUNICACES DE
PORTUGAL, PT; TELEFONICA DE ESPANA SA, ES; TELELOGIC AB, SE; TELEVERKET (SWEDISH TELECOMMUNICATIONS ADMINISTRATION), SE;
ALCATEL STC PLC, GB; NATIONAL TECHNICAL UNIVERSITY OF ATHENS, GR; THE GENERAL ELECTRIC COMPANY PLC, GB; INTRACOM SA, GR
//ACY
IE; GB; PT; ES; SE; SE; GB; GR; GB; GR
```

//UPD
1990—09—04
//TUD
1990—09—25

The features of CORDIS data can be described as follows:

Isolation – The RTD-CORDIS databases are isolated rather than integrated, such that the rich semantic relationships between the data items are ignored.

Large quantity – RTD-CORDIS data is very large (over 300MB), e.g. RTD-Publications is over 40 MB, including about 28000 documents.

Linear – As shown in Example 1, the supplied data is linear. Viewing each document as a record, each RTD-CORDIS database is a sequence of records indexed by the record numbers. Each record is a sequence of fields preceded by content indices. But records can differ from each other, because the optional fields can be missing. The data is poorly structured, because the fields are in the form of linear free-text, even though more information can be extracted from them. For example, the field 'PAR' in Example 1 is a linear text which implies a list of the partners of the project including the names of the organizations and the countries, as follows:

Organization	Country
BRITISH TELECOMMUNICATIONS PLC	GB
(CENTRO DE ESTUDOS DE TELECOMMUNICAÇES) CORREIOS & TELECOMUNICAÇES DE PORTUGAL	PT
TELEFONICA DE ESPANA SA	ES
TELELOGIC AB	SE
TELEVERKET (SWEDISH TELECOMMUNICATIONS ADMINISTRATION)	SE
ALCATEL STC PLC	GB
NATIONAL TECHNICAL UNIVERSITY OF ATHENS	GR
THE GENERAL ELECTRIC COMPANY PLC	GB
INTRACOM SA	GR

Inconsistency – The CORDIS data is inconsistent. Some inconsistencies are syntactical (e.g. for the isolation of RTD-CORDIS databases, missing of some fields, etc.), but some are semantic. Some invisible characters (e.g. newline, table) and blank can appear arbitrarily in the text, such that they give rise to confusion in string pattern matching.

3 A HyperModel of CORDIS

Instead of indexing, text-block referencing, i.e. hypertext description, is used by us to describe the profile of CORDIS data, and then stored in a relational database (RDB).

To create CORDIS hypertext, RTD-CORDIS must first be remodelled to a relational hypertext form, which is called CORDIS HyperModel. This is the template for data conversion.

Viewing a hypertext as a set of *domain objects* and a set of *information objects* [AK90], modelling RTD-CORDIS to the HyperModel means transforming RTD-CORDIS to a set of domain objects, i.e. object types (e.g. *Project, Program, project.ttl* (title of a project), *project.obj* (objective of a project), etc.) and their links. Data converting is a continual transformation to a set of information objects, i.e. object instances (e.g. 'NETMAN – Functional Specification for IBC Telecommunications Management' as an instance of *project.ttl*, cf. Example 1) and their links. This can be illustrated in Fig. 1.

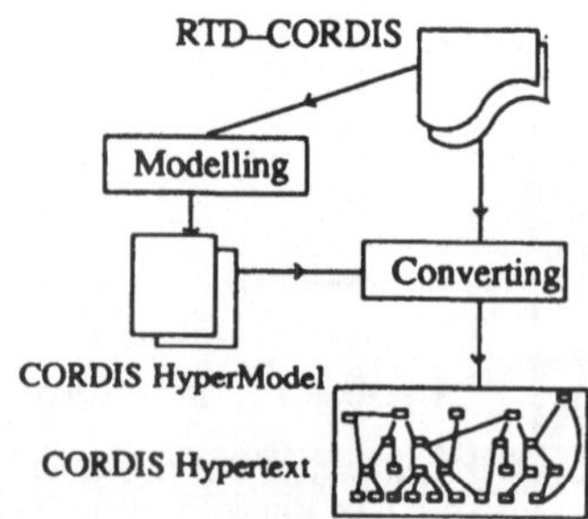

Figure 1 Modelling and Converting

3.1 Semantic HyperModel of CORDIS

Upon analyzing the semantics of RTD-CORDIS, we found:

In CORDIS the research activities are grouped by **Programs** (such as IMPACT, ESPRIT 1, ESPRIT 2, etc.); each program contains a group of **projects** as *members*[2]. Different CEC **commission services** are *responsible for* different programs. Programs and projects have their contractors, *i.e. primary contractors* and *member contractors*, called **organizations** *located in* some **countries** and some **cities**. There are some **persons** in the role of *contact* person of program, project, or commission service. The **publications**, including **reports**, **articles**, and **conference papers**, are *issued by* organizations, programs and projects, with some person(s) as *author(s)*. The programs, projects and publications can be classified to some *subjects.* e.g. IPS (Information Processing System).

In this way, RTD-CORDIS can be modelled to a node-link form, called the semantic HyperModel, as shown in Fig. 2, where boxes are nodes and the directed lines are links with identifiers representing the types of links. In practice, it should be refined continually, e.g. the

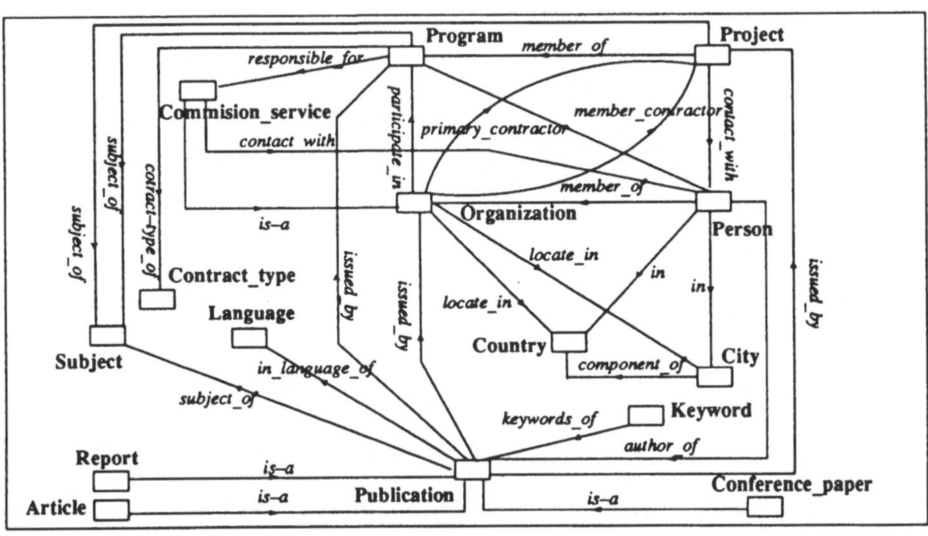

Figure 2 HyperModel (1) – Semantic HyperModel

node *Project* can be refined to the nodes *project.ttl*, *project.obj*, etc. and their links. Limited by space, it is unnecessary to go into detail.

3.2 From Semantic HyperModel to Relational HyperModel

Limited by the expressiveness of the relational data model, the links in Fig. 2 must be represented by relation objects and admissible relational links, such as *attribute-of; primary_key-of; foreign_key-of; common_key-of;* semantic links described by the integrity constraints (rules), etc. For example, the link between *subject* and *publication* in Fig. 2, *subject_of*, is evolved to a new object type (i.e. a relation), *publication_subject* constituted by the primary keys of both

---

2. The bold words (e.g. **projects**) are used to denote object types. Words underlined indicate the implied types of links, e.g. *member* means a *member-of* link.

original object types *publications* and *sic* (i.e. *subjects*), and the *foreign_key-of* links between it and *publication* (and *sic*) (cf. Fig. 3).

Therefore, the semantic HyperModel must be transformed to a relational node-link form, called Relational HyperModel. The overview of the relational HyperModel with regard to the link type of *key_of*, e.g. *primary_key-of, foreign_key-of, common_key-of,* can be illustrated as a hypergraph (Fig. 3), where each node is a *relation*; the link with double arrow represents that the

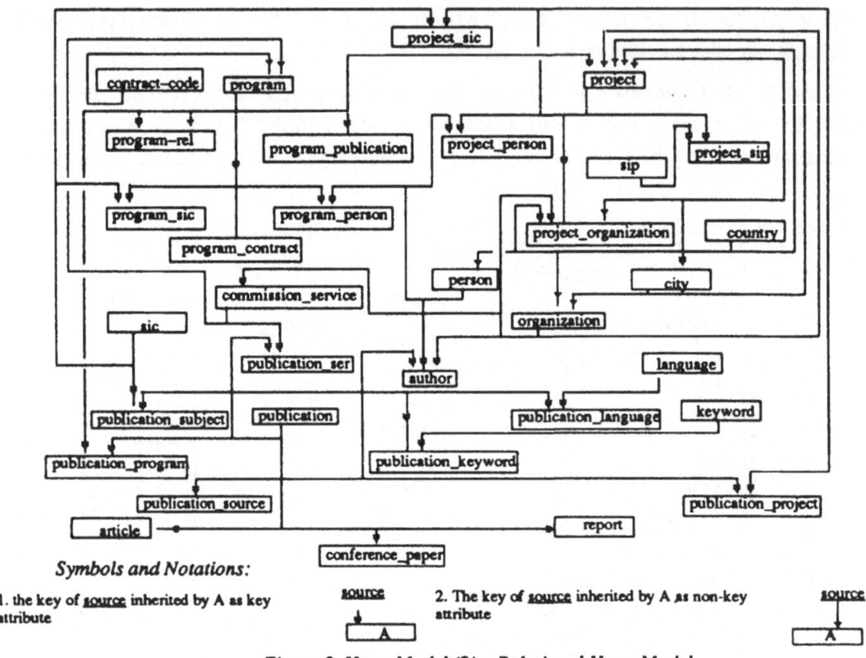

Figure 3 HyperModel (2) – Relational HyperModel

primary key of the source node is inherited by the destination node as (a component of) the primary key; the single arrow link means that the inherited foreign key is accepted by the destination node as an attribute but not (a component of) its primary key. In the relational HyperModel the indexing hierarchy of CORDIS has been replaced by *data nodes* – two dimensional tables (relations) and fields (attributes), and the relational links. The join operations and the virtual views are used as the navigation (operators) for accessing the hypertext.

4 Data Conversion

4.1 Approaches

To convert linear text to a node-link form, a *Node Selection Ahead* approach can be illustrated as in Fig. 4, where the text blocks are first selected as nodes from the linear text, then the links are created. Before the node selection, the text should be marked up, e.g. with SGML [ISO86] tags. The approach is used by some systems, e.g. Hyperman [SG91] and HEFTI [CNVW91], because usually the nodes can be generated statically, but most links are content dependent and generated dynamically.

Analyzing an IR hypertext, links between nodes (text blocks) can be generalized to five types [CT89]:

(1) Links between nodes derived by statistical "near neighbor" measures; (2) Links between nodes derived from citations in the text; (3) Links between nodes and thesaurus; (4) Links between nodes that represent a structure hierarchy; (5) Other links between nodes specified manually.

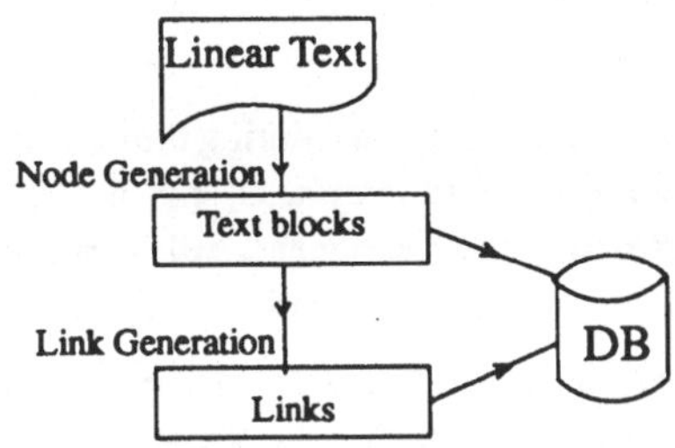

Figure 4 Approach 1 – Node Selection Ahead

Furthermore, we can classify such links in the following three groups:

Structure-Describing Links: Type (4) are *structure-describing links*, dependent on the structural syntax. In RTD-CORDIS they depend on the index architecture (e.g. record indexes, field indexes, etc.) and some not so explicit syntactic structure, e.g. the separators of sentences, sub–sentences, or words, such as semicolon ';' and comma ',' in the field '*PAR*'; the key words, e.g. 'tel:' for the telephone number, and 'fax:' for the fax number in the field '*CPJ*'; etc. as shown in Example 1.

Cross-Reference Links: Type (2) consists of cross-reference links. The cross-reference links in conventional documents are introduced by words such as *'see ...'*, *'cf. ...'*, *'see below'*, or footnotes. In CORDIS, they are mainly implied in the relationships between indexes, e.g. *project.pga* refers to *program.acr*.[3]

Knowledge-Based Links: Some links are knowledge-based, such as the type (1), (3) and (5).

Example 2: A user accesses CORDIS to get some information about the key word 'User Interfaces'. With a query, it is found that the key word is linked to the programs 'RACE', 'ESPRIT 1', 'ESPRIT 2', and 'ESPRIT 3' as shown in Fig. 5a. Then the four programs can be

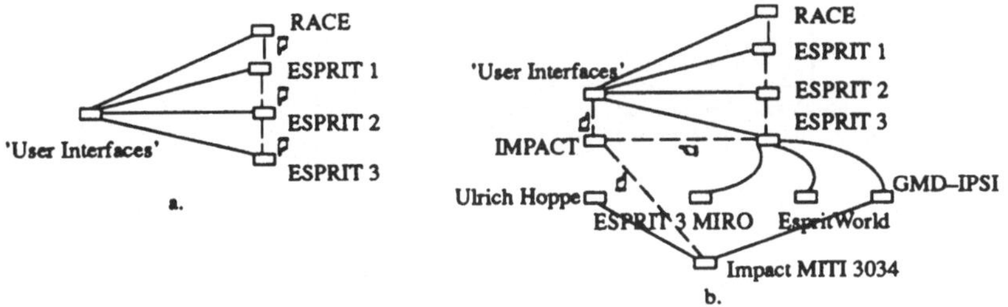

Figure 5 Creation of links during the User Session

linked together (indicated by dashes) automatically during the user session. After that, the user browses the projects of the program 'ESPRIT 3', listing the projects running in 'GMD-IPSI'. Continuing the navigation along 'GMD-IPSI', the user has found, that a project 'Impact MITI 3034' of the program IMPACT running in IPSI and with 'Ulrich Hoppe' as the contact person is also involved in 'User Interfaces'. Then the links between IMPACT and ESPRIT 3, 'Impact

---

3. project.pga: field *pga* (program acronym) in **RTD-Projects**, program.acr: field *acr* (program acronym) in **RTD-Programmes**.

MITI 3034', 'GMD-IPSI', and 'Ulrich Hoppe' are automatically created (as in Fig. 5b) for future IR searches.

Such links are created during the user session by the intelligent user interfaces, e.g. in TORI they are created by the components called *thesaurus system, history management* and *task supporting*.

The links of the first group can be created automatically during the text markup in one scan. Then the second approach called *Hierarchy–Ahead* as shown in Fig. 6 is used by us, i.e. first transferring the linear text to a hierarchic hypertext and then to a network form.

This process will be detailed in the next subsection.

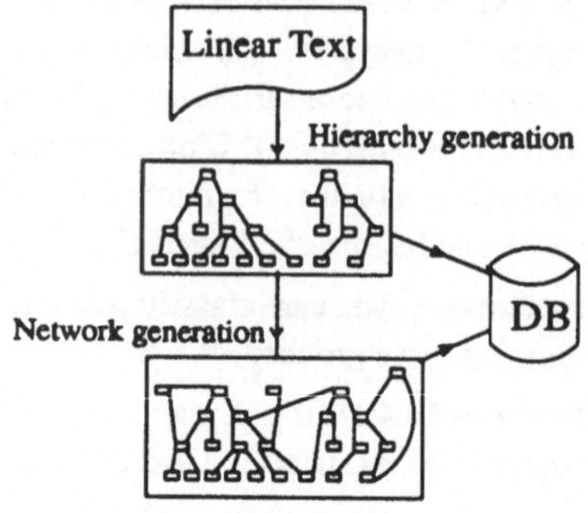

Figure 6 Approach 2–Hierarchy Ahead

4.2   Converting Mechanism and Data Conversion

Our converting mechanism is outlined in Fig. 7, where the text blocks with hierarchy-based links are directly selected and extracted from the linear text during the markup. It consists of several components, such as SPS (Scanner/ Parser/ Selector), Transformer, MLS (Merger/Link Selector) and ILS (Interactive Link Selector).

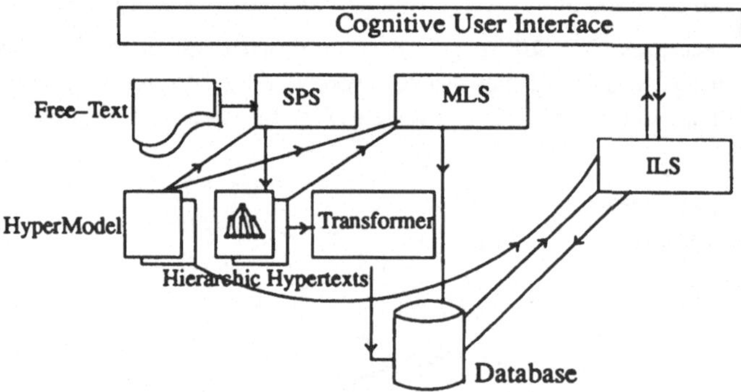

Figure 7 Architecture of Converting

SPS : SPS is written in the programming language PERL [WS91] to transfer each linear textual RTD-CORDIS to a hierarchic hypertext, such that the node- and link-selection are being done in a single text scan.

Transformer : The objective of the Transformer is to make the selected nodes and links suitable to the relational HyperModel.

MLS : The cross reference links between different hierarchic hypertexts (each corresponds with a RTD-CORDIS database) are created with the module MLS.

ILS : Other links are knowledge-based and created by ILS during the retrieval sessions (sometimes with the statistical knowledge) in the intelligent user interfaces, such as in TORI and MERIT.

Let RTD$_{cordis}$ be RTD-CORDIS, REL$_{cordis}$ be a relational CORDIS database, the conversion process can be noted as a mapping δ. In our implementation, it is divided into four phases, i.e. δ is divided into a sequence of sub-mappings (δ_1, δ_2, δ_3 and δ_4),

$$REL_{cordis}=\delta_4(\delta_3(\delta_2(\delta_1(RTD_{cordis})))), \text{ as shown in Fig. 8.}$$

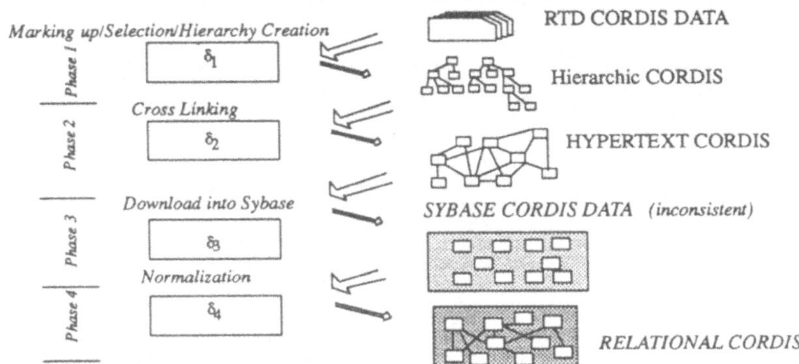

Figure 8 Conversion Process

Phase 1 : Converting to Hierarchies

The SPS and the Transformer are integrated in a single module and called in this phase. Here, each RTD-CORDIS database is transformed to its hierarchic form, e.g. the data in Example 1 are converted to a hierarchy as shown in Fig. 9 and the nodes in the hierarchy are linked to each other with HyperModel as the template. At this time, the missing fields are filled with NULL values, and incompatible data types (e.g. float, date–time, etc.) are transformed to the Sybase® acceptable forms. The output is the hierarchic links implied data files.

Example 3: Linking the nodes <PGA>, <RPG>, <POR> (and <PAR-ORG>) and <PCY> (and <PAR-COUNTRY>) in Fig. 9, as in Fig. 10, a data file *project_organization* is created by the SPS&Transformer:

```
RACE 1#R1024#Broadcom Eireann Research Ltd#IE ~
RACE 1#R1024#BRITISH TELECOMMUNICATIONS PLC#GB ~
RACE 1#R1024#(CENTRO DE ESTUDOS DE TELECOMMUNICAÇES) CORREIOS & TELECOMUNICAÇES DE PORTUGAL#PT ~
RACE 1#R1024#TELEFONICA DE ESPANA SA#ES ~
RACE 1#R1024#TELELOGIC AB#SE ~
RACE 1#R1024#TELEVERKET (SWEDISH TELECOMMUNICATIONS ADMINISTRATION)#SE ~
RACE 1#R1024#ALCATEL STC PLC#GB ~
RACE 1#R1024#NATIONAL TECHNICAL UNIVERSITY OF ATHENS#GR ~
RACE 1#R1024#THE GENERAL ELECTRIC COMPANY PLC#GB ~
RACE 1#R1024#INTRACOM SA#GR ~ 4...
```

Phase 2 : Cross Linking

Phase 2 (Fig. 11) is to link text blocks in different hierarchies according to the HyperModel. It is a recursive process implemented by MLS written in PERL. Then over 50 Sybase® compatible download files are created. Each file corresponds to a relation in Sybase®.

Phase 3 : Downloading structured CORDIS data into Sybase

Loading data into a RDB is implemented with the bulk entry facility in Sybase®. It should be

---

4. For convenient, '#' is used as field marker, and '~' is used as the record marker.

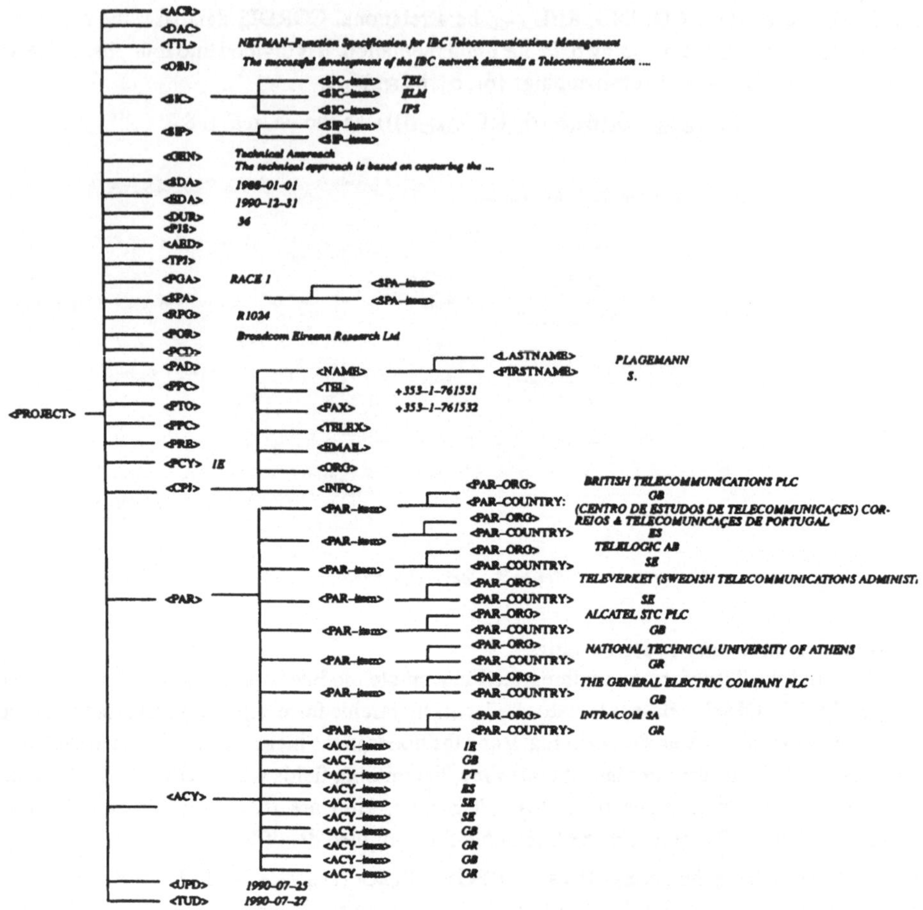

Figure 9 Hierarchic form of the data in Example 1

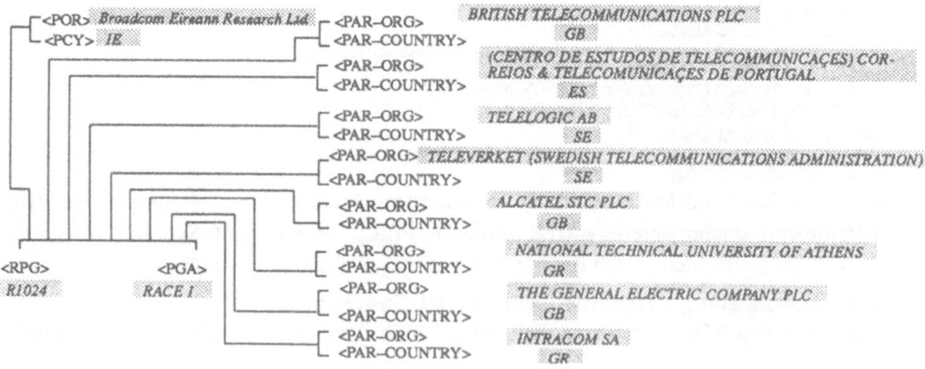

Figure 10 Project–Partner links

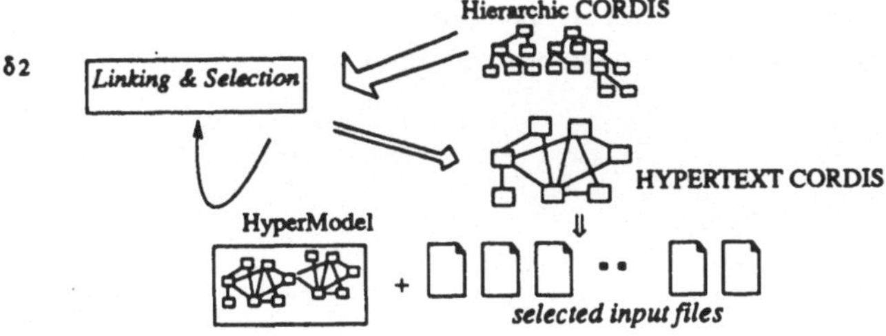

Figure 11 Conversion Phase 2

noted that even though the CORDIS data have been loaded into Sybase®, it is not a database which we expect, because it is still inconsistent. It has duplicate tuples and is inconsistent with the HyperModel. The fourth phase is needed.

Phase 4 : Normalization

The normalization is implemented mainly with SQL transactions.

Data Normalization and Deleting Duplicate Records–The textual fields in the database must be normalized. For example, the leading and the trailing blanks of each field must be are removed. Some fields should be transformed to their normalized form, e.g. after a comma only one blank remains, etc. Then the implied semantic equivalence of the fields in different formats are detected and reduced with SQL transactions.

Checking Inconsistency and Normalization–Inconsistency of data is checked with the DBMS facility. The detected inconsistencies in referential integrity are first eliminated. Then the database is transferred to its normal form. Both are implemented by customized SQL transactions.

Rules and Triggers–The semantic integrity of the relations are guaranteed by the rules and the trigger definitions.

After the 4th phase, the relational CORDIS is ready for use. It contains over 50 tables (relations). The largest table (*project*) is over 50MB, including over 14000 rows, with some long text fields (e.g. *obj, gen*) (allowed up to 2^{31} bytes).

5 Experiment and Future Work

Our target is a *multimedia* CORDIS. As the first step of this experiment we have visualized data. We have linked images (e.g. photos of project contact persons) and videos in the CORDIS Hypertext which were directly integrated in the relational CORDIS. Fig. 12 is a screen snapshot of MERIT, where the contact person entry of the project 'MIRO' is expanded to his photo and the contractor organization is zoomed to the located country (shadow area) in the map. From our experiment, some observations can be listed as follows:

Using a relational database (e.g. Sybase) for multimedia CORDIS, (1) full (multimedia) data (images, videos) retrieval can be implemented using an approach similar to that for conventional data retrieval, but *join, sort, grouping* etc. operations are no longer allowable; (2) flexible (multimedia) data retrieval, e.g. pattern matching with a sub-image, is possible but there is still much work to do; (3) the physical storage structure of (multimedia) data in a relational database system is still an open problem; (4) how to integrate CD-ROM[5] into a relational database system is also an open question.

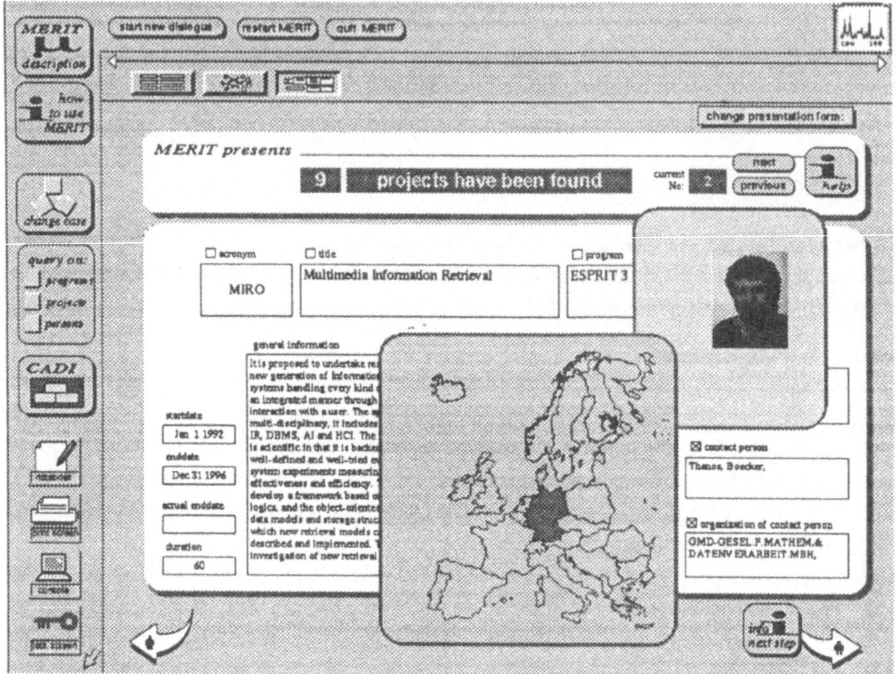

Figure 12 A Sample Screen of MERIT

In future, CORDIS as a multimedia database integrating text, pictures, images, animations, videos, sounds, music and speech, will also be implemented in the object-oriented database system VODAK [KNS90].

Another future task is the dynamic fine structuring of linear free-text nodes during the user session. For example, IR users prefer viewing the free-text fields (e.g. the field *gen* in the relation *Project*) with more readable format and layout, as follows:

Technical Approach
The technical approach is based on capturing the TMN functional requirements from the network management methods of existing ISDN, Mobile, OSI and other networks, from the IBCN Reference Model, from the needs of IBC users and from international standards. ...

Key Issues
+ Requirements capture.
+ Methodology.
+ ...

Achievements so far
+ Draft Network Management Functional Specifications;
+ Definition of Network Management Functional Areas;
+ ...

Expected Impact
+ Input to the development of TMN Reference Configurations (R1053 TERRACE).

---

5. RTD-CORDIS data have been also distributed on CD-ROM.

To satisfy the demand, flexible and dynamic structuring is necessary, i.e. the free-text nodes in a hypertext should be able to dynamically convert to a structural form during the user session. Two approaches are possible. One is to embed (format and layout) tags (e.g. SGML tags) directly in the textual nodes. When the marked-up data is displayed, an interpreter reformats the data according to the tags. The disadvantage is that the format and layout demands vary with different users rather than remaining fixed, but only one style for some users can be embedded directly in the text; when searching, tags matched as pattern may lead users astray. Another approach is to separate data and user-oriented format and layout description, i.e. the latter is used as a secondary hypertext, such that pattern matching is only applied to text without tags, but the output is automatically navigated to interpreting the secondary hypertext. We prefer such an approach.

Acknowledgements

Our most heartfelt thanks go to Dr. Martin Kracker. His preparation of the work, advice and close reading of the draft have been invaluable. The authors also want to thank Bernd Niessen and Peter M. Finch from the CEC for making the data and documentation available.

References

[AK90]   F. Afrati and C. D. Koutras: Formal Models and Query Languages, Proc. of European Conference on Hypertext, France, Nov. 1990

[CNVW91] Mark H. Chignell et al: The HEFTI Model of Text to Hypertext Conversion, Hypermedia, Vol. 3(3), 1991

[Co87]   Conklin, J. Hypertext: An introduction and survey, IEEE *Computer*, 20(9), 1987

[CT89]   Croft, Bruce and Turtle, Howard: A Retrieval Model for In corporation Hypertext Links, Proc. Hypertext '89, Nov. 1989

[FPS89–1] Richard Furuta; Catherine Plaisant; Ben Schneiderman: Automatically Transforming Regularly Structured Linear Documents into Hypertext, Electronic Publication, Vol. 1(4), 1989

[FPS89–2] Richard Furuta; Catherine Plaisant; Ben Schneiderman: A Spectrum of Automatic Hypertext Constructions, Hypermedia, Vol. 1(2), 1989

[Gl89]   R. J. Glushko: Transforming Text into Hypertext for a Compact Disc Encyclopedia, Proc. on Human Factor in Computing Systems, Austin, 1989

[ISO86]   ISO: Information Processing–text and office systems–standard generalized markup language (SGML), ISO 8879–1986(E), Int. Organization for Standardization, 1986

[KNS90]   W. Klas; E. J. Neuhold; M. Schrefl: Using an Object–Oriented Approach to Model Multimedia Data, Computer Communication, Special Issue on Multimedia Systems 13(4),1990

[SG91]   F. Sarre; U. Güntzer: Automatic Transformation of linear Text into Hypertext, Proc. of Int. Symposium on Database Systems for Advanced Applications, Tokyo, 1991

[SM84]   Salton, G.; McGill, M. J.: Introduction to Modern Information Retrieval, Mcgraw–Hill, 1984

[STT92]   Stein,A; Thiel, U.; Tissen: A., Knowledge–Based Control of Visual Dialogues in Information Systems, Proc. of the International Workshop on Advanced Visual Interfaces (AVI '92), Rome/ Italy, May 27-29

[Sy89]   Sybase Inc.: Sybase: Command Reference (release 4.0), Document ID: 324–4.0, Sybase Inc., 1989

[WS91]   Wall, Larry and Schwartz, R. L: Programming perl, O'Reilly & Associate, Inc., 1991

[ZKM92]   Jian Zhao et al: An Integrated Approach to Task–Orienred Database Retrieval Interface, Proc. on Interfaces to Database Systems 92', Glasgow, 1992

Hypertext und nichtkonventionelle Textstrukturen

Veith RISAK

Siemens Aktiengesellschaft Österreich, Programm und Systementwicklung

Universität Salzburg, Computerwissenschaften

A-1020 Wien, Lichtenauergasse 1/10   email: risak@mx39.geu.siemens.co.at

1 Einführung

Konventionelle Drucktexte haben lineare Struktur; sie sollen in der vom Autor vorgegebenen Reihenfolge vom Anfang bis zum Ende gelesen werden. Hypertext bietet die Möglichkeit zu interaktiv nutzbaren Verallgemeinerungen. So können nichtkonventionelle Textstrukturen mit einem Anfang und mehreren Enden (1:n), bzw. sogar mit mehreren Anfängen und mehreren Enden (m:n) neue Möglichkeiten für Autoren und Leser eröffnen, die insbesondere für literarische Texte ("*Hyperroman*") genutzt werden können.

Wichtige Strukturen werden angegeben und ihre Eignung für neuartige Literatur angedeutet. Auf vorhandene experimentelle Realisierungen wird hingewiesen.

2 Textstrukturen

Der Strukturbegriff geht vom *Textparadigma* aus. In diesem Sinne besteht ein Hypertext aus einem oder mehreren - meist längeren - Texten. Ausgehend von beliebigen Stellen im Text können Verweise zu beliebigen Stellen im selben oder einem anderen Text zielen.[1]

Ausgehend vom einfachsten Fall eines linearen Textes werden schrittweise Verallgemeinerungen eingeführt und ihre Eigenschaften besprochen. Die Klassifikation erfolgt nach der Zahl der Anfangs- bzw. Endknoten. Während im streng linearen Fall (2.1) die Lesefolge vom Autor völlig vorgeschrieben ist, hat der Leser mit den Erweiterungen (2.2 - 2.4) zunehmend größere Freiheit, die Lesefolge selbst zu gestalten; er kann den Hypertext jeweils auf andere Weise lesen.

2.1 Lineare (1:1) Texte

Streng lineare Texte - z.B. ein Roman - haben genau einen Anfang und ein Ende, dazwischen besteht keine formale Struktur. Der Leser hat keine Freiheit; der Text muß vom Anfang bis zum Ende gelesen werden.

2.2 Lineare (1:1) Texte mit Verweisen

Lineare Texte mit Verweisen haben genau einen Anfang und ein Ende (vgl. Abb. 1), dazwischen erlauben es aber Verweise, für eilige Leser unwichtige Textteile zu überspringen, oder

---

[1] Demgegenüber zielen Verweise in Hypertexten nach dem *Kartenparadigma* immer auf das erste Zeichen des Zielartikels. Dadurch sind dort eher kürzere Texte (z.B. ein Bildschirm) sinnvoll.

Hintergrundinformationen[2] nachzulesen. Es handelt sich um Vor- bzw. Rückwärtsverweise im selben Text, die dem Leser eine begrenzte Freiheit geben. Er kann zwar bestimmte Texte mehrmals lesen, oder andere überspringen, bleibt aber letztlich an die vom Autor vorgegebene Hauptleserichtung gebunden.

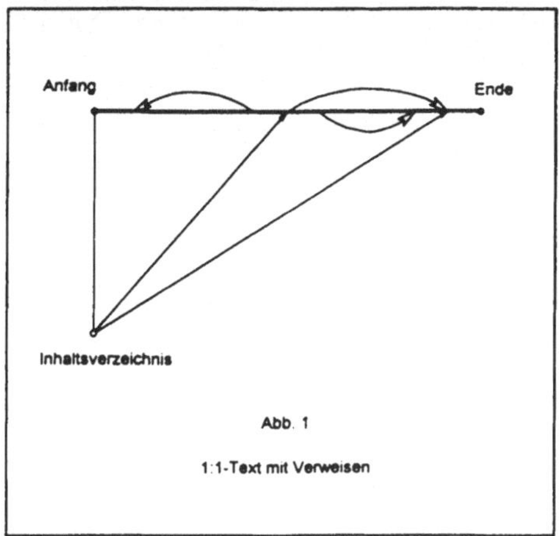

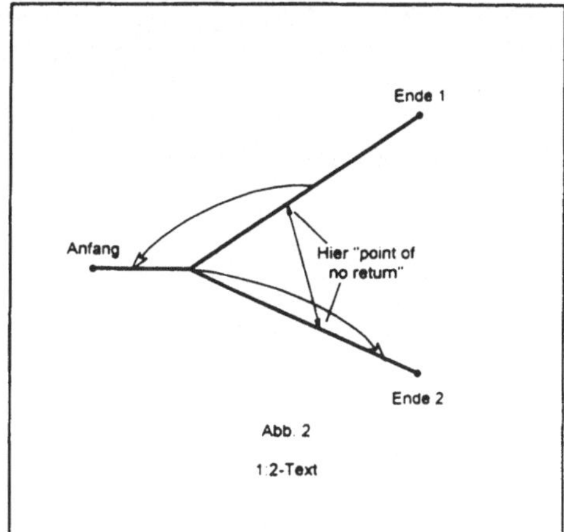

2.3 Verzweigte (1:n) Texte

1:n-Texte haben genau einen Anfang aber mehrere Enden (vgl. Abb. 2). Sie stellen eine qualitative, für interaktives Lesen als Hypertext besonders geeignete,[3] Erweiterung gegenüber 1:1-Texten dar. Mit derartigen Texten gibt es kaum Erfahrung; ein Beispiel wäre ein Kriminalroman, in dem der Täter je nach dem Navigationsverhalten des Lesers gefaßt wird, bzw. entkommt. Der Autor erweiterte, vgl. [RIS92], das bekannte 1:1-Märchen Aschenputtel zu einem 1:8-Hypermärchen. Die Realisierung erfolgte in GUIDE3. Zur Textstruktur vgl. Abb. 3.

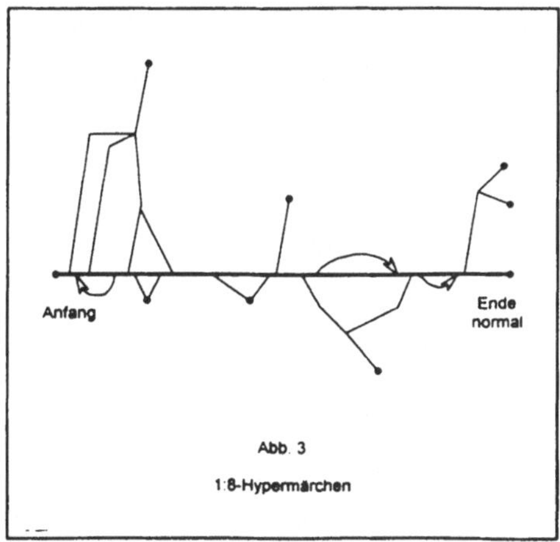

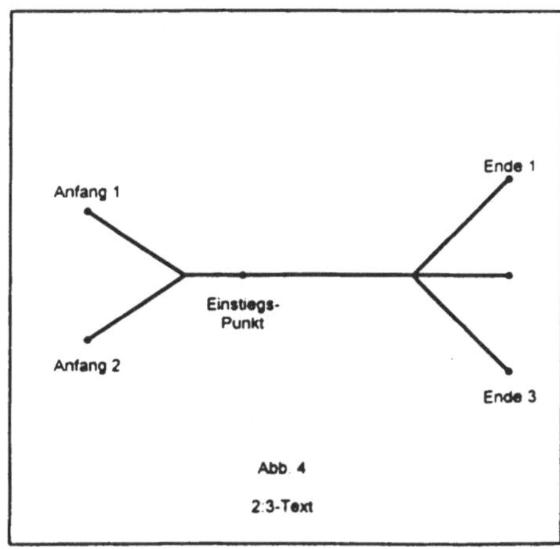

---

[2] Z.B. über das jeweils erste Auftreten handelnder Personen, usw. ...

[3] Versuche mit Verweisen finden sich auch in gedruckten Texten. Die Verweise werden dann als spezielle Symbole mit Zielangabe realisiert, vgl. hierzu [PAV88]. Das notwendige Umblättern und Suchen des Verweiszieles erschwert aber das Lesen gegenüber einem interaktiven Hypertext beträchtlich.

2.4 Verzweigte (m:n) Texte

m:n-Texte haben als Erweiterung der 1:n-Texte zusätzlich mehrere Anfänge (vgl. Abb. 4). Auch dies ist eine grundsätzlich nichtlineare, praktisch nur als Hypertext realisierbare Struktur. Ein Beispiel wäre ein - verallgemeinerter - Kriminalroman. Der Einstieg erfolgt in diesem Fall nicht an einem der Anfänge, sondern an einem Einstiegspunkt in einem gemeinsamen Teil, z.B. am Beginn einer Kommissariatskonferenz, in der mehrere Kommissare ihre Fälle darlegen. Der Leser kann sich nun mit einem der Kommissare identifizieren. Dazu kann er in einem der Anfangsstücke Hintergrundinformationen sammeln und auf dieser Basis versuchen, den Fall durch geschicktes Navigieren zu lösen.

3 Zusammenfassung

Neue Textstrukturen für vorwiegend literarische Anwendungen wurden angegeben und Beispielsrealisierungen[4] besprochen. Diese Verallgemeinerungen linearer Texte sind nur interaktiv mittels Computer möglich. Hypertext bietet dafür ein flexibles Werkzeug. Autoren sollten dieses zunächst experimentell erproben. Vielleicht nimmt sich einmal ein neuer Goethe oder Shakespeare dieser neuen Möglichkeiten an ...

4 Literatur

[OKO90]   Okopenko A., Kircher A., Nahrada F.: LEXIKON einer sentimentalen Reise zum Exporteurtreffen in Druden ROMAN. Als Teilrealisierung auf der Grazer Hypertext-Hypermedia-Tagung 1991 als Hypertext vorgestellt.

[PAV89]   Pavic M.: Das Chasarische Wörterbuch. Deutsch im Carl Hanser Verlag 1988.

[RIS92]   Risak V.: Aschenputtel, ein Märchen mit Alternativen. GUIDE3-Hypertext 1992.

---

[4] Vgl. die Verallgemeinerung des Märchens Aschenputtel zu einer 1:8-Struktur [RIS92] oder den fraktalen Hyperroman nach Okopenko [OKO90].

Flight preparation with *HyperCard*

Eric Griffiths

Department of Computing Mathematics, University of Wales College of Cardiff

1. Introduction.

This paper discusses the advantages and disadvantages of using a hypertext environment to develop application software. The chosen example application is that of aircraft flight preparation, details of which may be found in [Camp87]. Comparisons are made with a similar system discussed in [Grif90] and implemented using a spreadsheet.

A feature of the discussion in [Grif90] was that a significant amount of non-volatile data had to be re-entered each time the application was used, e.g. radio frequencies, bearings of destinations and intermediate points (checkpoints) along each stage of the route flown. In the hypertext implementation, the consistent nature of this data is exploited to generate reusable objects that are manipulated by the user in a user-friendly way to form the flight data log sheet.

2. Background.

In planning a flight between two locations, there are a number of factors which need to be assessed. Firstly, the aircraft cannot usually be pointed in the destination's direction and flown in that direction as the wind velocity ("W" for direction and "V" for speed in Figure 1) will cause the aircraft to drift off course. It is, therefore, necessary to calculate an appropriate magnetic heading ("HM") to offset the drift. Additionally, knowledge of the wind velocity also enables the calculation of other data items pertinent to the flight, e.g. (ground) speed ("GS"), time taken ("TM") and fuel required. Radio station frequency data is also required.

3. Automation.

This paper describes a system in *HyperCard*, to assist in the preparation of a flight. Originally, the system was implemented using a spreadsheet [Grif90] that required many static data items to be reentered manually. A major advantage of using *HyperCard* instead of a spreadsheet was that much of the detail for a particular flight could be stored in reusable objects. For example, consider the journey FROM Cardiff TO Swansea (Figure 1): the bearing (or "track") of Swansea from Cardiff ("TR") effectively remains constant (289°), as does the distance (26 nautical miles) and magnetic variation ("VR"). Thus, each time this stage of the journey was required, the appropriate data could be retrieved with knowledge of the start and finish points of that stage. Given the variable data items, namely wind velocity and true air speed ("TS"), the necessary calculations could then be made. In addition, associated data defining the radio service could be automatically retrieved (shown in Figure 1).

In comparison with the spreadsheet implementation [Grif90], preparation of the flight data is a great deal easier. The non-volatile route and radio data does not have to be entered in its entirety on each occasion, as was the case with the spreadsheet implementation. Another advantage that *HyperCard* has over the spreadsheet is its richer user-interface and functionality. The software developer is not restricted to a set of locations on a sheet, some of which are functionally related by formulae for the calculations discussed in Section 2. Instead, he can take advantage of the different types of object provided (fields, buttons, backgrounds etc.) to enhance the user-interface. The small drawback is that the programmer has to implement some of the spreadsheet's functionality, i.e. the functional dependencies amongst certain locations, in *HyperCard*, whereas this is a feature already built into the spreadsheet. However, a further consideration is that the software development time was greater using *HyperCard*, whereas a prototype with similar features (for the route processing) could be developed relatively quickly using the spreadsheet.

While traversing a stage of the journey, it is useful to have selected checkpoints which can be used to confirm that the correct route is being flown, and that estimates for speed are correct, based on the time the aircraft passes these checkpoints. Figure 2 illustrates part of a second page of *HyperCard* output for the Cardiff-Swansea stage. This has a checkpoint ("Bridgend") 7 nautical miles or 0.27 of the total distance from the start, taking 5 minutes to reach at a ground speed of 80 knots ("GS" in Figure 1).

4. Summary and conclusions.

The *HyperCard* environment is very versatile compared with that of the spreadsheet. The former, although resulting in longer implementation time, gives a fast data processing speed when retrieving information. Copious amounts of data need not be entered manually, rather, smaller amounts of data trigger the retrieval of associated data, decreasing retrieval time and potential error. This is desirable in a safety-critical activity such as aviation. Essentially, the original spreadsheet has been implemented using *HyperCard*, but with the added functionality of automatic data retrieval. The friendly user-interface provided by *HyperCard* for the programmer facilitates the development of the same for the application. This reduction of user-effort is made possible by reusable objects from which flight log data is obtained. Another advantage of developing the software in this fashion is that the developer may be able to visualise the data and functions more easily than with top-down functional decomposition, where data and functions can be considered independently.

A/C	G-ABCD	PA38 Tomahawk
DATE/GMT/TACH		Dec 12, 1990
1800	1915	1234.56	1235.70

FUEL		ASR	QNH
GPH	6.0	Cotswold	1010
Route time	53	Wessex	1018
Carried	30.0		
For route	5.3		
Reserve	9.4		
Required	14.7		
Remaining	15.3		

STATION	SERVICE	TWR	APP	RAD
Cardiff	ATC/LARS	125.0	125.85	125.85
Swansea	ATC		119.7	
BCN	VOR/DME	117.45		
Filton	ATC/LARS		122.725	122.725
Bristol	ATC/LARS		132.4	132.4
Gloucestershire	ATC		125.65	

FROM	TO	SA	ALT	TR	W	V	TS	DRI	HT	VR	HM	GS	DS	TM
Cardiff	Swansea	2300	FL45	289	270	10	90	2	287	6	293	80	26	20
Swansea	BCN	3000	FL30	76	270	10	90	2	74	6	80	100	31	19
BCN	Cardiff	2900	FL40	189	270	10	90	-6	195	6	201	88	20	14
Cardiff	Gloucestershire	2200	FL30	57	270	10	90	4	53	6	59	98	59	36

Figure 1: Flight data log.

CP	DS	FRA	TM	A	R
Cardiff	0	0.00	0		
Bridgend	7	0.27	5		
Swansea	26	1.00	20		

Figure 2: Route checkpoint data.

Acknowledgement.

To my colleague, Dr. Malcolm Brown, for useful discussions.

References.

[Camp87] R. D. Campbell (1987); Ground Training for the Private Pilot Licence, Manual 2, Air Navigation and Aviation Meteorology; Collins.

[Grif90] E.C. Griffiths (1990); *Flight preparation with a spreadsheet and HyperCard*; Proc. 12th British Computer Society IRSG Colloquium on Information Retrieval, Polytechnic of Huddersfield; A.S. Pollitt (ed.).

Hypertext in the Humanities:
TERESA

Herbert G. Klein
Freie Universität Berlin
Institut für Englische Philologie
Goßlerstraße 2-4
D-1000 Berlin 33

TERESA (<u>TE</u>xtual <u>RES</u>earch <u>A</u>ssistant) is a hypertext working environment developed predominantly, but not exclusively, for the needs of scholars and students in the humanities, especially for literary studies. It combines the functions of a multi-purpose tool for the organisation of most of the preliminary and preparatory stages of literary research with the features of an archive for the documentation of previous research and its results.

The application runs on all IBM-compatible computers and needs no more than 250 kb RAM. The first version was developed with North American Software's askSam 4.2 as a stand-alone solution, the current version uses askSam 5.1 and can be used in a network.

TERESA supports the fundamental activities of research for literary studies, which comprise the analysis of primary literature, the collection of bibliographical information, the excerpting of secondary literature, note taking, annotating and commenting. All these activities may be carried out independently, but more often than not they are connected with or dependent upon each other. TERESA therefore allows both separate or joint use of its individual components. The system is intended to support conventional ways of textual research by making all relevant information easily accessible and organising it according to the needs and wishes of the user. It does not require any fundamental changes in the user's customary approach, because it can be adapted to practically any work style.

The system provides four modules, which combine full-text retrieval functions with a bibliographical data-bank. The main task of the literary scholar, the analysis of primary literature, is supported by a module which allows the direct referencing of individual passages. Commentaries and pointers to related passages within the same text, to other works or to secondary literature can be directly included. There is no limit to the number or length of this additional material, neither does it necessarily have to conform to any given shape (although it is useful to maintain certain conventions). Information may also be added, changed or deleted at any later date. Similar features are provided for the excerpting and referencing of secondary literature, and for the storage and retrieval of other material.

The bibliographical module provides a very flexible tool for the compiling, sorting and processing of all types of bibliographical data, together with additional information of unlimited length. It can provide bibliographies in any format the user may need, including formats that can be used by other programmes. Bibliographical data from other sources can also easily be integrated. This module not only fulfills all the functions of a conventional data-bank, but adds to them the advantages of hypertext, i.e. searches can be undertaken from any unit of information, using any word or group of words within it, or any free format question. This allows an associative approach as well as structured browsing.

All nodes within the system can be linked to any of the others, both within one module as also between two or more. There is no limit to the number of these links and very few restrictions as to their form. These links can be placed anywhere within a given document, thus providing direct access not only to a particular unit of information, but also to a particular passage within it. Links may be changed or removed individually, within a selected group or globally. Explicit links and keywords can also be shown in the form of lists. TERESA allows free navigation in hyperspace within and between all modules, providing a history of the trip and the possibility of retracing one's steps and setting off anew from any previous point. A more structured approach is made possible by programmes which allow the selection of information according to key words, explicit or implicit links, data type or context. Boolean operators can be used, and different types of search may be combined. Units of information selected in this way constitute a sub-set which can then be used for similar retrieval operations or others. There is also an overview function which contains essential information on each node and allows direct access to it.

Output can be structured in a variety of ways and formats, depending on the needs of the user. Thus data on primary literature may be displayed alone or together with comments, quotations from other sources, bibliographical references, or in any combination thereof. This output can be directed to screen, disk or printer.

Through its versatility and openness, TERESA represents an easy to use tool for the basic tasks of the literary scholar, which becomes more powerful the more it is used. It allows quick and efficient access to all research material and makes it possible to provide output in different formats according to changing needs. Another advantage lies in its capacity to bring to light connections between separate types of data which might otherwise go unheeded. In this way, it makes work not only easier, but can actually help to enhance its quality.

Index of Contributors

Springer-Verlag und Umwelt

Als internationaler wissenschaftlicher Verlag sind wir uns unserer besonderen Verpflichtung der Umwelt gegenüber bewußt und beziehen umweltorientierte Grundsätze in Unternehmensentscheidungen mit ein.

Von unseren Geschäftspartnern (Druckereien, Papierfabriken, Verpackungsherstellern usw.) verlangen wir, daß sie sowohl beim Herstellungsprozeß selbst als auch beim Einsatz der zur Verwendung kommenden Materialien ökologische Gesichtspunkte berücksichtigen.

Das für dieses Buch verwendete Papier ist aus chlorfrei bzw. chlorarm hergestelltem Zellstoff gefertigt und im ph-Wert neutral.